PRAISE FOR

SOLITO

"A gripping memoir . . . *Solito* is special for many reasons, but the main one is [Javier] Zamora's voice and the energy of his vivid retelling of his journey. . . . And that makes it required reading."
—Gabino Iglesias, NPR

"The magic of this book lies not only in the beguiling voice of young Javier, or the harrowing journey and immense bravery of the migrants, or in the built-in hero's journey of this narrative. The magic comes from the deep humanity with which Zamora tells the story. . . . It's hard to reconcile the fact that this book hasn't always been with us. How can something so essential and fundamental to the American story not already be part of our canon?"
—*San Francisco Chronicle*

"An important, beautiful work."
—*The New York Times Book Review*

"Zamora's [*Solito*] is a distinctly American memoir, and he tells a distinctly American story."
—*The Nation*

"A monumental accomplishment."
—*Oprah Daily*

"Zamora's storytelling is crafted with stunning intimacy, and you'll feel so close to the boy he was then that you'll think about him long after the book is done. It's impossible not to feel both immersed in and changed by this extraordinary book."
—*Los Angeles Times*

"*Solito* . . . recounts in gripping and graphic detail [Javier's] boyhood travels to Gringolandia, that mythic land of big dreams and Big Macs. But it is more than a story about immigration, it is a coming-of-age tale about a 9-year-old whose journey toward maturity—another mythic land—was compressed into one season."

—*The Washington Post*

"*Solito* is an absolutely stunning immigration memoir told in beautiful prose." —*BuzzFeed*

"Engaging and beautiful." —*The List*

"Captivating, beautifully written . . . *Solito* is about family: family left behind, family waiting at the other end of the line, and the family that sustained Zamora along the long journey. . . . Readers will find it hard to set aside."

—*ReVista, Harvard Review of Latin America*

"In heartbreaking detail, [*Solito*] recounts the author's unaccompanied journey to a new country, supported only by strangers and his steadfast determination to see his parents. . . . Every step of his treacherous journey engages the reader's senses. . . . Zamora vividly evokes his childhood self: a curious, shy kid who is making the best of a situation that ultimately breaks a lot of the adult migrants around him." —*High Country News*

"A moving account of a child's perilous journey, [*Solito* is] also a reminder of how we can find compassion and family where we least expect it." —*Bookreporter*

"[A] beautifully wrought work that renders the migrant experience into a vivid, immediately accessible portrayal."

—*Kirkus Reviews* (starred review)

"Javier Zamora ventures through the fog of memory to reconstruct coastlines and jungles, deserts and drop houses, vividly conjuring the humanity and resilience that marked his childhood migration. As he journeys along the fraught desire lines that crisscross our continent, traversing borders that grow into evermore violent monsters, his story becomes that of a modern-day Odysseus in child form. *Solito* is at once blistering and tender, devastating and affirming—it is, quite simply, a revelation, a new landmark in the literature of migration, and in nonfiction writ large."

—Francisco Cantú, *New York Times*
bestselling author of *The Line Becomes a River*

"In *Solito,* Javier Zamora uncannily and brilliantly replicates his journey as a child traveling alone from El Salvador to his parents in the United States. In luminous prose, in harrowing and fierce detail, with tenderness and searing honesty he writes, for the first time, a *Salvadoran* account what it takes to reach the border, cross it on foot, and survive. Zamora chisels each moment into sharp relief, awakening us in the desert at daybreak, flooding our imagination with all that is seen and felt: every footfall, every sip of the last water left. His child narrator is shy, grave, acutely perceptive, still on the threshold, and already preternaturally wise. I cannot recommend this book enough, nor overstate its accomplishment."

—Carolyn Forché, author of *What You Have Heard Is True,*
finalist for the National Book Award

"This is a magnificent book. Clearly written by a poet, it puts the reader viscerally through every moment of Javier Zamora's epic journey. Every character is rendered with boundless care and love, and the result is not a book you should feel required to read but should rush to for a gorgeous, riveting tale of perseverance and the lengths humans will go to help one another in times of struggle. With this book, Zamora arrives at the forefront of essential American voices."

—Dave Eggers, *New York Times* bestselling author of
The Circle and *A Heartbreaking Work of Staggering Genius*

"*Solito* is a revelation, beautifully written, keenly observed. This powerful and searing memoir will stay with you long after the last page."

—Daniel Alarcón, author of
The King Is Always Above the People, co-founder and
host of *Radio Ambulante,* and MacArthur Fellow

"In *Solito,* Javier Zamora captures the voice of his nine-year-old self—a bit of magic—to tell a story all Americans ought to read. It's a harrowing but beautiful book that perfectly distills this moment in time; if there's any justice, it will someday be considered a classic."

—Rumaan Alam, *New York Times* bestselling
author of *Leave the World Behind*

"I have waited for a memoir like *Solito* for decades."
—Sandra Cisneros, author of *The House on Mango Street*

Also by Javier Zamora

....

Unaccompanied: Poems

(2017)

SOLITO

SOLITO

———

A MEMOIR

Javier Zamora

HOGARTH

LONDON • NEW YORK

2023 Hogarth Trade Paperback Edition

Copyright © 2022 by Javier Zamora
Book club guide copyright © 2023 by Penguin Random House LLC

Published in the United States by Hogarth,
an imprint of Random House,
a division of Penguin Random House LLC, New York.

Hogarth is a trademark of the Random House Group Limited,
and the H colophon is a trademark of Penguin Random House LLC.
Random House Book Club and colophon are
trademarks of Penguin Random House LLC.

Originally published in hardcover in the United States
by Hogarth, an imprint of Random House,
a division of Penguin Random House LLC, in 2022.

ISBN: 978-0-593-49808-8
Ebook ISBN: 978-0-593-49807-1

Printed in the United States of America on acid-free paper

randomhousebooks.com
randomhousebookclub.com

6 8 9 7

Book design by Barbara M. Bachman

To Patricia, Carla, Chino
& all the immigrants I met
on my way to the U.S. & never saw again.
I wouldn't be here without you.

The events and the people depicted in this book are real. To protect the identity of some, I've changed their names or used nicknames.

Our bodies are the texts that carry
the memories and therefore remembering
is no less than reincarnation.

—KATIE CANNON
(QUOTED IN *The Body Keeps the Score*)

Both boys and girls for example, made references to
the time lost and particularly to the uniqueness of a
mother's love. More than one also described feeling
as if they had a hole in their heart due to their
mothers' absence. In this way, they were
always enveloped by a sense of longing.

—LEISY J. ABREGO
Sacrificing Families

SOLITO

———

La Herradura, El Salvador

MARCH 16, 1999

———

TRIP. MY PARENTS STARTED USING THAT WORD ABOUT A YEAR ago—"one day, you'll take a trip to be with us. Like an adventure. Like the one Simba goes on before he comes home." Around that same time they sent me *Aladdin, Jurassic Park,* and *The Lion King,* alongside a Panasonic VHS player for my eighth birthday.

"Trip," they say now as I'm talking to them at The Baker's, where Abuelita Neli, Grandpa, and I go to call them—we don't have a phone at home, but we do have a color TV, a brand-new fridge, and a fish tank.

"¡Javiercito!" Abuelita Neli waves her hand at me. She's always called me that. I think my nickname, Chepito, reminds her too much of what the town calls Grandpa: Don Chepe.

"Your parents say you'll soon be with them," Abuelita says, and smiles, showing off her two top middle teeth lined in gold. Her dimples dig deeper into her round face. Tía Mali, who also has a round face, isn't here, because she's working at the clinic. She and Abuelita have been using the word more and more. Trip this, trip that. Trip trip trip. I can feel the trip in the soles of my feet. I see it in my dreams.

In some dreams I'm Superman, or I'm Goku, flying over fields, rivers, over El Salvador, over all the countries, over the people, towns, all the way to California, to my parents. I ring their bell. They open their huge door, tall and wide, made from the brownest wood, and I run to them. They show me their living room. Their huge TV. Their backyard with a swimming pool, a lawn, fruit trees, a mini soccer field, a white fence. I climb their marañón trees, eat their mangos, play in their garden . . .

Every night, between praying and sleeping, I lie in bed and think about them. ¿What type of bed do they sleep on? ¿Is it big? ¿Is it a waterbed like in the movies? ¿Are the sheets soft? I imagine cuddling right in the middle. The comfiest white sheets. Mom to my left, Dad to my right, a mosquito net like a crown covering all of us.

Whenever a plate breaks, whenever I find an eyelash, whenever I see a shooting star, I wish to be in that bed with both of them in La USA, eating orange sherbet ice cream. I never tell anyone—if I tell anyone my wish it won't come true.

I have bad dreams también. Bad dreams of growing a beard with my parents still not here. Bad dreams where I'm not up there with them—¡and I'm thirty years old! Bad dreams of being chased by pirates, or running down a hill during a mudslide.

"The bad dreams, those you have to tell first thing in the morning so they don't stay in your mind. And never in the kitchen, or else they get in your stomach. That's how you get indigestion," Mom told me, and I never forgot.

Trip. I've started using the word at school. I began telling my closest friends: "Fijáte vos, one day I'm taking a trip. Like a real-real game of hide-and-seek."

In first grade, I was the only one who didn't have both parents with me. Mali says they left because before I was born there was a war, and then there were no jobs. Now, most of my friends don't have their dad or mom here either. A few lucky friends have left to be with their parents in La USA. Most left inside giant planes.

At recess, my friends and I talk about eating our first pepperoni pizza like the Teenage Mutant Ninja Turtles, eating lasagna like Garfield, eating McDonald's, watching the new Star Wars inside a theater with air-conditioning, eating "popcorn" with butter. I've never tried any of these things except for pizza from Pizza Hut, and that was last Christmas.

"¿But will you miss me? ¿Will you?" my friends ask.

"Puesí," I say, but I don't really know.

I ask them if they will miss *me*. "Absolutely," they say, because no one who's left to La USA has ever come back to visit. Sometimes their grandma or grandpa will walk by on the street and we'll ask them how So-and-So is, and they respond, "So-and-So says hi"—that's the closest they come to remembering us. "Oh, gracias, doña, gracias, don. Tell them we say hi." But we never hear from them again.

The Baker is still here. His wife and all six of his kids también. They look happy. I want what The Baker's family has: everyone in the same room. All my friends and I want to be with our parents, where everything is new, fresh, where garbage is collected by trucks, where water comes out of silver faucets, where it snows the whitest snow, where people have snowball fights and cut real pine trees for Christmas—not spray-paint cotton branches in white like we do here.

It's because our parents are not here and we're not there that Mays and Junes are sad. For most of us, our grandparents are the ones who show up for Mother's and Father's Day assemblies. It's not that we don't love them. We do. I love Abuelita so much. I love her cooking. The way my face gets stuck in her curly, frizzy hair that she dyes black, her short hair that makes her look like a microphone, her hair that smells like pupusas when she hugs me. I love her two dimples when she smiles. Her wide and flat nose with its dark-brown mole in the middle that she has to check at the hospital every year to see it doesn't get too big. And I love her fake eyebrows she draws thin with a pencil first thing in the morning.

I love my mom, también. I've never met my dad—or I have, but I don't remember him. I was about to turn two when he left. He sounds nice over the phone. His voice is deep and raspy, but it's still soft, like a sharp stone skipping over water. I always talk to him second, after I talk to Mom. I remember everything about her. Her harsh voice like a wave crashing when she got mad at me. Her breath like freshly cut cucumbers.

Now I talk to her first, and then she hands the phone to Dad. Sometimes I'm so shy with Dad, Mom has to be on the phone at the same time. Other times Tía Mali whispers things I've done that week to tell him.

They send pictures every few months, and in the pictures Dad looks kind and strong. I like his thick mustache. His thick black hair. His big teeth. The gold chain he wears over his shirt, his muscles showing. Everyone in town tells me stories about him, but I haven't really asked him anything because I get shy when I hear his voice.

Now Grandpa is talking to them, trying to whisper something into the phone, trying to make it so I won't hear. But I do hear. I've been listening. My hearing is good. It's *really* good. I hear him whisper, "Don Dago," then something else I can't make out, then he blurts out, "By Mother's Day."

Don Dago is the coyote who took Mom to La USA four years ago. He's been coming around the house more often. I can put two and two together. I'm my grade's valedictorian; I get a diploma every year for being the best student.

Mother's Day. Since kindergarten the nuns have made us embroider handkerchiefs with *Feliz Día de la Madre* or *Feliz Día del Padre* in blue or red thread. Every. Single. Year. At least the *P*'s are easier than *M*'s. In second grade, my friends and I started writing our grandparents' names instead. It's easier.

But this Mother's Day will be different. ¡This is finally the year I see my parents! This year I will embroider Mom's name on a handkerchief and deliver it to her—in person.

"He'll get there before summer. He won't be cold like you were in the mountains," Grandpa tries to whisper, like I don't know they're talking about me. I hide my happiness, my smile, but it's hard not to run around The Baker's living room. Hard not to knock the tables over. Hard not to run the four blocks home. Hard not to run into the clinic where Tía Mali is working. I don't know if I'll be able to pretend once she gets off work at six P.M. But I do, I pretend, I walk back at Abuelita's pace, holding her hand. Clutching it. Squeezing it until both our hands sweat and the sweat says: *It's happening. It's finally happening.*

TÍA MALI RUSHES INTO our room, through the bedsheet hanging from a wire we use for a door, screaming, "¡Chepito! ¡Chepito! ¡I just talked to them!" She throws the black purse Mom sent her a few Christmases ago on top of the wooden dresser next to her bed.

"¿Who?"

"Your parents, tontito." I like it when she calls me that. The word sounds like rain slipping through holes in our roof, falling into tin buckets we place on the floor so the room won't flood.

"They've chosen the date. The month—"

She doesn't know I overheard Grandpa.

"¡Get excited! ¿You want to know how they chose?"

I smile because I want to know, but also because she's managed to untie one of her black flamenco shoes and is struggling with the other one.

"Your mom's co-worker at Toys 'R' Us said you should get there before August, so you can learn English before school starts." Mali sits on her bed as she reaches for the lemon half inside a small plastic bowl on top of her dresser—the half she didn't use this morning that's gathered fruit flies. She squeezes the juice on her feet then dries them with a towel.

"It's weird that gringos start school late, ¿right, Chepito?"

I look up at our roof, then look out the window next to my bed. "¿Why don't they start school in January like us?"

"Jaber," she says with a shrug as she slips into her clean plastic sandals and walks to the kitchen to throw the used lemon half in the backyard. The bedsheet door swooshes behind her as she runs back into the room and jumps on her bed.

"I guess this way, you'll be six months smarter than the gringui-tos." She *ito*-es everything. "And everyone is new the first day of school." She taps her mattress with her right hand, the signal for me to walk across the cold tile floor. The smell of pata chuca is mostly gone; the lemon has helped more than anything else she's tried. The talcum didn't do anything, and the weird concoction of vinegar, honey, and egg yolk backfired and made her feet stink even more.

We perform this ritual after she comes back from work at dusk. I lie next to her as she begins to tell me about the clinic's chambre: the sickness that each patient has, their test results, the new drama be-tween doctors, or when it's slow, how bored she was.

We lean our feet against the wall, our heads almost off the edge of the bed. We look up at the glass tiles in the middle of the terracotta tiles that make up the house's roof. We look through the glass and spot the night's first stars, which means it's close to dinnertime.

Mali is only twenty-three, but she's heard placing your feet on the wall like this helps with "cel-u-li-tis." I like that word, *cel-u-li-tis*. Every woman at Abuelita's pupusa stand seems worried about it like it's the plague. Abuelita has been selling pupusas in front of the clinic since Mom was a kid. Mom helped her sell pupusas. Mali did as well, until she went to school and started working as a secretary at the clinic. So now it's Tía Lupe—the youngest of the three sisters—who helps Abuelita make and sell them.

With our feet above us and the chambre done, Tía Mali begins to tell me about her suitors. "Fijáte que The Dentist came to visit me today . . ."

I zone out and remember she was late again this morning. ¡Even though our front door is only a few meters from the clinic! Most mornings, she forgets lipstick and I have to remind her. Then she looks at her gold Casio watch with its thin black strap and shrieks, "¡Puya!" which means she's late. She runs out the door, almost knocking the bedsheet out of the string it's tied to, and she's off, click-clacking across the street, fumbling her keys, running past the people already lined up so they can be the very first patients of the day. But she never forgets to paint a kiss on my forehead—which I leave for a few minutes before I wipe it off.

When Mali forgets breakfast, Abuelita sends her a pupusa wrapped in foil, or pan dulce in a paper bag, and I have to walk across the dirt street to Tía Mali's desk right next to the clinic's front door. When I'm not in school, I sell the best horchata, ensalada, marañón, and chan. I'm a good salesman; I learned from sitting on Mom's lap as she handed customers a plastic bag with whatever drink they ordered.

Every now and then, someone from the other end of town, near the pier where my dad is from, says to "tell Javierón I say hi." Dad has various nicknames, and I don't really know what they mean. Lelota is the most difficult one to decipher because it's not a real word. Then there are the obvious ones like Alacrán, but I still don't know how he got it, and of course I've never asked.

"So-and-So says hi," I tell Dad on the phone.

"Tell them I say hi back," he says, and asks about how many nines or tens I have at school and in what subjects. After we cover school, we cover my health, and then it's finally time to critique what they sent last time and discuss what new toy or clothes I want for next time they send me a package.

At the very end of our conversations, only then, when we say goodbye, I ask Dad when I'll finally meet him. It's the same routine with Mom. Other kids are already up there with their parents, or are about to leave. It feels like every month someone else disappears.

One day we're playing soccer at lunch, playing tag at recess, and then, poof, they never come back. They mostly leave by plane. ¿How? I don't know. Others leave by land in a car that picks them up. They go with a relative or the parent that was still here. At school, we only hear after the fact. They're here, and then they're not. No one ever lets it slip that they're leaving.

"Soon," my parents say. It's always "soon." But soon doesn't arrive, and I am still here selling pupusas to the same people Mom sold pupusas to.

"Be patient, Chepito," Tía Mali tells me every other dusk when I complain. But this time, today, it's different. After she's done telling me about another one of her suitors, she turns to me, looks me in the eyes, and says, "You'll be up there so soon, tontito, I'm so excited for you." I believe her.

We stare at the ceiling. Maybe Tía Mali notices I'm excited, because she begins to tell me about Mom's trip to California. It's the only north-trip experience Mali knows. No one knows how Dad got up there. Apparently, Mom made it in two weeks. "Fast. Quick," Mali says, slashing the air with her palm as she speaks, raising her normally soft voice to emphasize how fast it was.

"She crossed through San Ysidro, jumped a murito, walked up a hill-ita, and ran into a car-ito that drove her up a long road, the biggest road she's ever seen, past Los Ángeles, past San Francisco, to San Rafael, where your dad was waiting for her." As Mali says this, she acts out the verbs with her hands. Two down-turned fingers moving forward and backward means Mom is running. A wave is Mom jumping. An air steering wheel is Mom riding inside a "car-ito."

I've heard this story a thousand times, but never the details. I know the big picture: she left, got there in two weeks. She ran, she jumped, she hid, she drove. ¿Who drove her? I want to *see* the mountains she ran down, the trees that grow there. The fence. ¿Is it made of bricks? ¿Barbwire? ¿Is it tall? The roads, ¿are they dirt or asphalt? ¿Wide or narrow? I want details, but I don't think Mali knows more than what she's told me, and when she speaks, I stay quiet. It's something I don't like about myself. I'm too shy. At school, the cool kids make fun of me and I don't say anything. I hide.

I know my parents wanted me to wait until I got older. I hope they don't still think I'm too small. I'm not. I'm nine years old, but I can already jump the fence that separates our house from the neighbors' pretty fast. And it's made of barbwire. When our dog, La Bonita, chases one of the iguanas that live in our big avocado tree into

Niña Yita's land, I dive under it like she does, or climb the wooden poles the barbwire is wrapped around, and make it over. I've never gotten hurt. Not a single scratch.

"But it gets cold," Mali says. "Your mom says she got sick in the hill-itas and stayed sick a few days after."

"But she's okay now," I say. Mali plays with her wavy hair and looks at the skylight. She raises her black caterpillar-like eyebrows, something she always does when she's thinking. She takes a while, so I ask, "¿Want to look at the new photos Mom sent?"

"Yes," she says softly, and reaches for the album already on the bed, under her sweaty leg. Her skin sticks to the green plastic cover that's left a mark on her thigh. I don't get mad, because it's not her stinky feet on the pictures.

Mom sent this album for my ninth birthday in February. My favorite photo is the one where she's dressed up as one of the Toys "R" Us mascots. Not the big giraffe, Geoffrey—that costume is too tall for Mom. She's short, a little bit taller than Abuelita, but shorter than Mali, who is one meter and sixty centimeters tall.

In the picture, Mom is inside a smaller giraffe, *Baby Gee* written on the bib, where you can see her face behind a black screen. I laugh every time I see it. It's cute: Mom, a little baby giraffe.

My second favorite picture is of Mom facing the camera, dressed in an oversized blue polo shirt (maybe Dad's), the Golden Gate in the background. The Golden Gate is a huge bridge, *the biggest bridge anyone has ever built,* she wrote on the back of the photo. I tell my friends at school that.

I love Mom's black, straight hair. The bangs she used to hairspray into place in front of this mirror, and still does up there. I love when her hair is caught in the wind, like in this picture, and the bangs are frozen in place. She's smiling. Mom never smiles with her teeth showing, but always tilts her heart-shaped face a little to the right, like she's leaning in for a secret.

"See, it's great up there," I tell Mali, pointing at the mountains behind the Golden Gate Bridge. Her rounded face doesn't disagree.

"I'm gonna walk across that bridge soon," I say louder, like I just scored a goal. I point to the bridge's red, thick towers. "I'll send you a picture from right there, just like this one."

"Yes, please, Chepito, don't forget about me, ¿okay?"

I could never.

3-17-99

MOM AND DAD HAVE decided to use Don Dago, who visits our fishing town two to three times a year. Our town is not San Salvador, or even Zacatecoluca. It has one way in, one way out: a pothole-filled asphalt road that ends at the pier where fishermen leave hours before dawn and return around noon to auction the day's catch. In winter, when it doesn't stop raining, both the asphalt road and the only other road in town (the smaller dirt road we live on) flood. The entire town floods a few centimeters, and Mali and I go out to the street, where we cast off paper boats from Abuelita's flooded pupusa stand. We make boats from old school assignments or old newspapers, and I write the date in black Sharpie. Sometimes I name them weird things, like Mumra or Bulma. Other times I name them after one of my parents.

No one knows when Don Dago will come to town, but when he does, rain or shine, word spreads quickly and everyone knows where to find him: at Doña Argentina's cantina, drinking an ice-cold Suprema, smoking Marlboros with a glass ashtray next to him. People line up to ask if he delivers to Wa-ching-tón, to Jius-tón, to San Francisco, for the same price. If he delivers children, if he delivers women or men older than he is, if he can change all of our lives. Don Dago changed Mom's. Mali says she left because there are no jobs. Dad left because of "politics." "La USA is safer, richer, and there are so many jobs," Mali and Abuelita have told me.

Don Dago sits on a white plastic chair next to the white plastic table outside the cantina. The same cantina I ran to when Grandpa drank at home. I'd buy him the usual, a flask of El Muñeco, then I'd run the five blocks back home so he could drink it. When he finished the first flask, I'd run back to the cantina and buy him another one. We'd repeat until Grandpa passed out on the hammock. He always let me keep the change, which I stuffed into my Super Mario piggy bank I never cracked open, until last year when my parents said they didn't have enough money to bring me to them. Abuelita cried when I told her why I broke it. I cried because she was crying and because she told me it wasn't enough.

Grandpa quit drinking when Mom left, and Don Dago has been taking people from this town since before he took Mom, but now, when I walk by Don Dago sitting in his white plastic chair, he takes a puff of his cigarette and waves at me. Always at his side is a small white electric fan that Doña Argentina brings out for him, a bright orange extension cord zigzagging its way into the cantina to the nearest plug. The fan sits there like an obedient dog trained to lick the sweat showing through Don Dago's neatly ironed polo, unbuttoned to show off a bit of his graying chest hair. I want to have chest hair like that: almost curly, almost white as salt, like Santa's beard in Coca-Cola commercials.

On his left hand, a gold watch. On top of his chest hair, three gold chains, thin, but each one thicker than the last. Black leather boots match his black leather belt. This outfit lets people know he's not from La Herradura, not even from El Salvador. He looks more like the rancheros in Mexican novelas, except he doesn't wear a sombrero; a baseball cap covers his bald spot, and dyed black hair protrudes from the sides.

The most surprising part of his outfit, the part that doesn't match the novelas, is Don Dago's small, black leather fanny pack. In it, he stores his Marlboros, Bic lighter, Bic pen, sunglasses, Chiclets—everything except the small brown notepad he keeps in his back pocket. His notepad is the tool he uses to pause for suspense when people ask him questions like "Don Dago, disculpe, ¿how much to California?"

"¿What city? Rate is different," he responds, taking a sip of his Suprema.

"Los Ángeles," I've heard them ask, shyly, like they're scared of him.

"¿Gender? ¿Age of person?"

With just this bit of information, Don Dago has the excuse to scoot a little bit forward in his chair, lift up his left butt cheek, and reach for the notepad. He flicks it open like a switchblade to the inside cover, where he's written numbers only he understands. Sometimes they're crossed out. And his one rule everyone in town knows about is: *no negotiation*.

"It's not my rate. Can't change it," he says, showing customers his palms opened to the clouds, after pointing to the numbers, cigarette in hand.

"Can't change it," he repeats when they tell him the various reasons why their child, their brother, themselves have to leave this country. Grandpa says it's mostly poor people, often poorer than us, who need Don Dago but can't afford him. I overheard Abuelita say there's more violence now, so more and more people need coyotes. Just last October, Papel-con-Caca got shot in front of our house at dawn. "Because he had tattoos," Grandpa said. He was "bad people," a "marero," people say now, but he drove me on his bike whenever he got a chance. Then Pedro got shot in the market in November. And this past Christmas, Don Guayo shot someone in front of his pharmacy, then fled to La USA. Don Dago doesn't care about the reasons; he just repeats that he can't change the price, each time with a smile, showing the customers his perfectly straight teeth, big and a bit yellowed.

Don Dago was probably not lying when he told Grandpa, "I'm only one pearl in a long pearl necklace, Don Chepe." We were at home the second time he came over. Grandpa and Don Dago sat in plastic chairs under the mango trees in the backyard. "We all have to eat," he continued. I was playing by the marañón trees next to the mangos. Don Dago had visited us every time he was in town, ever since I turned eight. Before that, he'd only come here once.

I still remember that first time. It was days after my seventh birthday, after I'd gone to the U.S. embassy twice to get a visa and it became clear that leaving on an airplane wasn't gonna happen. Don Dago looked at me and announced, "He's too young." He was so tall. Taller than Grandpa, both of their polos tucked into their blue jeans. After Don Dago left, Grandpa said, "Apparently that coyote de mierda has a 'no one under ten' rule." Grandpa was pissed. His face turns pink and the veins in his temples pop out when he's pissed. I was sad. I had to wait once again.

"But ese cerote is still gonna take him, when the time is right," Grandpa said.

No one disrespects Grandpa. People in town are afraid of him. Mali says it's because Grandpa was in the military and he still owns a gun. I think it's because he's really good with his machete and whenever someone tries to steal our bananas, mangos, or oranges, Grandpa chases the robbers and shoots them with a slingshot. Kids or adults, doesn't matter. My friends' older brothers are afraid, my friends are afraid, even the dogs don't walk in front of Grandpa. I'm a little scared of him también.

I hope Don Dago has changed his rule. Being nine won't stop me from seeing my parents this May. Don Dago is "the best coyote in the central coast of El Salvador," I've heard people say at the pupusa stand, which means he's expensive.

Mali says he promised my grandparents that Mom would drive on roads, take buses, maybe hide in a trunk, maybe hide in a trailer, then run up a hill, run into a car, then make it to Dad. And Don Dago did all that. He was with Mom the entire way. "He's a good coyote," everyone says. Two weeks it took. Very fast. Very safe.

The adults don't tell me much. Tía Mali is the only one I can get any information out of, but sometimes even she doesn't know what's happening.

"We're saving, we're almost there, you'll be with us soon," my parents have said over the phone or in letters, over and over. I know my parents are saving, but I don't know the exact number. I make one up and write it at the top of every page of my school assignments. I flick my notepad just like Don Dago does, like a switchblade, and write the made-up number right below the date on the top left corner of the page.

3-20-99

I'M IN MALI'S BED while she waits for her friend to pick her up for the dance at the pier. It's the Saturday before the week before Semana Santa, and the town is already celebrating. Mali is in her going-out dress: black with shiny beads at the hem and a cut that shows off the top part of her back. Her black heels are next to the bed, her legs trapped behind black leggings. The lemon has already been applied and dried off with a towel, and her heels sprayed with perfume.

I like it when she purposely curls her thick black hair. It's curly regardless, but when she adds a little mousse and hairspray, it's *really* curly. On her lips, her favorite lipstick—not the peach or light-pink ones she wears for work. This one is red, but not too red. Looking like a bruja is always her biggest fear, so whenever she leaves the house for work or for parties, she stands in the mirror like she's doing now and asks me, "¿Do I look like a brujita?"

This time, she doesn't. I like this red, red like the red seen through my palm when I cover the end of the flashlight. I like doing that when I have to pee and have to walk to our outhouse at night. I like seeing all the blood flowing through me, trapped in there.

"The Dentist is pushy. He drinks. I don't want to run into him," Mali is saying, annoyed, her caterpillar eyebrows crunched together, causing her forehead wrinkles to show.

I look for stars through the skylight, only half paying attention to what Mali says.

"Your mom did her trip fast. Quick. It was a first-class mojado express," she says, laughing. Now she has my full attention. "You'll be safe. I'm not worried, Chepito."

Mali continues, says Mom called right after she crossed. I like that word: *cruzó*. I can see a crucifix. Maybe the fence is made up of a lot of little crosses.

"Your mom drank water from troughs, but she was fine," she says, now applying mascara, curling her eyelashes. When Mali says *troughs,* all I can see is Mom in the shape of a cow, then a horse, then in her giraffe costume, kneeling down, drinking dirty water.

"I'll be back soon, mijo, I'll come back, I promise," Mom said four years ago in this very room. The room was a pale indigo, the walls dark, the sun beginning to rise, light hitting the tops of the pink-and-white myrtle trees outside this window by the bed I shared with her.

My eyes were half-closed, but I remember Mom kissing the top of my head, then both my cheeks. She made a cross on my forehead with her fingers, whispered something to herself. Then she kneeled next to the bed and looked me right in my eyes and told me, "Te quiero mucho."

I regret not waking up for Mom. I liked watching her get ready when she went out. It's why I like watching Mali apply foundation, draw her eyebrows, put lipstick on, curl her eyelashes with mascara. Weeks before she actually left, Mom said she was gonna go away for a while, but didn't tell me when or for how long. I had just turned five. As she stood in the door for a few seconds, I closed my eyes and went back to sleep.

"¿Remember Roberto?" Mali asks.

At first, it wasn't Don Dago who I was supposed to leave with. Two years ago, my parents tried sending me by plane. There's another coyote who doesn't take people; he takes letters, videos, food from here to La USA. Don Leo is his name, and he also brings things: the once- or twice-a-year cardboard boxes filled with Legos, clothes, VHS players, toasters, and so on. The plane was Don Leo's idea. Grandma asked him after we saw Jeffrey—my older friend and neighbor—leave to La USA this way. Apparently, Jeffrey's family told people he'd gotten a visa, but Mali says the truth is he used someone else's.

Don Leo knew someone who had a son around my age. I memorized the kid's birthday, birthplace, family names, I even got a haircut that made me look like him—Roberto. I don't look like Roberto, I'm darker, so Roberto Sr. suggested I not play outside for weeks. I didn't even walk to school without an umbrella.

"Roberto got paid eight hundred dollar-itos to cover the fees," Mali reveals as she powders her face. "Then fifteen hundred more if you got the passport, and finally fifteen hundred more once you saw your mom," she continues with her same soft tone, like she's told me this before, but she never has.

I remember memorizing all the details of my new life as Roberto Jr. My parents knew many children who had gotten to La USA this way. I, fake Roberto Jr., would take a plane, get off in La USA, and mail the passport back to Don Leo, who knows someone at the airport who would stamp it for the real Roberto Jr. Like a ghost taking the plane back.

"I helped you practice, ¿remember?" Mali says, turning toward me, her makeup done. "¿How do I look?" Her voice gets softer when she's vulnerable, when she asks, like she does every morning.

"Bonita," I say. Our inside joke about my dog's name, but she knows I mean she looks beautiful.

We practiced my interview answers right on this bed. When the gringa behind the bulletproof glass at the embassy asked me all the questions, I didn't hesitate. I was proud of tricking the lady. I felt like James Bond, or La Usurpadora. But then, the gringa asked Roberto Sr., "Sir, is this your son?"

She asked in a soft voice, not threatening at all, in a beautiful accent, like the way gringos speak Spanish in Mexican movies. My pretend-dad started oozing large sweat beads from his forehead, his armpits; a small puddle seeped through his chest.

"Is this your son?" the gringa asked again, leaning closer to the glass, her voice harsher.

Roberto Sr. looked at me with almost a squint. His light-brown eyes, his face tilting to the side like he was already apologizing. I stared at La USA flag behind the gringa's light-brown hair. I counted the stars. Roberto Sr.'s hand pulled me from the bulletproof glass, across the linoleum tiles, dragging me out of the glass door, past the guards, past the turnstile, onto the street.

I was sad, but I didn't cry—not until I got home and hugged Abuelita. Then Mali. They hugged me at the same time. "Don't worry, everything is gonna be okay, you'll see them soon," they said, and picked me up, my legs dangling.

"La Migra—you know, the bad gringuitos—didn't catch your mom," Mali continues, now lying down next to me, her arms around me, her stiff hair on my face. She's wearing too much hairspray.

"Your mom says she doesn't know how she blended into the night so well." I picture Mom dressed in black, running to a tree, then a bush, molding into each shape. "Oh, and she saw snow for the first time when she crossed. ¡Snow!" Her entire face gets rounder when she smiles, her big eyes even bigger. "I want to see snow, ¿don't you?"

"Absolutely," I say. I want to make a snowball like in the movies. Mom did this in 1995, when I was five. My U.S. embassy interview was in 1997. And before that, in 1996, Mali and I tried to get a visa— a real visa, but the U.S. embassy said no like they said no to Mom. A much meaner gringa said there was "no way any of you are getting a visa. Next!"

It's 1999. I'm nine now, and I want to cuddle with Mom. I'm sad remembering Roberto. Mali looks sad because no one is showing up to take her to the dance.

"They left me with my curls made," Mali says.

"It's okay." I grab her sleeping clothes, an oversized, bright-orange T-shirt Mom sent with Don Leo from California. The shirt makes Mali look like a carrot. There's something written on it in English that we don't understand, except the word *love*.

Mali gives up hope and puts the shirt on. Our legs lean against the wall's bumpy surface. We count stars through the skylight Grandpa placed in the middle of the room and come up with stories for each star. I always name one after Mom first: Patricia.

3-23-99

MOM TRUSTS DON DAGO. Dad trusts him. Grandpa. Abuelita.

"That viejo is a rabo verde, fucking pícaro, but you know what, he's never done shit wrong besides groped someone's ass," La Chele Gloria—the fruit vendor across the street who I hang out with when Abuelita wraps up the day's sales—says with her loud megaphone of a voice, her hands constantly moving: cutting fruit, diving into her apron to give customers change.

"Always delivers the women safely," she continues. "Mirá, I see, I hear *everything,* bicho." She swipes the air to keep flies from landing on her sliced-fruit basket filled with pineapples, watermelon, cucumbers, mangos, oranges. "I know you'll get there safe."

"¿Where?" I say, already knowing the "there" she's referring to.

"Over there, cerotito, with the bridges, pizzas, swimming pools—you better not think you're a gringo." She grins, showing her full set of crooked teeth, her wrinkles cracked open when she grins. "You better not forget about me, cerotito." If anyone else called me that I would get mad, but if La Chele Gloria curses you out, it means she likes you.

Abuelita doesn't like La Chele Gloria's big mouth, and warns me against saying too much about Mom or Dad, about me leaving. "If you tell her A, tomorrow it will be J, the next day P, and finally it will come back to you as Z," Abuelita warns Mali, Lupe, and me whenever we come back with La Chele Gloria's fruit bags. But I love her stories. They're loud, filled with laughter, and every other word is a bad word.

"Vos, bicho, you'll hear bad words eventually, hijueputa," says La Chele Gloria. I like how she says the first part of the word fast, chewing the first two syllables into one. *Hijue* becomes *jue.* Then she emphasizes the *pu* with a popping sound, landing on the *ta,* elongating the ahhhh: *jue-pú-tahhhh.*

She says that to me now as I order a bag of sliced cucumbers sprinkled with alguashte, salt, and lime. "¿Anything else, juepúta?"

I shake my head.

"Ey. Vos. Cerote. *Shhhttt*." She's trying to get the attention of another customer, who's shaking his head because La Chele Gloria is cursing in front of me. She makes that noise by tightening her jaw, biting down on her teeth, then getting a little spit and pushing her tongue toward her teeth, her lips like they're getting ready for a kiss. As she says it, she nods. It's a thing everyone does, but when she does it, it's so accentuated, like she's performing at a talent show.

"Vos. *Shhhttt*. No te hagás el maje, cerote," she tells the guy, a regular, and they all laugh. Hers, a thunderous laugh that fills the air, rattles the ground, tickles my belly, and it's why I order fruit from La Chele Gloria every day. Not because she makes the best fruit, but because her joy is infectious. Plus, she *does* know it all. She's the one who first told me *the* story of the day Dad left for La USA.

"Bicho, cerote, mirá, you were little, like this." She calculates my height with her palm horizontal to the ground, which is how you measure animals.

"You measure people like this," I correct her, showing her the proper way to demonstrate human height, my hand erect, fingers pointed skyward.

"Mirá este hijo de la gran puuuta," she says, looking at the stranger. "¿You think you're better than me, cerotito? ¡Respect your elders! ¡Those fucking nuns don't teach you shit!" She says it loud enough so everyone in the clinic turns their heads, before she lets out a laugh that, kilometers away, people can hear. Her laugh covers the entire block, drenches it with her thick, moist, crooked smile.

"You were so fucking little," she continues, "your dad didn't want to go, but you know, the war. Dangerous. We didn't think it was gonna end. That mierda *hasn't* ended," she says, pausing to point with her knife to the pineapple she's cutting the eyes out of. "It was dawn, and your mom must've been asleep. Maybe she didn't know he was leaving, he's a fucker like that, he didn't want to make a big deal."

She slices the pineapple, yellow juice coats her hands.

"He didn't tell anyone. But he said goodbye to your grandpa. Then walked out, that way, with only his backpack." La Chele Gloria points with her lips pursed, nodding in the direction of my house.

After I heard this story the first time, I asked Mom; she confirmed Dad walked through our cornfield, toward the asphalt road, to the bus stop under the biggest ceiba tree in town.

"Then you walked behind him. No one fucking saw you," La Chele Gloria says, now cutting the pineapple slices into chunks so they'll fit into a plastic bag. "I remember your mom waking when the sun was about to be up over the volcanoes. I was setting up here. She was screaming. Maybe she thought your dad took you. Then your abuelita was screaming. Your aunts. Your grandpa. Everyone saying, '¡El niño, el niño, he's gone, help, help!' All of them freaking the fuck out. I thought your dad *had* taken you. But then I realized ese pendejo wouldn't do that. You had *just* learned to walk. I stopped everything and helped look for you, cerote.

"Some of us looked in your property, others up and down this shitty dirt road. We looked in the clinic. Then, finally, Memo The Mechanic started yelling that he had found you on the other road, so we all ran across the field." La Chele Gloria pauses with her knife in the air as she's cutting her second pineapple. Points it at me. "You were sitting on the roots of the ceiba, your arms crossed, waiting for the bus to come back. You must've waited an hour. I still remember the leafless tree filled with its cotton pods. Bursting. Putting that white shit everywhere in the air. And ufff, your mom. Oh, your tiny mom, I remember her face all crunched up like a prune." La Chele Gloria points the knife at her short, curly, dirty-blond hair to signal that she's got a flawless memory. "Your mom couldn't help but beat the shit out of you. But only after she hugged you. *I* would've beat the shit out of you. Bicho requetependejo, cerotón. Your poor mom, we had to stop her from hitting you more."

Except the last bit, I like hearing this story. A version of it has been told to me by so many people, but La Chele Gloria tells it best. The nurses, the doctors, the tamalera, La Belleza (my favorite drunk who stops at our house for water after lunch), almost every vendor at the market. Even the priest has heard it. I like it, it's like I'm famous.

"You've always wanted to be with them," La Chele Gloria continues as she stuffs chunks of the second pineapple into plastic bags. "You'll be up there, bicho pasmado. But you better wake the fuck up and grow before you leave, ponete las pilas. ¡Avivá! ¡Buzo! ¡Trucha!"

I'm not slow or little like she thinks. But I've learned my lesson. I don't correct her. Instead, I nod and grab my fruit and walk across to Abuelita's stand. Don Dago has promised a safer trip than Mom's. I'm almost ten. Almost in fifth grade. It's mid-March, Mother's Day is just around the corner. It's not a matter of *if* Don Dago will be taking me, but a matter of *when*.

3-31-99

I'VE ATTENDED ESCUELA PARROQUIAL Fray Cosme Spessotto since preschool. Mom used to walk me, or ride me on her bike. Now Abuelita or Grandpa walks me there. Mostly Grandpa. We walk and don't say much. When we get to the black iron gate at the front of the school, Grandpa points at my shoes and takes out his handkerchief so I can clean the dust off. Other times, he tucks my shirt in, or when there's nothing out of place, he dusts my shoulder.

"Always look bien pimp-it-is-nice," he says every time he drops me off. He likes that phrase, "pimp-it-is-nice." He smiles and watches me walk through the gate. Whenever he has to leave the house for any reason, Grandpa polishes his boots, irons his pants and his shirt, shaves, combs his hair with oil, and drenches himself in cologne. Every crease on his clothes is supposed to be there. He tops the look off with his clean handkerchief he also irons and tucks inside one of his back pockets; in the other one, his black plastic comb.

But when he's home, he wears the same pair of jeans, no belt, old sandals, and, if he wears one, an old white T-shirt—the ones he gets at the hardware store when he buys paint, always an XL, *Sherwin-Williams* printed on it.

"Big-bellied old man," Abuelita says, or my favorite, "stinky old man," whenever Grandpa is out in the backyard raking leaves, cutting old limbs from the banana groves.

Grandpa collects these shirts like he collects free calendars from every store he visits during his December errands. He stacks the calendars in his room next to the pile of folded shirts, and by May, starts using them as kindling for his afternoon fires where he also burns leaves or the day's trash.

I go out there when he's burning things. I like to see how different materials catch fire. Plastic is my favorite, but I hate the smell. It burns slow, turning black first, then melting a little. Sometimes the flames turn a dull green or a bright blue. I like it. But when Grandpa sees me watching him, he gives me a job: I collect the driest casings, like pods the coconuts grow out of. When the coconuts are mature, that part falls off. It looks and feels like coconut husks. I collect the casings from under the trees so the mounds of trash will light up. I like the sound the coconut casings make when they catch fire, like the fuse of a firework making its way to the powder.

Grandpa is out back burning trash right now, but I like swinging on the hammock with Mali. Walks to school, walks to church, walks to the barbershop, and trash burning: that's the only time I spend with Grandpa. He's quiet. I'm shy around him. Even though he's been sober since Mom left, I'm afraid he will go back to his old ways and yell at Abuelita, hit Mali, fire his gun in the air. But he's always been nice to me. When he drops me off at school, he gives me money, a colón or two so I can buy something. "Only if you need it," he says, and grins.

He leaves me at my Catholic school filled with nuns. Most of them are from Spain, but there are some from Costa Rica and Nicaragua. All of them are light-skinned, and they don't ever smile. They hit most kids with the knotted white cords tied around their brown habits, or with wooden meter sticks. The closest I came to getting hit was in first grade when, after watching too many novelas on TV, I asked Margarita to be my girlfriend.

"¿How's Margarita? ¿She your noviecita yet?" Mali asks as she rubs a cut piece of aloe on my skin, because yesterday we went to the beach and I'm peeling bad. Then she swings the hammock to cool the sticky liquid off.

"She's still not talking to me," I respond, short and stern. I don't like when Mali asks about Margarita, which is why I try to avoid asking her about her suitors. The nuns called my grandparents and Margarita's mom to tell them I was "too young for girlfriends." *I'm too young for love,* I wrote on the blackboard one hundred times after school, the first and only detention of my life.

"¿How is she?" Mali asks again. "You're getting red," she teases.

"¿Remember when I was good at grammar?" I change the subject.

"You're still good at it, Chepito," she says, kicking the ground with her much-longer legs, so we can swing harder. "The Grammar Whiz." My nickname at school. "¡You shook the president's hand, tontito!" she says, excited and proud.

That happened in second grade, during the biannual grammar contest. All the schools in El Salvador participate. First, there's a local competition, then a departmental competition, where the winners from all the municipalities across our department of La Paz compete for one spot at the national level. El Salvador has fourteen departments, so fourteen second-graders make it to the finals. I was the second-grader who represented La Paz. ¡Me! I got a medal that my parents have asked me to send with Don Leo. I was the first in my school's history to make it that far.

"¡You were on TV! ¿Remember? We looked on every channel, and there you were," Mali says, excited, her round face sweaty, smiling.

There was no footage of me in particular; just a brief story of the competition and a shot of everyone who participated, so quick I couldn't pick myself out from the crowd. The only proof I have that I was there is a picture Mother Superior took of me shaking President Armando Calderón Sol's hand.

The weekends before, I walked to school to study grammar for six hours each day. We had a month to prepare for nationals, which would be held in the fanciest hotel I've ever been to: El Hotel Inter-Continental.

The day of the competition, Grandpa was the only one who could come with me; Abuelita, Mali, and Lupe all had to work. Mother Superior picked us up in her small white Honda. At the hotel there was so much food, but I didn't eat any. I'd already eaten Abuelita's breakfast, but also, I was nervous. Abuelita and Grandpa eat with their hands. I eat with my hands. ¿What would the judges think? ¿Were they judging how we ate? Mother Superior used a fork and knife. Grandpa grabbed the scrambled eggs from his plate with the pan francés in his hands. I just sat there, watching them eat, silently repeating the grammar rules that still give me the most trouble: every word that ends with *-aje,* always a *j* not a *g.* As in *salvaje, ropaje, abordaje, masaje.*

When they called for us to enter the ballroom where the fourteen second-graders were going to take the test, Grandpa kneeled in front of me and said, "Do your best, we believe in you."

I knew the "we" included my parents, who had called the day before to wish me luck. I didn't want to let them down. I didn't want to let my school down. My town. First place got a thousand colones, plus an entire encyclopedia collection for themselves and their school. Second got five hundred plus the same books. Third place only got the books. I wanted something besides the participation medal.

At the other competitions I had fun, I was trying to solve problems, but this time it was after Mali and I had been turned down for the visa, after I pretended to be Roberto Jr. I couldn't stop thinking of the prizes. That maybe my parents would see how smart and ready I was to be with them.

I didn't even place in the top three. They didn't say how low I was out of fourteen, but I felt like I was the very last. I knew I lost the moment I sat down. It was cold. AC at full blast. My mind didn't work. I left a lot of questions blank.

"You did your best, we're so proud of you," Mali says to me now. I can smell the trash burning in the backyard. I think of the medal, how I've kept it locked with my favorite toys and now must send it to my parents with Don Leo.

"I love that medallita, ¿see? It's why the nuns called it a victory," she says. The picture of me shaking the president's hand is framed in Mother Superior's office. They've already signed me up for the grammar competition this year—but I don't want to still be here when the next competition is held.

"You can be a pet to your gringuito teachers," Mali says.

I plan to be. I hope the kids up there don't make fun of me like they do here. They call me nerd. Even my friends. They make fun of me for being smart, but also for being chubby. I just started playing soccer all the time, playing tag. I don't want them to make fun of how I look anymore. To flick my chest because I "have boobs." To call me "niña, niña" when I take my shirt off.

The smart part, that's not my fault. I want to make my parents proud. When I don't get a ten on an assignment, I get sad. Plus, valedictorians get free tuition and get the next year's books for free. Margarita has gotten second place every other year; she gets free tuition but she has to buy books. It's why I like her. She's smart.

Still, my parents send money, which Mali uses to buy me Yoplait, Kellogg's Frosted Flakes, and my favorite: strawberries. They don't have that stuff here in town, so once or twice a month we take a bus to Zacatecoluca or San Salvador, to a Súper Selectos.

"You're the smartest kid I know, Chepito," Mali says, smiling. "Your mom's work paid off," by which she means my "afternoon sessions," when Mom brought out a blackboard she bought the moment I could hold a piece of chalk.

The blackboard is now put away in the space between my bed's headboard and the wall. I still hate that thing. Mom purposely sat me here, out front, so people walking on the street could see me. She hit me if I got up before completing one of her assignments. She hit me if I got it wrong too many times. She hit me if I didn't do what she asked. It was terrible. But I could write the entire alphabet before anyone in preschool could.

Mali tried to do the same when Mom left. We sat here on our porch in front of the blackboard. We still do from time to time if I don't understand something. But Mali has never hit me. Abuelita and Grandpa have never hit me either. I listen to them. I listened to Mom también, but she was impatient.

Everyone in town reminds me how smart my parents are. They alternated being valedictorians every year. Both first place. Mali says, "You were always gonna be like them." I hope I am. "They're so proud of you," she continues, swinging on the hammock, and I hope they are. Our parakeet keeps chirping.

I don't want to let my parents or Mali or Abuelita or Grandpa or Lupe down. I want to be better than the gringos, to be valedictorian every year over there in La USA.

Abuelita always boasts about me at her pupusa stand. Grandpa también. "This one shook the president's hand. ¿Have *you* shaken the president's hand?" Grandpa asks our barber every time we visit him.

"Poor nuns are gonna miss you," Mali says.

I hadn't thought about that. The nuns don't know I'm not going to nationals. I wonder if they suspect anything.

"Everything will be okay, Chepito," Mali says, repeating what I was thinking. The aloe is dry. My skin still stings a little, but is better.

"Let's get ready for dinner," she says as she kisses my forehead like Mom used to and gets off the hammock, carefully, making sure I don't swing too much when she stands.

4-1-99

GRANDPA WALKS IN SILENCE. It's a humid and hot Jueves Santo. Today is the day the "Romans" run from house to house with their fake spears, spray-painted armor, red skirts, and cardboard sandals, shouting that they're looking for Jesús. Jesús is usually played by a local drunk with a long beard and long hair who needs a few colones.

I'm old enough to know that's not the real Jesús, but I like the sound of the matracas: wooden boxes with metal screws, nails, keys, washers trapped inside them. When the Romans twirl the matracas, it sounds like a thousand trains approaching. The Romans first look for Jesús near the pier; slowly, they make their way through town, entering houses, knocking their spears on the ground, twirling their matracas, asking kids if they're hiding Jesucristo.

It's still morning, so the streets are silent. Everyone is resting, the paletero's bells don't ring, La Chele Gloria won't set up her fruit stand, the drunks aren't asking for change, even the dogs aren't out walking, because it's already very hot and humid.

The school's front gate is unlocked, only for Grandpa and me. We walk to Mother Superior's office close to the front of the school. Her door is also unlocked, and when we open it, she is waiting for us on a large leather chair behind her wooden desk, a golden crucifix nailed to the wall. Wooden and crystal rosaries hang between framed pictures of Spain.

"¿How can I help you?" Mother Superior says in her serious voice. She looks Grandpa straight in the eyes when she says it. I remain standing.

With his handkerchief, Grandpa wipes the sweat from his forehead, then says, "Disculpe la molestia, Madre, especially on this day."

"No worries, Don Chepe," she responds with a faint smile at the very corners of her thin lips. "Anything for Javiercito."

"We're here to ask if you could please grant my grandson permission to miss a week of school," Grandpa says, quick but firm, like I imagine he gave orders to policemen when he was one.

"Oh," she says, sliding away from the desk on her leather chair. When the wheels stop, she continues, "But he's never missed a single day of school." She slides toward the fan, noticing Grandpa and I are sweating.

"Well, yes, I've made sure he comes to school every single day," Grandpa explains, stumbling at first, but catching himself midsentence, ending it full of confidence. He leans toward Mother Superior, almost whispering, "I've raised him as my own son. He's punctual like me. Well behaved."

She cuts him off. "One of our very best . . ."

"Which is why we're here, to show *you* respect. We wouldn't take him without asking."

"Thank you for taking the time, Don Chepe." She leans closer to Grandpa, arms on the chair.

"Our pleasure." Grandpa adds a smile.

"If you don't mind," she asks, "¿why is he missing an entire week?" Her eyes are fixed on Grandpa, the same look she and other nuns get when they're about to hit you with their knotted cords.

I've seen Grandpa rehearsing what he's about to say; he wants to get it right. I know he feels guilty for lying to a woman of faith, but someone at the market warned him that Jesuit nuns are infamous for calling the police on their students trying to cross the Guatemalan border.

Grandpa takes a breath, pauses. "Well, Madre," he says. Pauses. Continues, "Last year we didn't let Chepito go to that zoo trip in Guatemala City, because his mom dreamed he got lost."

"I remember," she says, nodding her head slowly, showing the top of her dark-brown habit, which makes her look like a penguin.

"We listened and didn't let him go."

"Premonitions are to be honored. God always sends signs." She places her hands on the desk, one hand on top of the other.

"He cried and cried. You know how much Chepito loves animals." Grandpa slows down when he says "animals." Making it sound like a ten-syllable word. He looks at me, which is my cue to look sad, which I do by looking down at the tiles in front of my shoes.

"Of course." She nods, showing the top of her penguin-head again.

"His mother felt so bad, she's sent us money to take him to Guatemala. I have some friends from my time in the military who live there."

Mother Superior acknowledges his service by pressing her lips together, moving her head down, the slightest nod.

Grandpa continues, "My friends will host us a few days. Hope you understand, Madre."

"Oh, I see. Okay. It's okay," she says, followed by "Don't worry about it. Javiercito, have a great trip." She stares as she gets up from her leather chair, shakes Grandpa's hand, taps my head, and walks us out. "Go with God," she says as she opens the door. "God bless you." We walk past her.

In the hallway outside her office, she calls my name. I turn around and she says, "Javiercito, I suggest you talk to your teachers so you get your assignments. You don't want to lose your first place now." She smiles again, not showing teeth, slightly moving her thin lips.

Grandpa laughs, but I don't find it funny. ¿What if I don't make it and I have to come back, behind in school? My family would have to pay for school. I won't be with my parents. No. I snap out of it as Grandpa opens the front gate and closes it after us. The matracas are not out yet. It's humid and hotter than when we entered Mother Superior's office.

He takes his handkerchief out and wipes his face. He's smirking. He's proud Mother Superior bought our lies. It's true Mom didn't let me go to Guatemala with my classmates because she dreamed a gorilla took me from the group. I was so mad at her. The zoo in San Salvador doesn't have gorillas, only spider monkeys. I've always wanted to see a gorilla. But besides that, everything else was a lie. Lying makes me feel cool. I hope Mother Superior doesn't suspect anything; that she won't call the police. My grandparents have said they remember, after I got to nationals, Mother Superior saying El Salvador needs kids like me, that people like me will make this country better, that it would be a shame if I ever left, like some kids at school already have.

WHEN WE MAKE IT home, the matracas aren't near, and as we open the gate Grandpa built out of barbwire and sticks, we see Don Dago on our front porch. The only other time he surprised me like this was when I came back from school and he asked me to open my mouth. He found a cavity I didn't know I had in the second-to-last molar at the bottom of my jaw, on the right side.

"Fix it, Don Chepe, I can't take him like that," he told Grandpa. It's how Mali met Daniel The Dentist—one of her suitors.

We say hi. Don Dago says hi to Grandpa.

"¿Do you want pepetos?" Grandpa asks.

"¡Indeed!" Don Dago always responds to the promise of fruit.

Grandpa, Abuelita, Mali, and Lupe—who's visiting with my five-year-old cousin, Julia—walk from the gate to the backyard, Abuelita leading the pack. *Indeed* is the signal for Grandpa to grab the long bamboo stick with a net he uses to cut and catch the ripe mangos without letting them fall to the ground.

"Gracias, Don Chepe." Don Dago fakes like he didn't know my grandparents gift him fruit first thing every time he visits.

"¿How are you, kid?" he says to me.

"Bien, señor," I say, trying not to act shy, to show him that I'm older and can have a conversation. But I am shy. I don't trust him.

"¿Your teeth good?" he asks in a detective's tone. Then, without warning, he grabs my jaw with his thick fingers and says, "Open."

He twists my head so he can see the top row. He nods his head yes several times. His mustache goes up and down like a caterpillar.

"Good," Don Dago says. "Let's talk inside, Don Chepe." And everyone follows except Lupe, Julia, and me, who stay under the trees.

Lupe is nineteen and younger than Mali. She had Julia when she was fourteen. She doesn't care when I pretend I'm a fly under the window outside the kitchen, where the adults talk. From this angle, if I stand on my toes, I can see their lips. They're whispering. Grandpa smiles to Don Dago, saying something about my assignments and a good idea.

Don Dago mentions a black backpack—but my Ninja Turtle backpack is bright green: Rafael, Donatello, Leonardo, and Miguel Ángel wield their weapons, frozen in a plastic patch near the backpack's handles. Their weapons are textured, which is why I chose it with Mali in San Salvador.

Don Dago shakes his head no at Grandpa. "No." Repeats it. They go back and forth. Abuelita asks something I can't make out because she's shorter and I can't see her lips. Don Dago paces.

The matracas are a few blocks away. Maybe they're about to split between the asphalt road and our dirt one. *Traca-traca-traca-traca* like a rain of mangos on the roof. Don Dago says something louder: "¿You got your passport in order, Don Chepe?"

Grandpa leans closer. Abuelita is almost crying.

"Yes," Grandpa says loud and firm, staring directly at Don Dago. They're almost the same height. Don Dago, two or three centimeters taller.

"Órale," Don Dago responds. It's the only time I've heard him say that. It's what Mexicans say in novelas. "Don't forget it."

Abuelita makes the sign of the cross in the air and looks up at the sky, which is blocked by the kitchen's roof. She whispers something. Grandpa walks closer to Don Dago and I think they're shaking hands. Neither of them smiles. No one says anything, and Don Dago starts walking to our front gate. He stops where Abuelita sets up her pupusa stand, turning to Grandpa. "Same thing like with Pati, don. I'll call two days before." Then he leaves.

The Romans come rushing down the street asking for Jesucristo, *traca-traca-traca-traca*. They walk past Don Dago. Stop in front of our gate—I'm too old to pretend. Julia laughs at the men dressed like that, the sound of the matracas so loud, like wrenches struck against a metal door.

4-4-99

IT'S BEEN THREE DAYS, and Don Dago hasn't called like he said he would.

"Coyotes take their time, like tortoises, tontito," Mali says as she swings us in the backyard hammock under the avocado tree, next to

Abuelita's bedroom. We're eating a bowl of green mangos Mali has sliced and drenched in lime, salt, and salsa Perry. "They have to get the other people ready."

¿What other people? This is the first time someone mentioned other people. I thought it was just gonna be Don Dago and me, walking, running, jumping over the fence, all the way to Mom.

"Don't worry, Chepito," Mali says as she stuffs another crunchy mango slice into her mouth, wincing as she tastes the sour lime juice mixed with the tart green fruit. But I *am* worried. ¿What are the nuns gonna think if I don't show up to school? ¿Are they gonna call the police?

I try to think of other things, like how Jesús got crucified on Friday and rose earlier today. Grandpa will walk me to church this afternoon so the nuns think I'm still a good Catholic. He's probably gonna tell them that my trip has to wait a few days. Mali is acting strange. Everyone is acting strange.

For Viernes Santo, Mali took me to the capital with one of her ex-boyfriends' parents. They still visit us from time to time. They drive from San Pedro Nonualco in Don Pablito's blue pickup truck to pick my grandparents up and eat cócteles de concha at the pier. Sometimes they take us to the beach. This Friday they took Mali and me to San Salvador. Don Pablito showed us the best pupusería he knows, which was only ok, definitely not better than Abuelita's. Then we went to Los Planes de Rendero and we caught the sunset at La Puerta del Diablo—two places I'd heard so much about but had never been to. It was windy and cold, and I saw my very first cypress tree.

It was fun seeing Don Pablito and Doña Luisita again. I like them. They love Mali and wanted Marlon to marry her instead of getting back with his ex and moving to Spain. Don Pablito and Doña Luisita seem happy and act how I wish my grandparents would. They share their food, their drinks, they hug each other, kiss, and hold hands, ¡even though they're old!

¡I've never even seen my grandparents hold hands! I sort of understand because when Grandpa still worked at the airport, whenever he was off the next day, he came home a little drunk, but not too much. He dropped off his things, changed, and walked across the cornfield to El Cumero's metal shop. He spent the entire night there, drinking. Close to midnight, he returned, banging on the kitchen door. Sometimes Abuelita opened it and didn't ask any questions. Other times Grandpa broke in. The real fights happened when he wanted to play music. He played his boom box so loud. Abuelita yelled at him. Mom yelled at him. He yelled back. Mali stayed in bed with me. Lupe put a pillow over her head.

The worst time, I cried after he pointed his gun at Abuelita. Another time, Mom broke a blender on his feet and Grandpa chased after her with his machete. I don't like to think about those nights. It's why I'm scared of him. It's probably why Abuelita doesn't even hug him. Grandpa doesn't hug anyone. Not even me.

"Don't worry, Chepito," Mali repeats again. She can tell I was thinking bad things. She hands me a slice. The mangos are crunchy, salty, bite-size, just how I like them.

"Plus," Mali continues, "Grandpa will be with you in Guatemala." She puts another piece in her mouth. "That's, like, almost half the trip," she struggles to say, almost spitting little green bits out.

Ever since Don Dago showed up on Thursday, my parents have called twice a day. Whenever The Baker's son comes over saying So-and-So is calling, I hope it's Don Dago. I think Abuelita, Grandpa, Mali, Lupe, even little cousin Julia, feel the same. They stick out their necks to hear what name comes out of The Baker's son's mouth. Then, when it's not Don Dago's name, they wilt like the ferns in Abuelita's garden when she doesn't water them.

IN BETWEEN LA BONITA's barks, through thick, humid air, The Baker's son yells, "¡Phone call!" from the street. I run to our front gate.

"It's Don Dago," he says like it's no one important. I scream Don

Dago's name at the top of my lungs, louder than La Bonita. Grandpa hears and rushes out of his room, rushes back in to get money to pay The Baker.

"¡I told you! ¡Let's go, let's go!" Mali says, her cheeks almost closing her eyes from how much she's smiling. Abuelita gets her things. La Bonita stops barking and circles in place.

From the front gate I run back to the kitchen to leave the bowl of fruit I forgot I was holding in my hands. Juices spill all over my shirt. I don't care. Everyone is ready. Lupe and Julia stay to guard the house.

In The Baker's living room, we wait for the beige phone to ring.

It rings once. The Baker picks up, hands Grandpa the phone. In less than thirty seconds, Don Dago says what he needs to say and Grandpa hangs up.

"It's done. Gracias a Dios," Grandpa says as he puts the phone back where it sleeps and turns his body to us. "Two days." His voice softer than usual, about to break. His words fall on the cement floor, his eyes wide open.

¡Two days! I start screaming. Spinning. Jumping up and down. Repeating, "¡I'm going to see my parents! ¡I'm going to see my parents!" Tears running down my cheeks. I don't care that The Baker's children look at me. ¡I'm so happy! Finally, the thing I want most is happening.

Grandpa has to hold me in place in order to keep me from running into The Baker's furniture. "Wait," he says, pressing his hands on my shoulder to anchor me, his thin eyebrows, his perfectly rectangular face closer to my face. "We have to call your parents."

"Yes, yeah," I mumble. My shoes feel like they have coals in them. I can't stay still. It's really happening. My trip. *The* trip. Trip trip trip.

The very first thing Mom tells me is "¡Finally, Chepito!" She's almost crying, I know she's happy, I'm happy. Her voice like a wet good-night kiss to my forehead. Full, like a hug. She says more things. I can barely understand. Dad says something similar. His voice, ¡his voice! I will finally see it come out of *his* mouth. Touch *his* mustache. *His* hair.

"Con la voluntad de Diosito en el cielo, everything, everything, will turn out as planned," both of them say. "You will be okay, we will see you soon, Don Dago will bring you here safe and fast. Te queremos mucho, muchisisísimo."

Then Mom asks for Grandpa.

He tells Mom something about me and him taking a bus to San Salvador, to Terminal de Occidente. "The same one," Grandpa tells her. "Noon." His voice back to normal. Stern, like he's annoyed to be saying details.

I get the phone again and Mom and Dad explain I will be with six other people. That everything will be ok. That they have toys and clothes waiting for me. I can almost feel Mom's warmth. Her laughter, her hands, her front bangs on my face as she kisses my cheeks. I can almost see Dad, his gold chain.

My grandparents and Mali walk back home, but I run. I run directly to my drawer where I keep the albums of pictures my parents have sent from up there. I make Mali look at them with me.

4-5-99

TODAY WAS MY LAST day of school, but nobody knows. At school I wrote:

JOSÉ JAVIER ZAMORA
LUNES 5 DE ABRIL, 1999

No made-up numbers underneath. At recess, I got the assignments from all my teachers. Everyone believes I'm only missing a week. That I'll be back next Monday. It's easier than I thought to lie to my best friends. Don Dago told Grandpa I could tell absolutely no one I'm leaving. My parents reminded me of the same thing yesterday and today again when they called.

But none of them said anything about inviting my best friends over to play with my toys one last time after school. Mom would've never allowed it unless I had finished all of my homework, I mean *all of it*. But Mali and Abuelita are different, always have been.

Alejandro, Torito, Alán, and Freddy walked me home from school. They all know how much I love my toys. I never bring my newest ones out to play, not even when family visits. Even if the president visited, I wouldn't bring them out; they're sacred. I keep the Spider-Man Dad and Mom sent when I turned seven in his box. From time to time, I slightly open the box so I can smell a little of La USA: a smell so new, fresh, like nothing that's here.

But since it's the last time I'll see my friends until I return, I show them my prized possessions: a Wolverine that can move all of his joints, my Red Power Ranger that with a push of a button can change his helmet into his real-life face, my ThunderCats Lion-O sword that glows in the dark, and *the* Jurassic Park T. Rex that walks and growls with a remote control. All of these I never, *never* bring out when my friends visit. These toys I keep in my "best toy" drawer only Mali and I have the key for, the drawer that will be waiting for me when I return—maybe Christmas. I *will* come back, not like my other friends who left and stayed in La USA.

Alejandro is two years older than me; he's my best friend. We're in the same grade because he flunked second grade twice. He's almost like an older brother. Except I'm smarter. I gift him my Classic Batman I never use anymore.

"¿Vieja, Javier, why?" he says with his fragile voice, shrugging his shoulders like he does when he asks questions in class.

"My parents told me to do something nice. *And,*" I add, to make it seem real, "*and* our moms were best friends," which is true, but they don't really talk anymore since Mom left. He nods and hugs me.

I do the same with the other three, reusing the lie about my parents wanting me to do something nice for my friends. To Torito I gift my Blue Power Ranger with a broken arm. Sometimes Torito gets jealous when I get first place. Maybe now that I'm leaving he can win.

Alán is better than me at soccer. He's the one who taught me how to curve the ball, and he likes cars—his dad drives a trailer truck like

Erik Estrada in *Dos Mujeres, Un Camino*—so I gift him a red Hot Wheels truck.

To Freddy, who never wants to play cops and robbers, I give a Robin action figure from the *Batman Forever* series. His cape is missing.

None of them suspect anything. If they do, they don't say much. I feel like James Bond again, hiding information. They leave and I say goodbye, like any other day.

It's late now. Mali and I are where we always are before and after dinner: her bed, staring at the sky through the skylight. The moon is halfway full.

"¿Will you miss your friend-citos?" Mali asks. It's after dinner, and we're so full from Abuelita's yucca frita, my favorite dish. She promised to cook it this morning after she asked me what I wanted for dinner. She promised she would make it extra special and she did; she added the fried smelt, hard-boiled egg, queso duro on top, everything. And, Abuelita being Abuelita, she also made my favorite pupusas: bean, cheese, and loroco.

"Yes," I tell Mali as I scoot closer to her, and I think I mean it. I *will* miss my friends. "But I'll be back to visit."

"You better," she says, and hugs me, her skin sticky from the humidity.

"¿Again?" Mali asks, holding one of the albums we looked at yesterday and left on top of the dresser next to the bed.

I nod. She's holding the small yellow album that says *Kodak* on it and has a picture of the Golden Gate. When she sits next to me, I realize the albums are going to stay, just like my toys, the fruits up on the trees, La Bonita, my friends, my cat, my parakeet, and my entire family.

We flip through the pictures, but it feels different. We pause on a picture of Dad in front of a garden. On the back it says, *This is one of the gardens I made.* He stands tall, his thick mustache, his big muscles and gold chain. His hands rest on his hips like Superman after saving someone.

I don't remember ever touching his skin. There are pictures of both of us, me on his shoulder or in his arms. In one picture, he's wearing a soccer uniform and we're standing in a soccer field—he's about to play a game, or just played. I've heard his voice numerous times, I can pick it out from a crowd, but I'm finally going to meet him.

Mali and I sit up in the bed, our backs against the wall. It's completely dark outside. The bats flap their wings, all of the stars are out, their light competing with the moon's.

"Let's look at the stars through the skylight," I say. Our arms touch. Mali kisses my forehead. When I feel her touch my skin, the wrinkles of her lips, I get sad. I didn't think I would get sad. I've been so excited to leave. This might be the last time we sit here looking up at the stars for a long time. I pay attention to her breathing. I try to match it. But now, I want to curse, I want to curse so bad that the nuns will make me say a thousand Hail Marys as punishment. But I don't. I stay quiet. I swallow it like a big gulp of cough syrup. We count the stars.

4-6-99

IT'S DAWN—INDIGO LIKE when Mom left. Mali kisses me awake and I have to get ready. The roosters crow, La Bonita barks, the birds sing, the world is waking up. The stars turn off one by one.

To shower, I pull water from a well with a bucket. Grandpa already showered. Abuelita dries me off. Mali irons my clothes. The outfit has been picked out: a nice dress shirt, dark blue. Dark-blue jeans. A black belt. Black dress shoes.

Next to the hard-boiled eggs, avocado, queso duro, and tortillas, a black backpack. Even the brand name has been crossed out. Inside it: a dark T-shirt, black pants, two pairs of underwear, an extra pair of shoes, the plastic toothbrush, a comb, soccer shorts, Colgate toothpaste, a bar of Palmolive soap, Head & Shoulders shampoo, and another dark-blue, short-sleeved dress shirt. There's a notebook, Bic pens, pencils, and the assignments my teachers gave me.

"Everything has to be dark colors," Mali explains. "Don Dago's orders."

I eat, and Grandpa waits by the door, holding my black backpack and his own regular one. He looks at his watch.

Abuelita combs my hair. Mali kneels in front of me to button my shirt. She tucks it in. Kisses my forehead.

Lupe is here, the earliest I've seen her come visit. She hugs me, kisses me, wishes me luck. Julia is sleeping in Abuelita's bed between two pillows to keep her from falling.

Abuelita kisses me, kneels to hug me. Then Mali and Abuelita hug me at the same time. Only now, I cry. This is it. The thing I wanted to happen, but it's happening so fast.

"Te queremos mucho, Chepito. Te cuidás. Que Dios te bendiga, here, everywhere, always. We'll be waiting for you. Praying you'll make it there safely, Javiercito." Their voices almost in unison, soft, breaking with every word, tears running down their round faces. I can't stop crying.

Then they make the cross over my forehead, over my head, over my entire body. Wiping my tears with their hands.

Grandpa grabs my arm. Walks me past the door. "Don't look back," he says. But I do. I see Abuelita and Mali in the middle of the door, holding each other, Lupe has a hand on each of their shoulders.

"Come on," Grandpa says. And we walk.

CHAPTER TWO

———

Tecún Umán, Guatemala
APRIL 6, 1999

———

WE GET TO THE TERMINAL EARLIER THAN WHAT DON DAGO SAID.
Grandpa asks a stranger which bus is ours, and he tells us all
the buses to Guatemala park next to each other. The buses look just
like La Costa Brava—the nicest bus in our hometown—except these
have polarized windows and hopefully no ripped seats.

We sit and wait for Don Dago. We wait from eight to ten A.M.
Grandpa buys chips, water, and two mata-niños sandwiches for the
road. Finally, Don Dago shows up. Behind him, six other people, just
like what Mom and Dad said. Two women, one girl, and three men.

Grandpa greets Don Dago, and as Grandpa is about to greet the
rest of the strangers, he recognizes someone from La Herradura.

"Buenos días, Don Chepe," says the man. He's taller than everyone
else in the group, has big muscles pressing against his shirt, a square face,
and black, wavy hair, short on the sides and a little taller on the top.

"I'm Marcelo," the man says. I notice his sharp nose, big and straight.
It doesn't protrude from his face like mine does, but it's still big and
makes his face look even more rectangular. His thick eyebrows are a flat
line across the top of his face. I don't like his eyes. Ojos de malacate.

"You're Doña Argelia's son, ¿right?" Grandpa asks.

Marcelo nods.

I stand behind Grandpa, so the strangers won't see my face.

"You're my group," Don Dago says in what he probably thinks is a loud voice, but his voice is so soft that it's hard to hear him with the buses parking and leaving, the people walking, the vendors in the terminal shouting about the goods they're selling. Pigeons and trash everywhere. It's noisy. It smells bad. My skin is already sticky and feels dirty.

"You have about thirty minutes," Don Dago continues as loud as he can. "We will stop twice in eight hours, once at the border and again in Guatemala City, so get water and snacks," he says. "I have your tickets. We'll talk more in Tecún. Sit separately. Remember, I'm not your anything."

Grandpa and I already got snacks and water, so we wait on a wooden bench in front of the buses spewing dark smoke. Everyone else fetches the things they need.

"That guy is from our town," Grandpa tells me. "That's good, you have someone you know." But I don't know Marcelo. I've never seen him in town and I get a weird feeling. He looks mean and scary.

The bus opens its doors and the driver shouts, "¡Tecún, Tecún!" A few people get aboard. We wait for Don Dago, who comes back first and tells us to go ahead, hands Grandpa our tickets. Don Dago waits for the other six to give them their tickets.

There's a mom, short like my mom, except this woman has very light skin, like an almond seed, and has what looks like dyed dirty-blond hair—I can see dark roots. She seems my mom's age, or a bit older. The mom has skinny legs and skinny arms wrapped around her daughter, who is tanner and looks a bit older than me. Their faces are long and thin. They come up the stairs, pretend to not see us, and sit a few seats behind us.

Through the windshield, we see Don Dago in his baseball cap give a ticket to the tall older woman, almost Don Dago's height, wearing a tight dress, her curly black hair flowing as she walks: thick black eyebrows, curved and plump lips, a sharp jawline. She's pretty. She walks past us, smiling. Behind her, men twist their heads.

Marcelo walks in with his chin raised and sits by himself. He doesn't look friendly. Hunched behind him is a light-skinned man who has a beer belly almost as big as Grandpa's. I don't know how old Marcelo is, but he looks older than Mali. This other pale man seems older than that, the oldest out of everyone except for Don Dago. He has a mustache and messy, light-brown hair. His face is rounded, full of acne, and he sort of looks like a plumper Marco Antonio Solís.

Finally, a skinny guy with short buzzed hair gets a ticket from Don Dago. He hasn't stopped smiling. Looks friendlier and younger than the other adults. His head is round, and from the bits of hair left, I can tell it's black. His skin is a little darker than the inside of an almond, closer to the mom and daughter's than it is to mine. After he walks past us, he sits next to the mom and daughter. They seem to know each other.

Don Dago comes in, looks at all of us, and sits on the front seat near the door. He sits alone and opens a newspaper—just like Grandpa does next to me. Everyone in the bus sits, no one talks. The driver doesn't play any music; it's silent. As the bus backs up, the driver announces we're headed toward our first stop, the Guatemala–El Salvador border: La Hachadura.

SUGARCANE FIELDS, COTTON FIELDS, barley fields, volcano, iguana hatcheries, oranges, flores de fuego, jacarandas, mangos, lemons, papayas, roses, mayflowers, myrtles, microbuses, horchata vendors, mototaxis, pupuserías, chorizo strings hanging from hooks, fried yucca vendors, another volcano, blind beggar, kid selling Chiclets, open-air garbage dump, vultures, more fields, cars, maquilishuat trees, furniture stands. I've never been farther from my town than San Salvador. I cannot miss what's outside this window. Houses, gas stations, roadside stands. Sometimes the bus stops to let a vendor in, only to drop them at the next stop where they get inside another bus. The green pleather seat heats up in the sun. My black backpack también. I hold it between my legs like Grandpa does with his. I've never been on a bus for this long. Minutes into the bus ride from the terminal, I am already the farthest I've been from home—ever. I hope I don't have to go number two. Whenever I go to San Salvador with Mali, I try not to go. I don't like using toilets, I'm scared I'm gonna get flushed down them. At home, I go number two behind the outhouse. Cover my poop with leaves and toilet paper, so Grandpa knows not to step on it. Mali said that I'm gonna have to go on a real toilet. She told Grandpa. I know I will have to at some point. I hope it's not now, not right now, on this bus.

THE BUS DRIVER SHOUTS that we're about to get to the border checkpoint and to get our passports ready. Two seats in front of us is a kid who's probably my age. His skin and hair are light, he looks like a gringo. He's sitting with an older man: ¿his grandpa? ¿dad? His breath has left a cloud on the window glass like mine has.

I look at Grandpa and squint. He says reassuringly, "I have them." I didn't know we still *had* my real passport from the time I applied with Mali to get a visa. I didn't know Grandpa had a passport también.

I look at Grandpa and ask why we need them.

"They have to check them," he says, almost whispering.

"¿Why?"

"We get fifteen days in Guatemala," he says, looking ahead as the bus approaches a bridge. In class I learned about this river that splits El Salvador from Guatemala. There's a building on the Guatemalan side that looks like a classroom. The bus turns and parks in the parking lot out front.

"Get your passports checked over there," the driver says, standing up, pointing at the building. "We leave in thirty."

Grandpa and I walk out of the bus—only Don Dago, the light-skinned kid, and his maybe-grandpa step outside before us. Don Dago lets us go ahead as he waits for the rest of the people. He reminds us to use the bathroom. We walk across the parking lot. There's a soldier at the door who checks our passports.

Inside the building, Grandpa hands a different soldier sitting at the desk some money. He stamps both our passports and tells us that we have fifteen days before we must leave Guatemala. "Fifteen days," he emphasizes, and asks if we want to exchange our colones for quetzales.

We are the second ones done. I see the kid walk onto the bridge, then onto something that resembles a balcony overlooking the river. I look at Grandpa and he walks with me. There's a sign that says the name of the river: *Río Paz*. From this lookout, we can see another sign that reads: *La Hachadura*. Over the bridge, on the side we came from, *Welcome to El Salvador*. The kid gets closer to us and asks me, "¿Where are you going?"

His light-brown hair almost touches his shoulders, his hands stiff on the railing as he looks over the edge. I imagined a huge river overflowing with water, maybe even waves, but it's none of those things.

"Tecún Umán," I answer, while also holding on to the railing, my hand closer to the color of the trickling brown water, his hand closer to the color of the dry boulders. I want to say more, but remember Don Dago telling me over and over: Don't talk to strangers on the trip.

I look at Grandpa, who doesn't say anything. My shoulders tense up. I stare at the rocks. The kid doesn't ask more. ¿Did I just mess up by saying I'm going to Tecún Umán? "Never say La USA," I remember Grandpa saying. My parents told me: "If someone asks where you're going, only say the name of the next place." That place *is* Tecún Umán.

"¿What's your name?"

"Javier."

"I'm Alejandro. Ale for short," he says, one hand brushing his hair to the side, both his feet on the lower rung of the metal barrier. His hair matches his light-brown eyes, almost caramel.

"I'm from Puerto Vallarta. We're going home." He looks and talks like the kids in *Luz Clarita,* my favorite pre-dinner novela.

"¿Where?"

"México," he responds. "Jalisco."

"Oh," I say. ¡He's Mexican! The first Mexican kid I meet. *Jalisco,* that's where Vicente "Chente" Fernández is from. I want to talk more. But his grandpa or dad might ask questions.

"I'm going back with Dad," he says, pointing toward the bus, where his dad is shouting Ale's name and waving his hand. That man looks older than I thought a father could be. ¡He looks Grandpa's age! Maybe my dad is gonna be much older than in the pictures. Dad is Mom's age, twenty-eight years old, but ¿maybe he looks older in person?

Grandpa and I follow Ale. On the way to the bus, Grandpa turns to me and says, "Chente is only famous because Javier Solís died."

I nod and don't say anything. Grandpa hates Vicente Fernández. Whenever Abuelita plays Chente, Grandpa makes her turn it off, saying Solís is the better singer. Then he makes me or my aunts play his favorite Solís song: "Payaso." Before Mom left, when he still drank, Grandpa used to burst out in tears singing that song. He was scary.

It's nice walking around in my first new country. Most of my classmates came to Guatemala City last year. Guatemala is so much bigger than El Salvador on the maps. "El Pulgarcito de América," the nuns said about El Salvador. But now, I'm going to a bigger country, and then México is bigger than Guate, and finally, I'm gonna live in the biggest country—La USA. I know because Grandpa had to buy two maps. One of Central America, where he traced a line from our town to Tecún Umán. And another map of only México. He says it's important I know "the Route," but also he knows I like geography. I memorized as many world flags as I could in class in third grade. I wanted to learn more after watching World Cup '98. It was the first time I'd seen the Croatian flag; it's so pretty. Made me want to explore and see the world. Of all the fourteen departamentos, before today I'd only been to three: La Paz, La Libertad, and San Salvador.

We walk toward the bus. The air here is dry, it's hot, but Grandpa says we're about to go up mountains. He's never been to Guatemala. I can't tell if he's excited, but when we get back to our seats, he doesn't pick up the newspaper. We leave the river. The road is flat at first, then we get elevation. I see a lake, coffee fields, pupuserías, tamaleras, lake, volcano, banana trees, bus stops, gas stations—not that different from El Salvador, except it's so much greener, the roads not as straight, and the mountains taller. I never knew roads could be built so far up, so close to the sun. Grandpa's eyes gaze out the windshield and out my window. His backpack sits on the floor, held in place by his legs, and he's placed my backpack on his lap. Guatemala might be prettier than El Salvador. We drive through small towns, bigger towns, and finally the biggest city, Guatemala City.

We briefly stop at the terminal. Same thing as the border, except we only stop ten minutes. Then more mountains, lakes, volcanoes, coffee fields on the side of the road, people picking them. After hours of Grandpa and me not talking, besides him asking me if I'm hungry or if I want water, he says, "Coffee grows at high elevations. ¿Did you know that?"

I didn't know that. I've never seen coffee plants, or bushes— ¿trees? I don't know what to call them. The leaves look fake, like plastic, like someone woke up early and stapled them on the long drooping branches. Yet the leaves glow, shine from how dark green they are, which makes the little red fruits stand out even more. Like ornaments on a Christmas tree.

Every now and then we see people with wicker baskets tied with cloth straps around their shoulders and waists. They balance the basket to one side of their hips. They pick the dark-red dots, almost purple, "which signals ripe," Grandpa explains.

He tells me that he used to pick coffee for work when he was a kid. I learn people can eat the meat around the coffee bean. "Technically, the meat is the fruit, a cherry, and the actual coffee bean is the seed people grind to make coffee," Grandpa says in a soft voice, almost a whisper, so no one else can hear, his eyes squinting now because of the low-hanging sun.

I like learning things from Grandpa. When he walked me to church or school, we walked in silence. This might be the most we've ever talked. Only now do I notice the different colors of the fruit on the drooping coffee-bush branches. They're like scattered marbles. There are rows of bushes that start next to the road and lead the eye into the hill, row after row after row.

It's like this for a while after Guatemala City. We go up mountains. I get scared of how close to the precipice the bus is. Sometimes there are railings, other times not. Then, as if the sun suddenly fell into a hole, it's night. I can't see anything outside my window, so I look through the windshield and try to follow the headlights approaching us. I'm scared. Every headlight a potential crash, but none come close enough. We've been traveling the entire day. I've been mostly awake since four A.M. Finally, the bus driver says, "Final stop, final stop." ¡I crossed an entire country in a day! ¿But where exactly are we going to sleep? It's the first night I won't sleep in my bed.

We enter a town that reminds me of Zacatecoluca. Don Dago gets up, takes a look at everyone in the bus, and walks out, his backpack on his shoulder. Ale and his dad get up and take their luggage with them. We stand up and walk out of the bus. Grandpa holds both our backpacks, one on his back, the other in his hand. Before we step out, Grandpa thanks the driver.

The night is warm but not humid. It's bustling with people, cars, vendors, bicycles. The air feels different. I want to wave goodbye to Ale, but he walks into the terminal without ever looking back.

A TEENAGER WITH STRAIGHT black hair that dances on his shoulders when he moves pulls up on his ¿bicycle? Instead of a front wheel and handlebars, it has a bench welded onto it, two wheels under it, and a canopy on top. It looks more like a tricycle.

"Bicitaxi," the teenager says. "It's a bicitaxi," he repeats to Grandpa, who seems as confused as I am.

"Ahh, va," says Grandpa, and smirks, almost a laugh. It's rare when Grandpa shows his small but straight teeth.

"A lot of people who aren't from here haven't seen one, so I tell them right away," the teenager explains as I notice the cloud of moths surrounding the dim lights of the lampposts.

The teenager seems to know Don Dago, who turns to Grandpa and says, "He knows where, go with him." The other six are getting off the bus, and one by one they crowd around Don Dago.

"Go, we'll meet you there," Don Dago repeats.

"Sit." The teenager taps the bicitaxi's bench. "I have to come back for Don Dago." He presses his whistle—¿horn?—that looks like a silver trumpet with a black rubber air cushion.

Grandpa and I obey Don Dago and sit. The bicitaxi is cool. It has mirrors to the side, lights on the canopy, and this horn. The teenager honks it every time we're about to pass a person walking in the street. We're moving fast; his straight black hair lifts off from his shoulders.

"¿What's your name?" Grandpa asks, turning his neck around to face the teenager. "¿And where you taking us?"

"Jesús, don, para servirle. And I'm taking you to Don Carlos's store," the teenager says without losing his breath.

After five minutes, we pull over to the side of the road next to a store, the walls topped with barbwire and broken glass. Jesús jumps out of the bicitaxi and knocks on the locked storefront's metal door with his closed hand, making a sound like hitting two saucepans together. Grandpa steps out, then helps me climb down. The teenager keeps knocking until someone opens the front door.

"Buenas noches, don, here are the first ones," Jesús says quickly, finally out of breath.

"Gracias. Go get Don Dago," the short chubby man with a dark mustache tells the teenager, who gets back in his bicitaxi and pedals away. The man opens the door more and turns to Grandpa. "Buenas, I'm Don Carlos. Come in. Con confianza. Come in, sit. Sit."

"Buenas," Grandpa responds in his firm voice, doesn't introduce himself.

"You must be the kid." Don Carlos points at me as he closes the metal door behind us. I don't know what to say, but I nod. He reaches over and grabs some chairs that are arranged around a table next to chips, batteries, cigarettes, liquor bottles, bread, bleach, soaps, toothbrushes, and phone cards, neatly stored in the cupboards on the wall.

Grandpa sits first, then me, then Don Carlos. "Don Dago is gonna come soon and tell you where you're gonna sleep." His voice is nice.

His teeth aren't: they're so yellow they're almost brown, and his belly is bigger than Grandpa's.

We sit and wait in silence. It's been a long day. I'm tired. I'm nervous but excited to know what bed I'm going to sleep in. Then we hear a knock on the door. It's the mom with her daughter and the skinny young guy with the shaved head. Don Carlos tells them to come in. Behind him are Marcelo and the pale older guy in another bicitaxi.

"Come in," Don Carlos says again as they walk through the door. Don Dago arrives in another bicitaxi with the tall, curly-haired woman.

"We made it to Tecún," Don Dago says triumphantly as he walks through the door. In the light, I can see his wrinkles. "It's late, so I'll make this quick," he continues. "You two"—he points at Grandpa and me—"will sleep here tonight. There's a room in the back, Don Carlos will show you."

Grandpa nods.

"This is Don Carlos." Don Dago points at Don Carlos, who raises his hand and hunches a little. "We will meet here every morning for breakfast, and in the afternoon for lunch. Dinner is on you," Don Dago says, pacing in circles on the tiled floor, trying to address everyone. He forgets to look at me.

"The rest of us will sleep in the motel across the street. Women in one room, men in another." He points at the mom, daughter, and taller woman. "Introduce yourselves."

"I'm Patricia, or Pati," the thin, light-skinned mom says in a scratchy voice, like she just woke up.

When the name comes out of her mouth, it startles me. It's Mom's name. She's short like Mom, maybe one or two centimeters taller. And I know she has an edge, like Mom, because her eyes are glazed over and when she speaks she stares directly at people. The whites whiter, and the dark-brown darker.

"This is my daughter." She points to the young girl with wavy black hair, but doesn't tell us her name.

"Carla," the girl interrupts her mom, glaring, her thick eyebrows scrunched together. She's really pretty and confident. She's probably the popular girl at school. Her voice is strong, but soothing. She's not scared of these strangers.

"Ajá, her name is Carla," Patricia says in an apologetic way, pinching her daughter in the process. Carla rubs her skinny arm. Patricia *is* similar to Mom, except Mom would've pinched me harder or hit me, even in front of strangers.

"I'm Marta," the tall woman with curly hair says as she awkwardly waves her hand at all of us, then looks at the ground. And that's it. The men stare at her, especially Marcelo and Don Dago. She doesn't say more. There's a brief silence, which is Don Dago's cue. He hands the adult women each a key to their room.

"You three, introduce yourselves," Don Dago tells the men.

"I'm Marcelo," Marcelo says in the deepest voice out of everyone. In the light I notice a scar on his cheek. All of us look at him like people look at Grandpa in town, with respect but also fear—which is why no one speaks until Marcelo nods at the skinny man.

"I'm Noel, but everyone calls me Chino," he says, pointing at his eyes. Everyone laughs. I don't get it. He doesn't look Chinese. He sounds young, older than Jesús, but younger than Marcelo. Under the lightbulb, I can see he doesn't really have a full mustache. The hairs are thin and darker only toward the sides of his upper lip, like a catfish. Reminds me of Diego, the eighth-grader who is my godfather's youngest brother. And like Diego, Chino looks kind, like a good person.

"And I'm Antonio, but call me Chele," the pale man says, but no one laughs. He smiles at his own joke, his cheeks big like Mali's, but pink and full of acne. He almost closes his eyes when he smiles. In the light, his skin looks greasy, like he's been sweating too much. "People with acne are dirty," I remember Mali saying. "Pale people are untrustworthy," Abuelita said. Chele nods like he doesn't know what else to say and smiles, showing us his big rectangular teeth.

"Don Chepe, ¿wanna introduce yourself?" Don Dago asks. Grandpa nods. Pauses. Looks at everyone. I look at him.

"Like Don Dago said, I'm José Ovidio Cortez, or Chepe," Grandpa says in his serious voice, looking straight ahead. "This is my only grandson, Javier, who will be with you after you leave this town. I won't be. We just met, but I ask, when I'm not around, that you please take care of him. He's little, and won't have family. *You* are his family. Please take care of him," Grandpa says in his stern, direct way, looking everyone in the eyes. I'm embarrassed. Everyone nods. Some say, "Sí, señor," or "Sí, don."

"Gracias," Grandpa responds, with one hand on his chest. "Va," he says, and nods at Don Dago.

"Okay," Don Dago says, and nods at Grandpa, still standing up in the middle of everyone. "That's it. Let's rest, and we'll talk more to-morrow. Meet here at eight-thirty in the morning."

Everyone gets up from their seats. The adults look excited and also tired. Everyone carries a dark backpack with them and nothing else. The girl, Carla, looks very tired, and doesn't stop holding her mom's hand. When everyone steps out into the night to walk across the street to the motel, I wish I had told them my name, like Carla did. After they leave, Don Carlos locks the metal door.

4-12-99

GRANDPA WAKES UP AT the same time he's always woken up: minutes before 5:30 A.M. He walks to the bathroom right next to our room and brushes his teeth. I can hear him flush after whatever it is that he does. Then he walks out into the red-tiled hallway and out the screen door that opens onto the backyard mostly made up of dirt, an out-house, and a well shaded by a huge almond tree. Grandpa showers at the well with his white underwear still on, his big, round, hairless, pale belly protruding from his small white underwear, his outie belly button like a cork in a wine barrel about to pop out. His skinny legs that from a distance seem to struggle to keep the rest of his body from toppling over.

Afterward, he shaves. By then, the sun is mostly out, so he can see his square jaw in the handheld mirror he brought with him. He makes funny faces in order to get all of his hair off. He shaves with his long single blade that he cleans in one of the plastic bowls, pulling the skin under his beard down with one hand and shaving the soapsuds off with the other. I don't understand how he doesn't cut himself, especially because he has an Adam's apple that sticks out of his neck.

Then Grandpa walks back into the room with the towel around his waist. He officially wakes me and says, "It's your turn, Chepito."

I flee the room before he drenches himself in cologne. He pours a small puddle into his hands, pats the smelly liquid all over his body. I can hardly breathe.

Before Mom left, she was potty training me. I was about to be able to use the adults' toilet, but we never got to that step. At school, I never went to the bathroom, except that one time in first grade I had to go so bad after I ate a bad pupusa. I was so afraid I was gonna be flushed inside, I panicked. There was no toilet paper, so I used my white-and-blue Donald Duck shirt Dad had just sent me for my fifth birthday. I left it right next to the unflushed toilet: white, blue, and brown. I always wore an undershirt. None of the nuns ever found out it was me who left a poop-stained shirt in the bathroom.

Just last week, before I left, Mali sat me down. "On your trip, you can't go to the bathroom like you do here. It's not normal, Chepito," she said one night in our room, emphasizing *normal* by making her voice deeper. I know it's not "normal," but it's easy, and there's no flushing yourself into the ocean.

My first morning here, I *really* had to go. I'd held it in the entire bus ride from San Salvador, and kept on holding it in for most of that first day in Tecún. At around dusk, Grandpa said, "You know the seat won't swallow you, ¿right?" his voice gentle, like a whisper. I'd been pacing under the almond tree the entire afternoon debating whether to go behind the outhouse.

"I can wait outside the door if you want," Grandpa said. I nodded, and for the first few days, he's been checking, listening outside the door. I talk to him to see if he's still there. "Sí," he responds. Nothing has happened. Yet. The seat hasn't swallowed me. Yet. I'm getting the hang of it.

So now I poop before I shower. I brush my teeth. By seven A.M., the rest of the group begins to trickle into Don Carlos's storefront. He opens the door, walks them to the outside patio with the red tiles, gets the plastic chairs, and places them around the foldout table. Breakfast is mostly a pot of refried beans, Guatemalan tortillas, avocados, and cheese. Sometimes we get eggs. The tortillas here aren't as thick as the ones in El Salvador. I miss Abuelita's, but these are also freshly made, still warm and steaming when Don Dago brings them in a plastic bag. Don Dago brings all the food from the open-air market and he's the only one who doesn't knock on the metal door before coming in—he has a key.

Don Carlos doesn't eat with us. He has to manage the store, so he gets a plate for himself and goes to the front of the house. I think he's related to Don Dago, because they call each other "primo," but they look nothing alike.

Marcelo and Chele sit next to each other. Both of them don't talk much, but in their silence, they act like distant cousins tolerating one another. Grandpa and I sit next to Marcelo. He calls Grandpa "don" and treats him with respect, which Grandpa appreciates.

Across the table, the women sit next to each other and talk as if they've known each other a long time. They're loud when they talk, which is how I overhear that Marta also has a son who's two years old.

I don't think Marcelo and Chele like Chino very much. Maybe it's his age, or that Chino talks a lot, and his voice sounds like there's dust in his mouth. Maybe it's his small Adam's apple that makes him talk like that. "Adam's apples mean people lie a lot," I remember Abuelita telling me. He asked Grandpa questions, asked Marcelo and Chele where they're from. Marcelo just stared at him. After the first breakfast, we learned Chino, Patricia, and Carla are from the same town, and Chino acts like an uncle to Carla, teasing her for not eating enough or eating too much.

Don Dago comes in after we eat. Sometimes he's already eaten and sits at the head of the table; other times he drops the food off and leaves. I'm still shy around the adults, I haven't said anything to them. The men we sit with don't speak, and at the other end of the table, the people don't leave room for anyone else to speak.

Lunch is the same routine, but with different food. Don Dago comes with tamales or a roasted chicken and tortillas. No one really spoke to Don Dago the first day or two, but after the third, at breakfast, people started to ask questions like "Bueno, Don Dago, ¿how long are we gonna stay here?"

We were supposed to be here only two days, but it's been almost a week. Don Dago says it's not up to him, that there's a holdup ahead. "Don't worry, we're taking longer because I'm thinking of your safety," he says in his soft voice. Grandpa believes him.

But Marcelo complains to Don Dago in front of everyone. Patricia asks the most questions. Everyone else stays quiet, even Grandpa— but he talks to Don Dago when everyone else is not around.

"The food is paid for, which is good," Grandpa tells me when everyone leaves. We speak under the almond tree, under the birds who dig holes into the ripe fruit. In between mealtimes, I fill in the worksheets my teachers gave me. I want to keep learning so I'm smarter than the gringos. I do one worksheet a day so I have something for the other days, even though I finish them quickly. Once I'm done with homework, Grandpa takes his México map out and makes me memorize the names of towns Don Dago told him we're supposed to pass on our way north.

"In case you get lost, you'll know exactly where you are," he says, pointing with his thick index finger to each town with his nail he keeps long only on that finger and his thumb. *Tapachula, Arriaga, Oaxaca, Puebla, México DF, Guadalajara, Culiacán, Ciudad Obregón, Hermosillo, Tijuana.* The names, underlined neatly in blue ink from the blue-capped Bic pens Grandpa swears by.

When we're done with that, Grandpa teaches me to lie better. Don Dago has given each one of us fake Mexican ID cards we have to memorize before we cross into México. We have Mexican names. Mexican birthplaces. But our same birth dates. On top of that, Don Dago gave us a photocopied sheet with the lyrics to the national anthem, "Mexicanos, al grito de guerra." We must know the chorus and first verse, as well as the number of soccer teams Guadalajara has in Liga Primera. We must love Las Chivas. We must know the name of the current president, Ernesto Zedillo, and who the best presidents have been: Benito Juárez and Lázaro Cárdenas. And if anyone asks, we vote for el PRI.

I miss school. I miss my friends. ¿Have they figured out I'm not coming back? ¿That I'm not at the Guatemala City zoo, but on my way north? No one has ever come back when they miss more than five days of class. I miss my toys, my clothes, having more than two pairs of underwear, two T-shirts, two pants, one nice dress shirt, sleeping shorts. I miss Mali, Lupe, Julia, Abuelita. The rain. The frogs at dusk, the bats eating the flies, the crickets at night, dogs barking at dawn.

Every evening Grandpa and I walk to the mercado or to the plaza to get something to eat. It was new and fun at first, but this town is small. We've run into Chele and Marcelo smoking silently, leaning against a wall. Grandpa says I should stay close to them, that they're strong, older, that they'll protect me.

We've also seen Chino walking with Patricia and Carla. They're the Soyapango group—it's why Grandpa calls them "Los Soyas"—who are always together. Grandpa says Chino will protect them because he knows them, but that they don't know me. Marcelo knows me. But I want to get to know Los Soyas because they're always smiling and laughing.

Marta never sticks around long after she finishes eating. She's always in her room. Marcelo and Chele try to flirt and tell her piropos; she never responds. Patricia has started whispering that there's something going on between Marta and Don Dago. "They can't trick me," she says. "They're definitely sharing a bed."

Grandpa doesn't think so. We did catch Don Dago eating dinner with Marta one night, but she said it was business. Don Dago is supposed to be my pretend-dad, but I haven't talked to him. Grandpa says everything is ok. The three of us had dinner our first night here, but that's it. Don Dago is still a stranger. He knows Mom, I've seen him for years now, but he's always felt distant. He ignores me. Doesn't look at me in the eyes. Makes me feel like I'm in time-out.

Tecún has one plaza, six benches around the main gazebo painted white, and a Pollo Campero food truck parked on the street alongside other vendors. People begging. People playing music. Grandpa and I sit on the bench and people-watch. Everyone here looks different. Grandpa calls them "indios" and when he says it, it doesn't sound nice. I think they look like us, just darker than Grandpa, a bit darker than me. All I know is that I'm an "indio" también. It's what Great-Great-Grandma Fina told me. She was the one who nicknamed Abuelita "Neli," which means "truth" in a language I don't know. "Indios" is what the nuns called us when we dressed up for El Día de la Virgen de Guadalupe on December 12.

Mom loved that holiday. She dressed me up every year until I turned four. "Somos indios," she'd say. I wore white canvas pants and a white canvas shirt. I wore a tecomate—a water bottle made from the morro tree—a cuma, and llinas. She even drew me a beard from shoe polish. Then all the kids dressed as "indios" walked in a procession to church. I don't understand why Grandpa, Don Dago, Don Carlos, a lot of people in La Herradura and here in Tecún, say that word with so much disgust. I like the dresses women wear. They're so colorful and pretty.

Grandpa and I sit on a bench and people-watch at the plaza every day. Even though he's never hit me, I'm afraid of his rage, of getting him mad. But these six days I've talked to him more than I have all those years in El Salvador. He's less strict than I thought. I've learned he was in the military, then became one of the first motorized policemen in El Salvador. I didn't know he was married before. That he was personal security for the president and other politicians during the war. That when he was security at the airport, people gave him gifts, like airplane dinners he brought home to us. That he "retired" in 1995; I don't know what that means, but he explains he still gets paid for the work he's done.

When the bats eat the moths and the lamps turn on, we walk back to Don Carlos's storefront and watch TV. Bicitaxis drive past us. We've seen Jesús's dark hair flash by. We watch TV in Don Carlos's front room, right next to the storefront, and watch whatever Don Carlos is watching—mostly novelas and the news. By 9:30 we make our way to our room. Ten P.M. is lights-out. Grandpa asks me what I think Mali, Abuelita, or Lupe is doing. I answer. Then he says we will call them the next day, but we've only called once. He says that we will call my parents up north, but we've also only called once. Then we say good night and fall asleep.

4-19-99

THIS MORNING, MARCELO YELLED at Don Dago and threw a warm tortilla at him; it landed on Don Dago's shoes. "Mire, cerote," Marcelo said, spittle in his mouth, "stop bullshitting us."

When the tortilla landed, everyone stepped back from their seats. Don Dago said he's done this a thousand times. That he's good. That delays happen. To trust him. Every day, Don Dago says, "We're leaving tomorrow," only to return at night to tell us, "Not yet." ¡It's been almost two weeks! Everyone has complained, but no one has raised their voice this loud or lunged at Don Dago besides Marcelo.

Marcelo wears a dark-green tank top, which shows his dark-green tattoos: one on his upper arm, another on his back. He reminds me of our town drunk, Crime Face, and of Papel-con-Caca and his tattooed friends who are from our town but had lived in La USA. People were afraid of them. "Tattoos are for bad people, mañosos, convicts, mareros, the ruthless, malacates, people without faith," Abuelita said back home when more men started showing up with words and numbers on their bodies. Then Papel-con-Caca got shot in front of our home at dawn while I slept, and his friends fled to La USA again. Marcelo looks like them but doesn't act like Papel-con-Caca—who was Mom's friend and my friend, and who was much nicer than Marcelo.

After cursing at Don Dago, Marcelo turned to Grandpa and said, "I'm sorry, Don Chepe, but this hijueputa is fucking up."

Grandpa nodded. On the park benches, Grandpa has told me Marcelo is the son of a tortillera and that he lived in Los Ángeles for years, that he got deported, no one knows why. It's how I learned that word: *de-por-ta-do*. "Means the gringos caught you," Grandpa said. I asked if *that* could happen to my parents. He said no because they follow rules. ¿But what if I get to California and my parents are gone? "That won't happen," Grandpa said.

Everyone is mad we're still in Guatemala. Marcelo threatened he wouldn't pay his second payment. ¡I didn't know there were payments! So Grandpa explained, "Half when you leave and half when you get there, is how your mom did it." I didn't know the number in Don Dago's notepad could be split. "But we paid everything up front for you, don't worry."

I *am* worried. And Grandpa is worried the two-week permit will run out and I will still be in Tecún. "That won't happen, don," Don Dago reassured Grandpa this morning.

Whenever the adults leave after Don Dago gives us bad news, Grandpa distracts me with stories. My favorite is the myth of the cadejo. Mom first told me about cadejos when I was four. The myth says God created a light cadejo to protect humans. The devil got jealous and created his own version, a dark one. Mom drew them like dogs or wolves, but with goat hooves and a goat tail.

Grandpa says cadejos have eyes "that burn like coals inside a stove," that the eyes are the only thing most people can see, if and when they see one. He says his cadejo is gray, that there are different colors, different personalities, that it's not so simple, not all good, not all bad, not all black, not all white.

"Listen," he said, pointing to his ear. "If you hear a whistle and it's high-pitched, it's a cadejo." I knew that. Legend says if it's far away, the whistle sounds close; if it's close, the whistle sounds far. "They protect you when you need it."

Today, because the fight was loud, instead of following everyone out of Don Carlos's store for a short after-lunch walk to the park like we usually do, Grandpa decides to stay here and hang out with Don Carlos.

"Jesús is coming for his break soon," Don Carlos tells me, turning around to face us inside the store. His breath stinks like a garbage can. Seconds later, Jesús honks and runs through the store's iron gate.

"Hola, ¿want to go to the maquinitas?" he asks me in his squeaky voice. "I have half an hour."

"*Buenas tardes, tío,*" Don Carlos says sarcastically. "¿Where are your manners, escuincle?"

"I'm sorry, tío, I'm sorry, don, buenas tardes," Jesús tells the adults, shoulders hunched over, touching his long hair. "Well, ¿*do* you want to go to the maquinitas?" he repeats.

I look at Grandpa without saying anything, but I'm screaming ¡*Let me!* ¡*Let me!* with my eyes.

"Come on, Don Chepe, let the kid play. ¡He's bored! Look, this is my nephew. I'm personally responsible," Don Carlos says, hitting the back of Jesús's head.

Grandpa chuckles, then calls me over. "Here," he says, pouring a few quetzales in my hand. "Be careful, but have fun." I don't remember him ever giving me money for maquinitas before; my family didn't let me play "those games."

¡It's the first time I'm hanging out with someone that's not Grandpa! I'll have to be by myself once he leaves. Grandpa says I have to get ready for that; it's why we practice my "Mexicanness" under the almond tree twice a day. And he also gives me this advice:

> Don't tell anyone how much money you have.
> Don't tell anyone where you were born.
> Don't tell them your parents' phone number, only in a
>   *real* emergency.

Emergency is if no one you know is around.
Or if you're apart from the group, only then, talk to
    the nearest adult.

Those are the biggest points. There are smaller ones like *Stay near Don Dago. If not him, Marcelo. Hold their hands when crossing streets. Eat as much as you can; you never know when you're gonna eat again.*

"It's the one good thing about this delay: we have more time to memorize," he says, particularly about my parents' address and phone number. But those were the first things I memorized. And just in case I do forget, Mali wrote their phone number *and* address along the zipper of the two pairs of pants I brought with me and also inside every shirt, in tiny numbers and letters.

"¡Let's go!" Jesús yells as the metal front door creaks open.

"Careful." Don Carlos wags his fat index finger at Jesús, who jumps into the driver's seat of his bicitaxi.

"Hop on," he says. I run to the plastic bench I haven't been on since that first night in Tecún.

As he begins to pedal, Jesús asks *the* hard question: "¿Do you have a school girlfriend?"

"No," I say fast, immediately wondering what Margarita is doing.

"¡¿What?! That's the best part of school. But you know what, school is not for me, carnal," he says as he pedals without sweating. "I was born working." He laughs. "I mean, ¿why go if you can make money?"

He has a point.

"But that's just my opinion."

Jesús makes sense. Some of my classmates already earn money helping their brothers cut cane in December when school is closed. Some take the fishermen food and get paid for that. I don't get paid for helping Abuelita, but I don't really do much. Mostly, I sit in a chair and fill bags with drinks. But I like school. I miss it.

"I know how to count, and *that's* the main skill in life: numbers," he says. "Numbers is money. I want to own my own bicitaxi company *and* an arcade."

"You have to learn to read first," I tell him.

"¿For what? I can pay somebody to do that."

I don't say anything. He pedals and I think of Dad's mom, Grandma Socorro, who is almost seventy years old, who never learned to read but whose math is impeccable. She has her own food stand. No one rips *her* off. I don't really see her much. She didn't even say bye to me when I left.

"¡Look, I did this myself!" he shouts, pointing at the thin plastic streamers taped to the corners of the bicitaxi's canopy.

All of the bicitaxis have colorful streamers, but none like Jesús's. Each of his streamers is a different bright color: red, green, yellow, blue. He's also added bright-purple side mirrors, a bright-teal car spoiler, and brightly colored plastic around his handlebars. "I bought all of these," he says, puffing his chest.

Then I point at the name written on the front of the canopy. At night, I couldn't see the name. But from walking with Grandpa, I know each bicitaxi has a name.

"Re-lám-pa-go," he says, pausing a second on each syllable, then quickly adds, "because I drive the fastest." Again he puffs his chest and smiles with his lips closed. Before I can ask *how* he wrote the letters, he says, "¡I know *some* words! No soy pendejo. ¡I went to school until fourth grade!"

"Grandpa only got to sixth."

Jesús nods back and grins. His teeth are big and a light yellow, not fully white.

"Back then, that's all you needed to become a cop," I tell him.

Jesús passes every other bicitaxi on the road, honking his horn whenever he has the slightest reason to do so. I couldn't have told him about Grandpa's sixth-grade education before this week. That and the fact that Grandma Socorro *and* Jesús are not in school right now makes *me* feel better about missing class.

He slows down. I can hear Grandpa under the almond tree telling me, "*You* don't be like me, ¿okay? *You* finish school, go to college." I like school but don't know if I want to do it for thirteenth, fourteenth, fifteenth grade. ¡I didn't even know there *was* school after high school! Grandpa told me Mom went to "universidad" for a little bit in San Salvador, but then ran out of money. "*You* don't be like your mom," Grandpa said. "*You* finish."

It's the afternoon, and kids walk in their school uniforms, their non-black backpacks, and I feel cool to not be carrying books, to be out already, with an older friend. When we get to the maquinitas, Jesús parks his bicitaxi next to an avocado tree and locks it with a metal chain he wraps around the tree's trunk. The arcade is inside a square building that appears to have no front door. We walk in. It's hot, and the sounds of the machines thicken the air. It's like I'm inside a television.

Jesús runs directly to the *Street Fighter* machine. Grandpa gave me extra quetzales; I offer some to Jesús so we both can play, but he shakes his head and takes out one coin from the bright-blue fanny pack strapped around his waist under his oversized shirt that says something in English we both don't understand.

"*This* is the only coin I'll need. Watch, carnal." His yellowish teeth are bright in his full grin. I know this game. The Baker's son had a Nintendo and had this game, along with *Super Mario Bros. 3* and *Duck Hunt*—the one with the plastic gun. The Baker's son was like me; he never let anyone else play.

Jesús chooses Chun-Li. I laugh when he picks her. "Watch," he says with a smirk. I put my coin in and choose Ryu. The first round I punch Chun-Li a couple times. *Ari-o-ken. Ari-o-ken.* I fly horizontally and drop dead on the ground after he hits me with a combination I've never seen. The second round, I don't land anything.

I turn around, and already there's a line of uniformed kids pushing against my back. "Don't worry, I'll be quick," Jesús says, his hands on the machine's buttons and handle.

"¡Okay, show me the coins!" he yells at the boy who's first in line. "¡If you're next, put a coin on the maquinita!" he yells again, louder.

I step to the side. I don't even want to play; I want to see if Jesús really *is* that good. No one makes fun of Chun-Li. The contenders pick: Ryu, Guile, Dhalsim, Akuma, Blanka. Some even choose Honda and Zangief, but none of the kids come close to beating Jesús. Finally, after about ten kids, Jesús screams, "¡Last game! ¡I have to work!" He quickly beats the last kid.

"Let's go, carnal," he says, and we walk toward the exit where he stands in the middle, looks back, and shouts, "¡That's all for today, see you tomorrow, losers!"

The sound of the machines can't drown all of the kids' jeers, their annoyance, their "yeah yeah"s. He unlocks his bicitaxi and we drive off.

"¿You have fun?"

I nod. I've never seen a teenager have so much confidence. He reminds me of Marcelo.

"¿See this?" He points at his bright-blue fanny pack where he keeps his money. "I only spent one coin, didn't waste any money." He laughs so hard his back teeth show.

"That's cool."

"It *is*, carnal." He says that word again. I've heard local people use it at the park; it sounds like carne. All the kids at the arcade used it también.

"¿What does 'carnal' mean?"

"It's like you're a good friend, ¿you know? Like blood. It's a Mexican term."

"¿Why does everyone say it here?"

"Most people think they're Mexican because—" He pauses, lets the bike chain make the noise it does when people stop pedaling. "Look, México is right there." He points at the trees on the other side of the river. The water is dark, almost brown. "But if you're born in Tecún, or drive a bicitaxi like me," Jesús says, pointing at his chest, "the guards sometimes let me cross the bridge and work over there for the day. I follow the money."

We're getting closer to Don Carlos's store, a few blocks away from the river. I look toward the bridge and can't see it, but I can see México on the horizon. Jesús knows I want to cross already. It's what we all want to do.

"It's okay, you'll cross soon, carnal, don't worry," he says, his voice softer as he begins to honk his horn to signal to Don Carlos we're here.

"TOMORROW IS THE DAY," Grandpa says when I walk through the metal door, his voice raspy. "Tomorrow," he repeats. I smile and clap my hands.

Don Carlos laughs, his teeth showing. "¿Why don't you go celebrate?"

"That's perfect," Grandpa says, and gets up from his plastic chair. "Go get ready, Chepito," he tells me in a happier tone.

We walk to the park, where the Pollo Campero food truck parks, but where we haven't eaten because it's expensive. "Today we feast," Grandpa says. It's near sunset. Grandpa buys a chicken breast, a drumstick, two thighs, six bread buns, and a tub of coleslaw.

We get the food and sit on a bench in front of the plaza's white gazebo like we have every afternoon the past two weeks. I love Pollo Campero because, for special occasions, Mom sent money for Mali and me to go to San Salvador or Zacatecoluca to buy chicken to bring home. I love the crunchy skin on the outside and I love the moist skin inside. *Mmm.* I lick my fingers every bite. Grandpa does también, and he laughs. I love his laugh. His small teeth show, his mouth opens, his belly rises up and down, and he cackles *ha, ha, ha, ha,* his shoulders and Adam's apple moving up and down, all of the wrinkles in his face showing themselves.

When he stops, he tells me, "Your mom ate so much pollo when she was pregnant. That, and green mangos with lime and salt. It's why you love both."

And I do. I smile with chicken grease on my cheeks. Grandpa laughs again. It fills the bench, the park. The pigeons come near us, hoping we drop something. I don't want to, but Grandpa throws them a piece of his bun, and more pigeons come. He doesn't mind them.

We finish eating and he says, "We have to call your abuelita *and* your parents."

It's not dark yet. This is an earlier-than-usual dinner, and I guess I must rest. I don't know *when* I'm supposed to leave, Don Dago didn't say anything. Just to have my bags ready by breakfast. Luckily, Grandpa did laundry this morning—our clothes are drying on the clothesline.

We get to the telephone at the corner of the park. We call The Baker's house first; that gives Abuelita and Mali time to make it there while we call my parents. After the third ring, they pick up.

"Pati, Javiercito leaves tomorrow—finally."

I listen to them talk, standing just outside the public telephone's bright-blue sphere.

"I go back to La Herradura tomorrow. Ajá."

It looks like a giant blue bean on top of a metal pole.

"He's been really good. Don't worry. Here, talk to him." Grandpa hands me the phone.

"Hola, hijo. Tomorrow Grandpa leaves, and you're gonna be alone . . ." *Alone.*

My stomach crunches when she says that. My eyes widen. I stare at the phone's metallic cord.

"But Don Dago and the others will be with you." ¡I haven't even spoken to them! "Grandpa is gonna give Marcelo money, so stay close to him, ¿okay?"

¡¿Marcelo?! ¡He's the scariest!

"¿Okay?"

"Sí, Mamá," I tell her.

"Don't worry. Everything is gonna work out, and in a few days you'll be here with us. Here, talk to your dad."

"¿How you doing, Super Mario?" I like it when he calls me that.

"Good," I say, and tell him about Pollo Campero and the maqui-nitas. I don't tell him I'm a little scared.

"Be safe, be good, listen to Don Dago and the adults," both of them say. "We love you, and you'll make it here so soon. Your toys and clothes are waiting for you. We love you very much, ¿okay?" They sound happy.

"I love you también," I tell them, and Grandpa takes the phone from me. He says he has to call La Herradura, and we hang up.

We repeat the same thing with Abuelita and Mali, who are already at The Baker's. I miss them almost more than my parents. My parents I'll see soon. But Mali, Abuelita, Lupe, Julia, my toys, my dog, my parakeet, my classmates, the cat, I won't see them anytime soon. ¿Maybe Christmas? ¡That's a long time! They're sad when we talk; both are listening and sometimes talk at the same time. Abuelita doesn't want to say goodbye. Mali either. They keep asking questions about the food, the weather, things we've already talked about. It's been two weeks. It will be longer before I see them again.

"Good luck, we're praying for you," they say. Grandpa gets mad, he has to keep adding coins and yanks the phone from me to tell them, "Enough. Wrap it up."

He hands back the phone so I can say goodbye. "Te queremos," they say almost in unison, their voices breaking. I know they're crying. My eyes start to water. I hold it in. Maybe Grandpa knows what's gonna happen next, because he yanks the phone from me again after I tell them, "Las quiero mucho."

"I'll see you soon," he says, and hangs up. Grandpa looks at me and pats my back, but then I realize I won't see *him* for a long time and I start crying-crying. He continues to pat my back as we walk, repeating, "It's gonna be okay, we're all gonna be okay."

When we get back to Don Carlos's, the moon is the thinnest fingernail, and the sun is still out. Both have been in the sky during most of the day at the same time; I've never seen that. The moon: white and thin. The sun: fat and yellow.

Grandpa says that because the moon is out during the day, the night will be mostly dark. Besides telling me stories I didn't know, he's been teaching me things like this. "Useful things" he says he learned during his time in the military and then in the police.

He's also taught me to point out the North Star. "It's not the brightest, it's not the biggest," he said, but I still don't know which one it is. What I do remember is that the farther north I go, the more the stars will change. I haven't noticed the difference. "Not yet," he says. I'm impressed at how much he knows, and sad I've never looked at stars like this with him before.

When we cross the street, I hold his hand—something we didn't do in La Herradura when he walked me to school, or when he walked me to church. I was always afraid of him, of his curt manner with Abuelita or his daughters. I was afraid of his deep, almost harsh voice, but I've heard other tones here. Seen him laugh a lot. He's more patient than I thought.

My favorite technique he's taught me, the one I've perfected, is how to tell how much time is left until the sun goes down. I have a watch with me at all times, a black plastic Casio Mali bought for me a few weeks before Don Dago picked me up. But just in case I lose it, Grandpa taught me to hold my left hand out far in front, my arm straight. Then, like a flag, I shift my fingers to the right. I line my index to the bottom of the sun, until my fingers reach the horizon. However many fingers there are, each equals fifteen minutes to sunset. Four fingers equals an hour.

It's what I do right now, on our walk to Don Carlos's: there's about thirty minutes left. Grandpa sees me put my hand out. He smiles and taps my back. "You've learned," he says in a soft voice. I love Grandpa like I love Abuelita. I didn't know I did. I didn't know he loved *me*. He's been patient like Mali. I'll miss him.

4-20-99

DON DAGO BRINGS US breakfast like he does every morning, except today everyone's backpacks are with them. Don Dago asks the people staying at the motel to give him the keys and wait at Don Carlos's until our bus leaves at eleven A.M., and then he walks out the steel door.

Everyone is broken into the usual groups: Chele-Marcelo, Patricia-

Chino-Carla, Marta next to Don Dago, and Grandpa and me. I see Grandpa take Marcelo under the almond tree to talk to him. Don Carlos is out front. We're *actually* leaving. Grandpa's packed the México map for me, makes sure I have everything, and gives me his handkerchief, his extra toothpaste, and an extra toothbrush. "Just in case."

I sit next to Grandpa, waiting. The men smoke in the backyard, Chino a few steps away from Marcelo and Chele. The women talk across the table from Grandpa and me. Patricia is telling Marta where she bought her lipstick. We're flies hanging around, waiting for Don Dago to come back to take us away.

Don Dago opens the metal door with a creak. We hear multiple bicitaxis, and I hear Jesús's horn. We stack the plastic chairs on top of each other and leave them at the corner of the patio like we do after lunch. Don Carlos wishes us all good luck. He turns to me, his breath at full power, and kneels, his shirt unbuttoned, his big belly drooping even more. "Good luck, niño, you will make it," he says in a whisper. "I know you will, ¿do you know you will?"

"Sí," I say, trying not to breathe. He grins, stands up, and shakes Grandpa's hand, telling Grandpa something I can't make out. Then Don Carlos says goodbye to everyone, and all of us step out onto the street.

"¡Finally!" Chino shouts. Patricia shushes him. Marcelo tells him to "shut up," hitting him hard in the back.

"¡¿What?!"

"Tranquilo," Marcelo says.

Jesús has been saving Relámpago for us. "Let's go, carnal," he says, tapping the passenger bench in front of his bicitaxi. Grandpa and I get on.

"Told you it was gonna happen soon," Jesús tells me when I turn to face him as we sit on the bench. He begins to pedal, his hair flowing in the wind like one of his streamers. We're moving fast toward the end of town where the arcade is, not the terminal where we landed our first night here. Banana trees are on both sides of the only road. We arrive and pull over. Grandpa tells Jesús to wait for him. Jesús nods.

"Bueno, carnal, good luck," he says to me once I step out. He steps off his driver's seat and gives me a fist bump.

Everyone gets off their bicitaxis, and their rides turn around and leave. No one else besides our group is here for the bus, which is small and old like the ones in La Herradura. We form a line. Don Dago walks to the front and says, "Get on," to each of us.

Everyone walks up the bus steps. Marta steps in first, then Patricia-Carla-Chino, then Chele, Marcelo is last. I stand next to Grandpa, outside the back of the bus. He's taught me so much. About the sky. About my family. About maps. I can almost tie my shoes correctly. I can poop and flush by myself now, I'm less scared. He's been on the other side of the door every single day. Everyone else is already inside the bus except for Don Dago, who waits for us, one foot on the ground, one on the bottom step.

I look up at Grandpa, who holds my hand. His face changes, an expression I haven't seen, not even in his drunken rages, not even when his tears promised Mom he would never drink again, not even when he chased Tía Lupe with a machete because she got pregnant with my cousin Julia inside her belly. In all of that, I've never seen his face like this: crunched up and wrinkled like an empty water bag, tense, his veins popped out, his skin pink, all of the emotions of those times tacked onto his face, but there's also a faint smile.

"Va. Ya," he says in his raspy voice that almost breaks. He smiles, a smile like when he knelt and prayed in church next to me. Grandpa is staying, and I'm going to walk up those rattling stairs. Black smoke spews from the exhaust pipe next to the spare tire.

We stand by the road, the banana trees on either side, raindrops still on the leaves, sliding down, dropping to the ground. It rained earlier in the day, but these drops haven't evaporated. Grandpa's eyes are doing the same, trying to hold his tears inside their corners. Grandpa who I got used to sleeping next to. He's no Mali, but he tried.

"Bueno, this is as far as I go, Chepito. Te quiero mucho, cuidáte, may God protect you all the way there."

He does the cross on me like nuns or priests do. He does it like Abuelita and Mali did that dawn I left them. I realize that he *is* religious. That he wasn't just going to church with me because someone had to.

"Remember: trust Marcelo. He's from our town, he knows us, listen to him."

I don't know what to say, what to look at. His face still red. The sky behind him like it hasn't made up its mind whether it will rain again or not. Dark-gray clouds next to bright-blue pockets of sky.

"Go," Grandpa says, wiping his eyes. I didn't see a tear, but he wants to cry. I want to cry. It's really happening. I'm really leaving.

"Come on." Don Dago hits the thick air downward with his hands. "Come on," he says again, tapping his blue jeans.

"Go, Chepito, te quiero mucho," Grandpa says, his hand on my shoulder again. He pushes me forward. A slight tap toward Don Dago. Then he grabs my hand, pressing it harder than usual; I don't mind. Each step so long, but there can't be more than ten.

Don Dago has both feet on the dirt, steps to the side, giving us space. "You're gonna get there safely. Tell your parents I say hi," Grandpa says. "You have a cadejo protecting you," he says softly. "Always remember that."

I turn around and reach for a hug. "Lo quiero mucho," I tell him for the very first time. I'm higher up. It's like I'm taller. Older. He hugs me back. His skin is warm. His fingers pressing into me, mine pressing into his back. I've never hugged Grandpa like this.

"Te quiero mucho," he says again, almost whispering. Hands me my black backpack. I hold it in my hands. Grandpa's face red red red. His veins thick like worms. Then he pats me again and I walk up the stairs. I look back and he's telling Don Dago something. They shake hands. Don Dago steps in. The driver closes the bus door.

The bus is empty except for our group and a few vendors. Everyone's eyes watching me. The back door has a window. I run to it. As the bus starts moving, through the dark puff of smoke, I see Grandpa in the middle of the wet and dry road, waving his hand. Jesús is behind him, sitting in his bicitaxi. The green on both sides of the road makes Grandpa's white polo look so white. The brightest non-rain cloud. His belly fat and so round, like a marble. His hand still waving. My face pressed against the back window's glass. I concentrate on Grandpa's light-brown hand waving. Grandpa getting smaller and smaller as the bus rattles forward. He becomes a cloud. A marble. A hand. A fingernail. A white dot.

I take a breath in.

Adiós, I whisper to myself. I stare at the road rushing underneath my feet. I stand there for I don't know how long, hoping to see the white dot, until I feel Don Dago's hand on my shoulder.

He doesn't say anything. Somehow he pulls me without pulling. The tires bump on every pothole. I sit next to Don Dago. I notice the green banana trees, all of those green leaves, on either side of the road. I don't want anyone to see me cry. I want my cadejo to appear. I change seats and sit across the aisle from Don Dago. I stare at the side of the road. At banana tree after banana tree. The blue or red or yellow plastic wrapping on the unripe bananas. Every now and then, I see a person cutting banana leaves, cutting the full bunches of green fruit. But that's not what I want to see. I look for two red dots. Two red eyes "burning like coals," Grandpa said.

CHAPTER THREE

———

Ocós, Guatemala
APRIL 27, 1999

———

We're in Ocós: a small fishing town. In La Herradura I heard the ocean waves crashing against the rocks only during big storms. The estero water underneath the pier was calm, sweet, and surrounded by mangroves. If I wanted to get to the ocean, it was a thirty-minute boat ride through the mangroves. Here, the ocean is walking distance, a few blocks away, the loud roar of the tides. The sand, the breeze, the salt in the air remind me of home.

Here, like in Tecún, at night I stare at the ceiling, waiting for something to fall on my bed—a cockroach in my mouth, a spider on my eye, a scorpion at my feet. There's no mosquito net hanging on top of my bed like back home. Grandpa isn't here to talk to me before falling asleep, to go out for walks and explore the town, and because of that I feel alone, lonely, solo, solito, solito de verdad.

The adults don't really talk to me besides "good morning," "good night," "pass the food," "wake up." And I'm too shy to talk to them, awkward, so I mostly keep to myself and stay out of their way. When the adults talk, I look at my hands. I hold them together and play with my thumbs. I don't know what to say. Who to stay close to. Marcelo pays no attention to me. All he does is smoke and drink. I feel like wet sand. Like mud. Like the corn dough Abuelita makes pupusas with, her fingers making and breaking clumps, *clap clap clap*.

I'm in a room with Patricia and Carla. Our room is small. We let the fan buzz all night, all day, in order to keep us cool and keep the mosquitoes away. My bed is across from theirs. I can almost touch where Patricia and Carla sleep, next to the window, with my arm. Patricia's and Carla's eyebrows get closer together whenever I do anything. I annoy everyone. So I just stay in the room, try to sleep, look at the map, memorize things. I want Grandpa to be here. I watch how Patricia makes sure Carla eats everything on her plate. How she tucks her in at night. Kisses her forehead before bed. In the morning, she brushes her daughter's black wavy hair, braids it or puts it up in a ponytail, lays out her clothes on the bed. Grandpa told me to stay close to Marcelo, but when I try to talk to him, he tells me to leave him alone. He only talks to me when he sends me out to fetch his daily pack of Marlboros.

Our first night here, Don Dago tells us the "new plan": we're crossing into México aboard boats. We're skipping Tapachula, Chiapas. Grandpa's blue line on the map is being revised and stretched into the Pacific Ocean toward Oaxaca, but Grandpa doesn't know. None of my family knows. They think we're taking the bus to cross the river on a raft. All the adults here thought that también.

Marcelo raises his voice, hits the plastic table we eat on—if he had something in his hands, he would throw it. Chino yells at Don Dago, and I'm scared. I didn't know Chino could get that mad. Chele stays quiet. Patricia screams at Don Dago también. Everyone's skin is now a bit darker, except for Chele, whose skin has gotten red, bright pink like a cooked shrimp. I listen, try to hide like a shadow when the adults speak.

It's weird staying in a room with a woman who isn't Mali or Mom. I don't feel comfortable. Plus, I think I like Carla. I'm worried I'm going to fart, or snore, or do something embarrassing. I don't want her or Patricia to see me naked, so when I shower I take all my clothes to the shower room, next to the last room on this side of the motel.

Inside, a showerhead lets water fall like rain on the cement floor. A curtain is the only privacy. There's a well with a motor like the one at Don Carlos's, but the pump fills a giant plastic tub behind the shower room. I shower only when no one else does. Pooping is the same. It's been hard without Grandpa to not be afraid that I'm going to get flushed down the toilet and out to sea.

I've been quiet. Patricia checks on me as much as she can, but she has her daughter to worry about. I try to do everything right. I wash my hands, I shower by myself, I don't ask for help, I eat everything on my plate, I clean up, make my bed, mind my own business. I don't want anyone to think I'm a little kid.

The next night, Don Dago brings the men a case of Negra Modelos—his favorite beer. When they finish it, they go out and buy cheaper beers, Gallo or Sol. Chele has to stop Chino and Marcelo from fighting over their tattoos. One doesn't like the other's, or something. Don Dago doesn't drink more than one beer with them, but by then, the men start asking questions about when we're leaving, and it escalates into screaming at Don Dago, who grasps his Negra Modelo and listens, picking at the gold paper wrapping around the bottle's cap. Marcelo is the first one who shouts, he's the loudest and drunkest. Chele threatens to return to El Salvador, says that he wants his money back. Chino throws a Modelo bottle at Don Dago's feet and tries to tackle him. Don Dago remains seated in his plastic chair. It isn't hard for the other men to stop Chino. He's so skinny. I'm afraid Marcelo is going to kill him—he could, but he's too drunk to land a punch.

It scares me. Like when Grandpa drank before Mom left, when he broke the kitchen door, shot his gun at the sky when Mom broke our blender across his feet. The next day I stay away from the men. I know Grandpa told me to "stay close to Marcelo," but he's the scariest one, always drinking, smoking, arguing.

The men fight again our fifth night. After dinner, Don Dago gets up from the table and in his almost whisper tells us, "Sleep. Rest. You're leaving in two days." He doesn't have a case of Negra Modelos and eats very fast. He gives us more details, and we just nod until he mentions that he's not coming with us. That it's better if he doesn't come on the boats. That he's a Mexican citizen, that he's going ahead of us to make sure our connections are made, that nothing goes wrong again like it did in Tecún, like it has here in Ocós.

"I don't want more delays," he says, and leaves for his room with Marta. The adults call it an "old thing" between them. A few nights ago, I heard Patricia screaming at Marta that the delays were her fault.

Patricia escorts me and Carla from the table like a train hurrying from the terminal, gets us in the room, tells us to stay there, and hurries back out. Carla and I glue our ears to the door. I can hear Marcelo barking like a rabid dog, "N'hombre, ya son puras babosadas, viejo," and everyone follows with their curses: "no joda," "puta viejo," "chorcha cerote," "hijue-sesentamil-putas." After a long hour, everyone calms down. I hope we're actually leaving when he says we are.

"Va. Ya, bichos. Shower, rest," Patricia says when she comes back into the room, calm, pretending nothing has happened. We don't ask anything. I grab my clothes and shower before everyone else. No one has picked up the glass shards on the ground, or the cigarette butts still burning on the floor.

It's our sixth night, and no one is outside drinking or smoking. Don Dago tells everyone to go to sleep early, to rest because we're leaving at dawn. After dinner he comes back to each of our rooms and brings us plastic water bottles and chips to eat on our trip and to stuff into our bags. Our backpacks are ready. Thanks to the motel owner, our clothes are clean and dry, because even though she didn't speak to us at all and no one knows her name, she washed our clothes today. It's 10:30 P.M. No one is arguing. I pray everything will be ok, but I'm scared. I'm showered, but already sweating because Don Dago told us to sleep with our clothes on. "Dark clothes," he said. I have my dark-blue jeans, my dark T-shirt, my belt, my black shoes, Grandpa's handkerchief.

I listen to Patricia and Carla talk until they go to bed. Patricia isn't snoring, so I know she's not sleeping. She always snores. Sometimes she also makes funny noises when she sleeps, but right now it's quiet. Carla never snores. I can't tell if she's awake, but I don't hear any whispers. The walls of this room and the entire motel are made of exposed brick, rough to the touch. In between us is a cement floor that's always cold, but coldest in the morning. There's a small fan next to their bed, the only thing making noise right now. I slow down my breathing to match the click of the fan's turning head. It reaches one side of the room. Click. Then it comes back to this side. Click. I like to put my feet up on the wall like I did with Mali, but not right now. I'm inside the sheets trying to stay still, because Patricia is awake, and I don't want her asking what I'm thinking about. ¿What is she thinking? ¿Is she worried like me?

Each bed only has one pillow. Patricia and Carla share theirs. I've never liked pillows, but I haven't told them because I like to hold my pillow in one arm. I sleep facedown and pretend the pillow is Mom, or Mali. There's one lightbulb in the ceiling. One small plastic drawer, a calendar above the drawer. Patricia likes to cross the days off with a pen. Next to their bed is a small plastic table where Patricia takes her hoop earrings off and leaves them overnight. Carla has small studs she never takes off. Next to the door, directly in front of my bed, are hooks where our black backpacks sleep. They're packed and ready for us to grab and go.

A few days ago, when the men were smoking at sunset, Marcelo said he'd heard rumors about boats capsizing. The locals told him more than sixty people had died the weekend before we got to Ocós. The same route. On the same type of boats we're taking tomorrow. Marcelo said it's why we didn't leave right away. The adults asked Don Dago about it, but he said it was mentira, pajas, chambre, porquería. That it was the Guatemalan police spreading rumors, paying locals to scare people like us—"migrantes" is what the locals call us. A word that's hard to say. The *gran* to the *tes* like a mountain that's hard for my tongue to climb. A word like there's salt water in my throat.

"You migrantes are like this," "those migrantes are like that," migrantes, migrantes.

Don Dago keeps saying not to believe "those indios"—again that word Grandpa also uses. Harsh. Don Dago says that *he* knows what he's doing, that we paid him, that he has done this so many times before.

The locals said it must have been the rough seas. The inexperienced coyotes. That there was a storm. But now it's about to be tomorrow, and I can't sleep. I hope Don Dago knows best. I don't want what happened to those people to happen to us. I can't swim. Even though I'm from the coast and my father is a fisherman, I don't know how. I was always too afraid of my town's dark water. I'm scared of sharks.

I focus on the fan head's clicking and think of my cadejo. I listen for him at night. But nothing. No whistles. No bright red eyes like coals burning. But that's ok. Grandpa said most people don't ever see their cadejo, which doesn't mean it's not there. *Cadejo, Cadejito, protect me,* I whisper in bed.

4-28-99

WE HEAR A KNOCK on the door. "¡Get up, get up, get up!" Don Dago tries to shout, but it sounds faint, drowned out by the knocks. Then the same thing, *knock knock knock*, the same phrase, but it's on the door next to ours, the men's room.

I wipe my eye boogers. I don't remember what I dreamed about, but it feels like I haven't slept. My neck hurts like there's a yarn ball tightening back there. Patricia wakes up right away. I can make out her shadow, her torso up off the bed, her legs straight.

"Ya, bichos, ¡wake up! ¡wake up!" she shouts. Carla snuggles the sheets crumpled in the space below her mom's back. Patricia turns the light on without warning. My eyes hurt. Patricia pulls the sheet off of her daughter.

"¡Mami!"

"Hurry up, wake up, Carla," Patricia says, not as loud but in her sharp voice. My watch marks 4:25 A.M. We're already dressed, but Patricia and Carla didn't sleep with their shoes on.

"Hurry up." Patricia shakes Carla.

My shoes are black, but with Velcro. I keep my boots with shoe-laces in the backpack, in case these get ruined. I don't know how to tie my shoes properly—just to make knots that I can't untie. Grandpa tried to teach me in Tecún, but I haven't completely learned.

Bats fly above our heads. We forgot to turn the room light off. Our lightbulb brightens the motel's patio. The men's shadows hover, little red dots in their mouths, smoke clouds above their heads. Everyone has their backpacks on, their dark clothes. I can see the overflowing garbage cans with all the beer bottles and cans the men drank this past week.

"Go go go," Don Dago keeps saying, walking in front of everyone, his baseball cap flipped backward. But we're not walking toward the street; we're walking to the back of the motel's property, toward a creek I didn't realize was there. So many trees and bushes, it looks scary.

"There," Don Dago says as he points to a light coming from the creek.

We walk fast toward the light under the coconut and mangrove trees along the creek's shores. Crickets chirp, and our feet crush the leaves on the ground. The water bottles Don Dago gave everyone slosh inside our backpacks. The men have extra jugs strapped to their shoulders. Chino carries two. Patricia carries two también. One of them is for me.

Don Dago has a flashlight, and mosquitoes, gnats, and moths surround it. The men's cigarettes can't overpower the smell of muddy water mixed with old fish. The sky is a very dark blue, the sun nowhere over the volcanoes. The air, like the entire week, heavy with salt. Bags of chips crinkle inside our backpacks.

"There won't be food," Don Dago said last night when he gave us each three small bags of chips. "If you want more, buy more. The store is open." I don't know if Patricia got more. I didn't. I have the money Grandpa gave me hidden in my clothes. We walk toward the light in the creek, which is coming from a boat. A boat like the ones we have in La Herradura. Six meters long. No roof on top, a long plátano split in half and the meat carved out. The same boats fishermen use to hunt sharks. A lancha tiburonera.

People sit along the length of the boat, near the edges, on wooden seats that look like soccer bleachers. There's a thick wooden board in the middle, another board near the front, and another thick one near the back, where big plastic containers sit directly in front of two huge motors. Chele's skin glows like a piece of paper when someone inside the boat points a flashlight at him.

"Buenos días, don," a man standing says. He sounds Mexican—like Jesús, but with a heavier accent. He speaks from his throat. Singing in a different way than we do. There's another man standing next to him, but he doesn't say anything.

"Buenos," Don Dago responds, tilting his flashlight up and down, like it's his head nodding.

"Come in, come in, sit anywhere," the man holding the flashlight says to us. I can't see his face, but I know he's wearing a hat—not a baseball cap but one of those hats that surround your head and give you shade from all angles. Then the man talks to the other people already sitting in the boat: "Make room, move, move."

Don Dago repeats the same thing. "Sit somewhere, find room," he tells us as he lights the wooden boards connecting the shore to the boat. People make room near the middle as we step inside. We sit and watch Don Dago on the shore, whispering to the men who are at the very back, near the motors. Marta isn't here. She didn't even say goodbye. No one has mentioned it. Maybe that's what the adults argued about last night.

Everyone has turned their flashlights off. We sit in the middle of the boat. Patricia, Carla, and me on one side. Marcelo, Chele, and Chino on the other, their lit cigarettes making little red dots. Mosquitoes bite us, the men blow their smoke this way.

"Bueno," Don Dago says as he takes a step away from the boat. "Go with God." He takes another step back. "I'll see you in México."

He taps the boat, and the men in the back pick up two oars and push us off the shore into the middle of the wide creek.

"Ey, vos," Chele says, tapping Chino. "¿Are they gonna give us more water?" I can almost make out Chele's acne and that red rash that's been around his neck the entire week. He's wearing a long-sleeved shirt that covers him to his wrist, but he never buttons his shirts to the top, and his white tank top peeks through.

Chino looks back at him and says, "¿Maje, why you ask stupid-ass questions?"

Chele play-punches him on his shoulder, then Chino whispers, "¡No! Pendejo." Patricia laughs. It's dark, but the light-colored articles of clothing people wear seem brighter, like Chele's tank top. Some people wear white socks. My wristwatch also shines. Some people have white lines in their dark shirts—they look like Christmas lights.

I've been good at not getting in the adults' way. I always listen to them, like Grandpa, Mali, and my parents told me to do. But I have to ask someone. I think of how to ask it the quickest way possible. I tug at Patricia's shirt. "¿How long is the ride?"

"I think sixteen to eighteen hours."

¡That's longer than our bus ride from San Salvador to Tecún! I don't want to be on the water that long. More time for sharks to show up. For a storm. For a big wave.

"Don't worry," she says, tapping my shoulders. I'm scared of sharks, anacondas, icebergs, alligators, anything that swims. Everything I was thinking about last night comes back. "These guys are good. Vas a ver. We'll get to México safely."

"Sí, vos," Chino says from across.

Cadejo, Cadejito, please protect me. I mouth it, so no one hears. Chino, Chele, and Marcelo mouth something to each other. I look up and down the boat. Everyone seems scared. I'm scared. The water looks black. The mangroves and trees on either shore create a tunnel. A current pushes us out toward the ocean. I hear waves.

The Mexican men at the back of the boat don't turn their motors on. Slowly, they lift an oar out of the water, then dip back into it, trying not to make any noise. We sit on the bench. Patricia hugs Carla. Marcelo, Chino, and Chele finish their cigarettes one by one and throw them in the water. The sound of the wooden oar entering the water is calming. Like water taking a breath.

THERE WERE NINE OF us before Grandpa left. In Ocós, we were eight. Now, Marta and Don Dago are gone. There's six of us left. *The Six,* I call us. It's my secret. Like we're the Power Rangers, Sailor Moon, or the kids with the rings that bring Captain Planet to life. We're a team. Our mission: get to La USA.

We sit next to each other surrounded by twenty to twenty-five strangers who don't talk to us. It's still dark; my watch says it's five A.M. The sun is nowhere over the mountains, it doesn't even peek through the mangroves and coconuts that cover the creek. The sky behind the Mexican men at the back of the boat is getting lighter and lighter. Hopefully, by the end of the day, we will be in México, the only country left between me and my parents.

Everyone huddles up, shoulder to shoulder, knee to knee, with the person next to them. Everyone holds their backpacks on their knees, their arms wrapped around them. It's mostly men. Adult men about the same age as Chele, Marcelo, and Chino. Exception: teenagers (no facial hair). There's also a few men who look older than fifty, closer to Don Dago's or Grandpa's age. Four women, counting Patricia. And two other children—shorter than everyone else and flat-chested like Carla and me. No one talks.

What separates us from the drivers at the very back of the boat is a double line of three bright-red gasoline barrels. Each barrel is almost my height. I'm far from them, but I can smell the gasoline, almost like paint, like glue, like smelling highlighters. At first, it smells good, but soon, it's overwhelming. Behind the barrels are the biggest motors I've ever seen, about half as tall as the drivers, who are the only people standing up.

They're also the only Mexicans. I thought that when one of them talked to Don Dago, but confirmed it listening to them talk to each other. They sound nothing like us and say "carnal" a lot. They haven't talked to us yet. As they row, they keep looking at the shores until the creek gets wider and the ocean waves get louder and louder. Near the motel, their oars touched mud. Now it's just water.

I try to find the moon, but it's nowhere. I want something big to look at. In two days it's supposed to be full. The calendar in our room had little red moons next to the black numbers. But nothing is up there. And it's cloudy. I hope it doesn't rain. I can't stop thinking about what the locals told Marcelo. *Everything is gonna be ok.*

It's warm already, even though there's a slight breeze that sends salt through my nostrils, on my tongue, on my cheeks. The waves are bumpier, it's not smooth like it was behind the motel. We're closer to the delta. It reminds me of taking a boat from my hometown to the ocean; that was the scariest part, the bumps. The Mexicans aren't rowing. One of them, the one with the round hat, walks up the boat toward Carla and me. When he leans closer I can see his beard is sprinkled with white hairs. He's old. Sunglasses hang from his neck, tied with a shoelace, and as he leans, they almost hit my forehead.

"Plebe," he says. His voice, his speech *is* different. Even more pronounced than Don Dago's. He sounds like the people in old Mexican movies, the ranchera ones Chente appears in. "Here," he says quietly. His voice reminds me of Grandpa's. Hard. Direct. He opens his fist, and two small white pills shine bright in the dark-blue light like eyes looking up at Carla and me.

"So you don't puke," he says, extending his big hand toward us. Carla grabs one first. Then he puts his hand closer to me, and I grab mine. He hands us water from a bottle tied with a rope to his belt. Before putting it in her mouth, Carla looks at Patricia, who nods. I look at Patricia and she nods again.

The small pill leaves a bitter streak on my tongue. I don't feel anything. He says nothing else but smiles, his teeth crooked and with big gaps in between each top tooth. The man hands Patricia one pill también. As she swallows, the man walks away, makes his way toward the front of the boat where the other children and women sit. We watch them take their pills. He makes his way back down to the middle of the boat, near us, and starts talking.

"¡Listen up!" His voice pierces through the sound of the waves and through the slight breeze. "There are a few rules." Everyone's head is turned toward him. "Once we turn the motors on, we will not stop. We will stop near sunset to give you a break, so if you have to piss, piss now." He speaks slowly. We listen to every word. "If you need to shit"—he stops there, looks around—"do it now, or hold it. We will not stop." He waits around for questions, but no one asks anything.

Then someone who sounds like us asks from the front of the boat, "¿When we leaving, pues?"

"When the other two boats get here," the Mexican says. I thought we were going to stop at the beach, stretch our legs, but no. "We've done this before, don't be scared," the Mexican continues, looking at Patricia, Carla, and me, then at the other women and children. His face is skinny and rectangular, and his hat is made of a light-brown cloth. No one asks anything, so he walks to the back of the boat.

It's almost 5:30 A.M. The sun's rays begin to highlight the edges of the waves—it's beautiful, the rest of the water looks like dark-blue Jell-O. From up the river, we see two boats approaching. They're identical to ours: no canopy, filled with people, and big red gasoline barrels near the back. The boats are painted white with a dark-blue rim and are nameless, which makes me remember what fishermen say back home: "A boat needs a name, or it sinks."

The boats drift until they float next to ours. We're so close we could walk between them. The Mexicans at the back of each boat— the coyotes—talk to one another. The other people look like the ones on this boat, mostly men. People my color, some white like Chele, others darker than me, some darker than anyone I've ever seen. Some say "vos" like us. Some call me "güirro." I don't understand. Others speak something that's not Spanish. Older men wear long-sleeved shirts and sombreros like the ones campesinos wear back home when they work the corn, cotton, or sugarcane fields. Mostly everyone else wears a dark T-shirt like Chino and Marcelo.

Marcelo is the only one on this boat who wears a tank top, the same dark-green tank top he wore in Ocós, showing off the tattoo on his left shoulder. The shirt makes him look like Rambo, or some other soldier ready for war. I try reading Marcelo's tattoo, but it's faded. More than once I overheard Don Dago telling him to cover it up, that people might think the wrong thing. Marcelo didn't listen, he shows it off like a badge. Some people stand up to pee over the side of the boat like the coyote said, but I don't have to go, not yet.

It's gonna be hot today. Marcelo has the right idea with the tank top. I wish I'd brought one. It's warming up, even with the slight breeze. The coyotes stop talking.

"¡Get ready, cabrones!" yells the younger coyote, wearing the backward baseball cap of a team I've never heard of. His voice is not as deep as the bearded coyote's. His face is round, and he also carries sunglasses tied with shoelaces around his neck. "¡Sit down! ¡Everyone, sit!"

The other boats drift away from ours. All of them turn their motors on. The older coyote tightens his hat—there's a chin strap he presses into his jaw—and sits. The younger grabs both of the motors' handles—the motors rumble, a noise that sounds like motorcycles. Everyone looks scared. People start whispering. The people next to us say "Diosito this," "Diosito that." Patricia mouths a prayer. Some look up at the sky, their palms opened and facing up. Others grasp the crucifixes around their necks or tied to their belts. Others pull out cards with saints on them. I pray I see my parents soon. I say, *Cadejo, Cadejito, protect me.*

We're moving closer to the delta, closer to the open ocean, where there's a break of big waves with white on their edges. Each wave feels harder and harder against our butts. The *bump bump bump* like a heartbeat that doesn't rest. Our boat is first in line. The coyotes both stand up. It seems like they're trying to read the waves, like the boat drivers do back home. I feel tingly. Numb. My face stiff like it's been smiling for too long.

"¡Get ready!" the old coyote screams. The boat waits, wobbles, lulls. The ocean is a small earthquake. My stomach churns like I'm about to puke. The sides of my stomach are an empty plastic pouch of mayo, a used paper plate with food smudged on it, a dirty window.

Then the Mexican with the rounded hat yells at the one with the baseball cap who has his hands on the motors' handles. "¡Ya! ¡Recio! ¡With everything! ¡Everything!" he screams at the baseball cap.

The boat jolts. The old coyote yells at everyone, "¡Grab the boat! ¡Grab the boat!" Patricia holds Carla with one hand, the boat with the other. I hold the boat with both hands. *Bump bump bump*, the waves bigger as they crash against the front. It's hard to hold on. Some scream. The older men with sombreros grab them before they fly off. I grab the people next to us. A shirt, pants, anything. Every single wave hurts our butts. A black cloud of gasoline smoke thickens the air. The smell. The boat breaks each wave, then there's a big one—

We're up in the air. The sky gets closer. Everyone holds their breath. Some fall into the middle. Then it's over.

The bumps quieter, smaller. But the smell stays. The stench of gasoline thick in our nostrils.

"¡That's it!" the old coyote says, celebrating, showing his crooked teeth. It happened so fast. We're over the break and in the open ocean. The shore is behind us. The volcano. Ocós. The cement buildings. The tower where the men smoked. Houses turning their lights off for morning. We watch the other boats break through the big waves separating river from ocean. The motors are loud. Everyone's smiling, crossing themselves, praying. Chele, Marcelo, and Chino pull out cigarettes and smoke. Everyone looks more relaxed.

My butt hurts. The motor in the background. *Rrrrrrrrr.* Splash. *Rrrrrrrrr.* Splash. *Rrrrrrrrr.* Splash, salt water on our faces. Wind on our chests. The sun warms our exposed skin. The old men keep their hands on their hats—it looks tiring. Some take them off for fear they will fly away. The sun is completely over the mountains, and every-thing on the shore, on the water, is closer to the color things are sup-posed to be. I'm trying not to think about the meters and meters of water, layers and layers of fish, sharks, alligators, monsters, under us. This is the farthest out at sea I've ever been. Nothing will happen to us here. Nothing will come and take us from these boats, throw us overboard. I'm going to land in México. I'm going to see my parents.

WE'RE IN THE MIDDLE of the Pacific Ocean, the ocean the nuns said is the biggest, the huge blue area on Grandpa's map. A month ago, I was at the beach for Semana Santa, when my skin peeled because I was afraid of stingrays and I didn't want to go in the water. Now I'm here. Surrounded by water and water and water. Sky sky sky. Clouds and more clouds. *Migrantes.* That word the locals in Ocós called us. We're that. *I'm* that. Everyone on this boat is one, like the people who drowned here before we got to Ocós.

I think about ants. My hometown's ants that live in holes in the ground. When it rained and it flooded, the ants held hands, or their antennas latched together, I don't know, but they formed a line like in red rover. *Red rover, red rover,* and the ants grabbed each other, float-ing in a made-up crowd that made them look like leaves floating in the flooded streets. Dark-brown ants on a light-brown current.

I feel like those ants now. The people in the boat, we're so close to each other. Shoulder to shoulder. Knee to knee. But no hands. I want to hold Patricia's, Carla's, Marcelo's hand. Some people talk to each other. Most keep to themselves. Marcelo sits across from me. The wind is cold, even though the sun is directly overhead. Carla sits on her mom's thighs. I don't know whether to scoot closer to them or not. I try nodding at Marcelo, but he looks over my head. Chino and Chele sit next to him, silent and with their eyes closed. ¿Are they sleeping? Patricia holds her forehead. I can't sleep with the waves hit-ting us.

Red rover, red rover. The only difference: instead of antennas, we carry backpacks, we carry water, we carry food, we're on a boat, our own paper boat, our own leaf, floating. We left our houses in cities, in towns, near the beach, near volcanoes. We left alone, then found a coyote, then a group, and now we're an even bigger group. A nest. A colony. There are at least thirty of us. Thirty more and thirty more next to us on the other boats.

One hundred ants, I whisper through the bumps on our butts, the splashes on our faces, the sun. The wind slaps a cold into my clothes that doesn't let my skin burn. No one brought sun lotion, but I like it that way. I like it when I peel. I want to feel like I'm back home, at the beach for Semana Santa. I like the flakes the next day and the days after.

Even though there's space under our seats, all of us hold on to our backpacks. Marcelo, Chele, and Chino grasp them tight. I can see Marcelo's veins on his hands even when he's "sleeping." I clutch my backpack when the boat slams down on a wave too hard and I get scared the boat will crack. It's my pillow. My shield against the wind and sun.

There are dark clouds over the west right now. I hope they stay away. Maybe it's true a storm drowned those people before we got to Ocós. The ocean *is* rough, it *is* scary. So many waves hit the boat, the seats hit our butts, our bodies have numbed. Some people sit on their bags. Others sit on their hands. Others put their sweaters, T-shirts, clothes, anything, on the seat like a cushion.

The sky, when the clouds break, is bright blue. I thought water got lighter the deeper into the ocean it was, but the opposite happens: it's an intense blue at the top of the waves, like the Salvadoran flag, darker closer to the water's surface like the Honduran flag, darker still under that.

Migrantes. It's hard to say. Like there's a lot of spit in my mouth, like I'm drowning. I keep saying it out loud. The noise of the motor in the back at all times. *Rrrrrrrrrrr.* Splash. *Rrrrrrrrrr.* Splash. Over and over. I feel dizzy, my head is spinning.

Gasoline feels like a finger in the throat. I want to puke. It's the reason the coyote with the rounded face and mustache yelled, "¡Every three hours, the last six people will rotate to the front! ¡The people in the front to the middle, the middle closer to the back! ¡¿Understand, cabrones?!"

"¡Rotate!" he screamed the first time, like he was yelling through a megaphone. The people in the back hunched over, grabbing legs, arms, hands, the boat, all the way to the front. No one dares walk upright for fear of falling over. We help each other. We push people toward the middle so a wave doesn't take them. We slide on the bench, to the back.

Every few minutes, someone throws up overboard. Others use plastic bags or hold their heads so they don't gag. Splash. *Red rover, red rover.* We're mostly centroamericano. "A la gran puta vos. No vomités. Pará. Dormite. Ya la cagás," people say when someone sounds like they're about to empty their stomach. But there's other people who talk funny. ¿Brazilians? Chele looked over at them the first time they spoke and said they sound like they have cheese stuck on their tongues. Chino laughed. Marcelo pretended to sleep.

Everyone is tired of puking. When people aren't careful, they spread vomit on the next person because of the wind. At first, fights broke out, but after a few hours, everyone has thrown up. No one argues anymore. We use the waves to clean ourselves. Patricia cleans Carla. Patricia cleans me. Marcelo, Chele, and Chino sleep. When they're awake, they constantly smoke. They hold their cigarettes in their fists so the light doesn't go out. They help each other by huddling, protecting the flame from the wind.

"It keeps the food inside," they say. Chele's face already bright red. Marcelo and Chino getting browner and browner. Maybe it's true. They've only puked once.

Every few hours the Mexicans take turns picking up a red gasoline barrel, balancing it on their knees in order to pour it into the motor's mouth. One does this while the other drives. We don't stop for anything. We're always at full speed. Because of this, they spill on their clothes, they spill on the boat. I've never seen gasoline up close. It's sparkly, like a rainbow that smells terrible.

I don't know where the other migrantes came from. I think they stayed at the same motel or maybe nearby. I can overhear people talking. Patricia and Carla don't say much, they just stare at where the land used to be. Sometimes I catch Chino, Marcelo, and Chele looking over our heads, out toward the rest of the ocean. Sometimes I look forward, north, where we're going, México, my parents.

Everyone hides what they carry in their backpacks. Grandpa told me to be careful, to hide my water, to hide my food. "¡Rotate, cabrones!" the mean Mexican yells again. He likes that word. We don't even have to look to know it's him. The bearded one doesn't call us that. People listen, they get up, hunched over. Sometimes with splinters on their hands. Some have taken their shirts off even though they know they will peel and burn. It's cold. Then it's hot. I'm tired. I'm sleepy. I'm fine. Awake. I feel funny. I don't. My stomach. I want to sleep. I can't. No one can. So much noise. So much blue. The same thing. *Red rover, red rover.* Our backpacks. Vomit. Splash. *Rrrrrrrrrr.* ¡Rotate! Splash. The sun. Sweat. The wind. *Rrrrrrrrrr.* Splash—

SOMETIMES THERE'S A FLOCK of seagulls or pelicans in the distance. "They're eating vomit," Patricia tells Carla, who leans on her mom, her eyebrows together like she doesn't understand. They both haven't thrown up, like me. By now, most people have multiple times. Vomit on clothes, on hair, on the boat. No one can sleep with that smell similar to ripe papayas. The coyotes told us to not eat anything before boarding. And to only bring light-colored foods: bananas, tortillas, bread. It's maybe why everyone's puke is light yellow.

"The birds," Patricia says softly.

I like the squiggly black lines circling in the water. The pelicans and seagulls look like vultures. They're far away—maybe they *are* vultures.

"No. There's fish over there," a stranger sitting next to Marcelo says, pointing at the cloud of birds, some dropping like missiles.

"N'hombre vos, it's 'cause you didn't shower," someone else in that group says. Some laugh. They smile. I smile. Marcelo doesn't react.

We've been out here for hours. No shade. My skin is sunburned. I keep my arms inside my shirt like I've seen others do. Everything inside our backpacks is wet. I wish for dolphins. I keep drifting in and out of feeling sick. The coyotes give Carla and me another pill.

Even Marcelo has thrown up. Chino, Chele, and he keep smoking, "to kill the taste," they say almost in unison when Patricia shakes her head at them. She doesn't like them smoking near us.

Everything smells bad. I'm afraid people will fall off when they reach for ocean water to clean themselves. I can't believe we haven't seen islands. I want to see one. I want to see a lighthouse. Maybe we can stop. Maybe we will poop there. Maybe then I'll throw up. I want it to get dark to see how far from land we are. To see the stars. The moon. I'm less afraid. I want to see more birds. I want to get there already. I wish for whales, because Abuelita believes they're good luck. I wish for anything that jumps out of the water besides the waves splashing into us. There are puddles inside the boat; when they get a few centimeters deep, we scoop them out with plastic bowls. It looks like we've crashed, like the *Titanic* when the iceberg hits, but "it's normal," the nice coyote said. "Don't worry," he told us when he showed us how to get the water out himself, his voice calm, which calmed me down.

"And if there *is* a crack, here's this," he said, holding up tar inside a plastic five-gallon bucket. He was smiling. "Don't worry," he said again.

"Puta," Patricia said. "No jodás."

That was at the beginning of the trip. We're hours in, and still no cracks. But sometimes a big wave scares me. Patricia doesn't seem worried. None of the other Six do, which makes me feel safer. I think about the time Mali took me to La Costa del Sol when the clinic was celebrating a birthday. One of her coworkers said he would teach me how to swim.

Without warning, ¡he threw me in the deepest part of a pool! I can still feel myself sinking. The taste of chlorine, the white of the pool's walls, the sky-blue water glistening above me in the sun. A fish tank.

Mali screamed loud, I heard her from the deep. The same man jumped in to save me. I was supposed to paddle, kick, punch, *anything,* but I didn't. While I lay next to the pool on the cement, choking, her coworker kept telling Mali to calm down, that it's how he learned to swim. She never talked to him again.

This is the *real* deep. It's so dark blue. Nothing else around. I try so hard not to think about what's below us. I repeat what I practiced with Grandpa: *Chiapas. DF. Los Mochis. Hermosillo. Tijuana. All the way to San Rafael, California.* Don Dago took our maps and threw them away in Ocós. "It's how La Migra gets you," he said. But I have names. I also practice my accent. *Órale. Popote* instead of *pajilla. Lana* instead of *pisto. Carnal* instead of *chero.* I listen to the Mexican coyotes speaking. I take notes. When we land, I will be Mexican. Tapatío. Headed to el DF. I know the anthem. The presidents. I repeat this when I get tired of looking at everyone. I want the sun to get lower so I can use Grandpa's trick to see how much sunlight remains. I want night to arrive so I can look at the stars.

THE MOON PAINTS THE waves platinum. The moon and the stars reflect on the water like jellyfish. Large tentacles reaching toward Asia. The stars' reflections on the water like tortillas on a comal. The motors are louder than every other sound. *Rrrrrrrrrr.* Our noses feel like someone stuck two gasoline-dipped cotton balls in our nostrils. A few people have finally given in to sleep. They don't sit on the bench for fear of tipping over if there's a big wave; instead, they're crunched up on the ground, wearing their backpacks to cushion the bumps.

It's cold. I blow hot breath into my hands. Some people have taken extra clothes from their backpacks and put them over their shirts. Each group sits even closer together, huddling. Women hug women. Women hug children. Some men hug each other. But not Chele, Marcelo, and Chino. They sit a bit closer, wearing all of their clothes, blowing into their hands, their arms crossed, but that's it. "¡Smoking keeps us warm!" they shout across the boat. They don't share their cigarettes with anyone, even though a lot have asked. The coyotes in the back also smoke. They haven't thrown up.

Patricia has a dark-gray jacket she pulls from her backpack. It's thin but big. She puts it on and then tries to get Carla inside it for warmth. They see me shivering and they try to squeeze me inside. Carla sits on her mom's legs, her arms inside the sleeves over her mom's arms. I sit on top of Carla's legs, but my arms can't fit in the sleeves, the jacket won't zip up. Patricia tries to cover me as much as she can, but the wind still hits my chest. She's like Mali trying to help. I didn't know she cared about me, not *this* much.

I'm cold, but not as cold as before we tried keeping warm like this: our bodies like blankets on top of each other. Carla breathes on my neck. I can feel her legs. I hope I'm not too heavy. I like us this close. I hope we're not too heavy for Patricia. This is the closest we've been. The closest I've ever been to another girl or woman that's not my family. I can smell them through the gasoline smell. I can feel their body warmth. My heart beats faster.

I try not to think about my nervousness by looking over the men's heads across from us, trying to spot a light, any light, to signal that we're close to the coast, but everything is dark over the side where the moon rose from. It's almost full. *Over there is México,* I whisper to me and only me. But there are no lighthouses. No islands. No other boats. No one has spoken in hours. Not even the coyotes have said anything. Not even "rotate." It's silent except for the sound of the motors, of the waves, and the boats that still follow us. We can hear their motors, fainter than ours, but they're there.

"¡Help!" breaks the silence. A shrill scream like cats fighting at night. It's a big man sitting near the back of the boat. "¡Stop! ¡Help me!" He's screaming like he's broken a bone, like someone is beating him.

I turn around and try to look at Patricia, who holds me closer. Tighter. Carla asks her mom what's wrong. She doesn't say anything. The men around the man ask him what's wrong, but he keeps screaming. People look at each other. Look at the coyotes, who pretend they don't hear anything.

The man says he sees fish. His mom. His brothers. He keeps repeating that he can't move. He can't get up. That he needs to shit. That he really needs to go. "¡Stop the boat! ¡Stop the boat!"

The man is bigger and taller than everyone. During the first rotation, the coyotes told him to stay near the back. "It's safer this way," they said. "Don't move." He hasn't moved. He's been near the gasoline the entire time.

"¡Help me, the sharks!" he yells. "¡Stop!"

In between each scream, a long pause. Like he's dying. My chest like it's a piece of ice about to break.

"¿What's wrong with him?" Carla breathes into her mom's neck. Patricia seems concerned. She presses her hands into both of us. Hugs us tighter. I see people cross themselves.

Everyone starts shouting, "¡¿Why can't we stop?! ¡Stop the boat! ¡Look, he's crazy! ¡He's gonna get us killed! ¡He's gonna jump!"

The men next to him try pinning him in place. The moon lights the man's chubby face. His cheeks. The ridge of his nose. Then the coyotes point their flashlights at him. They light his body. His thick arms. He's crying. Sweating. Begging. His hands like he's praying.

He tries to jump overboard, but more men press their bodies into him. The baseball cap coyote finally yells at the man, "¡Calm the fuck down, you dumbass piece of shit!" Repeats it: "¡Calm down! ¡Calm down!"

"¡¿Why can't we stop?! ¡Stop the boat!" someone yells.

"Because, pendejo, if we stop, everyone has to stop," the nicer coyote shouts, loud and firm like Grandpa.

"¿Can't you stop now?" someone else asks.

"No."

"¿Why?"

"No."

Marcelo, Chele, and Chino mind their own business. People keep arguing with the coyotes back and forth, until finally, the motors slow down, and the noise quiets.

The other boats almost rush past, but the older coyote talks into his shirt, flashes his flashlight. All the boats slow down. The ocean felt flatter when we were going full speed. The more the boat slows, the more we can feel the waves. Up—down. Up—down. It makes my stomach think I swallowed waves. People start puking. There's no wind. Nothing falls into the boat. Everyone empties in the water.

"¡Here it is, cabrones!" the mean coyote yells. "¡Your one and only stop! ¡Shit, piss, puke, but do it fast!" The other boats stopped far away, but we can see the shadows of people standing up. I don't *have* to pee. I don't feel anything, but everyone gets up and forms a line. Men, women, children.

"If you need to shit, use the back," the baseball cap yells. "Women, make a line there."

Patricia stops hugging us close. "Let's pee," she says. Taps me to get off. "Grab the boat." Carla gets off and we both grab the boat and each other, so we don't fall. Patricia hunches, making sure to balance herself, and walks toward the line with the women, to the front of the boat. We hold on to her jacket. The men unzip their pants and release wherever they stand. The wind is loud, but we can hear pee hitting water and The Screaming Man still complaining. He's quieter, but he's acting weird. He's near the very back.

"Let's pee here," she says, then turns to Chino, who is peeing right where he was sitting. "Chino, help me," she says.

She turns around and faces us. Grabs Chino's hands that hold her in place. He doesn't look at Patricia's ass facing the ocean.

"¡Hey! ¡Bicho! ¡Cover your eyes!" she says to me. I want to look.

I want to know what's down there. "¡Turn around!" she says again. "You too, cerotes," she yells at Chele and Marcelo. And they listen.

It sounds the same. The stream coming out of her. Carla stares at my face. I can make out the whites of her eyes. The other women are also covered by men. No one went to the back of the boat, closer to The Screaming Man who doesn't have to pee. "I have to shit," he says. "Help me," he begs the men around him.

"Pinche güey, you're a fucking pussy," the mean coyote says. The other laughs.

"No manches," the older one, the bearded one, says when he sees the chubby man trying to squat and shit off the boat. But he's too far away from the edge. He keeps almost tipping over, or falling back into the boat, his pants halfway down. It's dark where his thingy should be. The men around him, the ones who don't know him, laugh.

"No jodás, look," Chele says to Marcelo and Chino, pointing at the man whose underwear is now wrapped around his thighs. It's white, glowing in the moonlight.

"You're gonna fall in, just jump in, it's easier," the bearded coyote says.

"¡No! I can't swim."

"Then hold the boat."

"I can't swim. Señor, no, por favor."

"¡Jump in! ¡Don't be a bitch!" the mean coyote yells at The Screaming Man, who's still trying to back over the edge with his pants halfway down.

"¡The sharks!" he shouts loud.

I'm scared.

The younger coyote steps closer to the man. Pulls him by his shirt and whispers something. Some scream, thinking the coyote is gonna hit him. Patricia sits on the bench, she pulls us toward her jacket. I smell her sweat. Patricia releases us, the Mexican is still talking to The Screaming Man, who stares at the water, facing the edge of the boat, his pants still halfway down. He looks down at them. Takes the pants off. Everything off. He's naked from the waist down.

He looks at the men around him, at the young coyote. "Please, hold me, please, I can't swim." Then, little by little, he steps onto the bench, closer to the edge, sits on the edge, then finally lets himself drop.

The man lets out a scream like Abuelita waking up from one of her bad dreams. It scared me when Abuelita woke up like that. I think of a wave dragging him away. ¿What will happen if he drowns? ¿If there's a shark? The edges of the waves are lit, but everything else is dark dark dark. I'm scared for him. The boat moves up and down. The men hold on to his arms. His fingers dig into the boat's edge. The other boats are quiet, everyone is watching.

Cadejo, Cadejito, I whisper. I think of La Herradura. Of California. For a few moments, everyone and everything is quiet. The waves slap the boat. The wind brushes against Patricia's hair, against her jacket, against my backpack on the ground—a sound like running through cornfields, wind against leaves. The noise of the gasoline containers sloshing and hitting the side of the boat. Plastic against wood. The plastic bowls inside the boat, like drums. The loose oars on the floor. Wood against wood.

"¡Get in!" the older coyote shouts. It's an order. The Screaming Man listens. The boat rocks to one side as he tries to get in. He's pulling but can't make it.

"¡Con garras! ¡Huevos!"

People try pulling him up but can't.

"Dip, then jump," the nice Mexican says, mimicking the motion, "like this." More men try pulling. But not The Six. We watch. The boat leans. Rocks sideways.

"Everyone, on that side," the old coyote says. Patricia grabs us closer to her jacket. "¡Over there!"

More men try pulling him. Then push him into the water and pull. The second try almost makes it in. They push and pull again, and he makes it onto the edge of the boat and falls inside, wet, with a loud thud. Like dropping firewood. The man looks like a dead fish. He must have hurt something. He's not screaming. But he's crying. Softly. Whimpering. Patricia hugs Carla and me tighter.

"Está bien," she whispers in our ears. "We're almost there, bichos." Patricia rubs our arms, our hair. It's what Mali did when I was scared. Makes me feel safe. Like everything *is* ok.

The man says something, but I can't make it out.

"Okay, sit back down, sit. Sit," the old coyote says, flashes his light at the other boats. The young one starts the motors again. *Rrrrrrrrrr.* Twists the throttle all the way. The wind picks back up and kicks our faces. Patricia tells Carla to sit on her again. Then I sit on Carla. The jacket still doesn't zip up.

Chino sits across from us. Maybe it's because we stopped, or maybe because it's later, but the wind hitting my chest feels colder than before. Chino notices and he leans closer to us and asks me, "Bicho, ¿you cold?"

I nod.

"Vení, pues." He waves me over, his palms outside of his light-gray jacket.

I turn my head around and look at Patricia, who nods and smiles. "Está bien," she says quietly.

I don't know. Chino smokes. He gets drunk. Almost got in a fight with Marcelo and with Don Dago. He has tattoos.

The stars are bright. I taste salt. I can't feel my butt, all of the bumps, all of the waves. I've been sitting too long. Patricia's jacket isn't warm enough. Grandpa didn't tell me to trust Chino. But he's always with Patricia, who is nice to me. And Marcelo doesn't care—he leans on the boat, slouching, all of his shirts on. His arms are crossed and he looks asleep. Chele is also sleeping.

"Bicho, vení, I'm gonna cover you like Pati," Chino says, his voice soft, softer through the motors. He calls Patricia "Pati"—that's what people call my mom. It makes me miss her. He says this as he unzips his jacket. I don't know him.

"Go," Patricia says. "He's like a cousin. No seás bayunco."

"Está bien, I'm not gonna harm you." Chino knows I'm scared. His skinny face. His skinny frame. I nod. I let him wrap his bony arms around me. Let him zip the jacket up to my neck. His arms skinnier than Mali's. Almost skinnier than mine. I look up at the sky as long as I can, trying to find the same stars Mali and I did, pretending these are her arms. That I'm with her. He hugs me like Patricia did, rubs my shoulders inside the jacket so I get warm. I've never been hugged by an adult man like this. It's a hug like Grandpa's hug. I don't remember ever hugging my real dad. Patricia, Carla, and now Chino. Three strangers' hugs in one day. I tense up and forget to breathe.

"Breathe, bicho. It's okay, breathe," he repeats, rubbing his cold hands down from my shoulders to my elbows. "Puta, you remind me of my little brother."

I didn't know he had a brother.

"¿What's his name?" I ask. Chino's hands now almost to my fingers. It's working. I feel warmer.

"Oscar," he says, and stops rubbing. "You smile like him." He lets a long breath out and looks up at the sky.

"Oh. You'll see him soon," I blurt out.

Chino looks back at me, and his arms work their way back up through the sleeves and out into the cold air.

"He's dead," he says quickly, tapping his own legs, then crosses himself.

I don't know what to say. I remember Papel-con-Caca, killed as I slept. I didn't hear anything. But he was older, Marcelo's age.

"Está bien, Javier. We're almost there, don't worry. Sleep." Chino takes a long breath in, then lets it out.

After a while, he slips his hands back into the sleeves and rubs my arms again. His hands are freezing.

I remind Chino of his little brother. I've always wanted an older sibling. Chino reminds me of Mali. He can be so nice, tender. Patricia también. I think of everyone back home. My friends. I don't want to die. "Sleep forever" is what Mali said. I don't want to go to heaven like the nuns say. Not yet. On top of Chino's legs, the boat is softer, each bump not as big. Marcelo and Chele move every once in a while. They *are* sleeping. Chino doesn't. He keeps his hands inside the jacket, rubbing my hands. Every few minutes saying, "Sleep, everything's okay."

4-29-99

I TRIED FIGHTING SLEEP. Eventually, I gave in, but woke up when Chino nudged me.

"Bicho, bicho, look," he said, louder, his breath smelling of cigarette smoke. "Flying fish."

¿Flying fish? Fish out of the water, flying. Swimming in the air. Like dragonflies, but bigger. More and more of them.

"They're running from dolphins," the mean coyote says loud. I can't believe it. Maybe I'm dreaming. I thought they were a myth. I saw them on TV but didn't believe. They glide in the air for meters and meters. They ride the wind like bullets. Like skinny balloons. More and more.

We're gonna make it, I whisper.

"It's a good sign," Chino says. "Ya la hicimos."

People in the boat cheer. I don't know how long I've been asleep. Don't know how close we are to wherever we're going in México. "It's a good omen," some men shout. "¡A good omen!" People cheer and clap more.

Then the fish disappear. Like nothing happened. We wait for them to come back. I look over at Carla, her smile bright white in the moonlight. Patricia smiles también. Both of their eyes wide, glowing in the dark. We keep looking for the fish, but now the stars are up. The moon more than halfway over us, on the other side of the boat. I must have slept a long time. I look and look at the water— nothing. Chino says, "Sleep, bicho, rest."

THE BOATS JERK TO a stop. "¡Wake up! ¡Wake up!" both coyotes shout at the top of their lungs. The waves feel longer, the up-and-down comes back. I'm still inside Chino's jacket. The sky is bluer, the same blue like when we stepped onto the boat yesterday. I turn to the right, and ¡there! The shore. In the distance, some lights, but there's no city. In front of us, nothing. Just beach. No volcanoes. Everything is a bluish green.

We drift toward land. Everyone is on the floor or slouching on the benches. Marcelo looks at me, awake and already smoking. Chele is still sleeping.

"Va, ya," Marcelo says, shaking Chele. Carla is in Patricia's jacket, her eyes half-open.

"Wake up, hija," Patricia says loud.

Chino opens his jacket, and I climb out and sit next to him. I smell like cigarettes. Gasoline still thickens the air. The sound of the waves hitting the boat. The plastic bowls, the oars, but then there's a new sound—sand. It sounds like paper being ripped.

We're about to hit the shore. The waves are calmer. The sand is brown like driftwood. There's no one on the beach. As we land, we hear 4x4 trucks, which turn their lights on and speed to the shore. Everyone looks at the coyotes.

"¡Your rides!" they say.

"We're here. Gracias a Dios," the nice coyote says.

Coconut palms line the beach. Bushes everywhere—beach grape, I think. It looks like El Salvador, but the water is lighter and the waves not as big. It's beautiful. I want Mali to see. Abuelita. Grandpa. Lupe. My parents. Not a single house, no one else around.

"Okay, okay, okay, wait to jump out," the old coyote says. Then, a bump. The boat stops, and the young coyote jumps out and pulls the boat from the rope at the very front. "Vayan con Dios," the old coyote says, softer than any order he's given. People cross themselves. I cross myself. *Gracias, Cadejito,* I whisper. *Gracias a Dios.*

Marcelo has everything ready and jumps out. Everyone else follows.

"Vení, Chepito," he says, waving, putting both hands out for me to jump into. ¿Does Marcelo feel bad he didn't offer to hug me and Chino did? Maybe he remembers Grandpa giving him money.

I jump into his big arms, his muscles. The water beneath me like a puddle to leap over. Water splashes against Marcelo's shins. The waves on the sand sound like the ocean is whispering to us, *Shhhhh*.

Chino carries Carla. Patricia walks herself. Chele helps other people. So many legs moving. Shirts. Pants. Shoes covered in sand. Water coming out of shoes, water squeezing out of clothes. Sunlight hits us like a flashlight moving every which way. The smoke from the trucks' exhaust pipes. The palm trees sway slowly with the slight breeze, each frond an arm waving, welcoming us. The birds, perched and singing, telling us they're alive. As we wait for everyone where the sand is dry, the drivers from the trucks yell, "¡Get in a truck, get in a truck, the back, the back!"

Suddenly there's so much noise—waves, metal shaking as the trucks turn back on, feet running, feet in water, the rattle of the exhaust. People climb into the truck beds that also rattle. Marcelo puts me down and we wait for The Six to gather. Carla looks half-asleep.

"Let's go," Marcelo says, walking toward a truck, signaling everyone to follow him. Chino looks at Patricia, who grabs my hand, and starts walking behind Marcelo toward the red truck with the least amount of people. The sand is wet sometimes; other patches are dry. The air is cold, but not as cold as it was in the ocean.

"¡Hurry hurry hurry hurry!" the drivers say. They're Mexican: they sound like the coyotes driving our boat that's now empty because it was the first to make it to the beach. Our coyotes hand two backpacks to one of the truck drivers. Then the coyotes from the boat start their motors and wave. Seagulls fly over them. Real birds this time, not flying fish.

We wait in the back of the red truck for people to finish climbing out of their boats and into the trucks. Then a Mexican taps our truck. "¡Go!"

The driver starts moving. Some people from our boat are here, along with others we've never seen. Everything is happening so quick. Against the sand, the tires sound like they're about to rip open. The car lights are turned on; it's not fully morning yet. On the beach, our boat is gone, the second boat también, like they were never there. No volcanoes in front of us. Coconuts and coconuts. Then the tires glide onto an asphalt ocean, a road that reminds me of the road from Tecún to Ocós. I keep looking up at the sky. The stars are disappearing. We're in México. I'm almost to my parents. I'm almost to La USA. I'm Mexican. Marcelo, Chino, and Chele are smoking again. We're all Mexican. The lights of other cars on the road turn off. Sunlight begins to color everything.

———

CHAPTER FOUR

Oaxaca, México

APRIL 29, 1999

———

A FTER TWENTY MINUTES IN THE TRUCKS, WE'RE IN FRONT OF A one-story building painted with the same pattern as the clinic back home, except the colors are different. The bottom part of the wall is green, the second half white, and the paint over all of it is cracked and falling from the walls. ¿Another motel? ¿An abandoned house? The garden out front hasn't been cut in years. It's 5:50 A.M. Our truck got here first, but the others are arriving now. No one from the boats sits in the trucks' front cabins. The drivers are Mexican; the passengers in the front seat are Mexican. Only the drivers get out and yell, "¡Jump jump jump!"

Our driver walks fast through the abandoned building's doors. "Split up. Pick a room," he says as people rush in. There are two rooms. We split into two groups of fifty people each. When everyone is inside the main building, someone else shuts the door. Our driver, our new coyote, walks toward a door at the end of our small room, a little bigger than the rooms in Ocós.

"Lines start here," he says. "This is the bathroom."

Everyone leans against the walls. We look like the leaf-cutter ants in Abuelita's garden, but instead of holding bitten leaves over our heads, we carry our black backpacks. There's nothing in here. No beds. No furniture. Tiles on the floor and walls of unpainted cement. It's crowded, dark, and hot. The coyote doesn't let us turn the lights on, only one light in the bathroom.

"¡Listen up! Brush your teeth, do your hair, whatever, when you get there." The coyote points at a silver sink in what looks like a kitchen but without dishes or towels. "Then wait to use the bathroom here." He points at the door in front of him. "Shit. Shower. Whatever. But you only get three minutes. *And*"—he emphasizes the *and*—"put your nicest clothes on." He pauses and holds up three fingers. "¡Three minutes!" he yells before opening the bathroom door where the line starts. I see flashes of a sink and a shower.

"¡We have to be out by eight A.M.! ¡Let's go, let's go, let's go!" he screams as he snaps his fingers.

Sunlight slips through the cracks between the curtains covering the small windows at the very top of the walls. We can hear similar loud directions from the room next door. We wait together, The Six, close to the middle of the line. The group with The Screaming Man stays close to each other. Every group stays together like in the boats.

"Maitra, you three go first," Marcelo tells Patricia. He likes using that word. It's what he called Don Carlos, *maitro*. What he called Marta. I wonder where Marta is. If she and Don Dago are already in el DF. If they took a bus or a car.

Patricia holds Carla and me closer to her, and then nods.

"Vos, bicho, go first," Patricia whispers as she leans closer to my head and pushes me in front of her in line. I don't know what I will do. The coyote makes sure people only take three minutes.

He screams orders as he knocks on the thin wooden door with his palm open. He warns people like that before opening the door that doesn't have a lock. *He is the lock.* We wait for him to tell us we're next. We're lined up past the kitchen sink, so we don't brush our teeth yet, but behind us, people unzip their backpacks, brush their teeth, crinkle plastic bags they keep their toiletries in.

In the bathroom, some people shower really fast. The knob makes a funny noise when the water shuts off or turns on. The curtain must have metal rings because we hear rings sliding across a metal bar. Every now and then, the toilet flushes. Three minutes is not much. It's hot in here with all these people. We smell like the ocean. Like salt. Like gasoline. Like vomit. There's no wind. No fan to hide the smell. My hands and face are sweaty. I have a mustache of sweat. My eyes have eye boogers. My nostrils are full of dry boogers that will hurt if I pick at them. I'm thirsty. I don't remember when I last had water. We left the empty plastic water bottles in the boats.

I just want to wash the salt that's now thick on me like a mask. It's on the edges of my face, near my ears, on my sideburns I hope one day will grow into a beard. The Screaming Man was at the front of the line. We heard him turn the shower knob. Water falling on the cement. I didn't get much vomit on me. I didn't even throw up, but I still feel dizzy. When I stand, I feel the waves trapped in my body, in my legs, in my tummy. I feel like I'm swaying. My legs tingle. I'm spinning a hula hoop. I lean against the wall. Finally, it's my turn, and I still don't know if I'm going number two or taking a quick shower.

"You're next, ¡come on! ¡come on!" The Mexican likes to repeat orders.

Patricia's hand pushes me forward a little.

"Carnalito, apúrate." The coyote says *hurry up* funny.

I carry my backpack. I hold it tighter.

"Wash your shirt if you can," Patricia says.

I've never washed clothes. I stare at her face.

"Leave it in there then, I'll wash it."

I don't want to leave my Animaniacs shirt here.

"¡Hurry hurry hurry!" the coyote says, frustrated, banging on the door.

Patricia shakes her head, annoyed, sucks her teeth, *shhhck*. "Watch Carla," she tells Chino, then walks into the bathroom with me. Pushes the door shut, but it doesn't close fully.

"Take it off," she says, pointing at my chest.

I shake my head.

"No seás bayunco." She grasps at the air for my shirt.

I don't want her to see me naked. To see my boobs. My belly. At least Carla is outside. I close the plastic curtain and the metal rings make their noise.

"¡Take your shirt off!"

"¡Hurry hurry hurry!" the coyote yells and pushes the door open, pokes his head inside, but Patricia shuts the door on his face.

Patricia is angry. She hasn't talked to me like this. "Hurry up," she says, stern, like when Mom got angry. Her face also gets like a raisin when she's mad.

I hand her my shirt through the curtain, making sure she can't see anything.

"Here," she hands me a white soap bar she takes out of her backpack. "Your pants," she demands. I freeze.

Her hand now flaps inside the shower waiting for my pants. "Give them to me."

I drop them in her hand.

"Wash your calzoncillo," she says, quieter than the other things, but I don't take my underwear off.

The shower is like the one in Ocós: water drips from a showerhead. I'm thirsty, so I open my mouth. I drink and drink and don't care it tastes like dirt. I like showers like these. Patricia scrubs my clothes against the sink.

"Hurry up," she keeps repeating. I scrub with the soap she gave me, a thin white bar that smells like Carla and her: like Abuelita's roses in the morning.

"Ya," she says when she stops scrubbing and squeezing my clothes. I try to put soap on my underwear to "wash it" as I clean my parts down there.

"¡Out!" The coyote knocks on the door. "¡Out!" he repeats.

I take my underwear off and try to squeeze as much water out of it as possible before stuffing it at the bottom of my backpack I left just outside the curtain. Nothing got wet. I grab clean underwear and my nicest clothes: my dark-blue, short-sleeved button-up shirt. I don't have time to dry off, so wet patches leak through my shirt. I walk outside. Patricia stays in the bathroom. Carla switches with me. Patricia slams the door.

"Huele a tierra mojada," Chino teases, sniffing the air, the same thing Mali said whenever I showered to make it seem like I never bathed.

"Cabal," Chele responds, and all three of The Six's men laugh. I smile. I wait with them, holding my half-open backpack, walking in my socks. Patricia kept my wet clothes.

I wait the three minutes next to the door. I hear a flush as the showerhead remains on. The coyote tries to open the door, but Patricia stops him and tells him they get six minutes because it's two of them. They argue for a bit. "¡Five!" he screams at her face, and after five minutes, Patricia and Carla walk out in their nicest clothes. Patricia didn't shower. Carla has wet hair. Or maybe Patricia did shower, but didn't wash her hair. I don't know. Mali did that sometimes. She walks out with all of our wet clothes she washed by hand. Water drips from them, leaving a trail of droplets on the floor.

"My turn." Chino points at himself as he enters, beginning to take his shirt off. I see his ribs and spine. His six-pack, chest tattoos, and a flash of metal on his nipple. I didn't know you could wear an earring there. Marcelo and Chele make faces. Then Chino closes the door. The coyote also looked at Chino funny, but didn't say anything. I don't know if he was staring at his tattoos or piercing.

"Come here." Patricia pulls me by my arm. Carla walks next to us, and we form a line to brush our teeth. I finally have time to put my Velcro shoes on, that now smell like mildew because they got wet.

One by one, Chino, Marcelo, and Chele line up with us after they shower. All of us look "nice." We're wearing pants and our dress shirts. Patricia wears a black blouse over her dark-blue jeans, and Carla wears a black tank top.

As we wait, Patricia takes out the makeup case I've seen her use in the morning. It has multiple colors and a mirror she can look at when she puts on lipstick. Today she chooses the light-red one, my favorite. Then she brushes Carla's hair into a ponytail and ties it with a black hair tie with clear balls at each end. They both look pretty and they both smell like roses. I smell like them también. I like it. Makes me feel like I'm part of their family.

We get to the mouth-washing sink and it's nasty: dried toothpaste on the faucet and the sides; saliva with blood, gray boogers, and hair cling to the sides. The coyotes told us, "Only use the water you need. Nothing more."

It takes me two tries to get the gasoline out of my mouth. I can taste it. I can smell it on my skin, but the roses hide it. I got the salt out, but not this. Gasoline in my hair, inside my fingernails, between my legs, in my shirt, my pants, my underwear. Or maybe the smell is trapped in my nose, on my tongue. The smell from my washed clothes is mostly out. We're not the only ones who had that same idea. Others washed their shirts, their pants. Some flap them between their arms so they dry faster. Others lay them on top of their backpacks on the floor, but not much sunlight hits them. Someone tried to open the front door, but there was another coyote outside.

"Not until eight," the outside coyote said. Then the coyote inside, standing next to the bathroom, said the same thing but added: "You're pinches migrantes." That word again. "Locals can call the cops, who will take you, rob you, or kill you."

He didn't have to scream it, everyone heard. The word "kill." *Matar.* That's the word. Like a plant. Una mata de aguacate. Una mata de limón. Una mata de cristal. *Cadejo, Cadejito.* I don't want to die.

Carla hugs her mom, who pulls me closer to them. "Nothing's gonna happen," Patricia tells us.

Chele's face is the color of his tongue. He doesn't look like El Buki anymore. Even after he showered, his face is sweaty and greasy. His acne is pinker.

"Almost eight, get ready." The outside coyote's body halfway in, half out. He has a belly. That's all I could see before he closed the door. People start rising from the group, lining up at the front door.

"¡Last bathroom!" the inside coyote shouts. The last people in line wait to wash up.

Chele says a word I've never heard: *inminente*. "The bus to el DF is inminente." Chele sounds like a gringo saying it. A detective. Chuck Norris. Van Damme. Steven Seagal on a hunt for a clue to get the bad guy.

I don't think Marcelo or Chino understand the word either. "¿What you say, cerote?" Chino asks.

"That we're leaving."

"Let's smoke then," Marcelo blurts out, hoping someone around us has cigarettes. No one says anything. We're near the front. Chele, Chino, Patricia, Carla, and me. Marcelo is behind all of us.

A few minutes pass and the front door opens, this time all the way, lighting everything inside the room a bright yellow.

"¡Let's go!" the outside coyote says. He's wearing a T-shirt.

"¡Go go go!" the inside coyote says louder, banging on the bathroom door. The line starts moving.

"Told you," Chele boasts, looking at all of us, grinning, his thick teeth showing.

People have stuffed everything in their backpacks. Patricia took our wet clothes and put them in a plastic bag. They're almost dry but not completely. I hope they don't smell of mildew like my shoes.

Near the door, the heat hits our faces. A fire burning. When we cross into the cement walkway that leads to the dirt road where the trucks are parked, T-shirt coyote hands everyone a bag of Bimbo Donas or Bimbo Conchas. I hope I get the Donas. They're my favorite. That white powder is so sweet and gets on my lips. I like to dip them in milk or coffee. But there's none. Instead, another coyote hands out bright-yellow Tampico bottles. He's wearing tennis shoes, shorts, and a T-shirt. We haven't seen him before.

"Breakfast," the T-shirt coyote says as he hands me a green Donas package, green like they are in El Salvador. The crinkle of the plastic reminds me of home. Abuelita sells these, and most mornings, I split a package with her. I miss Abuelita. Her pupusa stand is probably already set up. La Chele Gloria's también. I like the green part of the package with the Bimbo bear on it, smiling.

"¡Jump on a truck!" all of the eight coyotes yell, two per truck. We make our way toward the same red truck that dropped us off. We repeat the same routine. Chino gets up, asks for Carla. Marcelo asks for me. Chele helps Patricia.

"Okay, listen up," the coyote who was handing out Tampico says. "We're going to take you truckload by truckload. At the bus terminal, one of us will stay with you and put you on a bus to el DF. You're Mexican now. Mexicanos. ¿Understand?"

It's what Grandpa and I practiced underneath the almond tree in Tecún. I'm from Guadalajara. Same age. Same birthday. I repeat the Mexican national anthem in my head. Las Chivas is my team. I'm in full Usurpadora mode. James Bond. We're supposed to say we're headed to Guadalajara via el DF. We're returning from the beach.

Chino sits on the edge of the truck bed like Marcelo. He looks at me and says, "Ó-rale, car-nal" with a thumbs-up, then smiles, showing me his teeth, skinny like him.

"Ó-rale," I respond, smiling back, remembering his brother Oscar.

"Ya vas, bayunco." Patricia slaps Chino's back and looks at him with her eyebrows furrowing. They act like family even though they're not. Carla smiles; her dimples form and then quickly disappear when she stops smiling. Everyone waits for the truck to turn on and move. We hold our backpacks. Everyone looks exhausted. It's hot outside. The wet patches from the shower have dried up and turned to sweat.

The people in the second motel group split into two trucks and leave first. Chino's left knee shakes up and down. Marcelo's knee también. They did this in Ocós when we ate dinner. With their nice shirts you can't see their tattoos. Chele sits on the seat made by the wheel in the truck bed, directly across from where Patricia sits. Carla is on her mom's left leg, I sit on her right one. We take up the whole seat.

We're now the last truck. The coyote in the T-shirt handing out Bimbo is the driver, and the coyote who was banging on the bathroom door sits in the passenger seat. He knocks on the roof of the cabin and yells, "¡Hold on!" and the truck rattles up the dirt road onto the asphalt one.

We drive past cars, bicycles, motorcycles, vendors, people doing whatever it is they do in the morning. The breeze feels nice. No one is asking anymore, but I wonder if Don Dago is actually gonna be at the bus terminal.

When we arrived at the old building, the first thing Marcelo asked the coyotes was if they knew where Don Dago was. Patricia asked también.

"Up ahead. El DF," one of the coyotes said. And that was it.

We drive a few minutes and get to the bus terminal that has tall cement columns and a tin roof. It's crowded. We pull over on the side of the road.

The coyote in the passenger seat gets out and says, "Don Dago's and Don Ignacio's groups with me." Three men jump out of the truck. I don't recognize them. They weren't in our boat. The Six jump off. "The rest wait here, your person is coming."

The three other men are short. We follow the new coyote, who hasn't told us his name even though he's been yelling at us for hours. He's a little chubby and walks slow. He's Chele's height, taller than Patricia and the three men I've never seen before. We look like we're not from here because of our backpacks. The people around us don't carry much, or they carry things they bought at the nearby market: chickens, egg cartons, vegetables, clothes.

We walk toward a metal bench. "Sit. That's our bus over there. That's the one." This coyote likes repeating himself. "We wait. Don't talk to anyone." His voice is raspy from all the screaming. We don't talk to anyone. No one talks to us.

The bus station is smaller than the one in San Salvador. No lines leading up to our bus; people look like a school of fish waiting patiently to swim through the door. I look around for the other groups, but I don't recognize anyone. Everyone looks like a local. It's noisy in here. The buses. The vendors. People walking. The stray dogs sniffing everything and everyone, but they're no cadejos.

I sit next to Carla, who sits next to Patricia, who sits next to the coyote. The warmth of the person who sat there before us lingers on the metal. The men of The Six and the three new men huddle around the bench.

"Cigarettes," Marcelo tells Chino and Chele.

"You're Mexican, cabrones, talk like us," the coyote tells them directly, but in a nice way. "Actually, don't talk," he adds quickly, with authority. "Remember, things are called different here. Say *aguas frescas* instead of *frescos,* and for *soda,* don't say *gaseosa.*" The men nod, annoyed. Don Dago told us this. "Go," he tells them, flicking his wrist. He looks old but not older than Don Dago.

Before the men leave, Patricia tells Chino as quiet and as Mexican as she can, "Comános agua, please."

"*Cóm*-pra-nos," the coyote says. "*Cóm*-pra-nos," he repeats, shaking his head. "Talk like you *are* from fucking Guadalajara."

She makes that noise with her mouth, *shhhck,* like she's smacking her lips, but it's more saliva and more tongue. Mali makes that noise when she doesn't like something.

As I sit and wait on the bench, the ocean comes back to my legs, my stomach. The waves. A hula hoop, or a Slinky that keeps moving down the steps.

"You have to be careful with your words," the coyote tells us and the new men. "¿You thirsty?" He looks at me.

I nod.

"¿What do *you* want?"

"Un fresco," I say.

"¡Chingue su madre! ¡No!" He tries not to shout, raising his hands in the air. The three new men laugh. Carla también. I look at the ground. I thought I'd practiced, but I forgot. "Aguas frescas. Aguas frescas," the coyote repeats. "¿Which one?"

"Horchata."

He walks to the nearest vendor and comes back with one for me.

"Share with your sister," he tells me. "That's your sister now. That's your mom." He points at Patricia. "Things have changed.

These are your new fake papers, morrito." He hands them to Patricia. "Everything's the same, except your last name. Hold them," he says firmly, handing her my new fake papers with her fake last name. I was supposed to be Don Dago's son. ¿Now I'm Patricia's son? That wasn't the plan. Patricia looks at the coyote, confused.

"You pass off as a family. It's easier this way. Better for all of you. Trust me."

Patricia looks at me, says, "Let's hope so," and stuffs the papers into her right pants pocket.

Coyote walks toward the drinks stand again. I don't want Patricia to be mad, to be annoyed at me like she was when we first got to Ocós. She did hug me and Carla like she was our mom on the boat. She's like Mali. Has my mom's name. It's a sign. She already helps me the most. Her and Chino. And Chino acts like her family.

"¿And what's this called?" Coyote asks Carla when he returns with drinks.

She shrugs. It's not called *pajilla*. We know that much.

"Po-*po*-te," he says in a quiet voice, holding the straw up.

I take a sip of the horchata and almost spit it back out. *¡It tastes like water!* I think, but don't say it out loud. It's lighter than ours back home. Coyote laughs at the face I'm making.

"¿You don't like it?"

"It's different."

Patricia takes the horchata from me and takes a sip. Makes a similar face. "Like water," she says.

Carla takes a sip. Same face.

Coyote laughs again. Locals walk past us, staring. They *must* know we're not from here. We look different. Locals look more like Marcelo. Like the three men. Sort of like me, but the locals don't look like Patricia, Carla, Chino, especially Chele. They're too light to fit in. A little darker now that we're tan, but still, light. Like the Mexican horchata. And the rest of us are like the Salvadoran kind. I think of my telenovela role. I don't want to get caught because of my skin. I want to blend in.

I hadn't really thought about skin in La Herradura. For the most part, I looked like everyone else. Except for my dad's brothers, the barber, and some classmates who are darker, and people make fun of them. But there are others who are way lighter than me. Like my school crush, Margarita. Like Patricia. Almost like gringos. I've always thought I look like coconut husks. Like wet driftwood. I thought Mexicans were going to look like the ones in novelas. The ones on TV. But right now, Mexicans look more like Marcelo, like Jesús, like Don Carlos. Chele, Patricia, Carla, and Chino stick out. I don't want them to get caught.

"Don't look people in the eyes," Coyote tells us as he catches Carla and me staring back at the people who look at us when they walk past.

"¿Why?" Patricia asks.

"So they don't talk to you."

Just then, we hear someone yelling, "¡De Efe! ¡De Efe!" in front of a bus. "¡De Efe! ¡De Efe!"

"That's us." Coyote looks around for Chino, Chele, Marcelo.

Patricia gets up and grabs Carla and me. "Let's go, hijos," Patricia says, smirking at Carla and me. "Sos—" She catches herself. "Eres," she says quickly. "Eres mi hijo," she tells me with a smile.

"Sí, Mamá," I respond. I'm a good telenovela star like Luz Clarita. The men come back, cigarettes in their mouths. Chino hands us our waters. He also bought chips and gives them to the three of us to carry on the bus.

"The bus ride is long—try sleeping. Or pretend to sleep. There are checkpoints, sometimes they don't wake you," Coyote whispers.

We know this already: checkpoints. In Tecún, Don Dago warned us of Mexican police and Mexican soldiers stopping buses to check for fake papers. But our papers are really good fake papers. We also know that they mostly check the people they suspect of not being Mexican. That they ask questions we've practiced for in the worksheets Don Dago gave us. I've practiced my fake snores, peeking through my eyelashes.

"But if anything happens, I will handle it, ¿okay?" Coyote makes sure we're listening, repeats, "¿Okay?"

We nod. The men try to quickly finish their cigarettes, taking long puffs. Then, one by one, they throw them on the ground around the bench and stomp them. Maybe they smoke to get the ocean out of them. Even Patricia asks Chino for a puff before he finishes his cigarette.

"Ah, vaya, señorita," he teases her, but hands her the last bit of his cigarette. She takes two puffs and doesn't cough.

"To the bus." Coyote taps Patricia's backpack. Everyone walks toward the school of fish crowding the bus's doors. Patricia grabs my hand with the same hand she was holding the cigarette with. She smells like crushed mango leaves mixed with smoke. Like the leaves Grandpa rakes and burns most afternoons.

It's what Chino's breath smelled like on the boat, his clothes, his fingers when he unzipped or zipped his jacket. What Marcelo's fingers smell like when he takes me down from a boat or truck. What Chele's hair smells like, and now Patricia smells like that también. She grabs my hand, then lets it go. I sniff my fingers, and yes, they're crushed green mango leaves mixed in with smoke.

The smell is growing on me. Chino looks at me and asks if I want to smoke as we're pushing against the crowd. I shake my head and get behind Patricia, who grabs my hand again.

"No jodás al bi—" Patricia stops, and her eyes get big. She looks around to make sure no one in the crowd heard. No one looks at us. Not even the coyote heard who leads us to the bus door.

I remember when the men asked me to fetch them "powdered gasoline" in Ocós. The entire week I fetched cigarettes for Marcelo. So when Marcelo, Chino, and Chele asked me to get them "powdered gasoline," I thought it would be something else like that. I went to every store asking "¿Do you have powdered gasoline?"

"We just ran out," "Not this week," "Let me look, nope, don't have it," the store owners told me. Until I went to the last store, where the owner burst out laughing. I've never been *that* embarrassed in public. I ran back crying to my room. I felt dumb. ¿How was I so stupid? I was tricked. *Me*. My grade's first-place.

Patricia asked me what was wrong. I cried into my pillow as silently as I could in case Carla showed up. I didn't want to tell her, but she kept asking.

"Oh no. That's it. Fuck them. Come with me," she said in a tone so much like Mom's.

She pulled me by the hand out the room, up the stairs, to the motel's second story where the men liked to smoke. She yelled at Marcelo, Chino, and Chele like they were her children.

"So he learns," they said. "It's a joke." She made them apologize multiple times, multiple ways. Patricia heard enough, and before she went back to the room where Carla had stayed, she told me not to trust them. Then Chele told me to stay and watch the sunset with them, so I did.

Chino kept saying that it was only a joke, not to feel bad. Marcelo said his uncles played that joke on him when he was five. "Don't be a baby," he said. He made me feel worse. Chele said his older brother had done that to him. Said it was a test. Then he asked me if I wanted to try a cigarette. Chino told him I was too small, but Marcelo stared at Chino, saying, "It will make him strong. An adult." So I took a puff.

Smoke filled my mouth, my tongue, the little punching bag at the end of my throat. A match. A fire. A furnace. I started coughing and couldn't stop. Marcelo hit me hard in the back to let the smoke out, saying, "You're a man now."

"You got hair on your balls," Chele said.

"Ajá." Chino nodded.

Then they laughed, but not like how the store owner laughed at me. They laughed like they were my friends. I started laughing when I stopped coughing. I felt older. That was two, three days ago. I *do* feel older. Like the smoke gave me courage to get on that boat. To not cry. To not vomit. To be here now in another country without Grandpa. I'm scared, but I've smoked. I know things. Hair is growing down there. I have Cadejo. I have Patricia here holding my hand, protecting me.

Finally, we make it through the crowd. The bus steps are clean. I feel the air conditioner. No bus we've been on has had AC. Velvet curtains cover the windows; it's so dark I won't have to pretend to sleep. This is the nicest bus I've ever been in. It's big. Even with this many people, seats remain open.

We split up the same. Patricia, Carla, and I share two seats. I'm squished against the window, but all three of us fit comfortably. Chino with Chele behind us. Marcelo by himself, but across the aisle from the other men. Two of the three men sit together, behind Marcelo. The other one, a seat behind them. Coyote is on a seat in front of all of us, two, three seats from the front door. No one sits next to him. We're not supposed to know him. Patricia is my mom, Carla is my sister.

The driver makes his way down the bus and looks at us, but doesn't say anything. Half my leg is on top of Patricia's leg. Carla closest to the aisle. It's cold in here. I take my thin jacket out of my backpack, the one that didn't keep me warm on the boat. I hold my backpack in front of my chest. Lean my head on the velvet curtains that are thick and soft. I pretend to sleep.

"CHECKPOINT," PATRICIA WHISPERS, BUMPING me with her elbow. "Sleep," she tells Carla and me.

It's dark and cold inside. I can feel the bus pulling over because the tires run over gravel. The velvet curtains bump against my face. Through the tinted windows, it looks like it's still day. I check my watch. It hasn't been more than three hours since we left. It's not even noon.

I feel like there's a fish bone or hair stuck in my throat. It's itchy. ¿Am I sick? It's probably the gasoline. None of us have gotten sick up to now. "A miracle," Don Dago told us in Ocós before he left. "Keep it that way."

"Because we ate dirt as kids," Chele joked. But I didn't. I get sick a lot. I hope I'm not now. It's a checkpoint. I need to clear my throat. Carla laughs as she watches me struggle to swallow what feels like phlegm, without making any noise.

"You sound like a cat," she tells me, softly.

"It's the air," Patricia whispers, pointing at the vents the AC comes out of.

I let a few coughs out before the bus driver opens the door. Through the windshield we can see two patrol cars blocking the two-lane highway, one truck looking at us, the other looking away. A line of cars, buses, trucks wait for soldiers to talk to them. Orange cones in the middle of the highway lanes.

"Sleep," Patricia repeats. Coyote doesn't look at us. All we can see is the back of his head, buzzed close to his scalp in the back and gelled at the top. We've practiced for this. If anyone asks, he's a stranger. I lean against my velvet curtain pillow. I don't scrub my eye boogers away in order to trick the soldiers that I'm really sleeping. I'm Guadalajaran. A real tapatío. I know the national anthem. I know the best presidents. The city's three soccer teams. Chivas is *my* team.

The motor turns off and the bus stops rattling. I close my eyes almost all the way, but leave room between my eyelashes to peek through. The doors swing open. The driver says, "Good morning."

The soldiers say, "Good morning," and that they have to check people's documents.

I hear two men, four boots make their way up the steps. They sound different than anyone else's shoes. These are heavy. Loud when they step. Rubbery.

"Good morning." This soldier's voice is loud. "We're here to check you are who you say you are." He pauses. "Documents out."

The driver turns the lights on. A flash to my eyelids, turning them from black to a light orange. I squint and hope the soldiers didn't see. I keep my eyes shut. Relax them to make my sleep seem real.

People shuffle their bags, unzip purses, plastic rustles, wallets flap open. My palms are sweaty. I don't want anyone in our group to get found out. The Boots squeak closer. With my eyes closed, I concentrate on the picture of the Mexican flag. Red, white, green. ¿Or is it green, white, red? An eagle eating a snake on top of a cactus. Cactus. Eagle. Eagle. Cactus. Carla and Patricia don't move. The AC feels like it's turned off. The jacket and the backpack on top of me make me feel warm, but I can't move. Sweat beads form in my armpits.

The Boots get closer until they stop at our row. They turn toward us. "Señora. Señora. Wake up." This is another voice.

I want to open my eyes. This voice is not the one that made the announcement. More nose than throat. He shakes Patricia awake, I feel it on my leg. I hold my breath. If I breathe, it means I'm awake; if I don't, I'm dead. I exhale, quietly and as "sleepily" as I can. Patricia hands him our fake papers. He flicks our "documents" to see if they're real.

"¿Your children?"

Patricia pretends she's sleepy and nods so much I feel her body shaking. A minute. Two minutes. The sweat is now a puddle in my armpits, but I don't move. I keep breathing. Normal. Normal.

He hands Patricia the documents and moves to the seat behind us. I want to open my eyes, but don't. ¿We passed? Patricia didn't talk. We're Mexican. Red. White. Green. I wait for The Boots to be as far back behind us as possible before I let out a sigh, but they never move—

"You and you. Get up."

"¿Why? ¿Why?" one of the men says.

"Get up." This is the original voice.

"Outside. Now."

I open my eyes and turn around as secretly as possible. It's two of the three new men who are with us. The short ones.

One soldier walks them toward the door. Their shoulders droop, eyes glued to the ground. Then the remaining soldier asks an old lady for her papers. She says she's from el DF, that she's Mexican, but the uniforms still ask her to get up and walk out. "I'm Mexican," she keeps repeating. Each time louder than the last. She refuses to get up and leave her grocery bags taking up the seat next to her.

"¡Take *them*! *They* are not Mexican. I am Mexican," the old lady says, nodding at the seat across the aisle from hers.

"¿Who, señora?"

"Them. Ask. *Ask them*. You'll hear."

"You. You. And you. Outside. Now."

"¡Now!" another soldier yells. "¡Outside!"

The bodies walk past us. It's them—Chino's buzzed head. Marcelo's height. Chele's belly. I want to scream, *They're Mexican. I know them*.

Patricia looks at Carla and me. Puts her hands on both of us. Shakes her head. Stares at us like she's saying, "Don't do anything." Presses her fingers into our arms. I don't move. I don't open my mouth. Everyone steps outside. Another soldier, a different one, comes up the steps. He has a mustache and big sunglasses on his rectangular face.

"¿Any other non-Mexicans?" He pauses. His voice is stern, his uniform clean and sharp. "If you get up now, it will be better for you. This bus won't move until we find everyone."

I look at Patricia, who doesn't look back, doesn't look to the side, who keeps shaking her legs. My hands are drenched. Coyote doesn't move. He keeps looking forward. No one gets up. The mustached soldier walks out.

People peek through the curtains, so we peek también. Outside, the soldiers make the men kneel on the dirt a few meters from where we're pulled over on the side of the road. The mustached one paces and asks them questions. No one says anything. The sun hits the men's faces. Marcelo, Chino, Chele, the three others. Coyote told us this could happen. That he would deal with it. But he's not doing anything.

The mustached soldier comes back up the steps and tells the driver to wait, then walks back out. All of the soldiers, except one stopping traffic the other way, surround the kneeling men. The cars behind us drive past, because the one soldier tells them to keep moving. Patricia looks over at Coyote, who looks back at her. She nods toward the window, her eyes big and white.

Coyote shakes his head. Doesn't do anything else.

Patricia's eyebrows touch, her face is red. She lifts her hands from our legs, suddenly turns toward the old lady, and says, "India pendeja, hija de sesenta mil putas, cerota mal parida." Her mouth like a rabid dog's, saliva spewing out from her like venom. I've never seen her this mad.

"Pinches mojados," the lady responds after a long pause. She clutches her bags. Her voice breaks like she's scared.

"If I didn't have my kids, I'd beat the shit out of you."

Coyote turns his head. "¡Sit! Don't say anything," he tells Patricia. Turns his head forward.

"India pendeja," Patricia says again.

"¡Sit!" he shouts again.

"Get these mojados out. ¡Out!" the old lady screams. "¡Out!"

Another soldier comes back up the stairs.

"Here." The lady points at us.

The soldier walks fast.

"¡Fuck you!" Patricia screams at the woman. The soldier tries to grab her hand.

"We can walk, hijueputa."

"¡Do something!" she yells at Coyote. "¡Get your backpacks!" Patricia yells at Carla and me. Then she pushes Carla into the aisle, pulls me off the window, her nails pressing into our arms. The ground moving fast, down the steps, through the bus door, onto gravel. Sunlight hits my cheeks, my nose, my forehead, my eyes adjusting to the brightness reflecting off the dirt. *Cadejo. Cadejito.*

"There's nothing you can do," the mustached soldier is telling the men, pacing. "This is México. There are laws here, and you're breaking them." He must be the soldiers' boss: five soldiers stand as he paces. He calls us "ilegales," "mojados," "criminales." "I have the power to send you all back to El Salvador, Guatemala, wherever the fuck you're from."

On top of the asphalt road, it looks like steam is rising. The bus is still parked. Cars wait in traffic behind it, one soldier is still checking papers. We were inside the bus, now we're standing in front of guns. Big guns hanging from shoulder straps. Little guns on belts. The soldiers *are* wearing boots, black ones, big leather ones. I remember the nuns telling me, "During emergencies you can pray without kneeling." Their guns shine when the sun hits the metal a certain way. Every night since Grandpa left, I've whispered a Padre Nuestro lying in bed. I start: *Padre nuestro, que estás en el cielo . . .*

"Throw your backpacks in front. All of you," the mustached soldier says, calmly, without shouting.

I watch to see if Patricia does. All of the men's bags are already black islands in the dirt.

"¡Do something!" she screams at the bus again before throwing her backpack. I throw mine . . . *hágase tu voluntad . . .*

"Kneel next to them," The Mustache says.

Patricia kneels next to Marcelo, who's on the outside of the line of men. Carla kneels next to her, then I kneel next to Carla. No one else next to me.

"Arms behind your head."

All of our arms behind our heads, in a line, on the dirt that hurts my knees. I try to scoot away from a rock pressing into my right shin. The sun warms up my hair. The back of my neck. My hands. I'm still wearing the light jacket. The dry air on my face, the heat—

"Nobody move."

"¡Stop, stop!" Finally, Coyote runs out of the bus, shouting at The Mustache, who whispers something to another soldier before talking to Coyote.

"¡Lie down!" this soldier yells, his hair buzzed at the sides and gelled back at the top. "¡Facedown!"

. . . nuestro pan de cada día . . . When I move my lips, they kiss the dirt. I wipe my mouth with my hand.

"¡Don't look up!"

"¡Spread-eagle!"

My arms in front of me like I'm Superman. Like I'm flying. Like I'm Goku. I peek from the side and see the bus. The traffic. Car tires, moving. Stopping. The old lady must be watching. The driver. Everyone else who didn't say anything.

Some of the soldiers look like Marcelo. Others like the three men. But The Mustache looks like a telenovela Mexican. His mustache thick like a bicycle tire. He's the only one not carrying a big gun but one like Grandpa's. The Mustache's gun is strapped in the holster that moves when he walks toward another soldier. Coyote behind him, begging.

The Mustache whispers something and a soldier runs toward the bus.

"There goes your ride. Now, listen," he says, looking at all of us as the bus shakes and speeds off. Everyone looks at Coyote, who stands and mouths, "Calm down," his arms pressing down against the air.

"Okay, okay. Let's work something out." Finally, Coyote speaks loud enough so we hear.

"I told you what." The Mustache fixes his sunglasses, his voice stern and louder than before.

"That's too much." Coyote shakes his head.

"Okay." The Mustache nods at the soldiers and all of their hands pat us up and down our bodies like spiders, touching, searching our pockets, our shirts, everywhere. The Mustache says they're looking for "contrabando." I don't know what that means. I try to repeat the word. *Con-tra-ban-do.*

When the soldiers lean to search us, I can see the tips of their guns. Long guns like in *Rambo*. Metallic. Black. The Mustache kicks up dust when he paces in front of us.

"You happened to catch me on a good day. I'm gonna make this very simple. Convince me *not* to deport you to your shitty countries."

"¿How?" someone at the other end of the line asks. I can't see who, and don't recognize the voice.

"You tell me, indio." That word again. Everyone says it nasty. Like a bad word. No one responds.

I don't know what to say. *Cadejo, Cadejito* . . . I close my eyes and fly far far very far away from here. Above the clouds. I'm flying over mountains, over lakes, over cities, all the way to the Golden Gate. I can't hear anything, I'm in California—until a small, dirt-colored lizard is close to my face, tan like me, blending in perfectly with the ground.

"This won't take long if you cooperate."

Co-o-pe-rate.

The lizard gets closer to my hands covering my eyes, my face, from the dust kicked up by The Boots. She's small. I name her Paula.

Hola, Paula.

Hola, Javier, she says, licking her own face. Her belly big, white, jutting from her sides like she's pregnant. Her tail thin like a strand of brown hair.

"¡Take your shoes off!"

"¡Empty your pockets!"

Paula almost licks my fingers.

"¡All your lana out!"

I don't know that word.

"Money. ¿That clear?" The Mustache clarifies. Coyote is shouting numbers next to him.

My tongue doesn't move. Paula freezes. Her hands and legs sprawled like mine. Like ours. Belly down. We look like Paula. Like lizards. Each breath lifts more dust onto my face, it gets stuck on my sweat. My big nose gets in the way. The sun is so bright. I keep my right eye closed as I tilt my head a little to the right so I can breathe. Paula doesn't move. Doesn't leave my side.

Paula says, *Everything is going to be okay, fine, just fine* with each lick of her tongue that wets her face. Then she runs away.

The Boots' hands enter my pockets again. My shoes. They open all of my backpack's zippers. Their hands, their fingers, search everywhere. Tap, tap, tapping away. I close my eyes. Their hands on the top parts of our bodies. The lower parts. Every crevice. They take longer on Patricia. Paula is still here, under a bush, hiding.

All of the bills and coins we carry in our pockets they pull out and throw on the dirt, drying in the sun.

Coyote is still talking to The Mustache, who asks if we have more. Says that this is our chance.

"No," the adults mumble.

Then The Boots pick up the crinkled bills, the shiny coins, and put them in their pockets. I don't carry much, only "snack money," like Grandpa told me to do, "enough to buy a drink or two."

But I have money hidden in places they won't find, I tell Paula. Then The Boots walk too close to the bush and she's gone. Their guns, big and metallic.

"¡Get up and kneel!"

"¡Kneel!"

Their guns pointed at us, like mouths, like eyes. The holes like Grandpa's gun. But these holes are wider. The guns are bigger. Longer. I close my eyes again. Coyote begs louder.

"If you still have money, now is your chance."

No one says anything. The sweat is everywhere inside my shirt, my pants, everywhere on my face. No one takes out more money.

"Everyone take your socks off," The Mustache says.

Green bills folded tightly into a square spill from the socks of one of the three men with us. The Mustache moves closer to pick it up.

Coyote tries to stop him, and the other soldiers point their guns. Coyote freezes in place and lifts his hands.

"Dólares," The Mustache says, stepping closer to the man in our group. I close my eyes. *Cadejo, Cadejito . . .*

"Don Dólares," he says sarcastically.

"Don't look," Patricia says. I look toward Paula's bush. A thud—

The man, Mr. Dólares, is holding his head. I hear him whimper, trying not to cry.

"Don't cry, maje," Marcelo tells him, loud enough for us to hear. "Con huevos."

"Macho man," The Mustache blurts out, raising his voice. "¿So *you're* macho man?" He moves closer to Marcelo.

"Okay. Okay. Enough," Coyote says in a deep voice. "Okay," he says, returning to his regular tone. "*Your* price then."

The Mustache smiles and walks away from Marcelo toward Coyote, who hands him a roll of money.

Padre nuestro . . .

The Boots finally lower their guns.

"There's been a misunderstanding, señores and señoritas," The Mustache says as he paces. "Please, please, get up."

Slowly, all of us pat the dust from our clothes. Carla hugs Patricia. Chino hugs her. Marcelo comes closer to me. "Todo está bien, Chepito." He pats me on the back. My legs are shaking. My hands.

Patricia walks toward me and says the same thing. "Todo está bien, bichito." The *-ito* like Mali. She hugs Carla next to me. Then she hugs me. Everything *is* ok. Everything *is* fine. We're in México. Mr. Dólares isn't crying. His head is fine. The other men with him help him get up.

But then The Mustache walks toward the three men not in The Six. "You three with me."

They look at Coyote, confused.

"Wait," he tells The Six. "Wait here." He runs toward the three men, each with a soldier behind them. Our coyote tells the three men something. They shake their heads. Yell at him.

"Not enough," he repeats.

"¡Let's go!" The Mustache says, and they walk toward the trucks.

The soldiers point their guns at the three men. I press my face deeper into Patricia's stomach like Carla is doing into her chest. She pats our backs, repeats the same thing, "Todo está bien," again and again.

The trucks turn on. I look away from Patricia's stomach. The three men climb in the back of one truck. Soldiers surround them. The trucks speed off. The three men are gone. No one tried to stop the trucks. No one says anything.

The sweat beads on my lips get bigger and bigger. I'm drenched like I showered again. I take my jacket off. I can't speak. I look for Paula. She's nowhere.

Coyote runs back toward us and says, "They didn't pay enough. I'm not responsible."

"Chorcha maitro," Marcelo says.

"You're still here, ¿no?" Coyote says. "*You're* my group."

Everyone from the boats is gone. The trucks and the orange cones aren't on the road. The bus is gone. Cars drive by like nothing was ever there. Like we're not here next to the road, walking toward the makeshift bus stop. Everything. Everyone. Gone.

WE'VE BEEN WALKING SINCE noon. One P.M. Two P.M. We watch for police and soldiers coming down the road. Not the main highway we were on, a different route, fewer cars, fewer towns, Coyote said. We've been on this road for hours. It's still asphalt, but there's dirt on both sides, cactuses, bushes, but no trees for shade.

If police or soldiers approach, we run away from the road and hide in the brush. We scream, "¡Hide!" if any vehicle comes from up front, or from behind. Marcelo walks backward, looking everywhere. Then Chino takes Marcelo's job. Then Chele. If it's not police or soldiers, Coyote holds his thumb out like in cartoons, says this is the safer thing to do, for him to put his thumb out and for us to run away and hide.

Coyote asks if we talked while getting on the bus, if we talked in the terminal. No one says anything. He tells us to always, *always* have our pinches Mexican accents on. "¿You know what? Just keep your fucking mouths shut. Now you're almost out of money." He explains he's done this a thousand times. That it's our fault we're walking. To let him be our mouth.

He still hasn't told us his name. Doesn't tell us much except that he's Mexican, but not from the "shitty" south of México where we are. We've been walking for hours. No one has stopped. It's very hot in the sun. Even hotter on the asphalt; our shoes feel like they're melting. We took our nice clothes off; Patricia thought it was smart to put our wet clothes on, the ones she washed for me. It did cool us off for a bit, but now we're hot again. We're sweating like we sweated when we were sprawled on the dirt. The guns. Their hands.

The plan is to make a car stop to give us a ride. It has to work. Coyote says The Boots took most of our money. That he had to give it to them. That it's the reason we can't pay for another bus. We must save.

Coyote says Mr. Dólares messed up, that he "royally fucked up." That The Boots just want to scare people and don't really want to deport us. "Too much paperwork."

"It's why you hide your money where no one will look. All they want is a little bite."

Even I remember Don Dago telling us not to keep our money in our shoes, in our pockets, in our socks. Or to double-sock it and hide the money between the socks.

"Cipotillo, don't worry," Chele says to me as we're walking. He's sweating, breathing heavily. *Cipotillo* is what he's decided to call me. No one has ever called me that. "We're from the only country in the world named after God. Think about it."

I didn't know Chele was religious.

"Cabal, it's a good sign." Chino backs him up.

"So that means He will help us get to ¡Los Estamos Unidos!" Chele screams the last part.

There aren't any cars, no people except us. No one tells him anything.

Los Estamos Unidos. I like that. It's where we're going. Together. To be with our families. I last spoke to my parents in Tecún when Grandpa called them. None of us have called north. When Grandpa left, that's the last day I talked to anyone: Abuelita, Mali, Lupe, Mom, Dad. I miss all of them.

¡*To Los Estamos Unidos!* I want to scream it like Chele did. But I just follow everyone. We walk until our legs say "no more" and Coyote says, "Rest, someone will stop."

"We've been through enough for one day," Patricia adds.

So we hide in the bushes next to the road as our Capitán Coyote holds his thumb out. All of us gather around Marcelo, who begins to explain what *faak* means. Whenever a car slows down but then keeps driving, Marcelo yells, "¡Faaaak!" No one knows the word.

"It's Inglish," Marcelo says. Tells us what it's like living in Los Ángeles, where he lived before he was sent back to El Salvador. That he didn't want to come back, but gringos caught him. I don't know what that means, but no one asks.

Grandpa was right. People in town say Marcelo didn't come back because he wanted to. "But up there, I learned *some* Inglish." Everyone's eyes are glued to him speaking. Then he says, "La USA is the best country, better than any we've been in." He leans closer to me. "The best country, Chepito."

It's my chance, so I ask him if what I've heard is true. "¿Is there pizza during lunch at school? ¿Do kids eat hamburgers all the time? ¿Are the streets clean and with McDonald's everywhere? ¿Is the beach blue and wide like in *Baywatch*?"

He says yes, yes, yes, and yes. Everyone smiles.

"Okay, but tell us what *faak* means," Patricia says.

"It's a bad word."

"Say it," Patricia pushes him.

"The kids." He nods at us, then leans closer to her and whispers it. She blushes and her eyes get huge.

Everyone laughs.

Another car slows but doesn't stop. "¡Faak!" Marcelo says.

"¡Faak!" Patricia shouts.

Then Chino. Then everyone in The Six says the same thing: "¡Faaaak!" We scream from the pits of our bellies. Up our throats. Out of our wide-open mouths. We can't stop laughing. I still don't know what it means. First, I hoped the cars would stop. Now, a part of me hopes they keep driving so we keep yelling: "¡FAAAAKKKK!"

It *is* getting late. Not dusk, but almost. Coyote gets an idea. "People want to help a mom and children, ¿no?"

"Puesí."

"Cabal."

A few minutes later, it's Patricia, Carla, and me next to Coyote hoping someone stops. We're so sunburned. Our water is running out. We've eaten all the snacks we bought at the terminal. The soles of our shoes hot like coals.

Then a light-gray microbus approaches.

"¿Where are you going?" the driver asks.

"Wherever you are, jefe," Coyote says, looking at us to make sure we don't say anything.

"¿How many?"

"Six plus me."

The driver taps the wheel with all of his fingers. Looks past the windshield, then flicks his head as if it's a tail. "Get in. You don't want to be here at night."

Patricia lets out a sigh. I smile. Carla smiles. Coyote waves at Marcelo, Chino, and Chele, who rise up from the bushes.

"They're harmless," Coyote tells the driver, making sure Patricia, Carla, and I are already in the microbus, his hand holding the door open.

The men climb inside. There's only one other person, in the passenger seat. ¿A customer? ¿The driver's brother? The driver doesn't say anything, but the passenger holds a backpack también.

"We're going to Acapulco, ¿está bien?"

"Órale," Coyote says.

Acapulco. I know that place. I sit in the back row, on Patricia's lap. Carla next to me. Chino next to her. The other men share the middle row.

There's no AC. The driver has all his windows down to let the air waft through the microbus. Chino opens the triangular windows in the back. They're small, and only some wind comes in, but it's better than hiding in the brush.

"Rest up," Coyote says, turning to look at Carla and me in particular. He still hasn't told us his name. "We're safe," he says, his voice still a little raspy. It's been that way all day, since he screamed at us when everyone from the boats was showering or using the bathroom. "Three minutes," I can still hear him saying.

"We're safe, rest," he repeats. No one says anything. The driver turns the radio on. It's Los Temerarios, "Como Te Recuerdo." I love this song. Mali loves this song. Abuelita loves it. The opening is so smooth, quiet. And then it increases in speed, in sound, and it's like a firework goes off before *Como te recuerdo, amor. Si tú supieras cuanto te extraño . . .*

The breeze enters through the crack in the window. I miss my home. My family. I want to sleep. I try closing my eyes. This is México. We're driving to Acapulco. The sun is a point in the sky, the same sun I saw rise today on that beautiful beach. Seems like days ago. The boats, the soldiers, the walk, the flying fish, the beach, the trucks, the shower, the three minutes.

CHAPTER FIVE

Waiting

APRIL 29, 1999

———

"Iᴛ's ᴀs ᴄʟᴏsᴇ ᴀs ɪ ᴄᴀɴ ɢᴇᴛ ʏᴏᴜ," ᴛʜᴇ ᴅʀɪᴠᴇʀ sᴀʏs ᴀs ʜᴇ presses on the brake, waking me in the backseat. He turns toward Coyote, who's crunched between Marcelo and Chele in the seat in front of ours. "I recommend you walk that way." The driver points with his head to the right side of the microbus. "I go that way." He turns and points to the left side of the car, motor still running.

"Gracias, compadre." Coyote reaches into his pocket for a handful of Mexican money: shiny silver coins with beautiful gold rings around them. I first saw pesos in Tecún when Grandpa exchanged quetzales for them at Don Carlos's store.

"Thank *you*," the driver says, turning to look at all of us as he lets a few coins fill his hand.

Coyote nods at Marcelo, who opens the microbus's sliding door. Each part of The Six says thank you. Marcelo. Chele. Chino. Carla. I get out before Patricia, and as she's stepping out, the driver grabs her hand and says, "Good luck. Protect your kids."

She doesn't respond, but nods without smiling. ¡We've tricked the driver! He believes we're family. I pull her hand and add a "Let's go, Mamá," loud enough so the driver hears. Patricia looks at me and squints her eyes while letting out a smile. *I'm a great actor,* I think.

"Welcome to Acapulco," Coyote says, spinning in place, his arms spread. We weren't supposed to be here. At least that's not according to Don Dago's original plan, or from Grandpa's map. But I know this city. Heard of it in movies and telenovelas. Luz Clarita had a field trip here. The wind rushes up from the ocean that looks like a puddle from this far up, like a crater or a hole. We're up on a hill that reminds me of the volcanoes back home.

Under the streetlamps, Patricia's hair is lighter, not quite blond, but close. She has dyed hair-tips that I first noticed in San Salvador, but now they're almost gone. I remember Mali wanting to dye her hair blond because everyone on TV was doing it.

"Don't mess up your hair like that," Abuelita told Mali whenever women with dyed hair walked in front of our house or waited in line to enter the clinic. Everyone made fun of those women behind their backs. "Look, a mutt thinking it's a purebred," Abuelita liked to say. "Viejas oxigenadas. Wannabe gringas."

It's dusk, almost completely night, and *right there* is the ocean. The stars begin to dot the sky. I like to think there's a giant holding the earth in one hand, a needle in his other hand, poking the sky there, there, and there—

"Walk uphill, I know a motel." Coyote's voice continues to be raspy. People walk past us in the opposite direction, toward the beach, almost dancing on the cement sidewalk.

When we arrive at a three-story motel, Coyote tells us to wait outside.

"Faak, we're in Acapulco, maje," Marcelo says to Chele as they each smoke a cigarette, Chino always smoking next to them.

"Chimeneas," Patricia says now, shaking her head. It's what she's nicknamed them. They don't react.

"Not in a hundred years," Marcelo continues, "did I think I'd be here."

He likes saying that, "Not in a hundred years." I don't *really* understand what he means. ¿Has he lived one hundred years? No. ¿Does he not expect to live over one hundred years? I don't wanna die before I'm one hundred.

"Same," Chele says. "It's pretty."

"¿Pretty? ¡No jodás, cerote! Está cosa seria," Chino tells Chele, nodding his head, making a gesture with his right hand like he's trying to point at something in the sky with his pointer finger and thumb out, in the form of a gun.

"¿Right?" Marcelo says, taking another puff.

"Puesí," Chino responds, then finishes his cigarette and throws it on the sidewalk. They're acting friendlier with each other. Usually, Chino stays with Patricia and Carla. I've seen the three of them smoking, but they don't talk when they smoke.

Coyote comes back out. "One room," he says. No one reacts. Coyote holds up two sets of keys and heads toward the front doors. We walk in behind him, into a corridor that opens into a courtyard. The courtyard has two tall palm trees. We can see the stars between the fronds. Ferns, Spanish flags, mother-in-law's tongues, and hearts line the edges of the yard. Abuelita has these exact plants in her garden. From the courtyard we walk up the cement stairs to our room on the second floor. Coyote turns the key and opens the door slightly, then looks at us, smiling. "Pinches lucky cerotes, that's the bay."

We can see the sliding glass door to the balcony. The tiled floors. I want to see the bay. The lights. The ocean. The moon on top of everything. The stars. Trees swinging in the breeze.

"¡I'm gonna see my parents!" slips out of my mouth.

"Sí, vos," Marcelo says, "we know, Chepito."

"Puesí," Chino responds, slapping my back.

"Ajá, cipotillo," Chele says, backing them up.

Patricia holds my hand tighter. Carla looks at me, laughing at what I just blurted out.

"¿What, morro?" Coyote asks. He didn't hear.

I don't respond.

I realize I've never slept on the second floor. ¿Is it gonna affect my dreams? ¿*Can* I dream? ¿What will happen if the earth shakes? ¿If there's a fire? I don't ask. I'm embarrassed I said my thoughts out loud. No one in The Six really talks about what they're going to do, who they will see in La USA.

We talked about it in Tecún, briefly, somewhat in Ocós, but only when the men got drunk. It's how I know Marcelo wants to build buildings, houses, roads, bridges, anything that's big and "will last." I think that's what Dad does. Marcelo says he used to do that in Los Ángeles. That he liked driving past a wall or sidewalk he'd helped build. "Hard work. Man's work," he said.

Chino wants to work in restaurants, serving "rich gringos, famous and pretty people." He loves food. Whenever we eat and he likes something, we can tell because he moans, nods his head up and down, smiling. His mom had a restaurant he worked at. She died. The restaurant closed, but he always wanted to be a chef. It's why I like him. It's why I like restaurants. I love helping Abuelita. Watching her make pupusas, curtido, horchata, chan. I love being her taster. Telling her what something needs. ¿Maybe I want to be a chef?

Chele loves cars. Big trailer trucks like the ones in *Dos Mujeres, Un Camino*. He mentioned that his cousin or uncle—I don't remember—has his own trailer he drives all over La USA. He wants to drive to different cities, towns, landscapes. "Choteando."

Patricia's husband has a job. It has to do with cutting down trees. I didn't know that was a job. I don't like when Grandpa cuts trees down. But *she* wants to cut other women's hair, style it, and do their makeup. Wants her own "salon." I think it's perfect for her. She looks pretty when she does her makeup. Carla, like me, is curious about gringo schools and wants to be with her younger sister, who is already up there with her dad. I don't know what I want to be, but I know I want to learn to swim so I can swim in my parents' pool in their big yard. ¿Does their house have two stories? ¿A balcony like this motel?

Everyone rushes outside to the balcony. Patricia, the last to enter room 205, closes the door behind her. It's difficult to lock. The living room has a small TV, a glass table, and two plastic chairs. The floor has half-broken tiles that aren't placed as squares but as rhombuses, their tips pointing toward the balcony. All of us look at the surrounding hills, the stars, the moon, the water, and some boats. ¿Did The Screaming Man make it to el DF? ¿Was he taken out of his bus? Since we landed on the beach, we've been walking or sleeping nonstop. I forgot about the ocean. I think I can see the waves. I know waves like I didn't know them back home. I *know them* know them. Dad was a fisherman. Maybe the ocean was always inside me.

Loud music reaches all the way up here from the beach. We can't tell what song it is, but it's probably Los Temerarios like it was in the microbus. Or Bronco. Or Los Bukis. It's what we've been listening to on all of the radio stations in El Salvador, Guatemala, and now here. Marcelo, Chino, and Chele have a thick cloud of Marlboro smoke around their heads.

I walk toward the metal railing surrounding the balcony. It's painted white. I stick my tongue out, I can taste salt. I like *A-ca-pul-co*. There's been salt in the air around us since Ocós. Here, it's colder, so far up in the air, closer to the sky. I pretend I'm the giant holding the earth in one hand as I watch the tiny faraway people on the beach.

When the cigarette butts are thrown off the balcony, the men walk back inside. I stay on the cement boat floating in the air, alone, standing on the lowest rung of the balcony's metal frame. I feel tall. Powerful. Like an adult. I can control the wind. The waves. The people on the beach who look like fruit flies in a garbage heap. I grab the balcony harder. With each push I make them move. I can make stars appear and disappear. My right index finger is the needle I poke the earth with. I squeeze the metal. Squeeze it harder so the people dance.

"LET'S GO FUCK AROUND," Chino tells the men as he leaves the bedroom where he was talking to Patricia and Carla.

"Let's gooooo," Chele responds, prolonging the *o,* slapping Chino's back.

Marcelo nods, Coyote nods, but before they leave Coyote says, "Put your fancy clothes on, just in case."

¿In case of what? I don't understand, but the men quickly rush to the bathroom and splash water onto their armpits, dry them, then splash cologne everywhere: hands, neck, chest, shirts. When they walk out, they leave behind a thick smelly cloud.

Patricia waits a minute to see if the men forgot something, and when they don't return, she explains that *we* get the room, *we* get the bed, that it's getting late, that it's time to get ready to go to sleep. But it's not even nine P.M.

"Vamos a la cama, que hay que descansar," she sings. It's the tune that plays right at ten P.M. on every Salvadoran channel—*Familia Telerín,* my signal to go sleep. The image of cartoon characters grabbing their things, walking in a line across the screen toward bed, flashes in front of me. I love that song. The older I got, the more I liked to stay up to watch it, proving I'm old enough for whatever is on TV after ten P.M.

"Vayan, bichos, brush your teeth," Patricia tells Carla and me, pointing at the bathroom that still smells like the men's nasty cologne. The bathroom is fancy: there's a mirror on top of the small silver faucet—next to it, the toilet and the shower. "Bien pimp-it-is-nice," the men said when they first saw it. Everything is here: toilet, shower, sink, walking distance from the bedroom. It's not outside like at home, like in Tecún, like in Ocós.

"Very convenient," Coyote said as he inspected the entire place. "And it's cheap."

I turn the faucet and water falls from it. It's like we're in a fancy sit-down restaurant like Pizza Hut in San Salvador. Carla walks into the bathroom, brushes her teeth next to me like we're actual siblings. I've always wanted a sibling, boy or girl; I just wanted someone to play with after Mom left to La USA. The closest I came to a sibling was Tía Lupe's daughter Julia, but she's five years younger than me.

Once, and only once, I accidentally knocked her off the bed and Lupe didn't let us play again. I was "¡pésimo, ajolotado!" Lupe yelled at my face.

Carla is old enough, stronger and taller than me. I don't have to worry about being pésimo if we ever get comfortable with each other. The problem is, I like her. I still don't want her or Patricia to see my chubby chest, my flabby belly, my thick legs. I don't know how to act around Carla. I think I annoy her. She has to share her mom with me, *and* she has to pretend she's my sister in public. I understand. If Patricia were *my* mom, I would be annoyed, even jealous. But I like pretending this is a novela. I like tricking people and getting away with it.

When Carla pretends she's my sister in public, she calls me "hermanito," like what Chino called me. In private, when it's only The Six, she calls me bichito, monito, or niñito. I don't mind. I *am* the youngest. Besides sleeping in the same room as Patricia and Carla in Ocós, and hugging on the boat, this is the closest we've been: brushing our teeth in Acapulco. The bathroom is small, the door is open, but our elbows almost touch. I can feel her small hairs right above her wrists brush against the hairs near the top of my elbows.

Carla's toothbrush is bright blue. My toothbrush is red. Her hair is in a braid she keeps tight with a black hair tie that has two clear balls at each end. Patricia has a pack of them clinging to a white piece of cardboard, like paternas or pepetos lined up in a row, like we were on the boats.

I've seen some of the things Patricia and Carla carry in their bags. Her makeup case everyone saw this morning. A small black purse with a picture of her younger daughter and her husband, which she hasn't shown me, but which she showed Carla one night when they thought I was sleeping. I like Patricia's hairbrush best: thick with tiny spikes, each spike with a gum-like tip, "to massage the scalp," she explained when I asked.

All of our backpacks follow us everywhere like shadows. Our shoes are shadows también. We haven't taken them off. I'm afraid that when I do, my feet will stink like Mali's do. I don't want Carla to think I have smelly feet. I don't want her to put up with what I had to put up with sleeping in the same room as Mali.

Carla brushes long, but I don't want to finish before her. Her teeth are perfect, so white, and unlike me, she doesn't have gaps between canines and front teeth. I don't like those gaps. Since Grandpa left, I only brush in the morning. I'm brushing now only because Patricia told me to. Carla brushes different: I'm gentler, she really digs into her teeth and spits more than I do. When she spits, I spit into the sink. When she gargles, I gargle. She turns the faucet on, I turn it off and wash our toothpaste-spit along the sides of our white sink, a bowl like the insides of a cracked egg without the yolk. I stop brushing seconds after she does to show her I have clean teeth también. Carla walks out of the bathroom, takes the three or four steps across the hallway into our room.

The mattress cover looks old. It has light yellow stains. ¿From pee? ¿Sweat? It's gross. Patricia throws the top sheet over it.

"Better," she says, and jumps on the sheets, then taps them, signaling Carla to get in bed. Carla takes her shoes off and lies next to her mom. I pause before taking my shoes off. There's only one bed. ¿How are we going to sleep?

"¿What you doing?" Patricia asks from the bed.

"Nothing," I say.

"Come here, bayunco." I really hope my shoes don't smell. I unvelcro the Velcro and hope for the best. I sniff around. Sniff. Nothing. Thank God. The tiles are cold, even with my socks on. My feet hurt. We walked and walked. Patricia crosses her legs as she sits up, using the wall for back support as she brushes her hair with her gum-tipped hairbrush.

I sit on the other side of the bed and distract myself by repeating words when I'm bored bored bored, but only say them in my head head head.

"Bichos, ¿wanna watch TV?" Patricia asks, even though she told us to go to bed. Carla nods. Patricia doesn't even wait for my nod and jumps off the bed. Carla walks quickly behind her. I follow them with my socks sliding across the cold tile floor.

Patricia sits on a plastic chair, Carla on top of her, and I take the other chair. The breeze bangs against the sliding door. Behind it, we hear the *boom boom boom* from the music playing at the beach. ¿How are we going to sleep? ¿Are all of us sleeping in the same bed? ¿Is that what Patricia expects?

"Nothing," Patricia says, flipping through the channels again. Things start to repeat.

"Mami, I'm sleepy," Carla says after a few minutes. I'm tired también, but I'm scared. ¿What if, when I'm sleeping, I fart and I wake both of them? ¿What if I drool? ¿What if they don't like me and leave me here?

"Sleep," Carla says again.

"Ahh, vaya, señorita." It's what Patricia calls Carla when she's mocking her. "A la camita pues." Patricia kicks Carla off her knee with a bounce. Carla walks toward the room. I'm frozen in place.

Patricia pushes the plastic chair closer to the wall. "Let's go," she says to me, and immediately starts singing, "Porque mañana será otro día y hay que vivirlo con alegría . . ."

I recognize the song.

"¡Topo Gigio!" I yell, raising my hand.

"¡Cabal!"

Topo Gigio is another show I watch—watched—with Mali and Abuelita on the weekends. During the week, it's Abuelita's novelas, then *Familia Telerín* comes on and it's my signal to go to sleep. On the weekends, *Topo Gigio* comes on before *Familia Telerín*. Patricia pushes my chair closer to the wall, turns the TV off, and pulls me by my hand into our room.

Carla digs through her backpack, searching for the clothes she sleeps in. I hadn't noticed she hadn't changed. Patricia is already in her sleeping clothes, but they both get up and walk to the bathroom. I know their outfits: dark-blue sweatpants and a dark-gray shirt with

English written on it for Patricia. Dark-green soccer shorts for Carla and a black T-shirt without any writing.

This is my cue to do the same and change into my dark-blue shirt with English and black soccer shorts before they come back. We did this in Ocós every night, except the bathroom was outside the rooms and I took all my clothes with me and came back changed. With the bathroom just steps away, they might barge in at any second. Luckily, all of my clothes are clean. I don't know *how* we're going to do laundry here. Patricia took her boat clothes out and hung them on the windowsill in the room. I take mine and hang them next to Patricia's. "Do what the adults do," Mali said.

I haven't washed my underwear. I take them off and stuff them in the bottom of my backpack, hidden under the plastic bag that's keeping my nice shoes clean. Back home, Mali or Abuelita did my laundry. In Tecún, Grandpa did. In Ocós, the owner of the place where we stayed took all of our clothes and washed them once. Sometimes I leave a trail of poop in my white underwear. Only Mali, Abuelita, Mom, Grandpa, and the motel owner know. No one else. I don't want The Six to think I'm little, that I can't wipe, that I need their help. Carla is going to think I'm a baby. Patricia will think I'm dirty. I don't know where Patricia's and Carla's underwear are. They hide them, but I want to tell them that I'm used to women's underwear. Abuelita and Mali hung them from our clothesline, and sometimes, when it was very windy, I had to pick them up from the ground and hang them up again.

I want to stay up until ten P.M. ¿Should I get in bed, choose my side? ¿Should I grab a pillow and make a bed on the floor? With none of the men around, I'm the man of the house. But the men will come back. ¿Where will *they* sleep? ¿When are they coming back?

"¿What are you doing, Javiercito?" Patricia's breath is minty clean. She rarely calls me that. Carla walks in behind her mom. "In bed, both of you," Patricia says, tapping the sheets.

Patricia looks at my clothes next to theirs on the windowsill. She gives me a nod and a smile like she's proud I followed her example. I like feeling like I'm doing something good, but I'm still standing in front of the bed, sweating.

"Let's sleep. But first, recemos." I didn't know Patricia prayed. I've been praying in bed, quietly mumbling words to myself, but now ¿she wants us to kneel? Carla and I look at each other, confused, but don't say anything. I kneel on Patricia's left. Carla kneels on her mom's right. We clasp our hands together, elbows pressed against the mattress, our fists close to our lips. My left thumb over the right one, the same for Carla, but Patricia's right thumb rests over her left one. The tile floor is hard on my knees and cold, but no one says anything or attempts to get up. We close our eyes.

Patricia mouths something, but I can't make out the words, only the wet noise of her lips touching, her tongue moving, reminding me of water dripping from the roof into cups when it rained back home. Carla mouths words también. I pray secretly, without moving my lips.

I pray we make it to La USA. That my parents are waiting at the border. That Mali, Lupe, Abuelita, Grandpa, are sleeping in their beds. That my friends are not failing class or getting hit by the nuns too much. I pray the nuns haven't called the police on me. That we don't get dragged out of a bus again. That Patricia and Chino and Marcelo keep being nice to me. I pray Cadejo keeps protecting us. I pray for the The Screaming Man. For Don Dago and Marta to come back and join us. For Jesús in Tecún, for Don Carlos. For the three Guatemalan men who got taken by the soldiers. I pray for the people in the boats. The people on the bus. That I don't fart sleeping next to Carla.

Patricia unclasps her hands as she whispers, "Amén" louder than anything else she's been mumbling. Then she lifts her right leg and pushes herself off the ground. Carla follows. I open my eyes and say, "Amén," loud like them.

The hotel is quiet. I listen for keys, for the men to walk through our door, but nothing. Carla jumps on top of the bedsheet. Patricia walks toward the door where the light switch is. I'm still frozen, standing right where I prayed. The lights turn off. I sit on the edge of the bed. Patricia's body like a shadow walking toward us.

"Sleep," she says as she scoots into the middle of the bed, between Carla and where I'm standing. "Sleep, bicho." She pats the side next to her. "Está bien, come here," she says, her voice soft, her breath minty and clean. It's warm in here, but not enough to turn on the fan.

"Buenas noches," Patricia says out loud.

"Buenas noches, Mami," Carla says.

"Buenas noches."

4-30-99

USUALLY I SLEEP FACEDOWN, but it's harder when sharing a bed. I wake faceup to someone knocking. I lift my head a little bit off the bed like I'm doing crunches. Patricia is sleeping facedown, her hands like rakes, each finger spread out against the sheets.

Knock. Knock. Knock.

When Carla sleeps, it doesn't matter *how* she falls asleep, her hands wake up looking like little dinosaur heads: an elongated circle, formed by her thumb touching her pointer finger. *Raaarrrr,* I want to say to her first thing in the morning but don't. Mother and daughter smell like meat cooking in broth, beef inside bean soup, oxtail soup, soups Abuelita makes "to sweat the bad out" when it's hot outside.

Knock. Knock.

I nudge my pretend mom with my elbow. Kick her a little. Finally, Patricia wipes the drool sliding from one corner of her mouth. When her bare feet touch the tiles, I know it's cold because she shakes a little. I keep my eyes slightly open, just like I did to trick the soldiers in the buses. ¿Where did the men sleep?

I can tell it's Chino because his head looks bald and the smell of green mango leaves and ash rushes through the door. His lips move, but I don't know what he's saying. Patricia walks to her backpack and searches for something.

"¿What happened?" I ask, my arms holding me up from the bed.

"Nothing. Sleep."

Carla wakes, yawning, rubbing her eyes, and asks the same thing.

"¡Ay, vos también! Nothing. Chino needs a nail clipper."

"Front pocket," Carla says. "Not that one. My backpack."

"¡¿Why did you move it?!"

"I didn't. Púchica usted," Carla grumbles, her eyebrows closer together. "No buenos días. No ¿how are you, hija? Nothing, usted mire."

Patricia doesn't respond. Continues searching. I try not to smirk. They don't usually fight first thing, but later in the day. It's funny. It's something *my* mom would do: get mad when I'm trying to help. And like Mom, Patricia is very particular. Likes everything in "the right place." In Ocós, every morning she slapped the pillows and made the bed. I don't understand. It wasn't our home, none of the places have been, but she treated Ocós like it was.

"Graaacias, Carlita," Patricia says when she finds the nail clippers, elongating the *a* and calling her "-*ita*." She's mocking her.

Carla buys her mom's tone, doubles down, and sarcastically says, "Sí, Mami, you're welcome," adding a fake smile.

Before walking back to the door, Patricia rubs Carla's legs. Their smell of oxtail soup wafts up from the bedsheets. I look at Carla, but she doesn't look at me. Patricia hands Chino the nail clippers, they whisper something, then she locks the door.

"¿Where did they sleep?" Carla asks when Patricia is back in bed.

"Living room."

"Oh."

I didn't hear them last night. It's better they stayed out there. They probably snore and would've kept us up. Grandpa snores a lot, but eventually I got used to it. Patricia snores, but it's faint. Carla looks funny in the morning. Her hair is always messy. Curls flattened on one side because she didn't sleep with her braid in. I want to tell her, "You look like a wet dog," but she'd get mad.

I look at my nails—thicker than crescent moons, the thickness of watermelon rind. I haven't cut them since Grandpa left. Mali packed me a nail clipper "just in case," like she knew the trip would take longer than what Don Dago said. At home, I learned to clip my nails when Mom left. Before she left, she cut them right after I showered because "they're softest then." She cut my hair también. The month after she got to La USA, Grandpa took me to his barber on a Sunday an hour before church. "Two birds with one stone," he said.

When Carla comes back, I'll shower and I'll cut my nails. I like having the shower two steps from this door. ¿Is this what it's like where my parents live? Fancy bathrooms. Tile floors. Patricia and Carla don't think much of it. In Ocós they complained because in their house in San Salvador, they have a bathroom like this. I didn't know what they meant. Carla called me a "chorreado," "una chusma." Made me feel bad. Patricia told her not to call me that, but whenever Carla got mad the rest of the week in Ocós, she whispered that to me. She hasn't done it since.

I liked pooping outside, hiding it under dried leaves, marking the mounds with toilet paper. I liked pumping water from the well to shower. It's why I liked showering in Tecún, it reminded me of home.

"You're next." Carla comes back with her wet hair and new clothes. Patricia walks toward me, pats my back.

I'm excited for this motel's showerhead. How easy it is to make it seem like it's raining inside, two stories up from the ground. I will enjoy and take my time. Not like in Oaxaca. I take my clothes, toothbrush, shampoo, streaked underwear, soap. The men are in the living room. Marcelo sits on a plastic chair, Chele on the floor on top of a blanket, next to another bundled-up blanket. Chino cuts his nails outside on the balcony. I rush into the bathroom. Coyote isn't in the living room. No one notices me. There's no one rushing to use the bathroom. I'll enjoy the rain. In my head I sing: *¡Que llueva que llueva, la Virgen de la Cueva, los pajaritos cantan, las nubes se levantan, que sí, que no, que caiga el chaparrón!*

WE'RE NOT ALLOWED TO leave the motel during the day. The men went out last night, but this morning Coyote told us we can't leave because it's Friday. "More people in the streets. It's safer inside. Only *I* leave that door," Coyote said, pointing at the locked front door, his voice worse than before.

At least Coyote bought Bimbo packages: Panqué, Doraditas, Mantecadas, Donas. It's back-to-back days we've had Bimbo for breakfast. Coyote also bought instant coffee, but no milk. There's no stove to warm it, so we drink the coffee cold. Back home, I hated warmed-up milk because of that thin layer of milk skin. But here, I miss that bright-yellow Nido can.

We dip our bread in instant coffee and sit around the color TV the entire morning. It's boring. At ten A.M., Patricia chooses *Marimar*. The same morning novelas that play in El Salvador play here, but they're episodes ahead. After, Marcelo chooses *El Show de Cristina*. He says he likes watching people talk about "stupid shit" in La USA. Cristina looks gringa, but she speaks Spanish and lives in Miami. ¿How far is Miami from San Rafael? I want to watch her show in person. Of course no one wants to watch *Blue's Clues*. I miss Face covering the TV screen. Back home, I flipped between *Blue's Clues* and *Nature*. I was hooked ever since I saw two snails kissing, their bodies intertwined, perfectly aligned, their four eyes moving every which way. When adults kissed on TV, I had to cover my eyes. With snails, no one told me anything. Abuelita was working. Mali was working. Grandpa was out in the fields. No one to say, "¡Don't watch that!" I couldn't look away.

Ever since that first snail kiss, I watch anything having to do with animals. *Nature* isn't on any channel in Acapulco. After *Cristina*, Chino chooses *Tom and Jerry*. After *Tom and Jerry*, Chele chooses the news. No one asks what Carla or I want to watch. Patricia at least gets a plastic chair. Coyote sits in the other. Carla gets her mom's legs. The rest of us lie on the ground on top of blankets.

Bimbo bread isn't enough. I'm hungry, but now everything is gone. Coyote leaves to get us lunch. The men keep going out to smoke. It's warm inside, so it's nice to have the breeze come in when they return. The breeze moves the one tiny Bimbo wrapper Patricia forgot to clean. I know what's next. She taps Carla to get off her leg, grabs the same plastic bag Coyote brought the bread in, and crushes the wrapper to fit in with the others she already cleaned. She's the Tasmanian Devil, folding blankets, grabbing the broom, throwing trash away, whispering to herself.

"Much better," she says when she comes back from the kitchen. This stillness doesn't last. She runs to the room and makes the bed, hangs our backpacks, folds our clothes, then starts cleaning the glass table with wet newspaper to get the coffee stains out. She reminds me so much of Mom, who would get in her "cleaning moods" that looked a lot like this. My pretend mom, who happens to have my real mom's name.

Chino is from Patricia's town, so he's always called Patricia *Pati*. The other men started calling her Pati only after the boats. I can't. Won't. Pati is saved for *my* mamá Pati. And when I have to pretend she's my mother in public, I call her "Mom," and only to trick soldiers. I know who my *real* mom is. But it's funny that they're both super short, they both have big tempers, and they both like to keep things clean.

"It's meant to be. It's a sign," Chino said when he found out. He always says that.

Whenever the men return from their smoke breaks, Chino tells Patricia to "stop cleaning and watch TV."

"We're mojados, but we're clean," she repeats. Reminds me of what Mamá Pati said in the dry season. It got so dusty in Abuelita's pupusa stand, so Mom swept the floors with a broom every twenty minutes. "We're poor, but that doesn't mean we live in filth."

We're still watching news when we hear keys digging into the doorknob.

"Eat eat eat eat," Coyote says as he opens the door, his voice like it's full of bees. His shoulders moving up and down like the dog in *Duck Hunt*. He rushes toward the clean glass table. He stops and, like an actual coyote on a nature show bringing food to its pups, drops two plastic bags filled with food. We gather around the table. We look like wildebeest drinking water from a river.

"Eat," Coyote says again, opening one of the bags, then the other. Oh, the smell: oil and salt, sea and lime. The two pairs of eyes are what I notice first, fried to a crisp, light-brown color of a guitar. The opened mouths with serrated teeth, like little saws. The potato chip consistency of the fried fins, the fried tails—my favorite part. Some of the tail-bits are crushed at the bottom of the Styrofoam container.

¡Fresh fish! I haven't had fish since I left home. Next to the two fish fried whole, there's another container of fries. Fish and fries. Limes sliced into quarters inside little plastic bags. Another small plastic bag filled with sea salt. And next to that, another bag filled with hot sauce that Coyote grabs, saying, "I know you cerotes don't like this."

"Yo sí, maitro," Marcelo bites back. "Learned in Los Ángeles."

I didn't know there were Mexicans in La USA. We haven't talked to a Mexican who's not a coyote or a microbus driver or a soldier. I want to ask Marcelo what he thinks of these Mexicans and what the Mexicans in La USA are like. But before I get a chance, the men each grab a paper plate and tear the fish apart with their hands. Eagle talons. Hyena jaws. Everyone laughs, oily hands, oily lips, smiling so hard because we're having fish. ¡Fish! Coyote is our Mr. Sabelotodo, our guide, the expert who knows when to spend enough money to eat the best meal.

¡Oh, the white soft meat, the crispy skin! I grab a piece of warm tail meat, still steaming, squeeze a lime quarter, and pour salt. Then I wash it down with fries. *Mmmm.*

"This shit is amazing, ¿ve'á?" Marcelo asks the group, meat in his hand, grinning. We all eat with our hands. Carla's eyes get big like mine do when he curses, even though he curses all the time.

"Puta, maje, it's better than . . ." Chele pauses for a long time. Everyone starts laughing. "¡The best fish of my life, pues!" He chews with his mouth open.

"Puesí," Chino responds, fries in his hands.

"Better than La Costa del Sol, ¿ve'á, Chepito?" Marcelo asks me as he chews. I nod and smile with food between my teeth. Everyone laughs.

"Like Barrabas's fish," I say once I've swallowed.

"¿Who's Barrabas?" Carla asks, cleaning her cheeks with a napkin.

"A fisherman," Marcelo adds. I forget he knows exactly where I'm from. Where *we're* from. He knows everyone, or mostly everyone, even though he left to live in Los Ángeles for five years. He's old enough to be my dad. Mom and Dad are twenty-eight, Marcelo is twenty-six. He didn't *know* my parents, but he knew *of* them. Marcelo is from the center of town, near the mercado. Dad is from the pier, Mom is from deeper into town. Three different barrios.

"Ajá," I say to what Marcelo answered.

He explains how Barrabas "catches the best jumbo shrimp, this big." He holds out his oily hand, moving his open palm up and down like there's a rock in it.

"Ajá," I back him up.

"¡And the best cócteles de concha! Vieja, you're making me miss La Herradura, Chepito."

"¿Where?" Chino asks.

"La Herradura, cerote," Marcelo answers, changing his voice back to its deepness.

"I think I've been. Good cócteles to get it up," Chele says, holding out his forearm.

"Usssh, ¡bayunco!" Patricia play-slaps him in the back. "¡Respect!"

Coyote lets out a big laugh.

I like this. We're all laughing, joking, and eating good. Marcelo is finally being nice. Grandpa gave him money, but he hasn't really taken care of me—but right now he's trying. He makes me feel like he's my friend. Like he knows me. Before we know it, there's nothing left in the Styrofoam containers besides bones and oil. We *are* hyenas.

"Good and cheap." Coyote taps his stomach with both his hands.

Everyone gets up, helps Patricia clean, throws the garbage back into the bags they came in. She hands the bags to Chino, who throws them into the garbage can. Coyote leaves again. Patricia goes into the room to nap with Carla, but not before taking newspaper and rubbing the glass table clean. I stay in the living room with the men, watching TV.

5-1-99

"¡ONE HOUR! ¡NICE CLOTHES, nice clothes!" Coyote shouts, knocking on our room door.

It's dawn, and it's already warm. Tiny sweat beads gather around my top lip and in the middle of my back. Patricia cleans her drool and grunts, "Sí. Sí."

Even though they make the bed warmer and their oxtail smell sticks to the sheets, I'm getting used to sleeping next to Patricia and Carla. Patricia is like Abuelita, grumpy in the morning without her Café Listo. She curls up next to Carla and whispers, "Wake up," then nudges me with her elbow.

We've established a routine: Patricia jumps off the bed. Brushes her teeth. Showers. Carla sleeps until her mom returns fully dressed but with wet hair. Carla brushes, showers. Patricia does her makeup and hair. Carla returns drenched. Then it's my turn to leave the room.

Taking my clothes to the bathroom works perfect. I'm ashamed of my chest. Every time I played soccer and changed out of the school uniform, boys taunted, "¡Boobs! ¡Boobs!" I've never forgotten it.

When I return, Carla's and Patricia's boat clothes are no longer on the windowsill, and someone has laid mine out on top of my backpack. Our backpacks wait next to the door. Patricia is usually done with her makeup by now, but today, she's still working on it. It's my chance: while they're both not looking, I stuff my poop-streaked underwear in the bottom of my backpack. I washed them yesterday and again today, but I couldn't get the mark out.

Patricia has a makeup case identical to Mali's, with a small brush that clips to the bottom of the palm-sized black case. Above it there's a flesh-toned rectangle filled with powder. Above that rectangle, four other colors in smaller squares, one red, one pink, one green, and one blue. "Makeup on the go," Mali called it when we went to the capital and she needed to "freshen up." The last part of Patricia's routine is the lipstick. She purses her lips, looking like a fish, to get it just right.

Don Dago and Coyote said to look sharp when we travel by bus, but that didn't work last time when we got dragged out. Maybe it's why Patricia is doing something I haven't seen her do: lining her lips with a small, crayon-sized colored pencil.

Then she uses my favorite tool Mali owned: metal clamps that curl her eyelashes. It's scary watching her do it. It was scary watching Mali. The metal clamping onto the thin eyelashes. ¿What if it pulls all of them off? And finally, after curling, Patricia darkens her lashes with a pen-like thing that looks like a hair roller, or like the metallic brush Tía Lupe uses to wash Julia's baby bottles. Patricia's eyes "pop out" more. She's beautiful.

We walk out of the room, everyone wearing our "nice clothes." Dark-blue jeans and short-sleeved button-ups for the men. Dark-blue jeans and black tank tops for Patricia and Carla. Bimbo bread and coffee wait for us on the glass table. By 4:45 A.M., there's still no hint of sunlight. The TV paints all of our faces a light-gray shade of blue.

"I'm smoking," Marcelo says, and the men fill the balcony. I walk out with them. It's warm but not as warm as it is inside. There's no breeze; the clouds of cigarette smoke linger. I look for the moon and realize that, just like the moon, Cadejo is sometimes around and sometimes not, but it doesn't mean he's not there. Cadejo is not around *right now* right now. Cadejo is like *that*. Like the moon. I know he's there. Watching. Listening. Cadejo *is* the moon. They will both protect me. Like on the boat. Like out of the bus. It's a good sign. The moon wasn't in the sky when we took the last bus. It's up there now.

Coyote throws his cigarette onto the balcony floor, stomps it, says, "Let's go," and walks into the living room. Everyone follows. He's already called a taxi that's waiting for us downstairs. Everyone puts their backpacks on. Coyote walks to the door as Patricia tries to gather the wrappers and coffee cups.

"Leave it," Coyote says, annoyed.

Patricia doesn't listen and throws the wrappers in the garbage can. "We're not animals," she says under her breath.

"Let's go." Coyote's voice is a little better than yesterday. "The taxi will take us to the bus station. From there it's twelve hours to Guadalajara."

¡That's longer than San Salvador to Tecún!

"Púchica," Chino says.

"¿What? It's better than the boats, cabrones. Perspective. Perspective," Coyote tells us, and no one else complains. "Don't worry, I brought you food." He opens the door and we walk downstairs.

"GUADALAJARA. GUADALAJARA."

A voice through the speakers wakes me—¿the driver's? Lights flash on. They weren't on when we left. Patricia and Carla are sleeping. The AC isn't too cold. The seats are big and comfy like a sweater. They're almost nicer than sleeping in that tiny Acapulco motel bed with Patricia and Carla, who always share a bus seat for two with me because we are a "family of three."

For the beginning of the twelve hours, I pretended to sleep, but soon, I don't even know when, I fell asleep for real. ¿Did I sleep half a day? I napped like I was back home. A nap turned to sleep, a deep sleep, and then—

"Guadalajara, Guadalajara," the driver repeats.

¡Twelve plus hours! ¿Was there a checkpoint? I would've woken up, ¿right? Patricia would've told me. I didn't even wake up to use the bathroom, I didn't even dream. I didn't know I was *that* tired.

This is a fancy bus. When we boarded, it smelled clean, like opening a new toy from La USA. Our plan was/is the same: split into three groups, pretend we don't know each other, pretend to sleep. If asked, we're from Guadalajara, but "absolutely don't talk," Coyote said when we got to the Acapulco terminal.

I look around, and Marcelo and Chele sit next to each other. Chino sits alone a few seats behind us. Coyote, alone next to a stranger but close to the front. No one dragged us out. The lights are on, but everything is still dark inside the bus.

Immediately, I pull the maroon velvet curtain to the side to take a look at the city, Chente's city, through the tinted glass. I remember the song I first heard in El Salvador, on TV, movies, and novelas, and from bayuncos or drunks that mess around and change the lyrics to make a joke:

> *¡Guadalajara! ¡Guadalajara!*
> *¡Guadalajara! ¡Guadalajara!*
> *Tienes el alma de provinciana*
> *Hueles a limpio a rosa temprana . . .*

It *is* true. It *does* look clean, even though we're stuck in traffic, waiting to get inside the bus terminal. But I don't see any roses, just regular flowers—red, yellow, white flowers, lining the street dividers. The bus finally stops. It's the biggest and most orderly bus terminal we've seen. The buses all park a meter away from each other and people walk through glass doors into the terminal—which is a building and not out in the open air. More lights turn on inside the bus, people get up, slowly, groggy, almost falling over into the nearest seat, or back down into the seat they sat on for half a day.

¡Half a day we've been sitting! I want to pee, but there's a hint of pee, shit, and soap coming from the back of the bus. I feel like I'm floating. I get up and my butt feels numb, the muscles tingle a little.

Coyote is nearest the door. He steps out without looking back. Then it's us. Carla in front of Patricia, Patricia, and then me. The men walk behind us. It's bright outside. Warm. Noisy. Bus motors and *ding-ding-ding*s, people talking on speakerphones, footsteps, cars honking.

"Welcome," the bus driver says from his driver's seat as we walk past him. We don't respond. Patricia feigns a wave. We're "home." Our birthplace: *Guadalajara, Jalisco.* That much closer to La USA. The air doesn't smell like wet earth like the song says. It smells of garbage, smoke, cars, too many people walking around, dog shit—it smells like San Salvador.

Like always, we have to make sure we see where Coyote is going. There are people everywhere. Women. Men. Kids. Backpacks. Plastic bags and cardboard boxes with all kinds of stuff inside them. I hold Patricia's sweaty hand. Carla holds her other hand. Chino was behind us, then sped up and nodded as he walked past. No words. We can see his almost clean-shaven head, skinny legs, black backpack.

Chele and Marcelo are a few steps behind us, and a few steps from each other. All of us walk past vendors. Shops. Food stands. Dogs. Flies. Trash cans. ¡And the noise! So many different types of shoes: boots, sandals, heels, sneakers. People's clothes rustle like leaves or doves flapping their wings. ¡We're in the middle of a huge beehive! People of all colors and shapes, but mostly people here *do* look lighter than in Oaxaca or Acapulco. Coyote was right. In the motel he told us, "Guadalajarans, we're *lighter* than other Mexicans."

Coyote said that Patricia, Chele, and Carla were fine. That they could "pass." That Chino and I could también, if we kept our mouths shut. But that he was worried about Marcelo, because he looks "Yucateco." "In public, all of you, just shut up," he said, his voice more normal, soft. First, I got used to him yelling or screaming at us. Then I got used to his throatiness. And now this version of his voice doesn't match, it's too nice.

We see him stop under a streetlight outside the terminal. Coyote taps the bottom of a cigarette box on his opened palm, right where the wrist meets the hand. The other men only do this when it's a new pack, but Coyote does it all the time. He takes his black lighter from his back pocket and starts smoking. He nods at Chino, who nods back like an iguana and stands next to him, searching for his own cigarette.

In Ocós, Chino liked to keep a cigarette behind his right ear. "Easy access," he said. But in México, he hasn't done that. Coyote nods at us and then at Marcelo and Chele, who start smoking. Patricia, Carla, and I stand a meter or so away from everyone. We're close to the street. We act like we don't know each other, until Coyote whispers something to the men and they walk toward us.

"I'll call a taxi," he says between puffs. "But inside, don't speak. ¿Entienden?"

We nod. As we wait, the men, almost collectively, say, "¡Twelve hours, maje!"

"¡Twelve fucking hours!"

"¡Puta!"

"Shhhh," Patricia reprimands them, looking around, holding Carla's and my hands harder.

Their puffs rise in the air, a thick cloud of gray. I want to be older so I can smoke with them like I did in Ocós. I regret crying. I want to like smoking so I can do it and not feel the pressure to say anything— *and* to make huge puffs of smoke that sometimes come out as rings. Marcelo and Chino are good at making thick rings that look cool, then smaller ones that look like gray Froot Loops. Chele can't do it. "Smoking is not a game," he likes to say.

Coyote waves down another microbus. This time, the men sit in the back, and Patricia, Carla, and I sit in the middle, my face glued to the clear glass window on the sliding door. It's right before dusk, and everything looks golden, painted in brighter colors like honey is covering everything.

This is cool: the colors, exploring another city, the people, the tall buildings. I can't stop looking out the window. Guadalajara is in a lot of novelas, in songs, in movies. Smoke fills the microbus. Ugh, I *love* that smell clinging to the men's clothes, to their breath, to their hair, to the tips of their fingers and anything they touch. Patricia grabs Carla and me, puts her arms on our shoulders. There's no AC. The radio is off. Coyote starts turning the knob, but finds nothing. The driver looks at him, shakes his head, flips the sun visor, and a cassette tape falls into his hand.

"¿You like Los Bukis?" the driver asks.

Coyote gives it a thumbs-up. The music starts playing. I know this one. It's the same cassette Patricia brought with her: *Quiéreme.*

As the song starts, Chino taps Chele on the shoulder and whispers, "It's you, cerote." The backseat and the middle seat try not to laugh. Marcelo shakes his head. I check if the driver heard the "cerote," but he didn't. Chele *really* looks like Marco Antonio Solís, "El Buki." They both have pale skin, brown hair, a big forehead, and puffy cheeks. The only difference is that Chele doesn't have a beard and Chele's hair isn't as long.

Outside, it looks less and less like a big city. The entire cassette tape makes it to side B. The road changes from asphalt to a dirt road with rocks that make our butts hurt. I don't see any Guadalajaran kids riding horses, no ranches along the road, or tequila farms like in novelas. Only some men wear boots and ranchero hats—I thought everyone was going to be dressed like that, ¡but more people dress that way in El Salvador!

It takes us over thirty minutes to get to where we're staying. It's officially dusk. Coyote gets out of the microbus first. He helps Carla. Patricia jumps out. Then I do. The men follow. No one says anything. Coyote gives the driver money and taps the car. As the microbus speeds off, it leaves a trail of dust. I bet these streets flood in winter like in my hometown. It's so hot.

There are houses and nothing else. Cement, brick, stairs, wind, dust, that's all. ¡No trees! ¡No people! Only stray dogs and garbage, mostly plastic bags swirling. It reminds me of a slow day at Abuelita's pupusería during the dry season, the hot season when all the little red dots appear on my body, when Mali rubs aloe on me every day because I break out with sarpullido. I hope I don't get sarpullido here. I don't want to rub my back on a pole or on the wall like a dog.

"We're experts at getting out of microbuses," Patricia says when we're alone.

"Veteranos," Marcelo says, his chin up, and maybe it's the lighting, but I notice his drastic clean-shaven jawline, his way to look "nice" for bus rides.

"Ajá."

"Sí, vos." Chele's brown hair looks lighter at dusk.

"Not so loud," Coyote tells the men as he walks toward . . . ¿his house?

"Va, maitro." Marcelo's jawline makes him look tough when he nods at Coyote. Then he takes a step back to walk next to me. "You're a veteranito," he whispers, tapping my backpack.

Ve-te-ra-ni-to, I repeat in my head. I like that. Maybe Marcelo *does* like me. I'm cipotillo to Chele. Hermanito to Chino. Marcelo is less scary now that he's been talking to me. Even with his tattoos. At first, I was more scared of Chino's tattoos, because Grandpa knew Marcelo. But Chino is so nice to me, and he looks like Olivia from *Popeye,* except Chino has acne and no hair.

Coyote keeps walking in the direction of what now looks not like a house but like a building. "It's not a motel, but it will do," he says as he walks up the brick stairs. We follow him up three flights. ¡I'm officially gonna sleep the highest I've ever been off the ground!

"This is your apartamento." Coyote points at a black metal door between unpainted cement walls.

A-par-ta-men-to. I only know that word from movies and from that show *Friends.* Another thing I've never done. It's a running checklist: Stay at a motel. Check. Use a fancy bathroom. Check. Shower with a showerhead. Check. Sleep in a two-story building. Check. Three-story building. Check. Stay at an apartamento. Check.

When Coyote unlocks the door, the inside is brightly lit, and there's a light-skinned teenager sitting next to an adult on a sofa covered with thick blue blankets. On the screen, two soccer teams are warming up and the commentators are talking.

"Hola," the man says, and gets up to help Patricia with her backpack.

"Gracias," she says. All of us walk inside and stand around the couch. Coyote locks the door behind him.

"Welcome, welcome. This is my son," the dad says, pointing at the kid, who is older than me and Carla. The teenager doesn't act surprised we're all here and waves at us without taking his eyes off the screen a meter away from his face.

"¿You're not gonna say anything, morro?" Coyote asks, and the teenager nods. The TV's blue light paints his short hair a pale brown. They know each other.

"Welcome," The Dad says again. "Come to the kitchen, sit, sit. You must be tired." The house is a long cement corridor. No tiles like in the motel; the cement is smooth and gray. From the door, it's a straight shot to the back of the place. Door, couch, TV, a wooden dining table with four wooden chairs around it. "Sit," The Dad tells Patricia as he pulls a chair out. The chairs have three wooden slats in the backrest.

"Gracias," Patricia says again, and he drops her backpack on the floor. Then she taps her thighs, signaling Carla to sit on her lap. Marcelo and Chino both grab a chair, drop their backpacks, and sit. Chele pulls the last wooden chair out and points with his lips for me to sit in it. With his backpack still on, Chele stands next to Coyote and The Dad, who stand in the corridor space closest to the couch. I hold my backpack. I like how it feels like a pillow or like a teddy bear in my arms.

"¡We made it!" Coyote says. "We stay here until I get the next orders." He paces up from the couch to the dining table, which isn't long; everything feels crunched up in here. "So for now, rest. You need to rest. There are two rooms back there, small, but you have two beds. The men together, you three together." He points at Patricia, Carla, and me. "There's also a couch. If you need anything, mi compa right here"—he slaps The Dad on the back—"lives downstairs. He will check on you, ¿entienden?"

The adults nod.

"But otherwise, don't leave this room. He"—Coyote stresses the "he" and points directly at The Dad—"*he* will check on you every morning, lunch, *and* dinner. He'll make sure you have everything you need."

"¿Where are *you* going?" Patricia asks.

"Around." Coyote grins. "I live here. But I'll check on you. I'll let you know a day ahead of time when we leave."

"¿Like, how many days?" Chino jumps in.

"Next few days, I don't know. But definitely not before Monday."

It's Saturday night. I'd forgotten it until Coyote said it.

"It's a modest place, but it's yours," The Dad adds. "There are a few supplies in the kitchen and that small fridge." He points at the black fridge, smaller than me, next to a propane tank. "I'll bring more pillows and blankets. Gets chilly at night." He's older than Don Dago, has a lot more gray hairs on the sides, but the top of his head is still mostly black.

"Órale," Coyote responds. "¿Any questions?"

All of us shake our heads.

"We're gonna leave you to it. Rest up, feel free to use the TV. Just keep it quiet. Our next stop is the border. Rest rest rest," Coyote says, grabbing his backpack tighter.

"If you need anything else, let me know," The Dad says louder, looking at Patricia. "Ándale, cabrón," he tells the teen, who hasn't taken his eyes off the screen. "Oh, and the bathroom is at the end, over there." He points to the end of the corridor, past the rooms. "¡Nothing to it!" he adds, looking and shouting toward all of us at the kitchen table.

"But the game . . ." are the first words out of the teenager's mouth.

"At home, morro." All three Mexicans walk toward the steel door.

Morro. I think it means something different here. At home, morro is a tree we use to make bowls, and the seeds we put in horchata.

"Always lock the door," Coyote says. "They have keys." He points at The Dad and son. "Don't open the door for anyone. *No one.* ¿Entienden?"

Chele, who's been standing this entire time, walks to the door with them and locks it. We can hear them walk down the stairs to the apartamento below us. Another metal door opens and shuts. Chino breaks the silence.

"¿Who's playing?" Chino asks Chele, who unfreezes from standing next to the door. Then Chele walks toward us. The TV was left on.

"Jaber," Chele says, squinting. "Can't see shit."

"Buy glasses in La USA," Patricia jokes.

"I need them."

Mom fed me carrot juice every morning, I'm far away but can see that next to the score it says ATL vs. AME.

Marcelo gets up and checks. "Atlas versus América. It's starting."

5 - ? - 9 9

THE ENTIRE PLACE SMELLS like smoke. I wake up with boogers in my nose, black and gray. While we were sleeping, the men took a small bowl and turned it into a bowl for cigarette butts they keep next to the couch. Patricia gets mad at them and we eat Bimbo bread for breakfast in silence. For lunch, The Dad brings a pot of beans; they're not the frijoles we eat back home.

Later, Coyote shows up with a carton of cigarettes for the men and tells us we are not leaving yet. "Rest, sleep, because the next step is the hardest." Then, while looking directly at Carla and me, he says, "Especially you, morrillos. I'll keep updating you, but don't expect to leave until late next week."

Before locking the door, he reminds us of The Rules:

Don't open the steel door without Coyote.
    (Unless someone's dying.)
Don't peek outside the windows. They must always
    be closed.
At night (or day), keep all of the lights off. In the living
    room, use the TV for light. In the rooms, one lamp
    only.
If we need something, Coyote will come once a day.
    The Dad will come every mealtime.
Stay hidden.
Only smoke indoors.
Alternate showering. The water runs out. The men shower
    one day, us the other.

That's it. No one can leave. We watch TV all day. Cartoons in the morning. Novelas in the early afternoon. Carla, Patricia, and Chino really get into them. They have discussions. Then, it's *El Gordo y La Flaca. Dragon Ball Z. Primer Impacto*. When they're playing, we watch Las Chivas—the team we're supposed to love. The Dad screams loud underneath our apartamento. It reminds me of Mom and Abuelita watching the World Cup final in 1994. None of the men of The Six react to the game. I don't think they like soccer.

5-?-99

I WISH THERE WAS a hammock because I keep waking up sweating. There's no AC. The fan isn't enough. Today is my shower day, but last time, I got out and immediately started sweating again. I miss home and the hammock Grandpa hung from the myrtle and sweetsop trees in the backyard. We've been here almost a week. The Six have split off into two groups: the men, and Patricia and Carla. I split my time between groups. When the men smoke while watching TV, Patricia and Carla stay in the room with the lights off, sleeping. Sometimes, I nap with them. Today, I've been in the room because I'm tired of TV and Patricia kept cursing at the men because they leave their clothes and trash everywhere. She's boycotting cleaning after anyone. She looks sad most of the time. Mostly, she sleeps. The fan spins and spins and it doesn't cool us, but it does get rid of the smoke and it drowns out the men's voices.

This room, but also this entire apartamento, makes me think of Abuelita's pupusa stand. Not the plancha she cooked the pupusas on, not the wooden table, not the six plastic chairs, but where we stored all of those things along with the chips and candies. Every afternoon I helped Abuelita put stuff away into that small storage room that didn't have light. Everything slept in there, locked away behind a huge silver lock at the end of the thickest silver chain only Grandpa has the keys to. We're like that room, except only Coyote and The Dad have the key. We're locked from the outside. "It's for your own good," Coyote said. "Groups have gotten deported," The Dad added.

In Tecún or Ocós, at least we walked around town and breathed fresh air. These past few days I've sniffed around this apartamento pretending I'm a dog. When the men get up from the couch, through the thick cigarette smoke, I can pick up some of their sweat. Marcelo smells like the ashes from Grandpa's firewood stove. Chino like the driest patch of dirt. And Chele like warm chicken feathers. What I can't get away from, and what has grown on me, is the way Patricia's and Carla's breath smells in the morning: like loroco. I try to remember what Mamá Pati smells like, but I forget. It's what I'm excited for when I see her again, to relearn her smells. Mali smells like freshly chopped wood, like sawdust—except for her feet.

At the pupusa stand, when I stacked the plastic chairs, I sniffed them. They smelled rancid, like mangos rotting. I stacked them in the corner of the dark storage room and made the pile look like a pile of white plates at the corner of the kitchen. It's my game. When I grabbed a chair, I'd grab it with its thick arms facing me, like they were about to hug me. I'd lean my face closer to sniff the plastic. Most patients at the clinic were recent mothers, young women I noticed from the table where I sold horchata, chips, and candies. I watched where they sat. It was like smelling the secret of where babies come from. I'm still uncertain where they actually come from, but those chairs convinced me they come out of butts.

¡Guadalajara! ¡Guadalajara! The men always break into song. Into rhyme. I'm so bored. So much TV. I can only play dog so much. I keep drawing cadejos on the newspapers Coyote brings. ¡No one reads them! I just hope this waiting doesn't take as long as Tecún. ¡Two weeks! I want to see the next town. I understand why Patricia and Carla stay in the room sleeping. My room. Our room. We eat the same thing every day: mortadella-and-cheese sandwiches, coffee and Bimbo, refried beans that don't taste like the ones back home, soft cheese that doesn't taste like queso fresco, like queso duro, like re-

quesón. Mexican crema is also different. ¡*And* the tortillas are even thinner than the Guatemalan ones!

"But this is better than being inside a bus," Chino said. He's right. It's better than not talking for hours. Although here, I don't really talk to anyone either. I just watch TV, eat bad food, sniff. *Guao guao.* I bark like the stray dogs outside. I tried nopales. ¡Guácala! Ate something else called a tomatillo that made me sick. *Guao guao. Guao guao.* More dog. More snout. More paws. More nose. Maybe this way Cadejo will finally show himself to me.

5 - ? - 9 9

I KNOW IT'S SUNDAY because soccer is on. Since morning, there have been commercials for the Chivas vs. Atlante game at five P.M., the last before playoffs. Every team will play at that exact same time. The men like Las Chivas more than Atlas because Las Chivas is doing better in the standings. No one likes Tecos. I think I like Atlas because of their black uniforms. I don't like Las Chivas' stripes. It's fun when there's a game, because the men pretend to bet with cigarettes and beer but they always end up sharing. The beer has also changed. Estrella Jalisco and Sol are what Coyote brings, but never enough for the men to get really drunk. I didn't like them almost fighting in Ocós. They talk more when there's a game.

5 - ? - 9 9

CHELE STAYS IN HIS room listening to music. The apartamento came with a small radio with a cassette player and he listens quietly but sings loud enough for us to hear in our room. He has a Bronco cassette. But ever since we made fun of him for looking like El Buki, he's embraced it and borrows Patricia's copy of *Quiéreme.*

Chino plays Vilma Palma e Vampiros. Chino's favorite band. He brought both of their cassettes, *Vilma Palma e Vampiros* and *3980.* I like that song "Auto Rojo" that goes, *Oooo-oh-oooo-oh-ohh, oooo-oh-oooo-oh-ohh, oooo-oh-oooo-oh-oh-ohh* . . .

Marcelo doesn't really listen to music. He just sits in front of the TV, flipping channels, chain-smoking. He's always in charge of the remote. But he also brought a cassette, Control Machete's *Mucho Barato*. "I like canciones pesadas, like rap," I heard him tell Chele once, while they were on the couch. I like pretending I'm invisible on the ground watching TV, listening to the men's conversations. *¿Pesadas? ¿How* is a song heavy? I don't know, but I know Marcelo's favorite song, "¿Comprendes Mendes?" They played it at school for the Mother's Day dance and everyone liked it too much—the nuns banned rap at all the other dances. Marcelo likes saying that: "Comprendes mendes." Coyote says it también.

Besides Los Bukis, Patricia also brought a copy of Los Temerarios' latest album, *Como Te Recuerdo*. We've heard it all over the radio. She liked to play it in Tecún and Ocós, but not anymore. I think it's what made her sad. The radio is always in the men's room and she never asks to borrow it. Whenever Chele or Chino is in there, I come to Patricia's bed and listen. Mostly, I try to stay out of everyone's way. I want them to like me.

5 - ? - 9 9

LYING IN BED WITH Patricia and Carla, I count the tiny hairs above their lips. I listen to their snores and weird sounds. I've never seen someone kick or twitch so much. Sometimes Patricia wakes herself, or wakes Carla. Both of them sleep more and more every day. When they're not sleeping, they stare at the ceiling in silence.

5 - ? - 9 9

I HAVEN'T CRIED, EXCEPT when I fetched powdered gasoline. Besides that, I've been good. Didn't cry when I saw the Mexican soldiers' guns. Didn't throw up on the boat. Didn't complain that we walked far. I've eaten everything, even when I got sick with the tomatillos. I've done all the things my parents, Grandpa, Abuelita, and Mali told me to do, "be good, follow the adults," and still Carla doesn't like me.

It's not like I want to marry her. I like her like I like the girls in novelas. But she's actually here. So I'm shy. ¡We haven't even touched! On the boat I sat on her lap, but that's because Patricia made me. In the bus, on the bed, Patricia is always between us. Patricia doesn't hug me either. I miss Mali. I want to go outside. I've learned to poop in the toilet, wash my underwear. The only thing I still don't know how to do is tie my shoes. I wear Velcro ones, but the other shoes in my backpack are for the border, Grandpa said. They have shoelaces. At school, I asked nuns for help. Carla already thinks I'm little. Carla's back to calling me "bichito" this, "monito" that. Makes me feel bad, but not as bad as when she walks past me and says, "Uuussh, chusma." I will learn to tie my shoes.

5-21-99

¡WE'RE FINALLY LEAVING! WE leave Guadalajara with our fake papers tomorrow. Thank God. It's been sooooo boring. No one even noticed when it was May 10.

"Vieja, ¿wasn't it Mother's Day?" Chino said one day.

"Felicidades," Marcelo told Patricia, and she shrugged. I don't even know when *that* day was. But now we know we leave tomorrow.

¡Guadalajara! ¡Guadalajara! . . .

I'm resting in bed thinking of rhymes when I catch Patricia hiding money in her bra. Abuelita kept her money in her delantal and said "women who use their bras have no class." Patricia sees me staring, but doesn't say anything. She trusts me. All she does is press her fingers to her mouth. I nod. Then, she farts.

¡She farted!

I don't know whether to laugh, walk away, or hold my breath. Patricia immediately laughs. The wrinkles in her forehead, the wrinkles next to her eyes, her dimples, everything shows. I can see the silver fillings in her mouth. I crack up también. She can probably see my fillings, silver, two cavities, both on the right side of my mouth.

The fart doesn't smell bad. Mali's farts are worse. Mom never farted. Patricia hasn't laughed like this in weeks. She's different now that we know *when* we're leaving. Everyone is. The men and Carla are watching TV. They didn't hear. We're still laughing. ¡We're leaving tomorrow! I make a fart noise and we laugh. Then, she farts—¡again! But this time she chases after me, wafting the air toward me. I'm laughing so hard I feel like farting, but can't, even though I've been holding them in. Mali didn't start farting around me until a few years ago. Then we had "fart wars" from across the room whenever we ate too much garlic or curtido. "¡It's the cabbage, pedorros!" Abuelita screamed from her room.

¡We're leaving tomorrow! ¿What are the towns and cities gonna look like? ¿What are we gonna do? ¿Eat? ¿How soon will I see my parents? Ever since Coyote told us we might leave this weekend, Patricia has been more herself. She's put most things back in their "right place." She's swept up all of her and Carla's hair that falls on the floor. Even in the shower, she takes it away, but she's still mad at the men, who leave hairs everywhere when they shave and pee on the toilet seat.

Patricia complains that Carla and I don't even thank her after she cleans the bathroom before we shower, but we do thank her. Mother and daughter pretend-argue. It's not loud arguing like Abuelita and Grandpa. Patricia never hits Carla.

Tomorrow, we're leaving early, like we always do.

"Dress nice," Coyote told us. We know already.

But it's what Patricia tells Carla, who is back in the room now because the novela ended.

"*I know,* Mamá. Gracias."

"De nada."

"Mucho nadar se va a ahogar usted," Carla says.

We laugh even though it's Carla's go-to joke. She leaves the room and gets ready for bed. I already brushed my teeth. The fan is on. We've learned the fan is useful to keep the men's noise down. They always stay up, especially the day before we travel, so they'll be able to sleep on the bus. The fan is a propeller. A helicopter. I've learned everything about this fan. The four spinning parts thicker than my nails, the thickness of a water glass. Dust gets stuck to the propellers that look trapped behind the white metal case surrounding the fan. There are three speeds. A button you pull to make the fan spin or stay in place. I stare at it. I can hear Mali's voice saying the fan can cut my fingers off. But she's not here. I can do what I want. Back home I put a pencil through the cage once, and Mali told me to never do that again. Mali, Grandpa, or Abuelita never hit me. But I think they came close that time.

At school, older kids dared each other to put their finger in the fan to stop it. They hung out in the classroom at lunch when the teacher left to eat. I watched with the younger kids, admiring how their thick fingers stopped the fan. ¿Are my fingers thick enough? ¿Old enough?

Old means strong. It's what the older kids said. My friends and I never tried. We need our fingers to play. To dance. To eat. To hug our parents. To climb the fence I will climb soon. Tomorrow we leave this place. I'm a veteranito, like Marcelo says. Patricia is in bed. Carla is in the bathroom. I change the speed of the fan to the slowest.

"¡Stop! ¡Bicho! ¡¿Qué putas hacés?!"

Patricia has never screamed at me like that.

"Come here, tontito." It feels like a bucket of cold water got poured on me. No one has called me that since Mali. Patricia taps the bed next to her legs. Her voice is softer. I sit but don't lie down.

"¿What's wrong?"

I shrug.

"¿You miss El Salvador?"

"Ajá."

"Yo también. But you'll see your parents soon."

"I know."

"¿You love them a lot?"

"Sí."

"I love mi hijita."

"¿Carla?"

"Sí, but I'm talking about the one over there."

I forget she has a daughter waiting for her. That Carla has a sister. I want to ask how her daughter got to La USA, but then Carla comes back from the bathroom.

"She left on a plane," Patricia tells me, holding her chest, the same part of the bra where she stuffed her money.

"¿A plane?"

"With visas," Patricia says.

"¿And you two?"

"Clearly not, bicho pasmado," Carla interrupts, shaking her head. Glaring.

"Don't call him that," Patricia snaps back.

"You love your parents, ¿right?"

"Sí. I'll be with them soon," I blurt out, looking at the ground, embarrassed.

"I believe you, Javiercito," Patricia says with a smile. "It makes me feel better. Your parents love *you*. ¿Entendés?"

I nod, trying not to look at Carla or what her eyebrows are doing.

"Let's sleep. A la camita."

Patricia rubs my head a few times, then gets in bed. I sleep next to her, Carla on the other side. I'm excited for tomorrow. To finally walk out of that metal door.

¡Guadalajara! ¡Guadalajara!

CHAPTER SIX

—

Guadalajara to Sonora

MAY 22, 1999

"HERE, THEN HERE, THEN HERE," COYOTE SAYS, POINTING TO THE cities we're gonna see on our way to the border. His fingers are the size of entire Mexican states on the pocket map he carries, much smaller than Grandpa's. A map of the northern part of México with these five states: Nayarit, Sinaloa, Sonora, Baja California Norte, and Baja California Sur. I didn't know California had Mexican relatives. While Coyote points out the route he's traced in pen, I notice his finger doesn't move to the left toward Tijuana. He never mentions that name, only Tepic, Mazatlán, Los Mochis, Ciudad Obregón, Hermosillo.

"That's where we'll stop and sleep," he says in the kitchen, all of us trying to get a glimpse. "Won't take long. Two days max to La Línea." He points at not-Tijuana. Tijuana was the last stop when I practiced with Grandpa.

"¿What happened to Tijuana, maitro?" Marcelo asks.

"We can't cross there."

"¿Why?" Patricia asks.

"Things changed."

"¿What?" Chino says, frustrated.

"I'm taking you to where the bosses told me to take you. New plan," Coyote says in a harsher tone. "From here"—he points to a town near La USA—"it's a straight shot across La Línea." He's not wearing a cap today, and his hair is styled with gel. I like that he's referring to the border as a line. It *is* a line on the map. "La mera neta, that other route is too dangerous right now. La Migra will definitely catch you there."

"Ajá," The Six say. Chino with a click of his tongue. Chele surprised. Marcelo sounds mad. Patricia says it sarcastically. Carla and I don't say anything. *La Migra.* I remember "migrantes." That's what we are, what the coyotes in Oaxaca called us. Grandpa made me remember the towns for a reason, but the plan changed in Tecún, changed in Ocós, changed in Oaxaca. Don Dago always reminded us that the plan *could* change . . .

¿And where *is* Don Dago? The adults don't even ask about him anymore. This is our coyote now. Coyote whose name we don't know. Marcelo only calls him maitro. Patricia and Carla call him señor. Chino and Chele call him don. Coyote told Patricia a name, but we all know it's not his real name. No one uses it. The one good thing is that we're leaving this apartamento.

I thought the naps were never gonna end. The boredom. I hold the straps on my backpack as I take my very last steps through this long corridor, past the couch, past the TV, out the metal door, down the stairs, onto the dirt. The Dad and teenager don't come to say goodbye.

We're finally outside. We're breathing air that doesn't smell like cigarettes and trash. It feels like we're breaking detention. Sunlight hits our skin. Our eyes adjust. We step into the microbus that will drive us to the terminal where Coyote says we'll take another bus.

"Ojalá no one stops us before La Línea," Chele says quietly in the microbus's backseat.

"Ojalá," Chino and Marcelo next to him whisper, before the driver turns the radio on. It's a little past eight A.M., the latest we've ever left to another city.

Capitán Coyote looks the nicest. He's wearing a silver watch, different from the black one he usually wears. His shirt is tucked in and ironed. Leather belt with a huge buckle. And, he's let a thick black mustache grow below his nose, his face clean-shaven everywhere else. The men wear a lot of cologne. It overpowers the cigarette smell even with the windows down.

"You've been wanting a call . . . today you get a call," Coyote says from the front seat. "But until then, keep your mouths shut."

The microbus drops us off in front of a huge church. A crowd waits to enter the cathedral, which Coyote says is famous. People sell amulets and sculptures of La Virgen de Guadalupe. Her image reminds me of drawing a shoe-polish mustache and beard every December 12. I had my own cuma, matata, caites, sombrero, and tecomate. I don't see anyone dressed up like that here. Trees jut out from huge cement pots that also act like benches. There's a fountain in the middle, the biggest I've ever seen.

"We don't have to pretend we don't know each other. Follow me."

We walk through the crowd, everyone close together. I'm holding Patricia's hand, she holds mine and Carla's. Some people pray outside the church on their knees. Others take pictures.

"Let's go," Coyote says as he walks up the steps toward the castle entrance. All the doors are gigantic, especially the middle one.

Everything is bigger than my town's church. Inside, everything is white, except for the hundreds of pews and the cement floors. And up front where the priest speaks, painted glass and dark wooden carvings of saints and Jesús. Polished. Shiny. Balconies of dark, shiny wood. Thick wood. Candles everywhere. Gold lining the thick white columns that hold up the ceiling. The smell of wax. Smoke. A crowd.

Coyote walks and sits halfway to the front, on a pew to the right of the center aisle. "Pray you make it there, morrito," Coyote tells me as he kneels. All of us kneel next to him.

It's quiet but noisy at the same time because of people's shoes squeaking on the floor, their clothes rubbing against each other, their breathing. The sounds travel up from the ground to the ceiling. The Six cross ourselves. *Tap, tap, tap, tap, tap.* It's hard to concentrate, but

I try. I pray for the same thing I pray for every night: that we make it north.

I open my eyes. The adults are still praying. I close my eyes and pray we cross La Línea as fast as possible, that we jump the fence and run so fast no one can catch us, especially the bad gringos. I pray my parents are waiting for me right after I jump. I want Mom's arms, I pray she hugs me, kisses me, and that Dad throws me in the air like I've heard he used to do every afternoon when he'd come home from his fishing boat. I hope Mom isn't mad I'm spending so much time with Patricia and Carla. I pray Mom doesn't mind I hold Patricia's hand in public.

Coyote taps my shoulders. I dust my knees. Everyone else sits on the pews. We're all done. Coyote looks at us and whispers, "Let's go."

We follow him outside. We don't talk and don't look anyone in the eyes. We're in public. We're hiding. We're Mexican. Our Mexican accents are back on our tongues.

"I'm Guadalajaran," I whisper to myself.

"*Tapatío,*" Carla corrects me. "*Tapatío,*" she repeats.

I nod, embarrassed but glad she talked to me. Then I practice the new story Coyote told us to tell soldiers: we're visiting family in Hermosillo, Sonora. That's where they moved. That's where we're going.

In the buses, Patricia is Mom. Carla is Sister. I don't know the men. In case we get separated, we stay wherever we are and we call the number Coyote gave Patricia and the other adults. Coyote or someone else will come rescue us. I don't have his number. I have Patricia's skinny hand that at the beginning of the trip had beautiful long nails painted red. Now they're colorless and cut short like the rest of ours.

"There's a Western Union near here," Coyote says outside the church, down the steps, past the fountain, and near a cement bench with a tree growing out of a cement pot. "But first call norte, ask for money. This is the last call before you cross," he says quietly as we huddle around him. "One call. Don't call home, call north." Then he looks at me. "We called your parents. They're okay. We don't need money from you."

¿Who is "we"? I want to hear my parents' voices, anyone's voice I know. But before I say anything, Coyote walks away. We're in public. Patricia looks at me, grabs my hand, and whispers, "That's good, your parents know you're okay. Gracias a Dios." She calms me. I trust her.

"Let's go," Coyote says. He walks us to the phone booth closest to the road but still in the church's plaza. The phone booths here look like the public phones in San Salvador, like giant blue kidney beans. Metal numbers on the pad, a metallic cord that leads to a black plastic phone the size of my head.

"Split. You three"—he points at Patricia, and we know he means Carla and me as well—"wait over there." He points to the cement bench a few steps away. "You, go first," he tells Marcelo, and hands him a phone card.

"Va, maitro," he says, and dials away.

I sit and watch the pigeons in the trees, pigeons on the fountain's ledge, pigeons eating trash. In the distance, a man feeds them. People keep walking onto the plaza on their way to the cathedral. Some stop to buy amulets of La Virgen. Patricia stares at the men. Chino and Chele smoke behind the booth. Carla looks at the church. Coyote listens to Marcelo. It's been so long since we've been outside. We've been in detention for weeks.

I look at everything: the pattern of the cement under our feet, the detail on the front face of the church, the bell towers, what people wear, what they're saying, how they're saying it, the types of cars stuck in traffic: microbus, taxi, car, bus, truck, bigger truck. But most important, I notice people's eyes. If they look at us funny. I'm afraid another soldier will drag us, ask us questions with guns, make us kiss this cement, take our money. But this time, we're out in the open. I know Cadejo is here. He's always here. I always listen for him. Coyote and Cadejo won't abandon us like Don Dago and Marta did.

Coyote hands Patricia the card and says, "Ask for this much." He doesn't say the number but shows her a number on a light-yellow piece of paper he has tucked in his back pocket. It's folded so small, the numbers flash by my face. "Tell them to send to here." He flips the page and points at something else. "This name," he says, and leaves the page there for her to make the call.

Patricia dials, and I notice the graffiti inside the booth written in Sharpie. There are stickers también, a lot of them in English with words I don't understand, but there's one with a heart and the word "love" in it, I know that means *amor*. Inside, the biggest heart has been carved with a knife and then traced with Wite-Out. It says *Flaco + Mara* or *María*. I can't tell. Near the bottom of the booth, under the metal thing that looks like a tabletop where the phonebook hangs, so many dried-up pieces of gum. White, hard, all the color sucked and chewed out.

"¿Aló? ¿Aló?" Patricia says, her voice frail like it's breaking up. I think it's her husband, Carla's dad. She talks for a while and asks for the amount Coyote pointed to. Explains why she hasn't called, where we are, and what the plan is.

Then she hands the phone to Carla, whose voice also changes. ¿Does mine change when I talk on the phone? Carla covers her mouth and the phone's mouth so I stop listening. Patricia motions Coyote to come over, her hand like a sock on a clothesline flapping up and down in the wind. No one pays attention to me. I want to talk to my parents. Patricia asks Carla to finish up and to hand her the phone.

"Here, amor, el señor is gonna talk to you," Patricia tells her husband. Coyote and he talk, and we just listen. As he hands Patricia the phone, I pull Coyote's pants.

"You're good, morrito. We talked to your parents."

I yank his pants again.

"They paid. Don't be latoso."

I don't know what that means, but how he says it makes me feel bad. I want to tell my parents I'm ok. That I miss them. Coyote's boots click on the ground as he walks toward the men. They're smoking. Laughing. None of them saw Coyote get mad at me. Not even Chino. I'm alone.

Patricia hangs up, and Coyote signals for us to go toward him. "We wait for them to call back. For the confirmation," he says. I don't understand.

I glare at Coyote, and he ignores me. I stand away from everyone, away from the bench, count the leaves on the tree growing from the cement pot. I want to cry but can't let them see me like this. I swallow it. I think of my parakeet, my dog, my toys, *Dragon Ball Z*. There's a soccer game today. Las Chivas must win the second game to make it to the next round. I yank Coyote again—

"¡No seas latoso! We talked to them. We can't waste time and money," Coyote tells me, annoyed. I continue to stare at the crowd. Everyone in The Six is thinking. Smoking. No one asks me to come over to them. No one cares. I want to run away. I squeeze my fists together. Concentrate on the ground. The pattern of the leaves on the trees. I can't cry. Don't cry.

Then, something warm on my shoulder.

"Come here." Carla waves her hand.

I look at her big brown eyes. She lets out a smile. Her hair is braided like it always is for these bus trips. It looks so much like Mali's hair, thick, black, curly. I hope she can't tell I'm tearing up.

"Come here, bichito," she says, but this time it sounds nice. I follow her to the cement bench across from where Patricia waits, a hand on her forehead.

"Mami said Coyote already called your parents," Carla says. "That's good."

"But I can't talk to them."

"I know." She taps my back. She *does* care. "Everyone is in their heads, look at my mom." She points at Patricia, who's staring at the phone booth like she stared at the ceiling in our apartamento. "It's okay."

She's right. Realizing this makes me warm, dizzy. No one talks. Cigarette after cigarette. Pigeon after pigeon. Person after person. The phone doesn't ring. And then it does. When it rings, Coyote gets up, walks to the booth, and picks up. He writes a number down on the same piece of paper. He doesn't hand the phone over to anyone. Then he walks back to tell us who called. We wait. And wait. Until everyone is accounted for.

WE'RE IN A FANCY bus again, with AC and velvet curtains. Coyote got everyone's money from the Western Union. We waited three hours. Then we went to the buses and finally left Guadalajara around three P.M. Patricia, Carla, and I sit together, separate from the men. It's not hard for me to pretend I don't know them.

Patricia and Carla fell asleep almost an hour into the bus ride. I can't take my eyes off the window. I concentrate on the same spot on the road, and it feels like I'm flying. The green landscape of endless hills reminds me of Abuelita's backyard past the mangos where the volcano stood. Green-green. But near the road, closer to the window: spikey plants like huge aloes or pineapples lined up in rows. ¡Tequila farms! Just like novelas. Row after row of spikey tips; silvery, blue-green crowns growing from the ground.

I stay awake and watch for checkpoints. Coyote said there might be some, said to "sleep." But it's day. I stay awake, hoping we don't get stopped and dragged out. Hoping we make it to Mazatlán safely. That's where we're sleeping tonight. Coyote is up front near the entrance. Alone. I'm still mad he didn't let me call my parents.

I'm still mad no one but Carla cared. Patricia tried a little, but to the men, I'm a rock in their shoe. A splinter. I don't like feeling like this, like there's something missing. An unfinished puzzle. A Lego set with pieces missing. When the adults ignored me and they got to talk to their families, it made me miss *my* family. My *real* family. I thought they cared about me. Chino called me his hermanito, but he didn't do anything. I want them to care like how Mali cares about me. Instead, I look outside—

Sometimes there are posters with *PRI* written on them. Red, white, and green. They look like the election posters back home. Reminds me of when Mali got paid to glue them all over town. She got a job with ARENA. Dad doesn't like them. I liked that they had cachiporras and handed out free plastic soccer balls. I try to stay awake. Coyote said it was gonna be four hours to Tepic, then four more to Mazatlán. We're used to longer bus trips. Tepic is in another state. That's four Mexican states we've been through: Oaxaca, Guerrero, Jalisco, now Nayarit. It's pretty here. México is big.

THE LIGHTS TURN ON, and Patricia says, "Despierta" to Carla and me in her best Mexican. We walk out of the bus and right onto the road. This isn't a fancy terminal like Guadalajara; it's a stop on the road. No tall buildings, just houses. My watch says it's ten P.M., so many people surrounding food stands; this is more of a market than a terminal.

Coyote stays near us, the nearest he's ever been in public, so we don't lose him in the crowd of people, lights, skillets, propane tanks. We don't pretend to be strangers, but we know not to speak. "Let's eat some tacos. This lady has the best ones, come."

We haven't had tacos yet. Mali was excited for me to try them. It's México's national dish. We've been eating tasteless meals. I want *good* food. Coyote walks us to the largest crowd. We look like flies, bees, ants, gathered around a plate. This reminds me of the pupusa stands in Olocuilta, next to the road, without roofs, people eating in their cars or standing around the skillet and propane tank.

It's just one lady cooking and counting the money, doing everything. There's a cooler next to her feet where she grabs the drinks and kicks the cooler's lid closed. We wait in the circular line. She's so fast with her hands. Flips the meat in the pan with a spoon, flips the thin tortillas with her hands, reaches into her bag to grab change, asks, "¿What do you want? ¿How many?"

She never forgets, always gets the order correct. The Six stare and stand outside the hungry circle. Coyote is the one that orders. He turns to us and asks, "¿How many? She only has de asada."

Everyone says four or five. I say, "Two, please."

We wait.

Coyote handles the money. He buys us food, gets us a place to sleep, buys us bus tickets. He's our wallet, our voice, our brain. The meat sizzles in the circular skillet, deeper than a comal. The little brown-and-red cut-up cubes smell so good as they release smoke and their juices. Then the lady grabs two tortillas that have been steaming on top of the carne asada, scoops a spoonful of meat into the double tortillas, and with her hands sprinkles diced onion and cilantro from a plastic container. One by one, she places the tacos onto a paper plate she adorns with radishes, sliced limes, and pickled jalapeños and carrots.

"¿Salsa?"

Coyote responds, "Not for these, but for the last five, yes."

She nods and hands Coyote a paper plate, then another. Through the crowd, he passes them to us one plate at a time. Then we push our way out of the circle, careful not to spill anything.

My stomach growls. Standing in the middle of the sidewalk, I finally bite into the meat, and oh my God. ¡This is the best thing! Better than the fish. Better than the chicken with Grandpa. Tacos *are* the best food in México. The juices from the meat drench the tortilla with so much flavor. I finally like these thin tortillas. By themselves, the tortillas are tasteless, but like this . . . And right then, a burning. An itch in the back of my tongue, traveling to the middle, to the front, to the roof of my mouth. I breathe air and fan my mouth next to Patricia, who asks, "¿You okay? ¿Do you want a Coca?"

I nod up and down, up and down. The men devour their food. Coyote también. An entire taco gone in one bite. They don't notice me fanning my opened mouth with one hand.

"Let's go." Patricia pulls me by my shoulder toward the lady and she asks for two Cokes.

The lady opens the caps with a bottle opener tied to the skillet with a nylon string. I remember Abuelita's advice to only drink out of a straw because you never know about the germs on the bottle opener. I pause and walk to the lady and ask for a pajilla.

"¿Pa—qué? ¿What you say, morrillo?"

I look over at Patricia. She pretends not to hear, points to the straws.

"¿What you say? ¿Pa—qué? ¿Pa—"

I messed up. I'm stupid. I don't know what to do.

"Ohhh, ¿this?" The lady holds a straw up.

I nod.

"You mean popote. *Po-po-te*." She lets out a huge laugh. Patricia is next to me. Stares at me and glares at the lady, who can't stop laughing.

"Gracias," Patricia tells the lady, yanking the straws from the lady's hand, who up-close looks older than Grandpa.

"Pinches mojados, learn to speak," the old lady tells us while Patricia pulls my shoulder away from the crowd.

"It's okay, caminá," she says, like we say back home: *caminá*. The old lady is still laughing. I can hear her through the crowd. I feel terrible. ¿Are we gonna be ok? ¿Is she gonna call the cops? She knows we're Salvadoran. Guanacos. Cerotes. Majes. Chambrosos. Chiflados. Cachimbones. There's a pupusa on our foreheads.

"It's okay," Patricia repeats. "They're called popotes here. It's okay." I don't even want the Coke or the straw. The white wrapper glows too much in the dark—a bright sticker soldiers can see.

When we get back to The Six, Patricia tells Coyote something. "¡Chinga su madre! Let's go," he tells us, then mumbles something under his breath.

We walk in silence toward the motel and Chele asks what time it is.

"It's ten-twenty," I answer Chele.

"It's nine-twenty," Coyote responds.

"Señor, it says ten . . ." I say, showing him my watch.

"It's nine."

"But . . ."

"¡It's nine-twenty! ¡Pinche morrillo latoso! You don't know shit. Time changes here," he says, annoyed. Harshly. The worst he's spoken to me. No one says anything. My watch says it's 10:21 P.M. I'm not wrong. I want to cry. But Coyote will think I'm weak, but I'm strong.

"All of you, change your watches, we're in Sinaloa, time is different than Jalisco," he says to the rest while looking directly at me.

Carla definitely must think I'm dumb, that I'm stupid, annoying. First the straw, now the time. ¿What's wrong with me? I'm a bad actor today. ¿How did I forget to say *popote*? I've been trapped inside too long.

Chino catches up to me and says, "I didn't know the time changes either." He rubs my back. Then he points to my watch. "That's a cool watch. Mirá, I have one también." He shows me his. Finally, an adult cares. I knew he cared. I could sense it at the booths, but he's different when he's around Chele and Marcelo—colder. Patricia got me the Coke. Carla asked me to sit with her. Now Chino is acting like he was acting on the boats, like he's really an older brother. He's better when Marcelo and Chele aren't looking. I just want to get to bed and sleep.

We get to a motel and it's the same routine: we wait for Coyote to get the key. The men smoke. We get the key. We walk to our room on the first floor. Coyote opens the door.

"¿One room?" Chino asks Coyote.

"Yes. To save," he says, locking the door once we're all inside.

"¿And the money we gave you, maitro?" Marcelo follows up. He's not nice to me, but I like that he asks questions that get Coyote flustered and sometimes mad.

"We have a lot more stops. You don't want to call north again, ¿right?"

Everyone nods.

"Let me do my job, you do yours." Coyote is in a mood. ¿What happened? This is the meanest he's spoken to all of us. "It's more dangerous the farther north we go. Just in case, tonight and every night, sleep with your clothes on, backpacks ready to go."

"¿De veras, don?" Chele asks.

"Yes, we must be better. There's soldiers everywhere. We can't lose too much money. Let *me* do the talking." No one says anything.

I'm rusty. I really *did* mess up. Everyone looks tired and full. ¿How is this going to work? ¿One room? The motel is tiny. The smallest one we've been in. Smaller than the apartamento. One skinny bed. One small TV and a sofa-like thing where only one person fits.

"I'm sleeping here," Coyote says, pointing to the sofa. "Arréglense ustedes."

"You three get the bed," Marcelo tells Patricia, nodding at Carla and me.

"Va," Chino and Chele agree.

This sucks. I want more than ever to be by myself. Run to the banana grove and cry like I did back home so no one will hear me. Carla will never like me. I have a solid white spot in my nail. A cloud. Only one in all ten fingers. It's official: I have a crush on Carla. It's what Mali believed when she looked at my nails and she found a white dot.

"The fainter the white dot, the briefer the crush," Mali said. Mali the nail-cloud reader, the crush adviser, the Walter Mercado of love. I want to cuddle her right now. Look at the stars and be far away from these people. Carla makes me feel weird. My chest like humming-birds fighting for the hibiscus in Abuelita's garden. I feel dumb, and now we have to share a much smaller bed. I hate watching Patricia and Carla help each other before bed. Patricia braiding and unbraid-ing her daughter's hair. I want *that* with Mom. With Mali. I just want a hug.

5-23-99

THE MEN SNORED LOUD. Loud-loud. The motel room walls were thinner than the apartamento's. I couldn't sleep. One of the men gasped for air until he woke himself. Another talked in his sleep—from the deep voice I think it was Marcelo. They sounded like cows. I'm so tired and we're in another city already, Los Mochis, Sinaloa, waiting for our next bus, sitting on a metal bench.

Los Mochis is small and hot. No wind. No clouds. The time is the same as Mazatlán. "Time won't change until Ciudad Obregón. Ten hours today," Coyote said before we left Mazatlán. That's more hours than yesterday. Three stops today: Culiacán, Los Mochis, Ciudad Obregón. We walk so fast, I want to be bored again. It's go-go-go. We wake up. Get ready. Walk out one door. Downstairs. Up another set of stairs into another door. Another bus. Another seat.

We're all wearing our nice clothes. The men showered with cologne. I brushed my teeth. Patricia redid her makeup and Carla's braids, but none of us showered in our motel. The taco lady didn't tell on us.

The buses to Los Mochis are fancy, but less so than the one out of Guadalajara. Culiacán was a big city, much bigger than Mazatlán and every other stop thus far. The roads are drier the farther north we drive. Right now, Patricia, Carla, and I sit on a metal bench waiting for the bus to Ciudad Obregón, in front of a TV that's playing the local news. The men smoke behind us. There's an "infestation" of scorpions. ¡Scorpions! Our eyes are glued to the ground. The men move as they smoke. The terminal has a metal roof, the ground is cement, but no walls; it's out in the open. ¡Scorpions!

Coyote is nicer today. No one talked to him last night and not much this morning. We keep to ourselves.

"Ey, mirá vos, bicha, they sell frescos over there," Chino whispers to Patricia, even though there's no one around. All of us turn our heads to where he's pointing with his lips. It's a drinks stand. Huge jugs of fresco. One of them light gray, whitish—Mexican horchata.

"Aguas frescas," Coyote corrects Chino. I won't make the same mistake again. I learned my lesson with the taco lady. I keep my mouth shut. "¿You want some? *I'll* get them." Coyote stresses the *I'll*.

We nod.

"¿What kind?"

"¿What flavors do they have?" Carla asks.

"Probably tamarindo, horchata, and jamaica."

"¡Vieja! ¿Jamaica?" Chino shouts, surprised, showing the wrinkles in his forehead. "Get me one, please."

Mmm. Jamaica sounds refreshing.

"I'll try the horchata again," Chele says.

"Señor, one jamaica, por favor," I tell Coyote.

"One horchata, four jamaicas, two tamarindos." Coyote counts the order in his hand and takes a step, then pauses and tells Chele to come with him. Coyote is being *really* nice. ¿Maybe he's trying to make up for yesterday?

Chele and Coyote come back with giant Styrofoam cups. We don't know what's what. Coyote looks at the tops and hands us our drinks. The jamaica is almost pink if you look at it through the plastic top. Patricia gets a tamarindo that looks darker than the rest of the drinks. The horchata blends into the plastic and Styrofoam.

My jamaica is amazing. Not too sweet and with a strong color. It paints Carla's tongue magenta; she shows her mom and smiles. I bet my tongue is painted también.

Chele makes faces. "Guácala vos."

"You fucked up again, maje," Chino tells him.

Marcelo laughs. He rarely laughs.

"This is not horchata, don," Chele tells Coyote.

"It's horchata," Coyote says again, tasting his tamarindo. Chele keeps making faces as he drinks.

"It's missing morro, pepitoria, a lot of things. This shit tastes just like water."

"You're still drinking it," Coyote says, not mad, almost jokingly.

"Puesí, got no choice."

I made the right choice. My jamaica is the best ever. I taste Patricia's tamarindo and it's too sweet. I miss Abuelita's fresco de tamarindo from the tree in our backyard. All of us finish our drinks and swirl our cups so the ice moves, so it melts.

"That's the bus. Last smoke, drink up," Coyote says as the bus parks, *CIUDAD OBREGÓN* written at the top of the windshield in giant block letters. All the buses look the same: a flat front nose, giant front windshields, steps, and tinted windows with curtains inside. We wait for the men to finish smoking before we line up. Patricia stands up and stretches. Everyone stretches. We've been sitting for more than six hours.

"Four more hours," Coyote whispers. Not many people line up. We're quiet. We must speak Mexican. *Those were good aguas frescas. Órale. ¿Comprendes mendes? Órale, vato.* We walk Mexican. Breathe Mexican. Our chests out in front, confident in our fake papers. It's almost dusk. "The day is fine. Night is when we watch out. If anything happens, let *me* speak," Coyote reminded us at the motel. He doesn't talk like that in public.

PATRICIA ELBOWS MY RIBS. I bump my head on the window's closed curtains. Her index finger is raised and perpendicular to her lips. *Quiet,* it says. She nods her head forward, toward the front of the bus, and purses her lips in the same direction. Through the windshield, red and blue lights circle and paint the night. The bus slows down.

Coyote said there would be checkpoints, said he would handle it. We're Mexican. We have *good* fake papers. Coyote showed us his real ones; ours feel just like his. The cops won't know. We've made it through inspection before.

"Don't exit the bus like in Oaxaca, no te pases de lanza," Coyote specifically told Patricia at the motel in Mazatlán. Every morning he goes over the rules, but I don't know what "pases de lanza" means. "*I* will handle it," he told all of us in the motel.

"But *that* bus left *us,*" Patricia responded.

"Because *you* got out. You got children. People don't want to see children dragged, kneeling, hands behind their heads. It's why the soldier waved the bus off. Then we're all fucked. Stay the fuck inside. Think."

Patricia's face reddened. The men laughed. Then Coyote turned to the rest of us. "I know these roads. I know the mordida here. I didn't know Oaxaca, but this is *my* territory. Pura neta."

I don't want to get dragged out again.

"Señores y señoras, documents out, please," the bus driver says over the microphone. There's a wooden barrier in the middle of the road, two trucks with lights, and men holding big guns in front of each truck. It's the same as Oaxaca. My hands and armpits start sweating.

"Sleep," Patricia whispers to Carla and me, pulling our papers from her pants pocket, sliding them under her right thigh so she can easily reach them.

The lights haven't turned on. I keep my eyes open until the soldiers come up the stairs. I want to see them. Carla rests her head on her mom's left shoulder. Patricia needs to use her right hand to show the soldiers our papers. I scoot closer to the window. My head rests on the velvet curtains, and I pretend to sleep.

"Buenas noches, we're here to check your documents and ask a few questions," one of the soldiers says. "If you cooperate, all of us can quickly go our way." His voice is softer than any other soldier's we've heard thus far. "My partner here will walk down the aisle."

I slightly open my eyes and see that both soldiers have flashlights they shine at each face. People shuffle their backpacks, pockets, to get their papers out. Sometimes the soldiers just shine a light on someone and move on. Other times, they ask questions like ¿What's your final destination? ¿Where are you coming from? ¿Where were you born? ¿Why are you going to Ciudad Obregón?

Today we must say our final destination is Ciudad Obregón. Our final destination is wherever our last stop is that day. Yesterday it was Mazatlán. Tomorrow will be different. The soldiers' boots move toward us. I close my eyes tighter, try to breathe slower so I look like I'm sleeping.

"Documents," a voice next to us says.

Patricia lifts her right thigh, the one closest to me.

"¿Family?"

"Sí."

He flips through the papers. Hands them back to her.

His boots step past us. "Documents," he says to the person behind us. It's over. We passed. I continue "sleeping." Carla doesn't move. Patricia stuffs our papers back under her thigh. I listen. More of the same questions. More steps. Then there's a commotion.

"Don't look," Patricia whispers.

Another soldier rushes past us toward the back. ¿Is it the men? Patricia holds us closer. I pray without moving my lips. The lights are still off. They keep arguing. The person doesn't want to exit. It doesn't sound like them. The person has a Mexican accent. *Cadejo, Cadejito.* The soldiers drag someone who bumps into our seat as they walk past. No one says anything. I shut my eyes harder. We hear the bus door open and they step outside.

I open my eyes.

"Híjole, it's Marcelo," Patricia whispers, her head like an owl's looking every direction.

I close my eyes and pray more.

"Ya valimos. Don't look, don't look." Patricia sounds scared. We can't tell what's happening. I peek through the space between the curtain and the window, but nothing. One minute. Two. Then Coyote and Marcelo walk back up the bus stairs. I thank Cadejo, Coyote, Diosito. ¿What does Coyote tell the soldiers?

"Everything's good," the soldier tells the bus driver.

Marcelo walks past our seat. I smile. Carla smiles. Marcelo doesn't look at us. He's mad. Mad-mad: eyebrows crunched, fists clenched, the veins on the side of his forehead jut out. His jaw the sharpest it's looked. Nostrils wide open. He blows past us. Across our seat, the passengers look annoyed. They glare at Marcelo like I look at mosquitoes after they bite me. *¡Slap!* Then they look at us and shake their heads as they whisper something to each other.

"Sleep." Patricia turns her head toward us, ignoring the people.

The door closes. We're moving. I try not to look—everyone around us is light-skinned. Coyote said "norteños are even lighter than tapatíos." I move the curtain to stare at the road.

"TODAY I GET YOU to La Línea," Coyote says first thing in the morning. We're in Sonora, the last state before the fence. Yesterday was our longest day since the twelve-hour bus ride to Guadalajara, but it felt even longer—three hours, plus three hours, plus four. I'm tired of sitting.

Coyote sounds proud. We've moved so fast. He got Marcelo back into the bus. He's in a good mood. He went to the market and got us actual breakfast: refried beans, eggs, and two types of tortillas. These tortillas are different than before: flour tortillas, flat and big. The burnt spots almost the size of eyes, and they actually taste good. Better than the thin corn ones we've been eating.

In Guadalajara, Coyote never ate with us. We never received a thin-tortilla eating tutorial. We've been stacking the thin circles on top of each other to make them thick like the tortillas back home. When Coyote was around to eat, we had chips, or bread, or tacos—self-explanatory. But now, we watch him lay a corn tortilla flat in his palm, then he takes the other palm and rolls it over the tortilla—it looks like a rolled-up carpet. Then Coyote uses his tortilla-carpet to move his eggs and dip into his beans. All of us watch him eat.

Marcelo, the least impressed, says, "That's what Mexicans do in Los Ángeles." He's always reminding us he's lived in La USA. That he's done this trip before.

"¿Simón?" Chino asks, tearing a part of the bigger flour tortilla and using it to grab eggs with his hands like we do back home.

Marcelo nods.

Coyote looks up and says, "¿What? Eat. We have seven or eight hours today, *and* we have to get you chamarras."

"¿Chamarras?" Chele asks.

"Chamarras," Coyote says again. We blankly look at him. "¿You don't know chamarras?"

We shake our heads.

Coyote looks at Marcelo. "¿Do *you*?" He's become our Mexican translator.

"A sweater," Marcelo says.

"Ahhh," all of us respond with our voices or our heads moving up and down.

"Kind of. More like a jacket," Coyote corrects Marcelo. "You need jackets for the desert. It's hot during the day, but cold as fuck at night." He pauses. "¿Don't you feel it? Nights are colder than Guadalajara here."

He's right. When we get off the buses at night, the air almost matches the AC. It was hot in Los Mochis, but at night in Ciudad Obregón, it was cold.

"Eat, and then chamarras."

The flour tortillas fill me up. We eat everything on our paper plates.

"La Línea," Coyote repeats again, wiping all of his beans with one last swipe of his rolled-up tortilla-carpet. "That's where I stay."

No one says anything.

"I drop you tonight in Nogales, where another coyote, un pollero, will take you across. Then I turn back around tomorrow. Today, we travel through Hermosillo to Nogales. Seven hours."

"¿What's a pollero?" Patricia asks.

"Like a coyote, but for La Línea. They walk you across."

"¿Why pollos?" Chele asks.

"You're our chickens."

When Coyote says that, the only thing I hear is: *Los pollitos dicen pío pío pío. Cuando tienen hambre, cuando tienen frío.* A rhyme Mom used to sing. We *are* like chickens. Coyote brings us food. We ask him for stuff. He brings it. Now we're cold. *Pío pío.* He gets us "chamarras." We're going to the store. ¡New clothes! So we walk across into La USA with our warm feathers.

WE BREEZE PAST HERMOSILLO. Then there are two checkpoints between Hermosillo and Nogales. Sometimes the soldiers are friendly.

Other times they bark like dogs. They sniff and sniff, and then they bark until the person they're barking at walks outside. Chino gets dragged out. My heart races. Sweat everywhere. But everything is ok. Coyote goes outside and gives them money, then the soldiers stop barking. Chino winks at us when he walks past us and sits back down a few seats behind. He isn't angry like Marcelo was. Patricia lets out a big sigh. She really cares about him. *I* really care about him.

The next time, none of The Six get sniffed out. It's someone else. A stranger. The soldiers come back up into the bus for the person sitting next to him, then two others sitting behind them. They're a group of four who sat too close to each other. I hadn't realized the people next to us, in all of the buses, might be trying to get to La Línea también. Maybe they don't have a coyote. Maybe their coyote is bad. The soldiers tell the bus to leave. The strangers stay there outside like we stayed outside in Oaxaca. They don't kneel but stand with their hands behind their backs as the bus driver speeds off. I pray for them.

WE GET TO NOGALES at dusk. The city looks crunched up, small hills everywhere, houses and houses. We don't wait at the terminal. A dark-blue truck waits with two men inside. They don't speak to us, but they already know Coyote and call him by the name he told us, "Pedro."

"Get in the back," Coyote says. "Hold on, it might get bumpy." Then he sits in the front cabin. We crouch down to shield ourselves with the truck bed. It's cold—good thing we have chamarras. Coyote said they must be dark-colored so we "blend in at night." And we do. Chino's is dark brown. Marcelo's and Patricia's are black. Chele's is dark blue, Carla's dark green. Mine is dark gray because it's the only one they had in my size.

Outside the city, more and more stars. We're speeding on an asphalt road with no streetlights. Barely any cars. Just grasses and grasses. The back of the truck is grooved, it hurts, so I sit on my backpack. ¿Are there more checkpoints? I remember the man in the boat. The Guatemalans on the bus. Strangers, but I remember some of their faces. The wrinkles when one of them cried. The people in the boat vomiting on their clothes. Shirts on top of shirts. Sitting on their backpacks like I'm doing now. It's like they're still here with us in the back of another pickup. I hope everyone is ok. That they're in La USA.

It's so dark, but the moon is a little more than split in half, a lopsided egg. I'm so close. The air feels fresher. Clean. Crisp. We've been on this road for thirty minutes, and only two cars have driven by us in the opposite direction. That's it. The road isn't bumpy. I don't know what Coyote was talking about. Chino and Marcelo sit on their backpacks with their backs to the front cabin. Legs spread. Their hands on their knees, cigarettes in their mouths. Their eyes look into the darkness of the road behind us. They look past Patricia and Carla on the right side of the truck bed. Past Chele and me on the left side. Chele doesn't smoke. He looks at the dark behind Carla's head. I look up and remember Scorpio, the constellation Mali and I knew by heart because of the stinger, "like a fishhook."

But I can't find it. I listen to the wind. The tires on the road. The occasional rock that gets kicked into the wheels. The coyotes or polleros up front don't talk. They don't even listen to music. It's quiet except for the breeze blowing past us. I put my hand out to feel the cold and high-five the wind. Then I see how strong it is by putting my palm flat facing up, then flat facing down. No one tells me anything. Mali got scared when I did this from the bus window. "¡A car might come and cut your hand off!" It never happened.

There's no one here. The back of the truck feels empty without all those people from the boats.

5-25-99

WE WAKE IN A house at the very edge of town—smaller than any town we've seen, smaller than Ocós *and* La Herradura. When we got here, the polleros told us where to sleep. There are three rooms.

Carla, Patricia, and I passed out in a bed, but this time Chino slept on the floor next to us, because Patricia said, "We don't know the other men in the house."

"Over there"—Coyote taps Patricia on the shoulder—"that's La Línea." He looks at Carla and me as he points at the bushes past the dirt road outside the kitchen window. Coyote looks sharp and smells good because he showered and hasn't put on cologne yet.

"¿That's La USA?" I ask, just to make sure.

"Sí, morrillo. Over there." He points at the endless bushes. "Way over there are your parents."

"¿There is no fence?"

"Not here. In Nogales you can see it," Coyote tells us. I don't know what I was expecting, but it wasn't this: there's nothing around. Just yellow-red dirt. Rocks. Some cactuses. A lot of bushes. Dogs barking. Roosters crowing.

"When you morros leave, you'll take that same pickup truck from last night and drive faaaarrr, all the way over there." He points even farther in the distance, a line where the sky meets the horizon. "And you'll walk and walk and walk."

I don't think there's gonna be hills like Mali says Mom had to cross. It looks flat. No green hills like *Born in East L.A.,* and no giant steel fence to jump. ¿Where are we? This isn't Tijuana like Don Dago promised. I thought my parents were going to be right over the fence waiting for me in their car after I jumped it. But there's no fence and no asphalt road with a McDonald's parking lot on the other side. There's nothing. ¡Not even big trees! Just cactuses and bushes.

"All of you have to rest," Coyote continues. "It's a long walk. You have to be ready."

"¿When?" Patricia asks.

"¿When what?"

"¿Are we leaving?"

"La pura neta, I don't know. Two, three days." Coyote grabs a chair from the dining table in the kitchen. "¿Maybe more? I'm not in charge anymore."

It's cold here. The tiled floor doesn't help. The two polleros who picked us up on the trucks gave us huge thick blankets when we got here. One blanket per person, but I still wore my chamarra to sleep.

"¿You hungry?" an older woman asks as she walks out of the fourth room. We were split into four rooms: our room, the men's room, the coyote/pollero room, and hers.

"Buenos días, doña, and yes we are," Coyote responds as we nod.

"I'll make chilaquiles and beans," she says quickly as she walks directly to the refrigerator.

"Órale," Coyote says.

"Buenos días, señora," Patricia says, and we follow.

"Buenos." The woman says without introducing herself. We don't introduce ourselves. She opens cans, grabs things from the refrigerator. She's old, but not older than Abuelita. Her slick black hair is up in a bun. I don't know what chilaquiles are. I hope they're good and not like the food in Guadalajara. Patricia and Coyote try to talk to the woman, but she's concentrating, gives one-word responses, so they stop trying.

The polleros come out of their rooms first. Then the men. I don't think any of them have showered. We haven't either. Only Coyote and La Señora look sharp. She already has her makeup on. When everyone is here, she starts laying down paper plates filled with what looks like cut-up tortillas in red sauce.

I bite down, and they're *really* good. The sauce isn't spicy. What is spicy, but I don't try, is the dried red chile Coyote crushes in a weird wooden thing.

"I miss these," Coyote says while he crushes the tiny red chile balls, and I don't know if he means the chile or the wooden thing. "Originally from Sonora, ¿no?" he asks as he taps the shoulder of one of the polleros sitting next to him.

"Ey," the pollero says, nodding up and down, chilaquiles in his mouth.

"Take some back. Our neighbor grows them," the woman tells Coyote, who nods.

"¿What is it, maitro?" Marcelo asks, reaching for the weird wooden contraption Coyote holds in his hands.

"Chiltepín grinder," the other pollero says, both their accents different from Coyote's. More singsong. Not like the Mexicans in novelas. Different.

"¿Chilte-qué?"

"Chil-te-pín," Pollero #2 tells Marcelo. "It's the name of the chile. The wooden grinder is so you don't touch your dick with the same hand."

He's funny. At night, I couldn't tell them apart. Still can't. They're both light-skinned, skinny, clean-shaven, and around the same age—older than anyone in The Six, but younger than Coyote.

"Look." Coyote takes the wooden thing. "Like this." He looks at Marcelo, placing a whole chiltepín on top of the wooden tool. There's a deep bowl on top of it. "Place it in here and crush with this." The stick breaks the chile into small pieces that look like salt. "Then sprinkle." Coyote takes the contraption and dumps it on his food.

"Órale," Marcelo says. I don't know if he's making fun or trying to blend in. He likes spicy food like Grandpa. All of us watch his reaction. He takes a bite of his chilaquiles with chiltepín on top. His face lights up. "Vieja, this shit is good."

"No jodás," Chino says. "Give me that." Then Chino starts crushing the chiltepín. Takes a bite. His face turns red, but he keeps eating. "Cosa seria," he says with his thumbs up. None of the rest of The Six tries it.

"Están chiflados," Patricia tells the men.

La Señora hasn't said anything. Hasn't told anyone her name. Coyote and the polleros call her Doña. She's still cooking, and occasionally asks if anyone wants more. I think this is her house. There are four rooms, but only La Doña slept in a room by herself. Chino kept us up. He didn't say anything when he was awake, but when he was sleeping . . . he's the one who gasps so loud, sometimes his lips flap and it sounds like a fart.

"Look," Coyote says when he's almost done with breakfast, "I leave today, but here, you're in good hands." He taps the polleros, who sit next to each other. "I've been doing business with them for years and never a problem. Never." He pauses. "They will get you there fast. Quick." Then he taps the shoulder of the one sitting next to him and says, "Tell them, Mario."

Mario is Pollero #1. His hair is brown. The other pollero's is black. And Mario's nose is skinnier and pointier than Pollero #2. "Bueno, right now, the plan is this: we walk a few hours at night, and our compas on the other side will pick us up in a van by morning and take us to Tucson." I'm distracted by the way Mario sings when he speaks, every other word like it's hard for him to get out of his mouth. I like how it sounds.

"We know the desert," Pollero #2 says. "My name is Paco, and you don't have to worry. We're from here. We've done this for years. Always safe."

Coyote looks at us. "¿Any questions?"

"¿How far are we walking?" Patricia asks. Coyote looks at Mario and Paco, waiting for them to answer.

"I don't know exactly, but I'd say like eight to ten kilometers. Fifteen max," Mario says.

"¡Fifteen! ¿Don't you see the kids? ¡¿How the fuck you expect them to walk that far?!" Patricia says, loud, pointing at Carla and me, her face wrinkling, reddening, the maddest I've seen her.

"Calm down, lady. I know. I know. We take kids *all* the time, and they make it. It's flat and easy. I've taken this route hundreds of times," Mario says in a softer voice that seems to calm Patricia, because she takes a huge breath before she says anything else.

"We've taken kids younger than them," Paco adds.

"¿Through the *desert*?" Patricia asks.

"Yes, but at night," Mario says.

"Makes a difference. It's why you got chamarras," Paco clarifies.

"¡¿Kids, in the desert, at night?!" Patricia raises her voice again.

Mario looks at Coyote, so he answers. "Pati, they do this all the time. They're the best."

"We *do,* señora," Mario says. "We're not walking long. One night. Then, the van. ¡Zás!" He moves his hands fast.

"We carry water, food," Paco adds. "What we need *you* to do is rest, so you're strong."

"¿Why at night?" Chele bumps in.

"Not as hot, and because of gabachos."

"¿Gabachos?"

I've never heard that word.

"Gringos, americanos, whites," Mario answers.

"So La Migra doesn't see," Paco clarifies.

La Migra. I know they're the bad gringos Mom and Dad and Mali talked about. ¿They're also called gabachos? But in the movies gringos are nice. The adults keep saying "desert," but a desert has sand like in *Aladdin.* There's quicksand and pyramids. No trees or cactuses or bushes. Walking at night doesn't sound too bad. It's not as hot. Easier than jumping a fence and climbing a hill.

"¿And after we cross?" Chino asks. "¿What's next?"

"We have other vans to take you wherever you need to go. There will be more people. It's not just you."

¡¿More people?! I didn't know that.

"¿And if we get caught?" Marcelo asks, crossing his arms.

"Won't happen," Paco says quickly.

"¿If it does, what's the plan?" Patricia pushes harder.

"If you get caught, but I know you won't—you have a number," Paco says.

"Someone in our network, our people, will pick you up wherever you get dropped off by La Migra and get you across," Mario adds. "You already paid for two tries."

"After that, it's not our responsibility. Your pedo," Paco says.

"¿What you mean?" Marcelo asks.

"That's *your* bad luck."

"But that never happens, and these guys"—Coyote points at Paco and Mario—"will say more when they know more. Right now, save your energy. This is the safest route right now."

"¿Who wants more food?" asks Doña, who's been listening to everything.

I raise my hand.

"Don't eat too much. You won't walk fast," Coyote says, ¿jokingly? Everyone laughs. I don't like it when the adults laugh at me.

"I'm kidding, morrito. Don't cry."

"I'm not crying," I say, mad.

"No, no. You *need* to eat," Paco says, staring at me. "You need to be strong. You too." Paco looks over at Carla while flexing his muscles.

"Sí, vos, eat more, Javier. More, Doña, please," Chino says, pointing at his plate. Patricia also gets more for her and Carla.

The chilaquiles are good. They almost taste like the enchiladas from El Mercado in La Herradura. The salsa on top, the crumbled cheese, are very similar. Except chilaquiles have scrambled eggs in them, but our enchiladas have boiled egg slices, sliced tomato, beets, and cucumber. I take a bite and almost forget the adults laughed. I don't like Coyote. I'm glad he's leaving. Paco and Mario are nicer. I trust them. They will get me to my parents. Fast and safe. I eat to be strong. To run fast. To walk far. But not that far. ¡I could see my parents as soon as three days from now! I haven't talked to them in weeks. I haven't talked to my grandparents in weeks. I hope they're not worried. Our third and final country is right there. La USA. The EE.UU. Gringolandia. The country of the movies, popcorn, pizza for school lunches, snowball fights, swimming pools, Toys "R" Us, and McDonald's. La Línea is right there.

CHAPTER SEVEN

———

La USA

MAY 29, 1999

I T's SATURDAY. TODAY WE LEAVE. COYOTE LEFT OUR FIRST DAY HERE, the twenty-fifth, a Tuesday. Said, "Good luck," and hugged Patricia, Carla, and me. Shook the men's hands. Since Coyote left, we've been eating Doña's cooking twice a day: late breakfast and early dinner. If we're hungrier, we have sandwich stuff, like we did in Guadalajara. This is the best we've eaten. Chilaquiles, carne con chile, tacos de carne, Mexican quesadillas, huevos rancheros, tacos de papa. I love the big flour tortillas. Doña pours a little lime on them. I'll miss her even though she doesn't talk. All she tells us is "Eat, get strong, sleep." And when she's cooking she asks, "¿Do you want more?" That's it.

"It's better not knowing you," she tells Patricia when Patricia gets frustrated. "It's for my own good," she adds.

"She hosts lots of people. Before you and after you," Paco explains. "She's not the only one in town. Other people in other houses will come with us."

The desert is cold at night, and it's cold in the mornings. Hot in between. Polleros tell us to sleep during the day so we get used to it, because "we're walking only in the dark." But it's hard to change; we still sleep at night. We haven't been watching TV, but yesterday it was the first leg of the semifinals. Because of all the buses and towns, I forgot about the tournament. My team, Atlas, beat Cruz Azul, but no one cared. The men don't bet. Mario and Paco like a player named Jared Borgetti because he's from the north of México like they are, but they won't watch Santos play Toluca later today.

Here, we can walk outside, look out the window. We don't have to hide from the neighbors. The men smoke out front or in the back-yard, no problem. The problem is when they smoke inside, Doña kicks them out and says she won't serve them food—but she always does. The houses across the street and the ones next to ours look empty, but we hear dogs and roosters. They're always barking or crowing. Mario said the air carries sounds farther in the desert. Told us when we walk, we can't talk. If we need to talk, we must whisper. The barks are loud. Both polleros tell us that if we get caught, we must say we're from Nogales, Sonora. That we're Mexican. Never Salvadoran. They give each of us another set of fake papers that prove we're from Nogales. Chino and Patricia are officially fake married. Paco said this was better. I hope people believe it, because he's nine-teen, but does look older. Patricia is twenty-seven, but looks younger. I think it works. I'm officially their child. Carla is still my sister—who's not speaking to anyone besides her mother.

"Just in case," Mario said as he handed us our new fake papers. I'm happy I have an excuse to hold Chino's hand in public. Now we're a little fake family of four. It already felt like that. Especially since Chino slept on the floor next to our bed. Marcelo is even more dis-tant from me. He was nicer in Guadalajara, but since the buses north, he keeps his distance. Smokes even more and doesn't say anything. And Chele is being Chele, despistado, in his own world.

We're from *Nogales*. The name reminds me of nuégados en miel. I don't know anything about Nogales. We were there less than ten minutes. Guadalajara has soccer teams, Chente, and tequila. Nogales was hilly and I saw the bus terminal, that's it. We're somewhere near Nogales, somewhere full of rocks, cactuses, roosters, and dogs.

Before the soccer game yesterday, Mario had to pick up tortillas and other things from the town's store so Doña could cook. He asked

Carla and me if we wanted to see the town. Carla didn't. Chino came with me. We rode in the back. There aren't big trees with full leaves here, just small bushes and skinny trees with thin tiny leaves. The dirt roads are full of rocks that turn the road into a roller coaster.

"Today we walk long," Mario says around the table during breakfast. "Paco and I will get you food and water. Shower. Rest. Sleep. You won't sleep tonight, we're walking till sunrise."

¿Sunrise? That's longer than the walk in Oaxaca, and my feet hurt after *that*. I need my good shoes, but I'm nervous to ask for help. My Velcro shoes stink and aren't as comfortable as the lace-up ones. I can't walk to La USA smelling bad. The adults are nervous. Patricia massages one hand with the other, switching as she listens. Chino's right knee shakes up and down as he sits. Chele looks dazed. Marcelo looks the same, doesn't speak, and occasionally rubs his head. Carla looks at her mom and tries to hold Patricia's hands so she will stop rubbing them.

"Wear dark colors. Eat. It's gonna be cold," Paco tells us in the kitchen.

"You three smokers, get it all out now, you can't smoke on the walk," Mario tells the men.

Chele breaks from his stare and nods. The other two make a face like they don't understand.

"The light. You don't want to stand out at night," Mario follows up. Then the polleros leave to get us the things we need and get what *they* need to walk with us.

Doña feeds us well. I'm so full, the news that we're leaving makes me nauseous. We're leaving México. Vilma Palma pops in my head. There's no tape player here. I want to listen to that song. *Déjame, déjame que te toque la piel* . . . I want to hug anyone like Coyote hugged us for good luck. It was the first hug I've gotten in a while. He squeezed me, and the rest of the day I smelled like him. Maybe that's why he wears so much cologne. I like that song best. And the title is in English: "Bye Bye." Everything else is in Spanish. I know that means adiós, salú, hasta luego. I'm finally gonna meet Dad. ¿Is he tall? ¿Short? ¿Is he gonna speak English?

When they finish eating, the men go out and smoke. They have one pack of cigarettes left. Patricia and Carla head to the bathroom to shower. I'm in bed looking out the window. It gets hotter and hotter until the bats show up at dusk. Bats smaller than the ones in El Salvador, but just as noisy. They bring the beginning of the cold. The dogs in the morning bark the cold away. Bats and dogs. Rocks and cactuses. Bushes and skinny trees that look like they're taking their last breaths. Doña doesn't speak, but she makes so much noise when she cleans up and puts everything away. It's hard to sleep. I have a knot in my stomach. Patricia and Carla return and we lie in bed motionless, even though we're all awake.

WE WAIT FOR PACO and Mario, dressed in dark colors, our chamarras wrapped around our waists. I'm wearing my black Animaniacs T-shirt with English on it in case a gringo sees me. It's hot and dry outside, hot and dry inside, so I go out to the backyard. I like it under the sun because everything has a fever: the rocks, the shrubs, the air, our shoes, our clothes, our tongues. But no one sweats.

The men wear a shield of cigarette smoke around them. I pretend to inspect the big cactus for red spikey fruits. The cactus is almost taller than the wall. Marcelo goes back inside. Chele and Chino remain. This is my chance. If not, I'll have to knot the shoelaces and cut them like Mali did before I was comfortable asking the nuns for help.

"Chino, come." I get him away from Chele.

"¿Qué onda?"

"¿Can you help me tie my shoes, please?"

"Sí, vos," Chino says. "¿Right now?"

I nod. Chele is looking at us.

"Va pues, go get them."

I run to the front door where all our backpacks wait, lined up in a row, for the polleros to return. I dig in my backpack for the shoes Mali wrapped in a plastic bag. They look brand-new. I've only worn them a few times. They're comfortable *and* tough. Almost like boots, but not high enough. Mom sent them for Christmas inside a box with a picture of a cute, white-and-light-brown dog with huge ears.

I zip my backpack, run outside, and drop the boots on the dirt.

"Va, take those off," Chino says, and I take my right foot out of my Velcro shoes. Chele looks at us, lighting another cigarette. His cheeks are red and full of acne that has gotten worse as the weeks have gone by. Chino has a lot more acne también.

"Puta, this heat fucking sucks," Chele says, walking over.

"Simón," Chino responds, tying my right shoe. Knotting it once. Twice. He has big pink acne-volcanoes on his forehead, just below his spikey hair he hasn't cut since Tecún. He looks up at me. "¿Like that? ¿Or another knot?"

"Another one." Three knots is definitely enough.

He taps my shoe, checks that it's comfortable.

I move my toes around. "Good."

"Va, other foot."

I take my left foot out and put it in the new left shoe. He does the same and taps after the third knot.

Chele leans over to look at the knots. "¡No jodás! He won't be able to take them off."

"Not even La Migra," Chino says, and they both laugh.

La Migra, that term again. "¿Who are they?" I ask only to make sure I know it's the bad gringos.

"¿La Migra?" Chino asks.

"¿You don't know, cipotillo?"

I shake my head.

"La Migra are mean gringos, hijueputas like the bad Mexicans that dragged us out of the bus," Chino says, standing up from the ground.

"Assholes," Chele adds.

Chino reaches for another cigarette. "But they won't catch us," he says, putting the cigarette in his mouth. "With these polleros, nah, they'll never catch us."

"Cabal," Chele says. "We have to be like the Road Runner."

"Like cops and robbers," Chino says.

I never thought of the Road Runner and Wile E. Coyote as cops and robbers.

"Vergón. Así merito." Chele nods his head. "We have to be faster."

I nod at everything. It makes sense. If we beat La Migra, I see my parents.

"But if they catch us, no nos ahuevamos, we try again," Chele adds.

"And again, until we fucking make it," Chino says.

I haven't thought about what happens if we get caught. I don't want to get caught. I'm good at hiding. I'm good at cops and robbers, I'm good at tag.

"It's why we're from Nogales," Chino says in his bad Mexican accent. "Mexicanos, órale, compadre."

"Mexicanos al grito de guerra," Chele play-sings the national anthem.

They're making me nervous. I don't want to get caught. I don't want bad thoughts.

"Walk around, morrito," Chino says, keeping his Mexican accent.

I stomp from one rock to another, until I get to the cactus with fruit. My feet feel good in these shoes.

"Va, bien pimp-it-is-nice esos caites," Chele says. It's what Grandpa says.

"Órale, let's rest." Chino puts his cigarette out and starts walking inside. We follow him. Patricia and Carla are in the bedroom. Doña and Marcelo sit around the kitchen table. We join Doña and Marcelo.

"Mario and Paco will be here soon," Doña says. "Pray, encomiéndensen a Dios. He will help you." She sounds like the nuns. But the men listen. They cross themselves. Then we sit in silence until Patricia comes out and tells me to go to the room.

"Pray like you've never prayed," she says once we're in the room.

I kneel on one side, Carla on the other side of her mom. I start by asking Cadejo to be with us. To protect us. I keep praying and praying, and Patricia doesn't get up. So I keep going. I press my hands hard, they get coated in sweat. Patricia's lips move loudly. I catch a word here and there. Makes me recite a Padre Nuestro.

Finally, she gets up. I haven't seen her cry like this. So much pink around her light-brown eyes. Carla hugs her.

"Está bien, Carlita," Patricia says. "Vos también, todo está bien," she tells me, and she hugs both of us. "God will protect us."

WE HEAR A TRUCK rattle down the street, then park out front.

"It's them," Patricia says, "gracias a Dios." I've never heard her say God's name so much. The men get up and put their backpacks on as Paco opens the passenger door.

"¡Come help!" he yells.

The men put their bags down and help carry plastic jug after plastic jug of water from the back of the truck. Mario drops a box of canned tuna in the living room. "Stuff these in your backpacks," he says, handing each of us two cans. Then he hands an entire loaf of Bimbo bread to Marcelo and another to Patricia. "Split these."

"Adults, one jug. You two, try to carry two," Mario tells Chino and Patricia, "for los morros."

Paco takes a thick roll of duct tape and starts making handles for the water so the adults can carry them easier. I pick up a jug just to try—it's heavy. "You carry these." Paco hands Carla and me smaller plastic bottles with a duct-tape sling.

"Drink from these two. Hydrate," he tells everyone as he passes two untaped jugs around. Everyone is moving. Backpacks open and close.

"Drink more," Mario says.

Even Doña joins in. "Drink."

As we drink, Paco looks around and says, "I'm not coming with you, but I'm driving you to where you're starting."

"He's taking us to the main pollero, who will be there with more people. We know him. We're in good hands," Mario explains. "Go to the bathroom. Take a shit. Piss. Because we're driving an hour, and then we wait for everyone to get there. And when we start walking, we won't stop."

The water, the instructions, everything makes it real. It's happening. I think of the boats. I was fine not pooping then. ¿What if I'm not fine this time?

"¡Come on! Use the bathroom," Mario says, clapping his hands. Patricia gets up and pulls Carla and me. The men let us use the bathroom first.

I can't go on command. My stomach growls even though I'm full. "Go first," I tell Carla.

She gets out fast. When it's my turn, I sit on the toilet until Patricia checks if I'm ok.

"I can't go," I tell her.

"Try to pee. Pee everything."

I do my best until nothing more comes out.

Then it's the men's turn. After twenty minutes, Mario yells, "¡To the trucks!"

Doña doesn't hug anyone but makes a cross on my and Carla's foreheads. "Vayan con Dios," she says as she kisses her hand before and after she makes a cross. She leans closer to Patricia and says, "The path is spiny and slippery like a nopal, but you'll make it."

"Gracias." Patricia nods.

When the door slams behind us, dogs bark, roosters crow—the sounds we've heard for almost five days. It's like they're saying goodbye. Chino helps me up into the truck. The metal in its bed is still hot.

"¡Adiós, Doña!" Mario yells.

"¡See you soon!" says Paco, who is driving, with his hand out the window.

The engine rattles, and we feel each of the rocks against our butts. The sunset and a cloud of dust behind us. The sky a bucket of water poured on the sun. The air is still hot. Bats don't show up just yet. The barks and crows get softer and softer until we can't hear them.

"It's finally happening," Chino says.

"Con todo a los Yunaited Estais," Marcelo adds, and it's the first thing I've heard him say in a while. He sits next to me and leans closer, puts his arm around my back and gets close to my ear.

"Chepito, I talked with Chino." He points at Chino, who's across from us and who winks at me. "He's gonna be next to you when we walk. Mario said it's best that way."

I nod and don't say anything. Chino puts his thumb out. ¿They talked about this?

"We're walking in pairs. Chino con vos. Pati con Carla. Yo y Chele." Marcelo says this to me, but louder so Patricia can hear.

"¿Is that what Mario said?" Patricia asks.

"Ajá," Chele answers.

"Sí, Pati," Chino says. "Vos y Carla up front behind the polleros, Javiercito y yo in the middle, and Marcelo y Chele behind us."

"Va," Patricia says.

There's nothing around. Just bush after small bush, small cactuses that look purple. More bushes. We drive toward where the moon should be, but we can't see it over the hills.

"¿Where's the moon?" I ask Marcelo.

"I don't know, but it's full."

"N'hombre, that's tomorrow," Patricia says. "I saw it in Donã's calendar."

¡Almost full moon! That's a good sign. Cadejo, the moon, will be big.

EVEN WITH THE CHAMARRAS ON, the breeze seeps into our skin. There's a checkpoint on the two-lane highway, but this time soldiers wave us off and we drive past their machine guns. We drive fifteen or twenty more minutes until there's an empty patch of dirt next to the asphalt. We drive up the bumpy dirt road for a few minutes.

The sun peeks above the hills, but it's almost gone below the horizon, painting everything bright red, deep orange, pink, lavender. It's like all of the dust behind our truck flew to the sky. With the sunset, the dirt road turns a bright orange for a few minutes. Then there's an opening. A clearing without any bushes. The ground redder and redder, brilliant, almost like blood. Ripped plastic bags, empty tin cans, pieces of shirts, single socks, plastic water bottles, litter the ground. Some are stuck in the bushes. People sit with their butts on the bright-red dirt, or under bushes. Others lie down, sleeping with their caps on their faces.

"¡We're here!" Mario shouts, banging on the roof of the truck's cabin. Paco parks and Mario gets out. "Here," he repeats with a ciga-rette in his mouth.

Chino jumps out and stretches his arms that, even through his thick brown chamarra, look thinner than all of ours. I notice he's wearing a silver ring on his left hand. I don't say anything and fall into his arms like a raindrop. Marcelo helps Patricia, who struggles with the position of the one-gallon water jug dangling across her chest, hanging by the duct-tape sling. Carla holds Chele's hand for balance as she jumps from the truck ledge onto the dirt.

We're ready. Patricia holds my hand and Carla's, the jug now to her left next to her rib cage.

Mario leans into the truck's open passenger window, tells Paco something I can't hear, and taps the door. Paco drives off, yelling, "¡Good luck!," his hand waving out the window.

Carla and I wave. The adults don't. Mario throws his cigarette on the red ground. "We can smoke until we leave. Follow me," he says, and starts walking.

We follow him toward a bush that doesn't have trash or anyone near it. None of the strangers speak to us. The bushes are bright green briefly, then change to darker greens. The sky above turns the color of rocks, then darker and darker blue. Over where the sun was, the horizon is red, deep orange, and yellow. The ground quickly changes from the color of my skin to blood to mud to gray. The air smells like sawdust mixed with water.

"Wait here, eat if you're hungry, I'll get the pollero," Mario says, his cap turned backward. It's the first time we see him wear it like this, and it's weird to hear him call someone else a pollero. All of us sit on the ground like other people are doing. Chele takes his backpack off and uses it as a pillow to lie down faceup.

"Usshh, vos, está chuco allí," Patricia tells him.

"¿So what?" Chele says, grinning with his thick white teeth. Then he takes a cigarette and lights it. I've never seen anyone smoke lying down. Marcelo and Chino follow. Chino makes rings. Marcelo doesn't, both his hands on top of his knees, staring out at the road we came from.

"¿Did you cross here?" Chino breaks the silence. Marcelo is the only one who's done this before. But even he's quieter than usual.

"No. Through the hills outside Tijuana."

The ground is warmer than the air, the rocks stuck in the ground even warmer than the dirt. Different types of birds sing, but there's a particular one that sounds like a person whistling. *Whuiiiitt-whuiiiitt. Whuiiiitt-whuiiiitt.* Everything is losing color, I can't see where the noise is coming from. Another *whuiiiitt-whuiiiitt. Whuiiiitt-whuiiiitt,* from another bush. It's the only noise around. People stare at the ground, the bushes, the sky. Then the birds stop. Birds that look like doves fly above us.

"They're going to sleep," a stranger says. He sounds like Jesús. Small brown bats take over, making noises like keys hitting keys, or like zippers hitting metal. Some even flap around our faces, but they never fly into us.

The lack of light turns everything gray. It's colder; I have goose-bumps, but it might be from nerves. It's just after 7:30 P.M. The sun is gone, and the moon is rising over the opposite horizon, but it's not yellow yet. I didn't realize how many people were here. Trucks fuller than the one Mario brought us in drop more people off. Everyone wears dark colors and carries water.

"There he is." Chino points at a man who's walking next to Mario and who's slightly taller and skinnier than him. They both stop at a bush with red dots under it, which means people are smoking. Then their shadows stop at another bush. The man also wears a baseball cap but with the bill facing forward.

"Hola, morros," Mario says with his hands on his hips, looking at me and Carla, who sits between Patricia's legs.

"¿What's going on, maitro?" Marcelo asks.

"Nothing. Introductions. This is the guide," Mario says, grinning. We know he means the pollero. "El Mero Mero," he clarifies, pointing at the man next to him, then taps his back.

"Hola," Mero Mero says, touching his cap's bill. He doesn't have facial hair, which makes him look younger than Mario. He wears work boots that look too big under his skinny legs.

We nod, and I notice stars beginning to pop behind his head.

"We're waiting for people. When everyone is here, I'll say more. Por ahorita, rest. Drink small sips, save water," Mero Mero says.

We nod.

"Órale, we'll be back." They both walk away.

"Let's eat," Patricia says.

"Take the bread out," Chele tells her. "Vos también," he tells Marcelo, who carries their bread.

"¿You scared?" Chino asks me.

I nod.

"Don't be, hermanito, El Mero Mero is the real deal, se nota que es vergón."

"Ajá," I say. He hugs me. Besides the boat, this is the first time I'm in his chest again, and he called me hermanito. I can smell his cologne. His cigarettes. But through all the smells, *his* smell: dry dirt before it rains. His hug warms me. Makes me feel protected, like it's Mali, Grandpa, or Mom here with me.

Patricia opens her backpack, and the white on the Bimbo plastic wrapper looks brighter than anything. I point it out to her.

"Oh," she says, surprised.

"It's your eyes adjusting," Marcelo says matter-of-factly.

"Like the boats," Chele adds. "¿Remember?"

"Sí," I say. Carla smiles at me without showing her teeth. I'd forgotten some colors shine, but none shone this bright. The ocean was cloudy then. Here, it's stars and stars. Our plastic bottles look white white white. The dry grasses. Some rocks también.

More trucks arrive. We hear them rattling before we see them.

Some park facing us, and the lights hurt our eyes. In the beams, the dust like stars dancing around Carla's face. She looks worried and cold now that she's not between her mom's legs. Patricia's eyebrows point downward as she struggles to open a tuna can for us to share. People jump off the truck and walk toward us. The lights pull away and the truck drives off, making everything dark again. We taste the dust. The new people don't say anything, choose a bush, and stare off like everyone else.

Chino opens his tuna can, the smell thickens the air. "I'll share with you, Javier," he says, tapping my shoulder. I'm used to Patricia doing things for me. Not Chino. He's really acting like my fake-dad.

"Má." Chino hands me a piece of bread with tuna on top. The bread is white and easy to see in the dark, but the tuna looks like a shadow. "Eat."

I didn't like canned tuna before this trip. In El Salvador, it's another brand, but Tuny tuna con mayonesa is good.

"Comételo, and after, we'll eat these babosadas," Chino tells me as he pulls out a Snickers bar. I tried those in El Salvador, stole them from Abuelita's stand. They're so good. I smile with tuna between my teeth.

Mario comes back and slides down next to Marcelo and Chele.

"Here's the plan. Eat. But don't eat too much. We have to be ready to run," he says, loud enough for all of us to hear.

"¿Run?" Carla asks.

"In case we see La Migra."

I can't get the picture of bad gringos chasing us like in *Born in East L.A.* out of my head.

"¿Here?" Patricia asks.

"No no no. We're in México." He points with his hand farther into the bushes. "We walk an hour that way. Then it's Gabacholandia."

Patricia hugs Carla. I look at Chino, who thinks I don't understand. "Gringolandia," he says. "¿You cold?"

I shake my head. Mario hears him and says, "If you're cold, you'll get warm when we start walking. We'll try to walk as fast as the group can. Stay with your person." He looks around. "You two, you two, and you two." He points at the pairs: Chele-Marcelo. Chino-me. Patricia-Carla. "I'll be in front of you"—he points at Carla—"so don't fall behind."

Patricia mouths something.

"For now, rest, smoke, get up, stretch, talk. We're in México. No Migra yet." He pauses. "I'll see when Mero Mero is ready." He walks toward the only other figure standing up.

The ground is colder. I can feel it through my pants. I see bunnies running away, small shadows. I finish my bread and tuna.

"¿More?" Chino asks.

I want more, but I have to run, so I say no.

"Jodéte pues," Chino says as he serves himself another one. I wait as long as possible, but he's almost done with all of the tuna.

"Okay, a little more," I tell him. He laughs and serves me more. Mario walks back.

"¿How long?" Marcelo asks him.

"Not long, he's about to talk. Pack up."

Chino wraps the bread and stuffs it in his bag. "I'll carry yours," he tells Patricia. Everyone flings the cans as far into the night as possible.

"¡Gather around, gather around!" Mero Mero yells, shining a flashlight around all the bushes. "Come up," he says. Mario and other men stand up—four other shadows next to Mero Mero, who is the skinniest and the second tallest.

"Everyone is here, I'm your guide," he says in a booming voice. The bushes move, people get closer, others stand, but we're close enough we can stay on the ground. "I'm gonna go over some rules," Mero Mero says, and pauses. "There's about fifty of us."

"¡Puta! Un vergo," Chino whispers.

"Un chingo," Marcelo responds.

"So," Mero Mero continues, "that's why these four will help us stay in a line." He flashes his light at the four men next to him, one of whom is Mario. "I'm gonna be up front, and they will be scattered throughout the line. One in front of the other. They"—he points at the four men—"should have paired you with someone. You and that person look after each other. They stop, you stop. One of you gets hurt, the other gets help. If you don't have a partner, choose a person in your group. Make sure you know where that person is. At. All. Times.

"Follow the group in front of you. Look at their shoes. Follow their steps. We almost have a full moon—you should be able to *see* the person in front. Don't. Get. Lost. Whoever stays, stays. We. Will. Not. Wait for you. If you fall behind, stay in the line. If you get lost, it's *your* fault.

"This guy"—he points at one of the shadows—"will be at the very end, making sure no one stays. Look at his hat. Memorize it." He's wearing a hat that looks like a beanie with a cotton ball on top. "You shouldn't see this hat. If you do, walk faster.

"If we see La Migra or hear cars, we stop and hide. Pick the nearest bush and get flat on the ground. La Migra has binoculars that can see at night. Helicopters. When I whistle, and only when I whistle, like this"—he makes a high-pitched whistle by squishing his bottom lip together and pressing it up against the top lip—"only then, get up.

"Don't worry. I've done this twenty-five times. This is *my* route. If you listen, by tomorrow morning we'll be in Tucson. We're walking eight to ten hours max, depending how fast we walk, to a road where vans will pick us up. Again"—he clears his throat—"if you're thirsty, drink one or two gulps. Don't get too full. Don't leave the line. If you need to pee, hold it. We will stop every two hours. Or walk faster to the front, pee to the side, and fall back in the line. ¿Okay?

"If you have questions, ask your polleros. Take a piss. Shit. Pack everything. Anything bright on your clothes, cover it with tape. Any writing, anything shiny, cover it. No flashlights. I have one because if we get separated, I will whistle first and flash the light like this." He turns it on and off. On and off. "Twice. Then I'll count everyone.

"Last thing: if we get caught, you don't know me. You don't know your polleros. And you're Mexican. ¿Okay? Ten minutes."

The moment he stops talking, the polleros walk to their groups. People stand up, pack up, throw trash. It's the loudest we've been. Everyone talks in their normal voices.

"Get up," Mario tells us. "Let me see your clothes." All of us get up and dust ourselves. "Turn around," Mario tells each one of us, shining his flashlight at our clothes, like the other polleros do to others. "Here." He looks at a shiny line on Marcelo's backpack. "Cover it with this." He cuts a piece of black tape with his teeth. "You're fine," he says, shining the flashlight at our faces.

"¿You have a flashlight también?" Patricia asks Mario.

"Same thing: if we get scattered, look for my signal. I'll flash it three times quickly. Go to where I am. ¿Entienden?"

"Sí," everyone says.

"Oh, and take this," he tells me and Carla, handing us each a white pill that shines in the dark. It's like the ones on the boats, except smaller. We look at Chino and Patricia.

"Gives them energy, it's safe," Mario tells them.

"It's okay," Patricia says, and Chino nods.

I swallow it and it tastes weird, bitter.

"Now we wait. I'll be in front of you. We'll be closer to the front."

My legs are shaking. My stomach hurts like I'm hungry. My forehead throbs. Or maybe I'm cold.

"Todo va' estar bien," Chino tells me. "Eight hours is nothing, hermanito." He taps my backpack that suddenly feels heavier.

I don't say anything. Maybe he's right. Eight hours. The boats were longer. The buses. It's nothing.

"You'll see your parents soon."

I look at Patricia, who whispers something to Carla.

"Va. This is it, bicha," Chino tells Patricia. He's pumped up. Excited.

"Sí, vos, vamos con Diosito," she says, trying to fake a smile. "Todos." She looks over at Marcelo and Chele.

"Eso." Marcelo nods.

"Con todo," Chele says loudly.

Some people from the nearest bush get closer to us.

"¿Where are you guys from?" a man asks.

"México via El Salvador," Chele says, laughing. The man laughs. "We're from México via Ecuador, hermano," he says.

¿Ecuador? ¡That's far! Wayyyy farther than us. ¿Did he take a boat? We met people from South America on the boats.

"We're from Guate," someone else says.

"¿Quiubo?" Chele says. No one else from The Six says anything.

"¿Everyone ready?" Mero Mero asks.

"Sí," some people shout back in unison.

"¡Line up!" Mero Mero shouts. A line begins to form. We're about fifty people, Mero Mero said, but the double line looks longer. A huge centipede. Everyone carries water and a black backpack. We're near the front. I look behind at Marcelo, who is shoulder to shoulder with Chele.

"Ya casi, Chepito," he says, resting his hand on my backpack.

We're in a double line. A fat centipede, a snake. I check my watch and can barely see its hands, but the white background helps. It's closer to 8:15, the moon is just over the horizon. The ground is still dark gray. Some things in it shine like diamonds. ¿Rocks? I look at my shoes, make sure they're tied. Look at Chino, who's looking at Carla, who's looking at Patricia, who's looking at Mario, who's looking at someone else I don't know. I'm cold, but the chamarra feels good. I'm full, but my stomach feels empty.

"¡Let's go!" Mero Mero shouts from the front of the line, and people begin walking.

"Padre todopoderoso," Mario says, crossing himself. Some people shout. People behind us, the ones who talked to us, whisper a prayer.

"¡Échenle ganas! ¡Con huevos!" Mero Mero shouts again, and the line begins to change from two-and-two into a single-file line.

"Follow me," Chino says as he takes his steps faster than me. Marcelo takes his behind me. They protect me. Our steps sound like eating cereal. All of our steps on the ground. Crunch. Our clothes rustling. Crunch. I can hear people's water bottles sloshing. Some carry plastic bags, and they rustle louder than backpacks or clothes. The stars are out. I whisper for Cadejo and Diosito to help us get to Tucson soon.

MY BODY FEELS FUNNY. Ants crawl inside my head. My eyes want to pop out. My tummy growls. I have a lot of energy. My heart beats fast. I keep thinking of different things, random things, like Michael Jackson's video where the sidewalk lights up. If we could do that here, each of our steps would light up the dirt. ¿A rock? ¿A bush? ¿Dry grass? Lighting the entire line. We're a fat caterpillar. Even the occasional cactus would be lit. Thick cactuses every once in a while that are my height, sometimes taller.

"Watch out," Mario says when he spots one of them. "Big cactus, big thorns." I like how lonely these ones look. They're never near other cactuses. Thick and with lines going up their bodies full of thorns. Some bushes have thorns también. We can't see them, but we feel them. "Watch out," Mario says again when we walk past.

We've been walking for an hour. We crossed train tracks, my first ever. I want to see a train, but nothing. "In a bit, we're in Gringolandia," Mario says, loud like Mero Mero. "Now we have to be quiet. There's Migra. If you need something, touch me, or whisper."

The Six nod. No one says anything. We're walking faster. The landscape looks the exact same everywhere. I can't tell we're leaving México. ¿Where are the cities? ¿Where are the signs saying we're in a new country? This is my third new country: Guate, México, La USA. The air feels different. Colder. But it might just be the night.

We snake through gray dirt, grasses, and bushes. Sometimes trees. ¡Trees! Like giant people watching us. Trees with skinny trunks, skinny leaves. Sometimes the moon hits something and the ground sparkles with jewels. None of the adults stop to check to see if they're real. Carla neither. I want to stop to check, but we can't.

I spot the first plants that don't look like anything else we've seen thus far. They're not like the bushes, trees, grass, and the lonely cactuses I like. These plants are tall. Taller than Marcelo. Taller than all of us. They don't really look like cactuses. Maybe they're not. Their silhouettes look like flores de izote because of their spikey leaves, but taller. Like big pineapples on a spike, but with a long skinny branch jutting up from the leaves. Sometimes they bend sideways at the top, making them look like they're bursting. Like party poppers. I like them. *Spikeys* I call them. There's the *Lonelies* and the *Spikeys*. The Spikeys always have friends. We walk through a party of them.

"Careful," Chino whispers to me when we walk through a group of Spikeys. I hear other people say the same thing in front of us. Mero Mero told us he would whisper messages down when we needed to stop. ¿How's Abuelita? I bet she's praying for me. She's always praying, morning and night. I'd hear her from my and Mali's room. Mali would like it here. There are so many stars, but no Scorpio. Grandpa wouldn't like that I still can't point out the North Star.

Twigs on the ground now mix with the crunch of the grasses and the sparkly things in the dirt. When we walk through a lot of bushes, their thorns get stuck to my chamarra, but the fabric's thickness protects me. Same with my pants. Mostly, I grab my backpack's straps. When that gets tiring, I rest my hands next to my waist. When we go through bushes I keep my hands in front of my chest in case a twig or branch is flicked at me by Chino, but he tries his best not to do that. I already got cut by thorns, but it doesn't hurt much. None of them get stuck inside my skin. Sometimes I pluck a tiny leaf from a thornless bush and crush it in my hands, then smell my fingers. It smells like dust mixed with a bit of dry soccer-field grass. But mostly dust. Everything smells like dust.

I watch the back of Chino's shoes. I don't know what color his soles are during the day, but they're brighter, a light gray now that the moon keeps rising. Everything is grayish blue. The moon is our flashlight just like it was when it peeked through the clouds inside the boats. It shows us the rocks we must avoid. Even the plastic bags some people carry look whiter. The water bottles like lanterns in people's hands. Chino has a jug on a sling and another in his hand. I can see him switching it from one hand to the other. Behind me, Marcelo does the same. I can't see Chele.

"¿Thirsty?" Chino whispers before he takes a sip. I like the sound of the plastic cap. *Pop.* Chino brings the jug to his lips as he walks, doesn't spill, then lets out an *ahhhh* after the cold sip.

Don't drink too much in case we have to run flashes through my head. It's what Mero Mero said. My tongue feels dry, I think I'm thirsty all the time, but I said no the first two times Chino asked if I wanted water.

After Chino's third sip, he makes me drink. I carry a small water bottle I keep in my backpack. I don't take it out. Chino passes his jug to me. It's heavy. I struggle to walk and bring it to my lips.

"Drink so you don't get tired."

I keep trying to lift it without stopping the line. Chino can't see me struggle.

"Tiny sips," Marcelo tells me from behind, making sure I don't fall behind, holding the jug up so I bring it to my lips.

The water is refreshing, cold, like it's been in the fridge. Gives me energy. I can't see Patricia or Mario. I can see Carla whenever Chino walks sideways to avoid a rock. Unless Patricia or Mario do that, I can't see them fully. Just bodies, shadows without faces. All the way up front is Mero Mero, but I can't see him. Behind me, more shadows. It feels like I'm only here with Marcelo and Chino. Between them, I feel safe.

Mario made sure we were in the middle. "It's the safest place," he said back at the bushes where the truck dropped us off. My legs aren't tired. We keep moving. The ground changes. Harder and less like sand, it's easier to walk on. I try not to think about it. And then, one by one, the sound of people's steps slow down.

"Pará, pará," Chino whispers. He stops, freezes in place. I stop. Marcelo. Chele.

No one says anything. A message gets passed down.

"Bathroom break," Chino tells Marcelo, who says the same thing behind him.

Then, more whispers from both sides of the line.

"Sit down."

"Sit."

"Sit down."

"Down."

"Sentate, Javier," Chino says, dropping his butt on the dirt.

Marcelo pees near a bush. We're in a ditch. Maybe it's why we stopped here; La Migra can't see us. I don't have to pee. I get up and try, but nothing comes out. I sit back down next to Chino and Marcelo. Patricia and Carla are in the bushes, peeing. Chele también. Shadows squat, and their underwear glows white. I drink more water even though I just drank. When I put Chino's water jug to my lips again, I notice my heart is racing. The stars move like we're still walking. My legs tingle. We were walking fast. I catch my breath. There's no breeze, but I'm cold. My skin like it's been dipped in cold water.

"¿Tired?" Marcelo asks me. He's sitting on the ground, legs spread out, hands on his knees like he was when the truck dropped us off.

"No."

"Eso es todo, veteranito," he says, giving me a thumbs-up. "If you need help with the backpack tell me." He's never asked to hold my bag or helped me drink water, not even in the boats.

"It's okay." My backpack doesn't feel heavy.

"Va pues," he responds. "You're a real machito." I like that. Grandpa would be proud.

Finally, I can look for those shiny things in the ground. Chele comes back. Patricia and Carla sit in front of Chino. I dig a handful of dirt and hold it up so the moon shines on it. It's nothing but twigs and dirt. I dig another handful. There are small flakes and more twigs. ¡They're like sparkles! Like plastic or confetti. Then Mario comes and checks on all of us.

"¿Everyone feel okay? ¿Everything okay?" he asks each member of The Six. We nod or say yes.

"¡Padre! Two more pee breaks, and we're there." He's excited. "Drink water, everything's going to plan."

"¿How's Gringolandia? ¿You like it, morrito?" he asks me.

"¡Sí, señor! It's pretty."

Everyone laughs. I can't see Carla's face, but she's looking over at me. Patricia's arms around her.

"If this is pretty, ¿what's ugly, bicho?" Patricia says under her breath. Then there's a faint whistle. ¿Cadejo?

People whisper: "Up."

"Up, up."

It's Mero Mero's call. But he said it was for after La Migra. I look at Chino and Marcelo. No one is worried. There's no flash of Mero Mero's flashlight. People dust themselves. One by one, we stand. I dust myself. Look at the pinholes in the sky's dark blanket. Stars twinkling. ¿Why do they blink like that? ¿Can they see the dirt under our feet? Like old newspapers. Crinkle. Crunch. Like walking on eggshells. Crack. The gallons of water in people's hands. Slosh. We're walking again.

Mice or bunnies sometimes cross our paths. Bats overhead. If I see them, I say they're my pets. I do the same with the strangers: we're all a family. Dad in front of me. Mom and Sister in front of him. The Six are my immediate family. I have so many faceless cousins, uncles, and aunts. Uncle #22 drifts off to the side to take a piss in the bushes. Aunt #6 steps to the side to take a sip of water. We push forward like a snake.

Then, minutes after our break, ¡a fence!

Not *the* fence like in movies but a cerco like the one back home separating our land from the neighbor's. I crawled under those wire fences to chase iguanas. Helped Grandpa repair them to keep the stray dogs out. A barbwire fence there. A barbwire fence here. Everyone spreads out, and we line up to get through the fence. The polleros have thick gloves to pull the sharp wires up from the ground so people can crawl under.

"Jump or crawl," the polleros say in their singsong northern accents.

Another pollero opens another section in the fence, next to this one. Chele and Marcelo follow him.

"Go go go," the polleros say in their normal voices. "Facedown, belly flat."

"Take your backpack off," Mario tells Patricia in front of us, but she's already on the ground. "¡Take it off!"

"¡Help! ¡Help me!" The fence is stuck to Patricia's backpack. "Don't leave me."

"We won't leave you," Chino loudly whispers. "Calmáte."

When Patricia moves, the fence moves. She looks like a lizard pinned down by a stick, trying to run away. Arms and legs up and down, but she's not going anywhere.

"¡Mamá! Cálmese," Carla almost screams. Chino grabs Carla so she won't touch the fence.

"No te movás," Chino whispers.

"¡Stop! Stop moving," Mario almost yells, lifting the barbs from her backpack, quickly dragging Patricia from under the wires.

"Throw your backpack," Mario tells Carla.

She throws it over the fence. Gets on the ground and crawls under. She makes it fast. Patricia pulls her hand and helps her up on the other side.

"Go go go," Mario says, looking at Chino and me.

"You first," Chino says, helping me take my backpack off.

"¡Throw it!"

Chino throws our backpacks. I drop on the ground and get dirt on my face. It's all dust. I like it. It's a game.

"Eso," Mario says, after Patricia pulls my hand.

Then Chino slides under. Everything fast.

To the right of us, people followed Chele and Marcelo, who helped each other and now pull people from under the fence. Some men try to jump over; they stand on a wire to climb over the other. Some get stuck but quickly get through. There's another man who is stuck and can't get loose to the left of us. We can hear his faint "Help, help." Someone walks back to pick the barbs from his clothes.

"Fast fast fast, go go go," the polleros say over and over.

"Let's go," Mario whispers to all of us.

"Walk walk walk."

"Hurry," Mario repeats, now a shadow in front of Patricia and Carla.

"¡Hurry up!" Marcelo pushes my backpack. Chino pulls my hand.

It happened so fast. My heart races. Legs tingle. Hands tickle. Some people get stuck like Patricia.

"¡Help!" I hear someone say louder than anyone else. "¡My hair! ¡My hair!"

"Shut up," the polleros say loud, but don't shout.

We're up ahead. I look back, and the fence and people are shadows again.

"¡My hair!"

"Help her."

"Shut up. Slide. Slide." The polleros' voices carry. We walk past the pollero with the beanie, who stays to the side to get to the back of the line. We walk until we can't hear the polleros behind us, or the people getting stuck. The line forms again but people are not where they were before the fence. There's more space between us. The Six are still a cluster, Mario up front and Chele behind, but the other groups are up ahead. More steps between them and our group. We lost our place in the middle, but we try to catch up. The twigs break under us, mice squeak, bats flap overhead. It's like the desert is playing a concert. I listen for Cadejo's whistling, but nothing. The crunch of our steps comes back. We're closer to the end of the line. Patricia getting stuck slowed us down. At least it wasn't her hair. At least it wasn't me who got stuck.

"More fences ahead," Patricia tells Chino—something Mario whispered to her.

"We must cross them faster," Chino says, telling Marcelo what Mario is telling Patricia.

"Va," Marcelo says, and passes the message to Chele. It's like telephone.

I'm ready. Avoiding cactuses is boring. I want barbwire. Thin, metallic, pointy. The smell of dust, thicker when our faces are in the dirt. Dirt in our noses. In our mouths. None of us got hurt. In Acapulco, when Coyote told us we might go through the desert, I never pictured this: bushes, trees, cactuses, bunnies, mice, bats, fences, mountains in the distance. I thought it was gonna be sand and sand only, like *Aladdin*. The fences are cool. I feel like I'm back home chasing iguanas. I've practiced. ¡It's the most exciting thing we've done all trip! It's a game. ¿Who can make it through the most fences without getting stuck?

My arms have markings of the rocks from when I crawled under. Imprints. It's worth it. My hands are scratched, and I can feel a thorn in my left palm, but that's ok. We keep walking. The fences can't stop us. We get to another one, and we're masters. Chele and Marcelo help each other. Mario helps Patricia and Carla. Chino helps me. None of us get stuck. Other people do, so we make up a few positions in the line. Cadejo protects us. I look for his eyes, but only find trash or a rock or someone's water bottle. I'm so awake. It's almost eleven, the latest I've stayed up since the boats, and I'm not tired at all.

WE CAN'T SEE MERO MERO, but he's up at the very front, he's the centipede's head. I don't know how he knows where to go. ¿How does he see? We trust him. Wherever he points his nose, our noses follow. I shadow Chino's shoes. Marcelo's hands on my backpack. Chele behind Marcelo's muscles. We don't rest. We've gone through four, five fences. I try to crawl without touching the wires. Then Patricia pulls my hand. I like getting pulled.

All of the fences were barbwire, except one was made only of thin wires. People thought it was electric. I was afraid to touch it. Mero Mero and the polleros had to convince everyone the fence was "just a fence." To "hurry up." "We can't just stand here."

"Last group, they told us it had electricity," a stranger said.

Mero Mero touched it, and when he did, people gasped, but nothing happened. People went under and the sound reverberated. ¡Slinky! Like thin metal hitting rock. Like a TV antenna on tough glass. Some people laughed. Others were mad at the person who said it was electric. Others still weren't convinced. The polleros didn't hold up the wires for us. Marcelo jumped it. Chele tried to, but fell over. It was hard not to laugh. But none of The Six did.

"Maleta," Marcelo told him, without laughing. "Hurry up."

The bunnies must laugh at us jumping, crawling under—they can just run under fast. All of our clothes are smeared with dirt only on the front. Our backpacks and the backs of our pants are clean. We've been walking almost four hours without a break. My legs are getting tired, but nothing else. ¡I'm wide awake! Then, all of a sudden— a high-pitched whistle. People freeze.

"¡Hide!"

"¡Tiráte, Javier!" Chino pulls my hand toward a bush. His head hits a branch, but he doesn't react. I hit some rocks, but I'm ok.

"¿What is it?"

"Don't know."

Mario, Patricia, and Carla are under a bush.

"Shh. Flat on the ground," Mario whispers. "Helicopter."

"Puta," Chino says.

My hands are spread out next to me like I'm crawling under an-other fence. I hear the rotor. I've never seen a helicopter. Only in movies.

"La Migra," Chino whispers, putting his arm over my backpack.

I want to see the blades spinning, but it's dark and the helicopter is far away. The sound like an old man saying *toh toh toh toh toh toh toh* over and over. No one moves. I look over to my right, and it's Mar-celo and Chele under another bush. Mario stares at the sky. Patricia's arm over Carla. Everything and everyone is still. No sparkly rocks. There are holes in the ground around the bush's trunk. Dried leaves scattered below it. Dry twigs. Thorns. The rotors are farther away. The dirt colder than when we started, but if I dig, it's warm. Through the sound of the rotors, the bushes keep saying *shhhhhhh*. The helicopter, farther and farther away. People look afraid, which makes my heart beat faster. Then—the high-pitched whistle again.

"¡Line up!" someone yells loud. Then, like a game of telephone, "Line up" is whispered from bush to bush. One by one we rise. Our backpacks make us look like the Ninja Turtles. The line forms again. I really need to pee. Chino's first water bottle is long gone; he tossed it as we walked. He hasn't opened his second one, strapped around his chest. For once, his hands are free.

We walk for a little bit and the line stops.

"¡Down!" We find the nearest bush.

"¿Are we okay?" I ask Chino.

"Sí. Sí. Todo está bien."

"¿Are we close?"

"Almost."

"¿Is it La Migra?"

"No, no. Don't think about that."

I grab a handful of dirt and throw it on myself and Chino.

"They won't see us," I whisper to Mario, who is under the same bush as Carla and Patricia.

He doesn't say anything.

"¡Stand up!" someone shouts. We walk again.

La Migra has helicopters. They have trucks. They have binoculars that can see in the dark. I want our own helicopter to fight against La Migra. To shoot those bad gringos making us scared. I really have to pee, but we keep walking and Chino has opened the second water jug. He hands it over to me.

"I have to pee."

"¿Want to stop?"

"Sí," I tell him.

"Va, vení." He takes a step to the side.

"Vamos a mear," he tells Marcelo.

"Hurry up," Marcelo whispers.

"Hurry," Chele echoes back.

We're off to the side, near a bush. People walk past us.

I walk far enough to make sure Chino is not looking. That no one looks. I'm so cold. My pee starts to come out and it's warm. When it lands, it's loud. The dirt is so dry, my pee starts to make a hole. I write my name.

"¿Ya?" Chino asks before I get to the *v* in my name. He's done. I push to let everything out faster.

"Ya."

"Let's go," he says. We didn't take long. We didn't take long, but we're near the end, we can see the guy with the beanie and other shadows. Chino grabs my left hand. He must be cold because he pulls my hand into his sleeve. I pull the sleeve over my right hand. It works. We're warmer, moving faster, almost jogging. People slow down and step to the side when we rush past. We make it back to Chele, to Marcelo, who taps my backpack.

"Eso es todo, Chepito," Marcelo says.

I feel better. Lighter. There's a faint breeze like the desert is breathing against our necks. I keep my hands inside my chamarra. It keeps me warm and protects me against thorns.

5-30-99

IT'S 2:30 A.M. THE moon over to our left. The light not as bright as it gets closer to the horizon. Chino and I finished the second jug. I still have my small bottle in my backpack, but that one is "for emergencies," Chino said. I'm thirsty. Carla and Patricia finished their water también. A lot of people have. At the last pee break, Mario told us not to throw our bottles away. Mero Mero told him that we're headed toward water, that we're close to the road where the van will pick us up, that we don't need to walk as fast anymore.

Our pace *has* slowed, thank God. My legs feel heavy. Both my calves hurt like I've been playing soccer nonstop. The middle toes on my right foot are numb. I don't know if it's from the cold or because of how far we've walked. They don't hurt—what hurts is the muscle behind my left shoulder, the left side of my lower back, and the back of my left thigh. ¿From sliding under fences? ¿Dropping to the ground?

Chino hasn't let go of my left hand. His pulling helps me walk faster. The empty bottle bounces across his chest as he walks. He knows I have water but doesn't ask for it. Mario, Carla, Patricia walk closer to us, Marcelo and Chele steps behind. In between, after the first fence, the line was a bit more spread out—not anymore. I can see Carla's and Patricia's faces when they look to the side. I can hear Carla asking her mom for water. They've all run out.

"We're almost there," I hear Patricia say.

The air is dry. My face doesn't sweat, but the patch on my back below my backpack does. My armpits a little bit también.

From behind us, we hear Marcelo let out a muffled scream: "¡Ahhh!"

"¿What happened, maje?" Chele immediately asks.

"¡Faaakk! ¡A la gran puta, my ankle!"

"Puta," Chele says as Chino lets go of my hand so he can tell Mario. Mario runs back and helps Marcelo get up. Strangers walk past. They don't stop or say anything. The Six lose more and more ground. We're at the back of the line, we see the shadow with the beanie.

"¿You good?" The Beanie asks.

"His ankle," Mario says.

"Está cabrón," The Beanie responds. "We're about to stop. ¿Can you walk on it?"

"No hay de otra," Marcelo says, grimacing.

Chele helps Marcelo onto his feet. Mario and Chele support him as Marcelo wraps his big arms around their shoulders. I can see his teeth as he takes his first steps. He doesn't look good.

"I'm good," he says. "I'm good." But he almost falls over.

Chele and Mario help him skip over a small hill, then down. People are farther in front of us but we can still see their shadows. The Beanie walks next to us. Marcelo hops on one foot until we get to an open area with trees. Different trees with thick and pale trunks. Everyone is already here.

"Water," The Beanie says. Shadows stand around what looks like a large metal barrel as wide as the length of a microbus. It's rusty and looks light gray, like the color of the metal sheets used for tin roofs back home.

"Refill your bottles here and drink," Mero Mero says, walking around. "The water is safe." As he says that, we walk up to the barrel. I can barely see over the metal. But at the bottom, there's a cement step. I stand on my tiptoes and look at the water. The barrel is almost completely full, a palm's length to the rim. But the water's top layer is filled with patches that remind me of the skin at the top of heated-up milk, except these are dark green. Where there aren't green patches, the water reflects the stars.

"It's safe, drink," Mero Mero repeats. "We're almost to the asphalt road. We walked fast, so we can rest."

Chino elbows me, gets near my face, and whispers, "Let's drink from the bottle in your backpack, and then we'll fill it with water. Ponete trucha."

I take my backpack off and lose ten kilos. ¡I can move freely! I crack my neck. Caps pop again and again. Everyone drinks bottled water—if they still have any—and refills their bottles with the new water.

I'm happy. We're almost to the vans. I will see my parents. Mero Mero walks around, telling his polleros something. He comes near us and checks on Marcelo. "Let's take thirty minutes," he says, and walks away to another group.

"¿You hungry?" Mario asks everyone. "We have time. Eat, if you are."

I'm not. I'm full of water.

"Thirty minutes," Mario repeats.

No one's whispering. The huge tree next to the barrel covers a big part of the sky. The moon nears the horizon more and more.

"¿Want to sleep a little?" Chino asks.

"Yes, niños, rest," Patricia says, looking at Carla, who sits between her legs.

I'm not *that* kind of tired. My body aches, but my mind is awake awake awake. Men sprawl on the dirt, their heads on their backpacks, just like we saw them when we got off the truck when Paco dropped us off.

Then a woman next to Patricia tells her something: "So good you brought your kids."

"Ajá," Patricia responds. All of us looking at the woman's shadow. I can't really see what she looks like, just that she has her hair in a tight ponytail and has a thin face.

"I want my kid to be born over there. Or, here. Aquí, pues."

"Un gringo," Patricia says.

And they laugh.

"I'll let your family rest." The woman lies down in her bush.

It's quiet again. The woman's belly isn't that big. ¿Is that man next to her her husband? None of The Six ask. Marcelo lies down, softly complaining about his ankle. The tree next to the barrel has big leaves. They move with the faint wind like they're clapping. We're almost where we need to get to. The moonlight is still strong, but less than before. I don't see as many bats. My watch says it's close to three A.M. Chele quickly fell asleep. Usual. Whenever he begins to snore, Chino kicks him. Chino closes his eyes, his hand on my backpack I use as a pillow. Carla rests between her mom's legs.

Mario keeps watch, although he's also sprawled on the dirt. I look up at the stars. Whenever we stop walking, it gets cold. The left side of my belly still hurts, maybe the cold helps. My stomach is warm, but when my hands touch it, I get goosebumps. My nipples harden. *Cadejo, Cadejito,* I whisper, looking at the moon. The biggest craters are two eyes on a white face. *Gracias.* I know he's guiding Mero Mero. I know he was the one who pushed the helicopters away.

"CHINO. CHINO."

Chele pushes Chino, whose hand is on top of me, so I wake up.

"¿What?"

"¡Marcelo is gone!"

"¿What happened?" Patricia quickly turns to face us.

"He's not here." Chele points at the ground where Marcelo was. "El hijueputa took my water and food."

"Puta."

"¡¿What the fuck?!" Mario shouts, the people next to us wake up.

"He's gone," Chele repeats.

"¡¿What the fuck?!" Mario screams at Chele, who springs up to his feet, picking up a lot of dirt that falls on Carla's face.

"I fell asleep, maje," Chele tells Chino. All of us sit up, pressing our hands against the ground behind us.

"¡Fuck!" Mario yells, shaking his head. He grabs his cap, takes it off, then puts it back on. "I knew that motherfucker was faking it."

I watched him trying to walk. His ankle looked bad. ¿Why would Marcelo trick us? He's part of The Six. Not the nicest. Not Chino, Patricia, or Carla, but he's been with us since El Salvador.

"Púchica."

"La caga."

"Hijueputa."

"Cerote took my food and water."

"I'll get you a new bottle. We got food," Mario tells Chele, pressing his shoulders down so Chele stops fidgeting, shaking.

Marcelo lied to us. He was talking to us more, was nice to me today, tried to help with my backpack, but he was *acting*. He tricked us. Stole from us. Marcelo doesn't care. He left us. He's supposed to be taking care of me. I want to curse. I'm mad at Marcelo like Chele is. He didn't care we've spent two months together. He made me smoke. I thought we were family. ¿Does this mean *all* of them could be lying?

"Hijueputa," Chino keeps repeating.

"Cerote de mierda." Patricia shakes her head.

Chele can't stop cursing and kicking the ground. No one trusted Marcelo. I feel dumb. Tricked like "powdered gasoline." ¿Who else is lying? Chele searches the ground like a dog. Mario looks everywhere for ¿I don't know what? It's a quarter to four. The thirty minutes are gone, but Mero Mero hasn't said anything. People gather around us. Chele keeps cursing.

"I saw him get up. I thought he was peeing," the pregnant woman tells Patricia. "He went that way." She points past the pale-trunked trees behind the barrel.

"Fucker can't be far," Mario says, walking toward the barrel, inspecting the ground, then heading toward the bushes.

"¡Ese hijueputa took everything!" Chele repeats, looking for his things. Other people wake up. The sky is dark, but one side looks lighter like it did on the boats.

"Ese hijo de la gran puta, ya la caga, me las va' pagar ese cerote de mierda," Chele says, grabbing a stick from the ground.

"Calmáte." Chino taps Chele's chest. "Calmáte."

"Calmáte, Chele." Patricia tries to grab Chele's arm to calm him down, and he pushes her off. She almost tumbles.

"Ey. Controláte, cerote." Chino grabs Chele's shirt, wagging his finger at him.

"Sorry. Sorry," Chele says, walking away, pacing, mumbling, punching the air. He's scaring me. My heart beats faster. ¿Why did Marcelo leave?

"He knew. Marcelo knew," Chino says, pissed off. "He speaks English, he planned this shit."

"Hijueputa," Patricia says.

"Mal parido." Chele looks through his backpack, making sure he has everything else.

Mero Mero comes back with Mario.

"¿Any of you know about this?"

"No."

"No, señor."

"No."

I shake my head.

"You better not be lying," Mero Mero says.

"No. No, señor."

"A la mierda ese hijo de setenta mil putas," Chele adds.

"He won't make it in the desert. Not during the day. ¿Where's he gonna go?" Mero Mero pauses. "Don't tell anyone. Don't say shit. You're good. Line up, we're leaving." He walks around to the next bush, telling people, "We're leaving."

"Last stretch. Last stretch. ¡Let's go!"

¿What does he mean Marcelo won't make it? I'm mad at him but don't want anything terrible. *Death*. Patatús. I hear that word, and I remember Great-Great-Grandma Fina. I took her coffee every night at dusk. When I was six, I found her with her dentures out. She wouldn't respond. Her skin was cold.

"Walk walk walk, the sun will rise soon," Mero Mero says loudly.

"Fast," Mario tells us. "Hurry up."

Everyone lines up. There's a hole where Marcelo was. Chele curses under his breath. I haven't forgotten Great-Great-Grandma Fina's hands. Marcelo *is* a bad person. His tattoos. Abuelita was right. But Chino has tattoos, and *he* hasn't lied.

We keep walking. Every few steps, something else comes out of Chele's mouth. "¡Even my fucking fork!" Chele carried a fork to scoop out the tuna. "Ese hijueputa de mierda." We're back in the grasses. After a few crunches under our feet: "Cerote mal parido."

"Ya." Chino turns back and tells Chele, "Cállate." Chino pulls my hand. Patricia holds Carla's hand. We keep walking. To our right, the sky looks lighter and lighter.

"Todo va' estar bien, don't pay attention to him," Chino tells me.

"Almost there," Patricia tells Carla.

"Not much left," Mario reassures all of us.

We're back in the middle of the line. The ground is flatter. No more hills and ditches. No trees. We're back in the bushes. Only Mero Mero knows what we're looking for, but he keeps saying, "We're near"—the message that travels down the line. Everyone keeps saying it, but we don't stop.

I'm thirsty. Chino makes me drink. I take a sip from the new water, and it tastes like metal and grass. It's closer to dawn. I helped

Abuelita water our garden every dawn; we saw frogs or toads. ¿Where are the toads? I can't hear any. There's a smell up ahead. Smells bad. Like roadkill but no vultures. The line gets uneven. It's a dog. A dead dog.

"Un coyote, Javiercito," Chino says after I squeeze his hand.

"Uy," I say, crossing myself.

"Coyote, the animal," Mario clarifies.

We walk past the rotting carcass. It smells bad. There's a hole in its stomach. The mouth is open, the teeth are really white. I can't tell the color; everything that isn't white looks a shade of gray. I've never seen a coyote. I've seen more people called coyotes than animals. It looks like a dog. *Not Cadejo. Not Cadejo.*

"¿Is it Cadejo?"

"N'hombre, vos." Chino pauses and laughs. "It's a coyote."

"¿Really?"

"Sí, vos. Look at its legs, they're not hooves." He's right. They're paws. We keep walking until Mero Mero stops meters from another barbwire fence. Everyone waits.

"It's the road," Mario whispers.

"We must run across," Mero Mero says. "Watch for cars. La Migra is on this road."

I keep squeezing Chino's hand without realizing it. "Está bien," he says.

"Everyone get a partner. There's another fence at the other end, so slide, run across, and then slide again. I'll go first. I'll check traffic. When it's safe, I'll whistle. Everyone run at the same time. No line, ¿entienden?"

People whisper, "Sí."

"Órale."

Mero Mero runs off, then slides under the fence across the street. We can't see him after that. He's in a bush. We wait. There's nothing on the road. It's my first road in La USA. It doesn't have any holes. The double yellow lines are so bright at night.

"Get ready," Chino says, which means I'm on the ground ready to elbow and knee my way across the fence. Carla is on the ground as well. We do what we've been doing, minus Marcelo. Mario and Patricia hold up the fence for Carla. Chele and Chino hold it up for me. Both Carla's and my backpacks are in either Chino's or Patricia's hands, waiting for us to crawl under so they can throw them at us. Then we hear Mero Mero's high-pitched whistle.

"¡Go go go go go!" people shout.

I crawl like an alligator and make it to my backpack.

"Wait," Chino tells me. Chele throws his bag over and crawls under. Then Chele helps lift the fence so Chino makes it. Patricia is over. Mario is over.

"Hand," Chino commands, and he starts sprinting. My legs are off the ground. He pulls me so fast, I don't touch asphalt.

We get to the other fence.

"¡Throw it, throw it, throw it!" I throw my backpack over just like he does. Carla throws hers. He grabs me under my shoulders. "Jump," he says, and throws me over the fence, then Carla.

"Under," Chino tells Patricia, already lifting the fence up from the ground. Chele catches up to us and throws his bag over. Crawls under.

"¡Hurry!" someone shouts. I look at the road, but cars are not coming. Chele holds up the fence for Chino, and everyone in The Six is across.

"¡Here!" someone shouts, and we run away from the road until we slide under a bush. I'm panting. My legs hurt. Chino picked me up. He didn't tell me, didn't warn me, but it worked. I landed on my feet. Carla landed on her feet. It was fast.

Chino sits next to Chele near a bush, both of them huffing and puffing.

"Vieja, it's faster like that," Chele says, and I know he means Chino throwing me over the fence.

"Sí, vos, just happened."

"Chivo," Carla says.

It's a bit past 4:30. A faint blue brightens the horizon. ¿Did Marcelo make it to this road? ¿How is he gonna make it to Los Ángeles? He was the only one who knew what fresh fish tastes like. He taught us to say *faak*. I don't like him, but I hope he makes it to his mom.

"I think this is it," Mario says.

"Gracias a Dios," Patricia says, crossing herself.

Mero Mero crawls from bush to bush. "Let's walk a bit that way, there's a ditch," he tells us. "Crouch, no standing. Follow me."

We crouch behind Mero Mero. People walk fast, almost run. Then the land dips. Some people fall. Chele falls on his butt. We didn't see the drop.

"Here." Mero Mero points to a ditch full of dirt. Bushes surround the edges. It looks like a moon crater.

"Órale," Mero Mero says. "¡We're here! The van will pick us up on that road. We're early. Rest."

People cheer. Cross themselves. Patricia hugs Carla and gives her a huge kiss. My heart is racing but not from running. I can't stop smiling. Everyone is smiling. Chino hugs me.

"Vergón," Chele says in the same place where he fell. We haven't moved. People kept walking past us.

"Gracias a Dios," Patricia says again, crossing herself.

"Va. Almost there," Chino says, looking at me.

"Mirá, you didn't need all that food," Patricia tells Chele.

"Ja—ja—ja—ja," he says sarcastically, his round face showing off his thick teeth. I feel lighter. My shoulders don't hurt. My stomach either. I feel good.

"¡No one get up! ¡Stay close to the ground, close to the edges of the hole!" Mero Mero shouts. "¡Be quiet!"

"¿How long do we wait, Mami?" Carla asks.

"I don't know," Mario responds. "Hopefully soon. Rest. We're here," he tells all of us. The crater has small bushes inside it. We're next to one. The dirt and air feel colder than before. The moon is gone and the sun isn't up yet. It's *really* cold. I put my hands in my sleeves again. Touch my belly to keep warm.

"Sleep," Chino says.

"I'm cold."

"Come here." He opens his arms to hug me. His chamarra is cold.

"Vos, get over here," he tells Patricia.

Others do the same. The Six huddle against the dirt, bunched together like bananas. I'm in the middle. Chele behind everyone, and Carla in front. I'm between Patricia and Chino. All of us faceup, our backpacks between our arms, over our chests, for more warmth.

"Rest, I'll keep watch," says Mario, who's still kneeling, watching us. "Sleep."

Huddling makes a difference. We're warmer. Our breaths smell like rust, like the barrel. Marcelo is gone. He was so close to the finish line. ¿Why did he leave? He's gone, but we're still The Six. Mario is our sixth now. He hasn't left. The sky begins to swallow the stars. The dirt feels wet, but it's not. Nothing moves. Nothing and no one makes a sound. We wait for the van to honk.

"¡LA MIIIGRRRAAA!" MARIO SCREAMS next to us, the sky light blue behind him.

"¡LA MIIIGRRRAAA!" someone from the other side of the ditch yells.

"¡RUUNNN!" Mario's eyes are wide and scared, then he sprints off.

Chele grabs his backpack. Chino grabs his backpack. Chele and Chino sprint into the bushes, lifting up dust. Wheels hit the bright orange dirt from all directions. Patricia grabs Carla's hand, grabs my hand. I try putting my backpack on. Patricia starts pulling. Everything's a tint of orange. Running. Everyone running fast. The white truck doors open. Men in green uniforms run after us.

"No mover! No mover!" two three four five uniforms yell. Then they release German shepherds—

Chino is meters in front of us, but then stops. Chele keeps sprinting.

"No mover!"

Everyone keeps running.

"Correr, disparar!"

Chino runs back in our direction.

"¡Jump! ¡Jump!" he yells. I jump on his back. Hold his neck. Chino grabs Patricia's and Carla's hands. We're running. My feet dangle behind him. So many backpacks on the ground, we almost trip over them.

"SI CORRER, DISPARAR! SI CORRER, DISPARAR!"

To our left, a gringo points his black gun at us—

"PARAR! PARAR!"

He's wearing a green boonie hat like the war movies. His gun, pointed at Chino's chest.

"¡NOOO!" Patricia lets out a scream and lets go of Chino's hand. She falls on the dirt. "¡Paráte, Chino! ¡Pará! ¡Pará, por favor!" she screams.

My heart pumps fast. Chino's heartbeat feels strong on his neck. He slows down. My stomach knots. Patricia screams again.

"SI CORRER, DISPARAR! ALTO!" another green uniform yells.

A German shepherd runs next to us, barking.

"PARAR," they say. "PARAR." Blond hair peeks from underneath the boonie hat.

I squeeze Chino harder. The dog keeps barking. The gringo yells in English. We don't understand. "Aba-ho. Aba-ho."

Chino unclasps my hands, tilts backward, and I land on the dirt. The dog growls at me. The gringo keeps yelling the same thing. Chino remains standing, puts his hands up. My hands are wet. My armpits. I can't yell—

Then the gringo's black boots hit Chino's legs. Drops him to his knees, pushes Chino flat on the ground, and gets on top.

Patricia screams, "¡Estap! ¡Estap!" She's hugging Carla.

I'm alone on the ground and can't move. Everything happens fast. Handcuffs on Chino. Uniforms do the same to the others who didn't run fast enough—like us. One gringo signals the dog and they both run after other people. I feel heavy. Frozen, but my stomach churns.

Another gringo wearing sunglasses walks toward us. "Todo

bueno," he says in a calmer voice. He doesn't wear a hat. He's not blond like I thought all gringos were. He has short brown hair. Then he talks to the uniform who has his knee on top of Chino's back. Boonie Hat steps off Chino and jogs toward the bushes, where more uniforms and dogs chase after people.

Short Brown Hair walks toward Patricia and puts both his forearms out in front of his chest. Taps her hands and places handcuffs on her. I watch everything from the red dirt. I haven't moved. I want to shrink. Blend with the ground. Carla is next to her mom, frozen.

"Estar bien," the uniform says, rubbing Carla's back. She still has her backpack on. Patricia is on her knees, sobbing. Carla hugs her. "Estar bien," he repeats, walking toward me. His black boots crunch against the rocks in the ground. My ears are ringing. Everything is so loud. The barks, the sobs, people's steps hitting the dirt, the beeping from the truck's opened doors. A thin green stripe across the length of the trucks. Everyone ran as fast as they could. *We* ran fast. The ground is cold, but I can feel it warming up, the air también. Everything is quiet and loud at the same time. My sweat dries cold on my armpits, on my back, my hands. Chino hasn't said anything. He lies flat. Dirt on his face. Patricia sobs and mumbles something. This isn't happening. My entire body moves with each heartbeat. It's hard to breathe. My head feels huge, the sides of my forehead like they're about to explode. I want to wake up.

Short Brown Hair walks away from Patricia to tell Chino something in English. Helps him up to his knees. "No correr, okay?" he tells Chino. "No correr," he repeats, looking at Patricia, then points at the nearest dog: brown body with black face and a black tail. Its teeth big and scary. The gringo pushes Chino toward Patricia and begins to walk both of them toward two trucks facing each other.

With his hand, he motions Carla and me to follow. The ringing. My stomach. I have to pee. I think I have to go number two. I can't take a step. He says something in English I don't understand, then says, "Aqui."

Carla walks toward me. Her hands jolt me awake—they're ice. "Let's go," she says, tapping my shoulder. My legs are wobbly.

"Estar bien," the gringo tells Carla and me. "No malo." He points at his chest.

We follow the adults toward the two trucks. They're not like the ones we've been on. They don't have beds, their windows are tinted, and both have red-and-blue siren lights on top. I look at the remaining trucks across the ditch, and two of those have a metal cover in the back where the bed should be.

Uniforms return from the bushes. Some with only their dogs. Others with people in handcuffs. They tell each other something. Five cars surround the ditch, our red-dirt crater is sprinkled with black backpacks and water bottles. I don't know which is mine. Patricia left her bag like me, but Carla has hers. ¿What am I gonna wear? I want my things. Grandpa's extra toothbrush I never used. I can't speak. My tongue like it's cut off.

We get to the car. The gringo opens the back door, motions Chino to get in first. His uniform is dark green, but the sun hits its creases, lighting them lime, almost yellow. I'm so close to him, his skin lighter than mine, I can see his veins—green lines. Chino stands erect against the opened door. He doesn't want to get in. Short Brown Hair says something in English, then presses Chino's dirt-covered head down below the car's roof, pushing him inside.

"Dentrar," he says, looking at me and Carla. I look inside, and besides Chino, there's nothing in the backseat. No seatbelts, and the seats look like they're made of plastic. Dark-gray plastic, almost like leather.

Carla helps me toward the door. There's a black metal divider between the front seats and the back. The gringo grabs me and lifts me by my armpits. I almost pee when I touch the warm seat. Carla walks in after, makes me scoot over. I slide on the dark-gray plastic.

Patricia follows, tears and dirt covering her face. Short Brown Hair shuts the door loudly and walks away. It's warmer in here. All of us look around in silence. Chino leans toward us so his handcuffed hands can try to open the door. It doesn't work.

"¡PUUUTAAA!"

Patricia tries to open *her* door; it's locked. Carla tries opening the metal around her mom's wrists; she can't. We're trapped.

"¡PUUUTAAA!" Chino screams again. I've never seen him like this. I've only seen Grandpa act this way drunk. Chino keeps trying to open the door. Kicks the seat in front of him. Kicks the metal divider. Kicks the door. He's a rabid dog. The entire car shakes.

"Ay, no. Ay, no," Patricia repeats, crying.

I want to cry, but nothing comes out.

"Calmáte, Chino," Patricia begs. "¡Por favor! ¡Los niños!"

Chino stops. Takes huge breaths. He's so red. The acne on his face even redder. Veins on the side of his forehead, just like when Grandpa gets mad. He looks at Carla and me and, slowly, calms down.

"We fell asleep," Chino says, shaking his head. "La cagamos." He kicks the driver's seat one more time. Then stares out the window. He's angrier than Chele was when Marcelo left. Chino's been so kind. He ran back to pick me up. Grandpa didn't even pay Chino to take care of me and he has. He's the complete opposite of Marcelo. In the boat he hugged me. He's been making sure I drink, I eat, I sleep, just like Patricia has. I trust him. I like it when he hugs me, when he asks me questions to make me feel better. But now he's mad and sad, and it makes me mad and sad también.

No one speaks. Everyone stares out the window. I stare through the windshield, look through the metal divider. The uniforms handcuff people lying on the ground using plastic ties. Then the gringos walk people to other trucks that look different from ours; their back doors open to what looks like a cage with two metal benches. The gringos throw the people inside. I see faces for the first time. These men were shadows last night. None of them are Mario. None of them are Chele. None of them wear beanies. None of them the pregnant woman. I don't even know what Mero Mero's face looked like, but none of these men are that tall and skinny.

Patricia takes a few breaths, gathers her voice to say, "We're Mexicans, a family, remember that."

Chino nods.

"Sí, Mami," Carla says.

"Practice your names," she says, and in my head, I repeat my fake name written in my fake papers.

Boonie Hat hasn't come back. Short Brown Hair is still helping the other green uniforms put people in trucks. It's getting hot. We must have slept a long time. The vans never honked. ¡*Faak!* ¡We were so close! Now we're trapped like parakeets. We can't open the doors, we can't open the windows, we can't do anything.

Short Brown Hair returns, saying something in English, turns the car on, and talks into his radio. The passenger seat is empty. The dashboard lights up. The AC begins to blast. We start driving. More uniforms walk out of the bushes empty-handed. They didn't catch everyone. We drive through the bushes we walked past last night and then merge onto the asphalt road, the road where the van was supposed to be. Short Brown Hair asks questions we don't understand. Then he tries to speak Spanish.

"Donde . . . pais?" He sounds like a toddler saying his first words. No one responds. I try to move my tongue, but it's frozen. *We are Mexican. She's Mom. Chino is Dad. Carla is Sister. We don't know who the coyotes were. We're from Nogales.*

"México," Patricia responds in a singsong way, just how we've heard real Mexicans say it. Chino keeps staring out the window, clutched fists behind his back, the handcuffs bright against his dark shirt.

"Familia?" the gringo asks, looking in the rear-view mirror, then briefly turns around to point at all of us.

"Sí," Patricia says, looking at her hands. She's wearing her ring. Chino también. Carla looks at her mom's hands. She hasn't spoken since she last talked to me. Maybe Carla's tongue is also frozen. I feel like I'm gonna melt into the seats.

"Mex-xi-co?" The gringo's tongue gets stuck on the *x*.

"Sí. Familia," Patricia responds, elongating the vowels, singing them, followed by the best circle motion she can make with her head. With her free hands, Carla rubs her mom's back.

"Está bien, mija," she tells Carla, adding the "mija" to make it sound from Nogales. Carla doesn't respond, stops rubbing her mom's back, and stares out the windshield. ¿Where is the gringo taking us? ¿When will I see my parents? ¿When will Mero Mero come back to help us? Everyone is quiet. I don't know who to look at. *What* to look at. There are binoculars on the passenger seat. We haven't driven past a car yet. Bush. Tree. Grass. Grass. Bush. Bush. Grass. Sometimes there's a fence, the fences we crawled under. The dirt is red in the sun.

WHEN THE GRINGO FINALLY stopped asking questions, we drove in silence except for an occasional beep followed by voices coming from his radio. We merged onto the asphalt road to another road to a much bigger one, until we got to a town. We took a lot of rights and lefts that got us here: two black gates with a bricked booth in the middle. A sign above the booth with English written on it, and below it: *Nogales, Arizona*. ¿We're back in Nogales? But this is La USA, not México.

The gringo inside the booth waves Short Brown Hair in and opens the gate. A lot of white cars with green stripes are parked in the huge parking lot in front of a two-story building. La USA flag droops on a pole next to doors made of what looks like tinted glass. The gringo parks and takes the keys out, and when he opens the door, a whiff of hot air rushes in. Inside the car, the sweat in my chamarra has dried because of the AC. I still have to pee. My stomach hasn't stopped grumbling.

The gringo opens Chino's door.

"Fuera," he says calmly, followed by English. "Ir. Camino," he says, a little louder, this time pointing at the dark asphalt in front of the door. It's not correct Spanish, but we understand.

Chino looks back at us and says, "Wait for me."

"Sí," Patricia says. We nod. Then Chino steps out.

The gringo grabs Chino's handcuffs with one hand, then motions us to wait with the other hand. Closes the door with a thud and grabs Chino's neck as he pushes Chino toward the front doors that slide open.

"Todo va' estar bien," Patricia tells us, switching back to our accent. "Dejen que yo hable." She repeats our fake names. We nod. She asks me to say my fake name, but I can't.

"Podés," Carla says, tapping my leg. "You can, remember it." I mumble the name. It's my first word since Mario yelled "¡Migra!"

"Todo va' estar bien," Patricia repeats over and over.

My jaw feels heavy. Everything, my body, my legs are sore. My stomach. I feel sick. Like I have a fever. My head hurts. I have to pee—bad.

The gringo walks back toward the car with another gringo wearing sunglasses. Their uniforms are dark green like the skinny trees with small green leaves next to the building.

"Remember," Patricia tells us one last time.

Short Brown Hair opens the same door, and the other uniform walks around the front of the car toward my fake mom. I have to pretend. With both doors open, hot air rushes in and it feels like a stove. It's hot in La USA. My parents' country. I was expecting snow, the North Pole like in Coke commercials, but it's hotter than El Salvador.

The new gringo tells Patricia something in English and pulls her out, quickly closing the door after her. He puts his hand on her neck and starts walking her toward the front of the car.

"Salir, por favor." Short Brown Hair reaches inside with his white hand. He has trouble saying the *r*'s. "Tu tambien, dos," he says, looking at my fake sister, expanding his fingers into the number two. "No malo," he says, placing his palm on his chest next to a yellow patch with English writing on it.

Carla tries to push me. The gringo grabs my forearm. He's warm. His palms are soft and smooth. I slide across the dark-gray seat, across where Chino was. Short Brown Hair helps Carla out. When her feet hit the asphalt, the gringo shuts the door and grabs Carla's hand. There's sweat in my armpits and my lower back. It's so hot. All of us walk toward the tinted glass doors that slide. I've never walked through one before.

The doors open by themselves. The air inside is like the air inside the car, cold like opening a fridge. Chino is here, handcuffed and standing next to a counter with a computer on it. He's talking to another green uniform on the other side of the counter who's typing on the keyboard. The screen is black and big, the size of a small TV. I don't like these uniforms. More behind the counter. They hit Chino in the desert. They caught us. They brought us here. They're bad.

Short Brown Hair stays with Carla and me as we sit on a metal bench. The gringo holding Patricia walks her toward Chino, then walks away down the long tiled floor. Counter Gringo asks them questions and types into the keyboard. From here, they look like a married couple. I've never seen my real parents together like this. I can't stop looking at Chino and Patricia. ¿Do we look related? He stands so close to her, their handcuffed arms touch.

"Agua?" the gringo asks Carla and me. She nods. But I don't want water. ¡I need to pee! But I'm embarrassed and don't know how to ask.

"Comer?" We both nod. He gets up and walks down the same hallway Patricia's gringo did. Gets to a wooden door and opens it as more uniforms jog toward the sliding door.

"Okay," Counter Gringo says out loud. I know that word from the movies. "Aqui." He motions us to come. Carla looks confused.

"Vengan," Patricia says like she's singing.

Short Brown Hair is not back. Counter Gringo tells us something in English. "Aqui," he says, annoyed. Carla gets up and grabs my hand, walks me across the tiled floor to the counter where Chino and Patricia stand shoulder to shoulder.

"Madre?" Counter Gringo asks.

"Sí," Carla responds.

"Madre?" he asks me.

I nod.

"Okay." Then he says our names out loud.

We nod.

"Años?"

"Doce," Carla says.

"Tu," he asks me, pointing a pen at my face.

I freeze.

"Nueve," Patricia answers for me.

Short Brown Hair comes back with two paper cups and cookies. I don't drink my water. I hold it out in front of Chino's legs. He nods at me to drink. I shake my head. I push the cup closer to his chest. Finally, he bends down to drink.

"Okay," Counter Gringo says, then calls another green uniform from behind him. He looks like us, browner than Patricia *and* Chino, and has dark hair. ¿Is he gringo? He doesn't have blond or brown hair. No green or blue eyes.

"Ho-la, ustedes son familia?" He speaks with a funny accent. Like a gringo, stressing each syllable.

"Sí," my fake parents say, almost in unison.

"Okay, entiendes que eres detenido?"

They both nod.

"Entiendes si cruzar otra vez, diez años carcel, okay?"

They look at each other. Brown Gringo's Spanish is slow, he mispronounces words. It makes sense most of the time, but this I don't understand. Patricia shakes her head and says, "¿Puede repetir?"

"Lo que hicieron"—he makes the motion of people walking—"es ilegal. Cruzar. Malo. Crimen."

Chino and Patricia nod.

"Otra vez, es carcel, diez años." He holds up ten fingers.

Counter Gringo snickers, crossing his arms.

"Sí," Chino says, annoyed, his veins popped. Patricia doesn't understand fully, tries elbowing Chino, who gets closer to her and whispers, "Ten years in jail if they catch us again."

Her eyes widen. She shakes her head.

"Entender?" Brown Gringo asks again. "Crimen."

Patricia nods.

The gringos talk to each other and Counter Gringo types something into the computer.

"Tu firma y manos aqui," Brown Gringo says, taking Chino's handcuffs off. Then Brown Gringo takes each of Chino's individual fingers and presses them onto a purple pad, and puts a pen in Chino's hands so he can sign a paper.

Once Chino is done, Brown Gringo takes Patricia's fingers and does the same.

The doors slide open again and uniforms enter holding handcuffed people in dark clothes—mostly men, some women, but no children. ¡It's the people from the centipede! The gringo who hit Chino is with them. Boonie Hat.

"Todo bien," Short Brown Hair tells us, rubbing our backs. The handcuffed men are told to sit on the floor next to the bench we were just sitting on. Others stand. There's a lot of them.

I was ready to press my fingers onto the purple pad, but no one asked me or Carla. Brown Gringo walks from behind the counter and starts pulling Patricia's forearms. Grabs Carla.

"¡Estamos juntos! ¡Juntos!" Patricia shouts at Brown Gringo. "¡Familia!"

Chino takes a step closer to me.

"Sí," Brown Gringo says, slips into English, and then back to Spanish: "Separar hombres y mujeres."

"Procedimiento," Short Brown Hair says, rubbing my shoulders. Chino gets closer.

"Nos esperan. Cualquier cosa, nos esperan," Patricia tells Chino and me, loud, in front of everyone. The gringo carries Carla's backpack. She's not crying. Patricia isn't either. Chino doesn't say anything. He nods and leans his body on my head. ¿Are we going to see them again? ¿Where are they taking them?

Brown Gringo walks them down the tiled floor, past the wooden door where Short Brown Hair got us water and cookies. I still have my cookie in my hand. I'm not hungry. I'm not thirsty. I need to pee.

"Está bien, we're together," Chino whispers.

Short Brown Hair grabs Chino by the back of his neck, holds my hand, and walks us down the same hallway. Everyone is looking at us. The uniforms. The handcuffs. With each step, everything feels colder and colder.

I'M IN A ZOO. A cage. I'm a monkey with at least twenty-one other monkeys. Everyone wears a long face. No one smiles. When someone else comes in, we're more than twenty-one. Some leave. I'm the only kid. This is our room. It's like the back of a trailer, if the back door was made of black metal bars. Three walls. One tiny window at the back of the room lets some sunlight inside. The walls a bit more than a meter stick apart, three meter sticks long. We're locked in. If we want freezing water, we drink from the metal sink on top of the metal toilet seat that reeks of piss. Patricia and Carla are in another room. They screamed our fake names and Chino screamed back. She recognized his voice the very first time.

"If you're out first, tell us, we'll tell you también," she said, and we haven't spoken since. Everyone's quiet. People stare across the room at nothing. Some stare out the small window with metal bars. Others hide their faces—if they were with us in the desert, I wouldn't know. No one knows if the gringos can pick up our accents.

My body is cold and it hurts. My back. My arms. My calves. My thighs. Even my butt cheeks. My left side hurts more. Everywhere, sore. The lower part of my neck like I'm still carrying my backpack. My bladder is full. My belly grumbles. I hold my pee. I can't do what adults do: pull their zippers down ¡in front of everyone else! When Short Brown Hair brought us here, he took Chino's handcuffs off. We leaned against the door's metal bars. The toilet is right there. A man got up and unzipped his dark-blue pants. His thing—so big, much bigger. Thick. But brown, and pink at the tip like mine. ¡Everyone could see it! His thick yellow stream hit the toilet's metal with a loud force like rain falling into a saucepot. The piss, yellow yellow yellow, almost orange. And the smell—

I couldn't look away. ¡I'd never seen an adult penis! I'd seen my friends', accidentally, when we went to the beach, or when we played soccer and we pantsed each other. We were always the same size. Mamá Pati called mine tortolita or palomita. This man's was a big pigeon. I didn't know it could get so big. Now I'm embarrassed. Ashamed mine is small. Ashamed I looked. It was so close to me. I asked Chino to move away and we did.

We walked to the back wall under the window, past everyone in the cage, some standing, others lying down or crouched against the walls. My head so close to the strangers' waists who were standing up. All I could think of was how much bigger than mine their things were. ¿Will mine get that big? ¿Does it hurt to have it behind underwear?

I want to melt into the bricks. Squeeze out the other side and be in the sunlight, in the hot air, with the birds. When they fly, their shadows enter our cage. Maybe doves. Maybe crows. They sing. Squawk. Caw. It's cold and dark in here. I keep my hands inside my chamarra. All of our shoes, all of our dark clothes, are dirty and dusty. The desert clings to us. Dirt. Cactus. Sweat. Brush. Rocks. Blood. Spilled tuna juice. Piss. All of it on our skin.

The monkeys in here stare, they sleep, they doze. This cage. This silent and stinky room. The monkeys next to the door wait for their names to be called. Then a gringo comes and takes them away. The uniforms are clean and green, their boots black and shiny, their black guns hang from their black belts. Sometimes the monkeys come back. Sometimes they don't. When they return they don't know why. No one knows why. But they say we're all getting "deportados."

"Back to México," a monkey says.

"Órale, güey," another says in his best Mexican, laughing. Hopefully, the gringos can't tell.

¿Where's Mero Mero? ¿Mario? The uniforms walk more and more monkeys down the hallway. New monkeys from green-striped cars into more rooms like ours, to the left or to the right. None of them Marcelo. None of them Chele. None of them the polleros. But Coyote and Mario said we would try again. ¿When are we gonna go outside? ¿How long will we stay in here?

The gringos have black radios. They look like walkie-talkies. I wanted walkie-talkies for my ninth birthday, to play with my friends, but my parents never sent them. ¿What would my friends think of this? I'm a monkey. The gringos watch us pee. I can't hold it anymore. I don't want anyone to see. Only Mamá Pati has seen me. She showered with me. No one else has seen my thing. I'm embarrassed, but it's more embarrassing if I piss myself.

Sunlight slips through the iron bars in the window, warming my hands, my bulging need to pee. My tongue is a rock, but I must—

"I can't," I whisper to Chino, who leans against the cold wall. His wrists are marked by deep lines where the handcuffs were.

"¿What?"

"Me hago pipí," I whisper into his ear.

He points with his lips. His eyes are blank. "Over there," he says, cold.

I shake my head. "Tengo pena."

He doesn't respond. Keeps staring at the space in front of him: a square of cold cement next to a sleeping monkey on the floor.

"Chino," I say, pulling his brown chamarra.

He looks at me, doesn't say anything. "Va," he says before he walks across the room toward the toilet. The sunlight hits the metal toilet seat, making it shine like real silver. He signals with his hands for me to walk to him. "Come," he finally says.

I gather the strength and walk past the monkeys, who stand with blank stares or lie on the ground, sleeping.

"I'll cover you," he says as he stands tall behind me, unzipping his chamarra, angling it so that no one can see.

"Don't look."

I make sure Chino keeps his eyes closed before I unzip. My bladder is pressed hard against my pants. I've been waiting for this since Mario yelled, "¡La Migra!" I hold my thing in my hands. The man's penis flashes in my head—

"Hurry," Chino says without opening his eyes. He's helping me pee. I don't remember my real dad doing this.

Finally, a drop turns into another, then a stream, an open faucet hits the toilet water. My piss is yellow. But not as yellow as the other man's. His thick brown thing. Its pink tip. I feel lighter. Like a balloon letting air out. My stomach doesn't feel as bad. It smells bad in here. I keep going until nothing else comes out. I flick my thing up and down, looking everywhere making sure no one sees.

I pull Chino's brown chamarra. He doesn't say anything and starts walking toward the back, his hands on my shoulder, guiding us toward our old spot below the window. I listen for the birds. Look for their shadows in the cage. I'm trapped. I want to leave this room. Be with Patricia, Carla, and Chino, together. Our little family. I want all of us and all of the people in here to walk out down the hallway, past the counter, onto the road, into a van to drive us where we're supposed to be right now: Los Ángeles, San Rafael, Wachingtón, Nueva York . . .

Sunlight doesn't brighten the toilet seat anymore; it lights up a patch of the cement floor next to it. Another man unzips, releases a stream less yellow than mine. Everyone's head is tipped toward the ground. It's cold. Warmer under the window because the outside air seeps in, but I still have to wear my chamarra. I wish I had my backpack to use as a pillow. ¿What am I gonna do? Wish I had all my things: shorts to sleep in, more underwear, clean dress shirt, Velcro shoes, Colgate toothbrush and Colgate toothpaste, Head & Shoulders shampoo, my Bic pen, the toothbrush Grandpa gave me, his extra toothpaste, his handkerchief. I want to be clean. I miss my family in El Salvador. I want to draw something. I haven't slept. I'm the most tired I've ever been. I couldn't sleep because I had to pee.

Another monkey tries to get the attention of the gringos at the end of the hallway. He hits the metal bars with his shoes, he whistles at them, no one tells him to stop. Nothing is loud enough for the gringos. We can see them. They can see us. Chino hasn't moved. He's mad. He's sad. I rest my head against the wall. Try to close my eyes. Through the monkeys' dark clothes, our black hair, our brown or light-brown skin, I count green uniforms. One. Two. Five. Ten. Their black boots, their black guns, their handcuffs, their black radios with nothing but English coming out.

"TU." A DARK-BLOND AND clean-shaven uniform points into our cage. "Todos," he says, and pushes the air toward us. We stand back. One monkey walks to the front and is taken out in handcuffs. I don't know how long I slept, but the sun is still shining through the window. I dreamed I was still in the ditch. I had my backpack. Marcelo was there. Chele también.

Some people are gone, others replaced them, the room is still full, uniforms walk up and down the hallway with more people for more cages. We wait for the gringos to call our fake names. I wish an earthquake would crack the wall so we could run outside, but nothing comes—just snores and piss hitting the toilet.

Chino leans against the back wall like he did before I passed out. Dark bags under his eyes. I don't think he's slept. Keys open the cage next to ours. "¡They're taking us!" Patricia's voice echoes. Chino springs up to his feet and runs through the crowd to the front.

"Mijo," Patricia says, looking at me and handcuffed. "Es mi hijo. Mi marido," she tells the same dark-blond gringo as before, trying to hold her ground. She won't take one more step. Dark Blond's hand pushes against her neck as Patricia tries to nod toward us.

"¡Mamá!" I scream, but it doesn't come out loud.

"¡Mujer!" Chino shouts, reaching his hands through the metal bars, but Patricia and Carla are too far.

"Papá," Carla says softly as she lets go of Patricia's shirt and takes a step toward Chino.

"Está bien," Chino says, playing with Carla's hair.

Dark Blond whispers something in English and pulls Carla by her arm. She doesn't let go of Chino's arm. I believe they're family. *My* family. Another uniform comes running and lifts Carla off the ground.

"¡Noooo!" I find myself screaming. ¡I *can* scream!

"Está bien," Chino repeats, hugging me.

The uniforms say something in English followed with "okay." They keep repeating it, patting Carla on the back as she sobs.

"Ya, mija." Patricia leans closer to kiss Carla's hair.

Dark Blond shouts in English, and both uniforms pull Carla and Patricia away from our door, down the hall, toward the counter. Both of the gringos' yellow badges flash in the hall's darkness. My heart beats like a trapped dragonfly. Chino hugs me, says the same thing everyone says, "Está bien," but nothing *is* ok. They're taking them away. ¿When are we gonna see them?

"¡I'll tell them to take you out!" Patricia screams. The people in our room don't react. It's like nothing happened. Like nothing *is* happening. I want Patricia. I want my real mom. I want Mali. I don't want to be here. This nasty toilet. This cold cement floor. These uniforms.

Then Dark Blond walks back down the hall with a different gringo. They stand right in front of our door. "Hey, tu," Dark Blond says firmly, pointing at me. "Tu, niño."

I look at Chino, who takes a step closer to me.

"Tu, no." He shakes his head. Dark Blond's arm stretches toward Chino, palm raised up, brows closer to each other, fingers pointing at the ceiling.

"Soy su papá," Chino tells them.

"Tu, todah vee-ah no," he clarifies with a thick accent.

Chino doesn't move at first. Looks at the ground. Looks at my legs, my knees, my chest, my head.

"Rapido," the other gringo says.

Chino gets closer to my ears. "Go with him. Tell Pati and Carla to wait for me," he whispers, wrapping his arms around me. I sniff his dry dirt smell. He doesn't stop tapping my back.

"Todos, atrás!" Dark Blond shouts at everyone else. The door shrieks open. Scratching the floor.

"Salú," Chino says, giving me a last squeeze, without hiding our accent.

I take a step, Chino's hand on my back until I'm outside. The door clicks behind me. Metal hits metal. The gringos' keys like chalk scratching a blackboard.

I'm outside our stinky room, the trailer, the cage. I look back. Some men lie down or lean against a wall like nothing happened. Like Chino and I don't exist. Others look at me, smiling. Chino smiles and waves, his hands through the metal bars flapping like a fan. I walk up the hallway. Dark Blond pulls my sweaty hands. The other gringo walks behind us. The counter is in front; the sliding doors let bright light in. Patricia and Carla look like shadows, but I recognize them.

"Goh," Dark Blond says as he pushes my back toward them. I run. Carla hugs me. She smells of dust like Chino. Patricia leans her upper body to touch my head.

COUNTER GRINGO SITS BEHIND his computer talking to more hand-cuffed people. Dark Blond stands with Patricia, Carla, and me. We're waiting, I don't know for what.

"Okay, el, Mexico," Dark Blond says, making the motion of a steering wheel, then pointing at another uniform, who carries Carla's backpack. Gringos look like all types of things. Not just blond with blue or green eyes like I thought. This uniform looks more like us. Short black hair and light-brown skin like Chino's.

"¿And yours?" Patricia points at Carla's backpack.

"In the desert."

Dark Blond tells Short Black Hair something, and both start walking out toward the front door.

"Marido. Esposo," Patricia says without taking a step.

"Salir mahs tardeh."

"Mi esposo," she repeats, taking a step toward the hall, pointing with her head toward Chino.

I'm scared we will never see Chino again, like the people in the boats. Like the Guatemalans taken by the Mexican cops. Like Marcelo, Mario, and Chele. We can't leave him.

"Papá," Carla says.

"Papá," I join her.

"Mahs tardeh," Short Black Hair repeats.

"Todo es bien," Dark Blond says after him.

"Mi esposo todavía está allá." Patricia points at the cages. Counter Gringo turns his chair, looks at us, and yells something we don't understand. He's pinker, redder, like a pig's skin. He turns his head and calls another gringo over.

"Calma. Cálmate," a new gringo says. "Todo está bien, es que papeles toman más tiempo." He has a thick mustache and speaks in a singsong like Mero Mero, Mario, and Paco. It's the best Spanish a gringo has spoken.

"Mexicanos, verdad?"

"Sí," Patricia says quickly.

"Okay, pues, él no tarda. Hoy o mañana, deportado de aquí." There's that word again. It's what Marcelo was. *De-por-ta-do* back to El Salvador. Bad people get *deportado*.

"¡¿Mañana?!" Patricia tilts her head back and stomps the cement floor.

"Sí, toma tiempo." His eyes are dark brown like ours.

"¿Pero lo dejarán ir?"

"Sí," Mustache Gringo says.

¿Why are they taking longer with Chino? ¿His tattoos? ¿His piercing? I don't understand. But he hasn't taken his shirt off. They're all on his chest. The uniforms haven't seen them.

"Mi marido," Patricia says again.

"Prometo lo saquen más rápido," Mustache Gringo promises, and explains there are a lot more men than women and kids. He signals Short Black Hair and Dark Blond to take us out to the parking lot.

"Buena suerte," Mustache Gringo says.

The uniforms walk us to the entrance. A hand on Patricia's neck. The doors slide open. A thick cloud of heat hits our faces. The flag is there on the pole, unmoved. ¿How long did I nap? It wasn't minutes, it wasn't a few hours. The brightness confuses me. We're in the furnace again. The asphalt feels sticky, the heat crawls up our shoes. We walk to another white truck with a green stripe. Small birds rest on skinny green trees that look like they haven't drunk water in years. There are cactuses, tall and plump. ¡They're like the ones in *The Road Runner*! I didn't see this type of cactus at night. It's not a Lonely or a Spikey. They look like people. Thorny old people looking down at us. One of them, growing out of the parking lot, has his arms up like he's scared. Another has four arms with more arms growing out of them, like a weird octopus.

Short Black Hair opens the front door. Automatically, the door starts beeping *ding-ding-ding-ding*. Dark Blond opens the back door and helps Patricia in. She slides across the seat to the right back window. Dark Blond helps Carla, then me. He shuts the door behind us and waves at us before telling something to Short Black Hair, who's already sitting in the driver's seat.

The car turns on and the AC blasts cold air. The back of the car is the same: no seatbelt, dark-gray plastic seats, metal divider separating the front cabin from the back. My throat is dry. I'm thirsty again. I should have drunk water in the cage. I haven't brushed my teeth. My tongue is filled with a thick layer of the white stuff that makes breath stink in the morning. ¿How am I gonna brush? ¿Shower? ¿Get clean? All my stuff is in the desert. Patricia's backpack is lost también. Only Chino and Carla have all of their things. I know I stink. I want to shower. The desert is in our clothes, in our skin. We start driving. We are *de-por-ta-dos*. My stomach growls. I feel like I'm still next to the silver toilet. Zippers. The yellowest liquid.

We left Chino. He never left us. He ran back to pick me up. Chele and Mario ran. Chino could've gotten away. But he came back. This feels wrong. We were The Eight. Then The Six. This morning we were The Four, briefly; now we're The Three. I'm afraid it's gonna be just me. That Patricia and Carla will leave. I don't want to be alone. I'll do anything. I want to cry. I want to cuddle. I want to be with my parents. I don't want to go back to México. I'm in La USA. It's not supposed to feel like this. I want to be laughing, jumping into my parents' arms.

It's quiet in the truck except for the occasional radio beep, the sound of the AC, and the tires. We drive out of the parking lot onto the road with trees like the trees in the desert. We drive toward hills filled with houses. The real fence, the one from the movies, crawls up the ridge. From here it looks small and rusty. The ride isn't long. We drive closer and closer to the fence and the hills, until we take a left. We're in the town we drove past on our way to the cage. A Burger King. We take a right before we get to a McDonald's. We drive past a Shell gas station and wait at a stoplight next to a palm tree.

To the right of our car, a row of stores with awnings. The road gets wider. Two lanes then three lanes go through a two-story building that looks like a beige shoebox. At the end of each lane, there's a booth filled with uniforms. A lot of cars wait to drive through. It looks like the building swallows the cars, each booth a large tooth, the windows on the second story the building's eyes. The five lines of cars are five long tongues sticking out from the shoebox's mouth.

The light is still red. In front of us, a park with a gazebo and trees; different trees than the ones in the desert, full of leaves and taller than any building. Pigeons perch on telephone lines and some fly overhead. The light turns green and we take a right into the traffic waiting to be eaten by the building. *MEXICO* is written on a green sign with an arrow pointing forward. To our right, past Patricia, who stares at the seat in front of her, a store with headless mannequins in the display window. Above the white awning, written in huge black letters: *COQUETTE'S*. On the awning, written in red: *Mayoreo-Menudeo ropa para toda la familia.* ¿I thought we were in La USA? The people shopping look like us.

We take a left onto a road that leads to the park. Ahead, another hill with the rusty fence crawling up it. To the right of the fence, houses and houses. To the left, bushes and dirt. We pass two pairs of train tracks right next to the park. ¿Are these the same tracks we crossed at night? The road ends in front of a store named *Victoria*. This doesn't feel like a victory. We drive closer to a concrete wall with curly barbwire on top; the Mexican flag hangs from a pole on the other side. Chino isn't here. There's so much room in the backseat.

The road curves left. To our right, the concrete wall has silver-blue metal sections that start above the heads of adults waiting in a line. Where the line begins, there's a house-like building with terracotta tiles on top. We park where the last person is waiting.

"Aqui," Short Black Hair finally says. "Aqui dejar." He looks at Carla and me. "Caminar otro lado." Then he smiles, showing us his white teeth, almost no space between each tooth.

Patricia glares at him. "¿Y mi marido?"

The gringo leans closer to the metal divider, looking at her. "Esperar otro lado. Aqui lugar donde deportado."

"¿Cuándo?"

"Mas tarde." Then he mumbles something else. "Antes de noche."

¡¿We might wait until night?! He turns the car off. None of the people standing in line look like us. He walks over to Patricia's side, knocks on her window, and opens the door.

"No correr," he tells her, pointing at the booth. *MEXICO* is written in black next to a black arrow pointing into a door that looks like the turnstiles at supermarkets, except this one has a lot of metal bars from the bottom all the way to the top. Each time someone walks through, the metal teeth click.

"Afuera," the uniform says. Our door is still open, his hand on Patricia's handcuffs. Carla and I step out. The gringo grabs Carla's backpack strap. I hold Patricia's shirt. He kicks our door closed.

Now there's only one woman waiting to get through the turnstile. She looks back at us and tells the gringo something. When she turns back to face the booth, her oversized red shirt fills with air. Her face has a lot of wrinkles and is missing a tooth. She's scary. I don't like her jean shorts that look too tight. She's swallowed by the metal mouth and into the little house with the terracotta roof.

Once she's on the other side, the red-shirt gringa walks into a store where some people walk out with bags. We're in front of the turnstile, and finally, Short Black Hair takes Patricia's handcuffs off. She rubs her hands.

"Caminar," he says as he pushes Patricia in front of us. "Buena suerte." He taps me on my shoulder. Patricia looks back, trying to stand her ground. "Nada estupido," he says, and signals with his finger where to go.

She goes through the metal teeth. Click. Carla. Click. It's my turn. Directly behind the turnstile is a booth with a person inside it, behind glass.

"Caminar," Short Black Hair says. I take a step, touch the warm metal. "Goh."

I push and make it through. The booth is narrow like an outhouse. The gringo behind the glass doesn't look at us, but looks at a much bigger line of people trying to get into La USA.

Patricia grabs my and Carla's hands, pulling us deeper into México, away from my parents, away from Chino. But she's still with me. We're still a family. She will protect me. She called me hijo.

We walk toward a Mexican guard who waves us off, saying, "Caminen, caminen," and we walk out of the booth. There are only two streets. One to our right, parallel to the concrete wall, the other directly in front of us. So many people walk in all directions. On this side, the little house doesn't have terracotta tiles like on the American side; this side has rows and rows of curly barbwire. The gringo gets in his car and drives off. Carla and I look at each other. There are a lot more people. People here wait on the street, not doing anything. On the other side, everyone was in their cars or inside stores. But here, Patricia's hands are free.

The pole with the Mexican flag is right in front of us. We're back in our pretend country. The air is the same as four steps ago. Pigeons fly above the wall and sit on telephone wires on this side también. Patricia hasn't said anything. We rush past the people trying to get to where we just came from. ¿How can they just walk through? Some look like us. Some are speaking Spanish. There's a paletero man. I ate the cookie, but it's only woken up my stomach. Patricia keeps walking fast without saying anything, keeps pulling both our hands. I know not to ask. The paletero rings his bell. There's no wind, the sun is directly over our heads. Patricia's face is sweaty. She looks lost.

"Mamá," Carla says.

Patricia doesn't hear.

"¡Mamá! ¡Stop!" Carla snaps at her and lets go of her hand. Patricia stops.

"¿What?" Patricia lets go of my hand.

"It's too hot."

Patricia looks at her, then looks at me.

"Sí," I whisper.

"¿What the fuck do you want *me* to do?" she almost screams.

"I don't know," Carla says softly. Then she starts taking her chamarra off.

All three of us take off our dark chamarras and wrap them around our waists, the linings and zippers already hot to the touch. Patricia pauses and looks around.

"Give me the backpack," she tells Carla.

"¿Why?"

"¡Give it to me!"

Carla hands it off, and Patricia wears it on her back.

We keep walking, and after a few steps Carla asks, "¿Where are we going?"

"Stop asking questions."

Patricia stares at the ground, looks everywhere, scratches her head.

"There." She points at a string of stores. Some look closed, a palm tree growing behind them. Men sit on a waist-high broken brick wall that seems to be an old demolished building. Others sit on the sidewalk, or stand with one foot against a store's locked metal doors. Smaller birds fly overhead. I don't understand how they can fly when it's so hot. Only now, I miss the coldness of the room where Chino is still trapped.

The men look at us funny. Most wear jeans and either baseball caps or cowboy hats. Patricia walks us to the shade under a store's awning. I feel like we're naked. Like people know we're not from here. Like they know I saw a man's thing. I'm sweating, but sweat doesn't stay on my skin—the air licks it away fast. Stray dogs wander the street. I get closer to Patricia; I don't want them to be the German shepherds from the desert. The orange dirt, the dust kicked up. We're back in México, where we were yesterday.

Patricia sits on the sidewalk, leaning against the store's wall. Carla and I sit next to her. The paletero keeps ringing his bell. Other vendors walk by selling chips. I'm hungry. Carla looks at her mom but doesn't say anything. Patricia has my pesos, my snack money. I carry a few dollars Mali zipped into my pants in secret places.

The men sitting on the brick wall whistle at Patricia, shout piropos, things like "mamacita." She ignores them and hugs both of us. We keep a close watch for a skinny, tall, almost bald man with thick black eyebrows and very small eyes—an Olivia-from-*Popeye* look-alike.

The men get closer. Now they're not shouting things at Patricia but prices.

"¡Five hundred dollars to cross!"

"¡Six hundred dollars to the other side!"

"¡Coyote! ¡Coyote!"

"¡Pollero!"

She doesn't respond. We wait for one man and one man only to exit that gate. The man who has been with us since San Salvador and didn't leave us. The only person left who has lived through everything we have.

Another man comes up to us wearing Mexican boots, a belt, and a tucked-in dress shirt. He's short and has a scraggly black mustache.

"Hola, señorita, ¿do you need to cross?"

Patricia shakes her head.

"I got the best price. The best coyote."

He walks closer, and Patricia shakes her head, tries to ignore him.

"No, gracias," she says as he takes one step closer.

"Look, because you have plebes, fifteen hundred dollars for you three."

"No, gracias, señor," she tells him in her best Mexican.

"¿Who are you waiting for?"

"Mi marido." Patricia leaves it at that. Looks away from the man, who understands and walks away toward the other men. He tells them something and they point at us and laugh. One of them shouts something at Patricia. She looks away. After a short while, they forget about us and shout their prices at other people walking back from the gate. Mostly men. Some women and children. They walk out of white cars with green stripes like we did. None of them Chino.

"Excuse me." Patricia reaches out to the man who talked to us. He runs over, his boots clicking against the sidewalk.

"¿Mande?"

"¿Where can we buy water?"

He smiles. "Over there." He points to a store down the street, farther away from where people wait in line to cross. "Or wait for a vendor."

"Gracias."

The man walks back to his spot on the bricks.

"Let's wait," Patricia says. Last time I drank water was in the cage. The water from the metal sink was so cold, but now it sounds good. The Water Man is nowhere. Chino is nowhere. Pigeons and smaller birds have stopped flying, it's so hot. We fan ourselves with Carla's clothes from her backpack. I think they're clean, but they smell like the desert, like dust and more dust.

We don't take our eyes off the turnstile, the barbwire roof. Gringos cross into this side. The Mexican guards know them; they wave at them. These gringos don't look like the ones in movies or the ones in uniform. Their clothes are ragged, old, dirty. Their faces wrinkled like the woman waiting in line, all of them skinny like Chino. Some of them have shopping carts. They remind me of the drunks from my hometown: Crime Face, The Beauty, The Milk, Water Bag. They talk loud and shout things in English. They go into the store to buy beer or other things they carry in plastic bags. Then they wait in line to cross back into La USA. Sometimes they cross with their carts. Sometimes with nothing but their two feet. They come to this side, where we're hungry. Thirsty. They walk back to that side, where my parents are. Where Carla's dad and sister are. These gringos make it look easy. It doesn't look like they show documents on the way to La USA. There's another gate that's not the turnstile; the uniforms open it for them if they have a shopping cart. The wheels make as much noise as they do. They talk loud and sound drunk.

Finally, The Water Man comes and Patricia buys us three bags. After an hour, a lady selling chips comes, and Patricia gets us Doritos. She still has some pesos. The sun drags across the sky. We keep fanning, but the shade keeps moving, so we scoot over to lean against the store's metal gate instead of the wall. Hopefully the store doesn't open soon.

So many gringos with loose clothing, wrinkles, and carts walk back and forth. Sometimes, it's the same one back for another trip. ¿Why can't *we* do that? All the gringo guards need to hear is English. ¿Why didn't my parents tell me to learn? I could walk across easy. No one would notice. I don't look like the gringos, but some people in line look like me. They *must* have papers. We don't have real ones. The men shouting prices must know that about us. We've been here long, and some men have left and new ones replaced them. They also whistle and shout piropos at Patricia. After a while, they say the same thing: "¡Six hundred dollars! ¡Six hundred dollars to cross!"

"Do it for the kids," the one woman who stands with the men tells Patricia. But Patricia doesn't respond. This woman has black curly hair and wears red lipstick, blue jeans, and a white shirt she tucks into her pants, held up by a black belt.

Patricia shakes her head at all of them. On the street parallel to the concrete wall, other men shout their prices at people walking out of the little building we walked out of. They can tell who is like us. I think I can también: it's the people looking down at the ground when they walk out. They don't smile. Mostly they're brown and sunburned like us. Some have backpacks, others have nothing. They're not like the gringos, who smile and shout as they walk into the store to buy things.

Minutes later, the curly-haired woman walks back toward us, trying to stay in the shade. She tells us there is a place with beds and free food where we can wait. She says we don't have to use her services, but that there are coyotes there también. Patricia pretends not to listen, but the woman with the red lipstick points to where it is. "Down this street, then take a left. Ask for el albergue."

"We have to wait for mi marido."

"Wait, then go," she says, and walks away.

It's getting late. Patricia, Carla, and I have to be the eyes, the mouth, the shadow, the hunger, the brains of The Three. I'm mad at Cadejo. ¿How could he let this happen? The moon was there, full, but she didn't do anything. I never saw Cadejo's red eyes, heard his faint whistle. We wait and we wait. We follow the shade from one side of the street to the other. The sun is softer now, but the air is still warm. We get another water bag, but no chips. More people cross to this side, more people wait in line to get through the booth to La USA.

It's 5:35 P.M. We've been here since the sun was on the other side of the sky. We keep drinking water, but my tongue feels dry. My throat has ants inside it scratching the punching bag at the back of my mouth. My breath stinks, the white remains, I swish the water like I'm gonna spit it out but swallow because I'm thirsty. Patricia's and Carla's mouths stink también. It's why Patricia looks away when she talks to us.

"Puta, I haven't showered in two days," she says, sniffing her armpits.

"¿Two days?"

"Sí, Javier, ¿you don't remember?"

I don't know what she's talking about.

"One night in jail," Patricia says, looking away. "It's Monday."

"Two stinky days," Carla adds, looking my way but pointing her words at the ground. "We showered on Saturday."

¡¿Two days?! ¿It wasn't a nap? ¡I slept in a cage an entire night! *That's* why there were different people when I woke. Why I smell so bad. Why I'm so hungry. My armpits smell rancid. I'm still dirty. All of our pants are dusty. Our shirts.

Another white truck parks and lets more men out. All of them line up to enter the turnstile. Two green uniforms next to them. They make it through one by one. ¿Is it? Dark clothes: check. But all of the men have dark clothes. Skinny: check. No hair: check. Patricia stands up. Carla and I follow. I think it is—

"¡Chino!" Patricia shouts.

"¡Chino!" Carla and I shout, using our hands as megaphones.

People look at us. We don't care. Patricia waves her hand. "¡Aquí! ¡Vení!"

Chino lifts his head. Grabs the handles of his backpack. ¡He got it back! He walks faster. I want to run to him.

"Careful, there are cars," Patricia says, holding me back.

It's him. He's back. We didn't leave him. He didn't leave us. We're a unit again. A family.

"¿Quiubo?" Chino says, nodding his head at us. "¿We fucked up, ve'á?"

"Calláte, cerote," Patricia tells him, but we all laugh. He's right. We got caught.

Patricia hugs him. "I was scared we weren't gonna see your ugly-ass face again," she says. I didn't know that. She made it seem like she knew he was coming here for sure. ¿What if he hadn't? Uyyyy. ¡No! Dios mío. I don't know what we would've done.

"No jodás, vos. Mala yerba nunca muere."

I hug both of them. I don't ever want to be separated again. We smell of dirt and dust. Carla hugs them. We're The Four.

"Ya. I'm not dead, bayuncos," Chino says, his small teeth, his dimples, his acne pockmarking his face. He looks better. He's smiling.

"¿How was it?" Patricia asks.

"Javier can tell you."

I shake my head.

"He's not speaking," Patricia says. "Almost mute."

"¿Verdad, bicho?"

He kneels to talk to me face-to-face. It *is* harder for me to speak.

"No," I whisper, and shake my head.

"Va. He's good, you're the one with chiripiorca."

Patricia shakes her head, smiling. Carla smiles as well.

Chino tells us the uniforms weren't lying. He waited because there was a long line to "process." I don't know what that means. We waited a long time.

Carla looks at Chino up and down, touches him. "¿You eat?"

"Puesí, but ¡those sandwiches tasted like cardboard!"

We laugh. They did taste like cardboard.

"Pero, mirá, I talked to that man." He points at a man that came out of the truck with him. "He told me there's a place with free food, beds, and they even have polleros."

"Un albergue," Patricia says.

"Cabal. Let's go." Chino points at the crowd of men, who seem to know where they're going. They walk down the street the woman with red lipstick pointed out.

"Vení," Chino says, looking at me. "Let's eat and sleep." Chino says the last part looking at Carla. He nods at Patricia, and she knows he means to grab Carla's hand. He grabs my hand. His hands are rough. It's like the desert: he's our leader, he knows what to do. We walk down the street, deeper into México. Past cars. Past stores opening up. Past stray dogs and vendors.

"¿You talked to them?" Chino asks Patricia as we walk.

"¿Who?"

"The number Mario gave us."

"No," Patricia says, embarrassed. "You just got out and ¿you're already asking?"

"Ajá."

"When we get there, we'll call," Patricia tells him. I think they mean the coyote's number. But Patricia and Chino don't tell Carla or me anything. Maybe Carla knows. We keep following the men. We're like a wave. Walking past everyone on the sidewalk. People look at us. They must know we're not from here.

One of the men asks, "¿To the albergue?" I think he's chapín.

"Sí," Patricia responds, and he starts following us. We're a wave that will crash on a bed.

5-31-99

WE WAIT IN LINE to get into the albergue without saying hi to anyone. A nun at the front of the line says, "There are beds, showers, food, and water inside, but"—she pauses—"you must wait in an orderly fashion. No cutting."

We followed the wave of mostly men. Here, Patricia, Carla, and I aren't the only women and children standing next to the building's bumpy walls. The one-story building is painted white and looks like a big warehouse or school, with a tin-metal roof. It's almost dusk; we're wearing our chamarras but with zippers open. The line moves slowly. Like in the desert, we aren't the first ones, but we're not the last. Light-brown doves make a funny noise when they fly off from the roof's ledge, like windup toys that chirp when released. The building's black iron doors are wide open. We look through and see lots of mattresses on top of a tile floor.

Another nun walks down the line, checking how many people per group. She gets to us and asks, "¿Together?"

"Sí," all of us say. She smiles, showing off her dimples. She's not that old, her skin is still smooth.

"You're almost inside."

"Gracias, Madre," Chino says.

She responds with another smile.

These nuns are nice and they all wear white. Back home, only Mother Superior wore white, and not all the time. She must know I'm not coming back. I don't want to go back to El Salvador. We take a few steps forward. Chino smells bad. I smell bad. The people in front también. Sweat. Dust. Sardines. Piss. I can't wait to shower. I look at Patricia's lips, and there's a flower bursting through them. A fire. The beginning of a cold sore. Mamá Pati gets those. I get them. ¿Did she have a fever in the cage? ¿The temperature change? I don't want a fever.

Chino pulls my hand. We're moving-moving. We make it to the door where the other nun hasn't moved. She's short and has a round face like Abuelita Neli, who must be worried. I want to tell her I'm fine, that I'm with good people. I want my real family to meet Chino, Patricia, and Carla.

When we get to the nun, she greets us with a "buenas tardes" and hands us each one water bottle, one plastic toothbrush, and one white Zote soap bar, plus two white towels and a small Colgate toothpaste tube to share. ¡I'm gonna be clean again!

"Gracias, Madre," Patricia says.

"Gracias," the rest of us follow.

"It's nothing. Choose any bed that's open." The nun points into the room with row after row of mattresses on the floor. "Preferably one per family. Oh, and the bathrooms are through that door." She points to the far left corner of the room.

Patricia rushes in front of us in order to choose a bed. It's warm inside. Other single men or families choose their route through the mattress maze. There isn't much room to walk. All of the beds have white sheets and one white pillow. A lot have people resting on them, who look at us as we walk past. It's a race to the freest mattress. The floor is terracotta, which makes it easy to see the dust on each tile. The roof is tin, held up by black iron bars. The walls are white or beige, I can't tell with the sunlight, and every two meters, standing fans spin their heads.

Patricia zigzags to the back left corner. People claim beds by sitting or jumping on them and tapping them twice. The person in front of us takes one. Another. Patricia keeps zigzagging. I feel naked like when we first made it through the turnstile. Everyone stares, especially the children. Children smaller than me. Sitting next to their moms, they point at us.

There are open mattresses near the right corner of the room. A man and a kid eye the white rectangles. Patricia notices and speeds up. We speed up behind her. "Everyone gets a bed," the nun said. It doesn't feel like it. He picks up his kid and beats us. Doesn't matter, Patricia takes the white patch next to them at the very corner of the large room. She spreads her arms and legs, tapping the bed twice.

"Here," Patricia says, loud enough for the dad and kid to hear.

"Vos, take that one," she tells Chino, nodding toward a third open mattress.

"La Madre said one bed."

"Agarrála con Javier."

Chino sits on the bed and I sit next to him. The mattress feels thin, but it's long. Bigger than Chino. I nod at the boy lying next to his dad. He doesn't nod back. I don't care and let my weight go behind me. The mattress is comfy. The sheets smell like detergent and bleach. Everywhere, movement: people's footsteps, people talking, the fans shaking their heads. The room has some columns in the middle and a high ceiling; it feels like the church back home. Windows let the sun in, painting the room more and more orange. I'm tired. We waited hours for Chino. I'm hungry. The chips helped, but I want real food.

"Bichos, rest," Patricia says.

"I'm hungry." Carla points at her belly.

I just nod.

"¿Where's the food?" Chino asks.

The man with his son looks at us. "¿First time?"

Chino nods.

"You better start lining up, the line gets long," the dad tells us. He doesn't sound Mexican.

"¿Why aren't *you* up?" Patricia asks.

"The middle is where they give more food."

"We'll get up with you then." Patricia smiles at him.

"¿How long?" Chino asks.

"Any minute. The nuns shout when the food is ready. Never past seven-fifteen."

I look at my watch. It's about to be seven. ¿What's dinner gonna be? As long as it's not those green tomatoes we had in Guadalajara, I'll eat anything. I hope it's tacos like in Mazatlán. Or Doña's chilaquiles.

"¿The food any good?" Chino asks the man.

"Más o menos," he says, the corners of his top lip pressing down against the bottom lip.

"¿Y de dónde es usted?" Patricia asks. *Usted.* She must think the man is older. I look at him, but I can't tell.

"El Salvador."

"Vieja. Nosotros también. ¿What part?" Chino interrupts.

"San Miguel."

"¡Garrobero! Nosotros somos de Soyapango."

"Oh." The dad nods and leaves it at that.

I've never been to San Miguel. I miss Abuelita's tortillas. Some of them salty like how Grandpa likes them. Warm tortillas with half an avocado from our backyard, a chunk of queso duro, and refried beans. That's what I *really* want.

I lie down and stare at the slit between the wall and the tin roof. ¡There's a dove's nest! Over at the front end of the mattress maze, someone starts playing their radio. People get quieter. I know this song.

"Vieja, Los Yonic's."

"No, vos, it's Marco Antonio Solís," Chino corrects Patricia.

"No fregués."

"Sí, it's Jesucristo."

Carla chuckles. I laugh.

"No seás bayunco." Patricia slaps her pillow.

I think Chino is right. I'd recognize that voice anywhere. These lyrics:

> *Pero te vas a arrepentir, cuando veas que no es nada*
> *Su riqueza comparada con lo que a ti te di.*

"It's Los Yonic's *featuring* Marco Antonio Solís," the dad next to us says.

"Ohhh." Patricia and Chino nod and smile.

I think of Chele, the times he played Los Bukis and everyone made fun of him for looking like Marco Antonio Solís. He ran. He was always distant, but it's strange not having him here, not knowing where he is. ¿Did he make it to the vans? ¿Where's Marcelo? He stole Chele's food and water, that's a sin. He was "deportado." My town was right; he's a bad person. But we're deportados. I want him to make it to his mom.

Everywhere we've been, the same artists follow us. Los Temerarios. Los Bukis. Bronco. Control Machete. Vilma Palma e Vampiros. Los Yonic's. Grupo Límite. Now they're here. I close my eyes, let the nearest fan's breeze touch my skin.

Then, with their hands around their mouths, the nuns shout, "¡Diiinnner!"

The music is still playing. Everyone shuffles to the back of the building where we are. Directly to our left at the end of this final row of beds, there's a kitchen. A room with stoves, a giant griddle, and a fridge. The nuns stand behind a plastic table with giant steel pots, stacks of paper plates, boxes of plastic forks and spoons, and a container of tortillas. It's like a birthday party. We're lining up for cake.

"Vamos a hartarnos," Chino says, slapping his tummy. All of us sit up and look over at the dad.

"Not yet," he whispers, holding out his palms like he's pushing air toward us. "Trust me." The line gets bigger and bigger. "Now," he says, and stands up, pulling his son's arm.

Chino pulls my arm. Patricia and Carla behind us. We stand in the middle of the line. Some people smile at us, others talk to each other. Most of them carry their things with them. If I had a backpack, I wouldn't leave it unattended either. Chino has his. Patricia carries Carla's, but left a shirt on her bed and threw another on ours.

The pots release thick wafts of steam. My mouth waters. Ugh, I'm soooo hungry. I want everything. The young nun grabs a paper plate, dips her scoop into one pot: ¡refried beans! Then she dips another scoop into the other pot: ¡yellow rice! Hands the plate over to us. The older nun, the one that looks like Abuelita, reaches over to our plate and drops a thin slice of queso fresco *and* two flour tortillas— ¡my favorite!

"Gracias, Madres," I say.

They smile back. The paper plate heavy in my hands. At the end of the table, there's a stack of paper cups and a water dispenser. I place my full plate on the table and press the blue handle in the dispenser for cold water. I fill my cup. Chino is behind me. He points to our bed with his lips. I walk, making sure I don't trip on anything.

All of us make it to our beds. Chino stuffs his face, makes a *hmmppphh* sound with his first bite, and can't stop nodding. Patricia nods también, gives me a thumbs-up. I grab beans and rice with a piece of the warm tortilla. *Mmmm.* The spices. ¡Everything is sooo good! I follow the bite with a piece of queso fresco. The entire room's gone silent. Even the music stopped. Everyone's eating. After a while, the music starts again. This time, a different song. It starts off slow. I know that voice. It's José Guadalupe. Then, the keyboard.

Traigo en el alma pena y llanto, que no puedo contener . . .

¡Bronco! "Que No Quede Huella." Abuelita loves this song. We keep eating. Smiling. Moving to the rhythm of the keyboard. The fans shake their heads. Our fingers dive into the food, dancing and singing.

AFTER DINNER, PEOPLE LINE up again; there are showers for men and for women. It's colder. I thought I wanted to shower, but I'm so tired

I don't want to move. Patricia and Carla are already in there. Chino and I watch our beds. He asks me what team I think will play in the Mexican final.

"Atlas is gonna win it all."

"N'hombre, Toluca and Cruz Azul in the final."

I disagree. We playfully argue until, after a few minutes, Patricia comes back with Carla. Their hair is wet, but Patricia is wearing the same clothes, her shirt wet in patches: I can see her belly button screaming through the dirty shirt, her bra like two wet eyes.

"Vieja, it's gonna rain," Chino tells Carla, then looks over at Patricia. "Huele a tierra mojada." His two favorite jokes. It's funny now only because he said it all the time at Doña's and in Guadalajara, but *he's* the one who rarely showers.

"Bayunco." Patricia is pretend-mad, but she smiles. It makes me smile, which makes Chino smile, which makes Carla laugh. Now all of us are laughing in our own white sheets: our private boats or white-sand islands in the middle of a terracotta-colored ocean.

"We have to buy clothes," Patricia says between laughs, raising her right hand to sniff her armpit. "Todavía jiedo."

We burst out laughing. I grab my stomach. Chino throws himself on the bed. Carla wipes her tears. People look over at us. Some shake their heads. We're the loudest boat. Others smile. Slowly, we quiet down, and then pick up again, but not as loud as the first burst. I can't breathe. My stomach hurts from laughing.

"Ya, bayuncos," Chino tells us, shaking his head, looking over at the people near our bed. "Let's shower." Chino grabs the towel we must share and the wet bar of Zote soap Patricia and Carla just used. I grab my new toothbrush. Carla hands me the Colgate tube. Chino and I walk to the back of the building, behind the kitchen.

Outside, it's dark and colder than it is inside, where the fans are still rotating. I have goosebumps on my arms, my nipples are hard. Men wait in line. A green plastic curtain acts as the door in front of the cement walls that make up the showers.

"Wash your shirt," Chino tells me. "Go first."

I untie my shoes and put my socks inside. The moment I touch the cold cement, my nipples harden even more.

"Bicho, má." He hands me the socks. "Wash them." He's smart; I can leave them drying overnight. The man in front of me gets out of the shower, fully clothed. I look at Chino, who nods, and I understand he means I should change inside.

"Don't wash your pants, they take too long to dry."

I walk barefoot toward the green plastic curtain. The cement is rough. Soapsuds and shampoo foam drip down from the curtain as I open it. At the corner of the bathroom, leaning against the cement wall, there's a huge plastic barrel filled with water, a smaller plastic bowl floating inside it. The water is still moving from the man who just used it. Luckily the barrel is not taller than me and the water is almost to the brim. I can scoop it. Above me, an uncovered lightbulb hangs from the ceiling. Moths fly into it. The brown cord is wrapped around a wooden beam so many times it will never fall on me.

I hand Chino my belt, my pants. I keep my underwear and shirt on in the shower, so I can wash them, but also, so people can't see me. The curtain doesn't cover the door entirely. I pour a bowlful of water. My skin tightens. I remember my well. Then Tecún Umán and Grandpa. Water makes it all the way down my body. My thing shrinks. I feel like I can't breathe, it feels good. Chino bangs my pants against a wall to get the dust out. I scrub dirt and more dirt from my armpits, legs, crotch, belly. My hair releases the most dark water. I'm so dusty. I wash my body, then my shirt. My socks I hand over to Chino after I'm done squeezing the dirt out. I get as close to the middle of the curtain as I can and take my underwear off and try to scrub everything. These aren't the ones I left a mark on, they're not stained, but I hate that they're white—they show dirt so easily.

"Towel," I say, reaching my hand out.

Chino hands me the towel and I dry myself.

"Pants."

He hands them over. They're still dusty, with some needles and grass stuck in them.

"Belt."

I put everything on, including my wet shirt and underwear, and walk out.

"¡I forgot to brush my teeth!"

"No, no," Chino says, showing me his teeth. "Over there." He points at a sink with a faucet. I hand him the wet towel. I feel clean. But Patricia is right: my pants still stink. My belly presses against the shirt. If my shirt wasn't black, my belly button would look like a mouth, like Patricia's did.

"¡Walk to our bed when you're done!" Chino shouts from behind the curtain. I brush my teeth at the sink and walk back. The room is warm. It's not as cold here as it was in the desert, but it's also not as late. My shirt feels like it's drying fast. I get to the bed, and Carla is already sleeping. One of Patricia's arms is around her, and she brushes her daughter's hair with her other hand. I lie down on the sheets. Because of my shirt, I feel like I'm wetting the bed. I sit up. Patricia's shirt looks completely dry.

"Sleep," Patricia says without looking over at me.

I stay quiet and pull the front of my shirt away from my skin so it dries faster. Chino doesn't come back.

"Sleep," she repeats.

The front of my shirt isn't as wet as the back, so I flip the Animaniacs' faces so I lie on top of them. I try to get comfy on the side closest to Patricia and Carla's bed. They're so close, only a tile between us. I want to cuddle with them like we did in the days before the desert, but these beds are skinnier and thinner than the ones we're used to. I look up at the ceiling and follow one ridge of one piece of the tin roof down into the next piece and into the next, until I get to the roof's edge. The doves are gone. They must be sleeping.

"¡Lights out at nine P.M.!" a nun shouts.

¿It's not nine yet? It feels like midnight. My stomach is full. My legs are sore. My shoulders. My neck. I lie down and I'm on a cloud.

Rain waiting to drop from my wet shirt. I flip the shirt back so the
Animaniacs' faces look up at the tin ceiling. I close my eyes and wait
for Chino's weight to press down on the mattress.

6-1-99

"EXPENSIVE," THE DAD FROM San Miguel with the son says about
our pollero, Mario. Which makes Patricia feel better about our services. "Expensive things are better than cheaper ones," Abuelita said.
I hope it's true. His pollero didn't allow for a second try if he got
caught. Ours does. Mario gave Chino and Patricia a number. Everyone eats breakfast slowly, maybe because the eggs don't taste like anything, but the beans are good. When we finish, Chino gathers our
bean-smeared plates and throws them in the trash.

"Stay here, Pati. I'm gonna call."

Before breakfast, Patricia told Chino she wanted all of us to go
look for a phone. Chino told her it's safer if we stay. It's what most
people are doing: one person leaves, the rest stay on the white islands.

Patricia keeps talking to the Migueleño who's resting next to his
son. It turns out he's used three different polleros, but not ours. None
have worked. He's tried to cross three times. His walks sound longer
than ours. I don't want to do it more than twice.

"Just be careful. Carry enough water for the kids," the Migueleño
tells Patricia as he stares at the ceiling. The kid, who is younger than
me, sleeps below his dad's armpit.

It's quiet. Like breakfast had pitos in it. *Mmm.* Abuelita made the
best bean soup with those flowers that look like thin green tubes of
lipstick with their red or orange tips. After a bowl, everyone took a
nap. It's how I feel right now. Music would help, but I think the person with the radio is sleeping, or is out looking for a pollero. Fans and
doves make the only sounds. Carla hugs her mom. I miss their oxtail-
soup smell that seeps into the sheets. This bed is so small, but it feels
huge without Chino. I don't know how to ask them if I can snuggle
like everywhere else we've stayed. I was so tired last night; if Chino

snored, I didn't notice. But there's a patch of drool on the sheets. I don't stretch in that direction. His backpack is still here. Patricia has threaded her arm through the straps of Chino's and Carla's backpacks. Chino did the same last night. They're all we have left.

I feel like we're back at Doña's. I can't sleep. Everyone else is passed out. ¿When are we gonna walk again? ¿When is Chino gonna come back? ¿Is someone gonna pick up the phone? ¿Is Mero Mero back in México? ¿Mario? ¿Is someone else gonna take us? ¿How can Patricia sleep? She's probably not asleep. She does that: makes us go to sleep, but she stays up thinking. Her lips move as she thinks. I look over. Her eyes are closed. Her hair is loose. Every brownish-red strand is spread out on the sheets. Her black hair tie is on her left hand; her ring is on the finger it should be on. So many wrinkles. Her hands look cracked. I look at mine and they're dry. The air is dry. We need lotion. I think it was in Patricia's backpack. Maybe she *is* sleeping. She hasn't moved. Her breathing smooth and in the same pattern. Fine. I'll try closing my eyes. Try not to think of anything. Nothing. The tires come back. That man shouting "¡La Migra!" and then Mario. No. Think of stars. So many of them at night. *Okei,* like the gringos say. *Okei.* Nothing. Sleep. Sleep.

6-2-99

"COMÉ COMÉ COMÉ," CHINO tells me as he swallows a handful of tasteless scrambled eggs and beans he's grabbed with a piece of flour tortilla. Breakfast is the same every day. But what we didn't know our first day was that if the food doesn't run out, we can get more. It's what the nun said yesterday at dinner. They made too much food. We always line up in the middle, behind the Migueleño and his son.

This morning, the silver trays still have scrambled eggs, and the silver pot still has beans. Chino and Patricia get up again. They bring back two more plates for us to share. But no tortillas.

"For strength," Chino says with food in his mouth, smiling. He's right. We must eat.

Yesterday, Patricia and I gave Chino our dollars for the call and for supplies. I don't have any left. Chino made contact with the number Mario gave us. We get a second try. But it's our last. We have to make it this time. The man on the phone knew Don Dago, Coyote, Mario, and Mero Mero, but hadn't heard from the last two. The man told Chino we could leave today, which is what we're gonna do. But told Chino to buy food and water with our money.

"Same thing." We're gonna drive out to the middle of the desert and walk from there. All day yesterday, Chino turned into Mario and Paco, telling us to sleep, to rest, to eat for our new walk. We ate and slept all day. I tried my best to nap. It got easier. Chino napped next to me. His body on the bed makes a difference. I don't feel so alone.

"¿You're leaving already?" The Migueleño is surprised we're leaving so soon. We still don't know his real name. We just call him Migueleño and he calls us Soyas. He thinks I'm from Soyapango también. He believes we're a family.

"Ajá," Patricia responds as we finish our second paper plate.

The Migueleño is staying at least one more day.

"Be careful, take a lot of water," he reminds Chino and Patricia, then lies down on the bed.

We're leaving at noon. Chino hasn't told us where we're going. Says he knows. To trust him. Says there's gonna be a man with brown leather boots, a black cowboy hat, and a red truck.

I'm getting nervous again like I was at Doña's, but it's different this time. I didn't know what the desert was gonna be like at night. I didn't think we would get caught. That if we didn't run fast enough we could get left behind and then thrown into the back of a Migra truck. That we would sleep in a small cage like animals. I don't want that again. I want to see my parents. I don't have a backpack—I'll walk faster this time. My stomach grumbles. I hope the eggs didn't make me sick.

"Sleep, hermanito," Chino whispers. He's lying down next to me, but his eyes are wide open. Patricia's eyes are closed, but this time, I catch her moving her lips. She's thinking. I can't see Carla because she's on the other side of the mattress. ¿Maybe Patricia is praying? We did last time, but that was before we left. I close my eyes and imagine I'm in church praying with my classmates.

CHINO SHAKES ME AWAKE, whispering, "Javier, Javier."

Patricia and Carla sit up on their mattress, their hair wet, Zote soap thick on their skin.

"¿Wanna shower?" Patricia asks.

I shake my head.

Carla turns her head and pretends she smells something nasty, her nostrils flaring.

"Bañémonos," Chino says.

"Sí, par de monos," Patricia jokes. "Ufffa," she adds, flapping the air.

I don't want to shower. But I don't want to be the only one who doesn't. I rub my eyes and stand up. Carla laughs at me as her mom combs her hair. The comb must've been in Carla's bag. If Patricia still had her backpack, she would be curling her eyelashes, lining her eyes, covering the almost-gone cold sore with lipstick. I miss watching her like I watched Mali.

"Má." Patricia hands Chino the soap. "El zopilote," she snickers. It's what she calls the soap bar. Zote does sound like zopilote.

I follow Chino to the showers. It's hotter today. There's no line for either shower, but Chino lets me go first. Same thing: I shower, and he hands me my pants. I don't wash my shirt, but I do wash my underwear. I scrub everywhere, I have to smell good if I meet my parents tomorrow. This is my last Mexican shower. I dry up and hand Chino the towel and soap. I brush my teeth because I forgot to this morning. No one woke me. My heart beats faster. My head feels funny. I want someone to tell me everything will be ok. No one has in a long time.

When I get back to the bed, Patricia is brushing her hair. It's still wet. "¿Ready?"

"Sí," I say.

"Sí, ¿qué?"

"Sí, Mamá."

She laughs, leans closer, and says, "You're a good fake son. Let's pretend again, ¿okei?" Since we heard the uniforms using it, all of us say *okei* more and more.

Chino looks like he didn't even shower. There's not one wet mark on his shirt.

"¿Ready?"

"Sí," all of us say.

"Va, let's grab our things."

The Migueleño and his son lift their heads up from the bed. "See you on the other side, Soyas," he says. "Good luck." He gives us a thumbs-up.

"Gracias, maitro."

Maitro. I wonder if Marcelo's already building houses in Los Ángeles. Chino grabs his backpack. Patricia has Carla's on her back. Carla grabs her mom. I hold Chino's hand and he leads us through the mattress maze, past people sitting up, mostly lying down. Some of them wave.

CHAPTER EIGHT

——

Second Attempt
JUNE 2, 1999

T HE POLLERO DOESN'T SAY MUCH, JUST "JUMP IN THE BACK."
He's wearing a black cowboy hat and brown boots, smoking a
cigarette in front of a red truck. People are already sitting in the truck
bed.

We don't leave right away. We wait for more people. Another man
sits in the passenger seat, smoking. Each time more people arrive, the
pollero counts us, and when the number is finally the one he wants—
around one P.M.—we drive off.

We've been driving an hour and a half now. We drove away from
Nogales, toward the mountains, then past small towns, next to dry
riverbeds, through valleys between the mountains. Brown mountains to our right, brown mountains up front, dusty mountains everywhere. Up, down, side to side, the curvy road. We drive and
drive—longer than our first try—until cactus and skinny trees are
the only things growing. The tires hit gravel and we drive on a flat
dirt road.

After a few minutes, we stop at a big tree with a white trunk. The
tree's hand-sized leaves shade a run-down house with broken wooden
slats and no windows. Doves scatter from the house's roof, and I notice people sleeping on the floor.

"We're here," Black Cowboy Hat says. The other man is still up front, silent. "Rest, eat, sleep, we'll come back at sunset."

Chino jumps out onto the dirt the color of sawdust. It's three P.M. The sun is high, but we can now tell which way it sets—past the big tree, toward the horizon. It's hotter here than it was in Nogales. Hotter than El Salvador. Chino helps us out of the truck, one by one. No one else offers to help. The strangers step slowly. The polleros don't tell us to hurry. This is different from last time.

It's mostly men again. Men everywhere. But there are some women and even some kids—older than me and Carla, teenagers. We walk toward the house that looks more like an oversized outhouse. The front door is unhinged and rests sideways against the wall. Sunlight pierces through what once was a roof. "Five-star hotel," Patricia says.

"At night it's more," Chino jokes.

We stay outside where most people wait in the tree's shade.

"Careful," Chino says, pointing at the nails sticking up from the floor. Every other wooden slat is missing or half-broken, and we can see the ground is covered in trash: water bottles, soda cans, tuna cans, plastic bags, ripped shirts, bras, socks, and underwear. We pick the corner closest to the house, where the shade hits most, where some slats remain whole.

Chino and Patricia sit with their backs to what used to be the house's front wall. Men sleep with hats on their faces. I remember men doing that our first try, when Chele and Marcelo were with us. They smoked so much. No one is smoking here. Chino's knee shakes. He hasn't bought a pack of cigarettes, but smoked a few at the albergue. Even though Chele didn't really talk to me, I miss his jokes. Maybe it's why Chino has been joking more, but it's a different humor. Chele didn't mean to be funny. And Marcelo . . . I'm still mad at him. But not as much.

Patricia thinks it was smart Marcelo left, because he probably didn't get caught. Without him I feel less safe. When Marcelo was around, people looked at us differently—with respect and with fear because of Marcelo's big muscles, scary face, tattoos that peeked out from his sleeves. Now no one looks at us like that. Chino's tattoos are hidden. His face is friendlier, and he's younger. He doesn't look as tough, but he tries—whenever a man looks at Patricia, Chino glares at him and then flaunts his fake wedding ring. "¿Quiubo?" he says, nodding at people staring at Patricia on the street. In the truck, no one talked; everyone stared at the landscape. Here, everyone sleeps. The leaves on the trees flicker with the breeze, and it sounds like rain. Green and yellow rain.

"Rest," Patricia tells us.

I look at Carla. She looks at me.

"That's all we do," Carla complains. She's right, we're pretty rested. My legs don't hurt. My tummy is almost back to normal. I gather the courage and back her up with an "ajá."

Patricia doesn't tell us anything. If I complained like that, my mom would've hit me.

Carla has her hair tie around her right wrist. I point at it. "¿Wanna play?"

"¿Play what?"

I put my hands out and form a circle.

"Ohhh." She smiles and starts pinching the front of the hair tie with her thumb and index finger. Does the same on the other end with her other hand. Then lets it go. Carla misses the circle and hits my belly. We laugh. She sounds like a chicken clucking. I like her laugh. Chino and Patricia look over at us and smile.

We play whoever makes the most out of five. Then to ten. Then fifteen. She wins every time. After the game, we take sips from one of Patricia's big water bottles. We bought two big ones for Chino. Two big ones for Patricia. One medium-sized for Carla and me each.

"Mami, play with me," she says to Patricia after we both realize I'm never gonna win. Patricia pretends not to hear until Carla looks sad and crosses her arms.

"¡Mona mimada!"

They play, and I look at the horizon where a hawk circles. ¿A good sign? The sky is blue and blue and blue. No clouds. The air is still hot. More trucks come with people in the back. A gray truck. A dark-blue truck. Our red one hasn't returned. Five to ten people each truckload. Maybe some of the people we saw during our first try waited this long before we lined up and started walking. It's four P.M. and trucks keep coming. We're at least thirty people. It doesn't feel like there's a coyote here. A pollero. No one talks to us. No one talks to anyone. Some eat. Drink water. We're not hungry yet. I lie down on the wood and spread my legs to the side, pointing at the sun. Instead of resting my head on a backpack, I use my chamarra. It smells like sweat.

Patricia loses to Carla, who is happy and finally rests. She lies down next to me, her head on her backpack. "Todo va' estar bien, bichito," Carla says without looking at me. I look at her, but she keeps staring at the sky. I haven't heard that in a while. I point at the hawk, farther away but still circling. Carla smiles and taps her mom on the arm so she can take a look.

"Good omen," Patricia says.

No clouds and no moon. It's weird. I look all over, but nothing. Last time we had the moon, almost full, and we got caught. Maybe this is better. Cadejo wasn't there. He isn't the moon. I saw a hawk. Everything will be ok. We're gonna make it.

I don't want to get caught again. Don't want that cage. That cold floor makes me want to walk faster, make it to the van quicker. I'll take smaller sips of water. I *should* rest more. But here, under this big tree, I'm less nervous than the first time we were driven out and we waited. I didn't know how far we were gonna walk. How cold the desert gets at night. That we were gonna follow a single long line. Now I know. I'm ready.

ONE TRUCK RETURNS AND parks next to the other three already here. Brown doves fly off from the tree and the roof; their wings flap bright white. I love the sound they make. They fly toward the mountains painted orange by sunset. The hawk should be out now, but he's gone. Every truck has a driver and a man in the passenger seat. All of them exit and walk toward us. I napped, but had nightmares of dogs—I'm less rested. There's nothing to do but lie down. No one gets up. No one makes any unnecessary movements. We know what's coming: walking, walking, and more walking.

I think I know who the new Mero Mero is: a short man with skin like Chele's, reddish-brown wavy hair, a scraggly beard, and a mustache. A group of seven men—¿the polleros?—follow him. He carries a dark-blue backpack that looks longer than his torso; it almost matches his dark-blue jeans. Tucked into his black belt, a dark-green, long-sleeved button-up shirt. He's chubbier than Chele, less than Don Carlos. A dark-brown baseball cap covers most of his hair, some curls sticking out above his ears.

"¡Listen up! ¡Hey! ¡Attention! ¡Everyone!" The new Mero Mero's voice is raspy like Coyote's was when he yelled too much. He's hard to understand. "¡Everyone!" he repeats, taking his cap off to wave it in the air. ¡He's bald! ¡Mero Mero #2 is bald like Don Dago! It's why they wear hats. But he doesn't look as old. "We're leaving soon. Gather your things."

Black Cowboy Hat stands next to Mero Mero #2 and yells, "¡You heard him! ¡Pick a truck! ¡We're driving to La Línea!"

Finally, backs, knees, hands start moving. People walk, avoiding the holes in the ground. Some shake their heads; others slap their cheeks to wake themselves up. Some have tied bottles to their backpacks with duct tape, others with shoelaces, someone with a belt.

"Segunda es la vencida," Chino says, puffing his chest.

"No nos salés," Patricia says, opening her backpack, checking everything.

Chino checks his water bottles—at the store, he wrapped both gallons with so much duct tape that the tape looks like a gray snake choking the bottle. He did the same to Patricia's. He stuffs one of his gallons in his backpack and straps the other around his shoulder like a sling. Carla and I stare. No backpacks for us. I feel naked.

"¿Ready?" Patricia asks us. We nod so fast our brains hit our foreheads. "¿Vos?" she asks Chino.

"Cómo no."

We stand up and follow the crowd toward the four trucks. No one hurries. The polleros don't tell us to. Chino leads us to the same red truck we came in. He leans closer to me. "¿You see El Coco Liso?"

I don't know what he's talking about.

"Coco Liso, vos. The pollero."

Carla and I laugh. Patricia shakes her head, whispers, "Bayunco"— that should be Chino's *real* nickname.

Black Cowboy Hat stands next to the red truck, smoking. The same man sits in the passenger seat. There's some blue in the sky, the sun hasn't dipped over the horizon, but the birds are gone.

When everyone is in the back of a crowded truck, Mero Mero #2 takes a last look inside the outhouse. Checks every nook. As he steps off the broken slats, he whistles by putting his index finger and thumb at each corner of his mouth. It's loud. My third-grade nun whistled like that to get our attention.

"¡A la chingada!" he yells at the other trucks as he walks toward the dark-blue one.

Coco Liso, I whisper. Chino *is* funny. That's what we'll call our new Mero Mero, because he's bald: *Coco Liso*.

Coco Liso gets in the truck, slams the door, puts his window down, then slaps the side panel. "Hold on," Black Cowboy Hat yells as he presses the accelerator. All of the trucks start moving. The sun hits the dust clouds, painting them gold as we speed off to La Línea.

IT TAKES ABOUT THIRTY minutes to get to a dirt road no one drives on except us. The same bushes that were everywhere last time are here: skinny branches with needles and hard leaves. There's a lot of trash and clothes where the trucks park. All of us jump out and the trucks linger for a bit, then leave. There are only four polleros this time. Black Cowboy Hat left like Paco did—he was just the driver.

"¡We leave in fifteen!" Coco Liso yells as he smokes a cigarette. The other three polleros stand behind him. They look about my parents' and Patricia's age, older than Chino. All of them wear dark jeans and baseball caps. One of them looks like Marcelo, curly-to-wavy hair, dark-brown skin, square jaw, but not as buff or as tall. The other two polleros are light-skinned like Coco Liso, except they have black hair.

It's getting dark. Some people sit around Coco Liso, others stand. Bats hiss and flap their wings as they swallow bugs flying over our heads. I hope they eat the fruit flies and mosquitoes swarming our bodies. No one talks except Coco Liso. A thousand crickets chirp from the bushes.

"First, check that you don't have anything that reflects light. These three will check and give you tape to cover it up.

"La Migra have night binoculars. Helicopters. Infrared cameras," he warns us like Mero Mero did.

I'm an expert, I know what's on the test.

"We walk as far as we can until dawn, or into the morning. Tomorrow afternoon, we'll get to a ranch where vans will pick us up."

"Different," Chino whispers to Patricia, who's standing and paying close attention.

"¿A ranch?"

"Coco Liso seems more professional," Chino says, nodding up and down, doing the thing with his lips that means he's impressed.

Carla and I look at each other and mimic Chino, nodding and pressing down the corners of our mouths, adding a thumbs-up. We laugh.

"We walk in a single line," Coco Liso continues. "We stop every two hours for bathroom breaks."

"If you see me, you're at the end," Marcelo Look-Alike interrupts, raising his hand. "Don't be at the end."

"If I think there's Migra, I'll yell 'hide' or 'run.' If we run, I'll whistle twice like this." He does his whistle. "Then I'll do this call." He opens his mouth: "Oooo-oh. Oooo-oh. Oooo-oh."

¡He sounds just like an owl!

"Three times only. Then a minute later, I'll hoot again." Coco Liso hoots again.

"If you can't find us, do this call and we'll look for you."

"Practice," the other polleros say.

We start hooting. Owls under shrubs, owls standing up. *Oooo-oh. Oooo-oh. Oooo-oh.* I hoot at Carla. Patricia and Carla hoot at me. Chino hoots at the sky.

Then Coco Liso whistles and it's quiet again. It's getting chilly. There's a faint wind. I put my chamarra on. Carla follows. Chino and Patricia must still be warm, because they keep listening and don't look at us. Everyone listens to Coco Liso like nuns listening to a priest. I don't remember Mero Mero making owl noises. I feel better about Coco Liso. He's a professional.

"Save your water. Tomorrow is gonna be hot like the devil's asshole."

"Uffa," Patricia says, looking at me.

I pinch my nose.

"The more we walk tonight, the less we walk in the heat."

Another pollero whispers something to Coco Liso.

"We're walking north and looking for a peak to our left that looks like a horn. A rhino's horn."

¡¿A rhino?!

"There will be barbwire fences," Coco Liso continues.

I look up at Chino, who looks down at me with his big eyes and bushy eyebrows, then winks. "I'm picking you up like the last time," he says, mimicking the motion he made when he threw me over the last fence on our first try.

"Ajá."

"A vos también," he tells Carla.

It *is* faster that way.

"You go under, don't get stuck," he tells Patricia.

"Try to help each other," Coco Liso says; he hasn't stopped talking. "The faster the better."

We're ready.

"Take a last piss, drink water, five minutes."

People start moving. The rustling drowns out the crickets and bats. The polleros spread out and check people's clothes. One of the pale polleros comes up to us and hands Carla and me small white pills. We take them without looking at Chino or Patricia. We know they help.

"Bichos, recemos," Patricia says, huddling us together. "Vos también." Chino gets closer, hugging all of us. Patricia starts praying. We close our eyes. We're so close and I'm the shortest; I feel like I'm in the middle of a forest. Carla's and Patricia's hair smells like Zote soap. Or maybe it's Chino. All of us used the same bar. But our chamarras still smell like dust and dry grass. I pray we make it, that La Migra doesn't find us, that I finally see my parents.

When I open my eyes, some people have pulled out rosaries from their pockets. Others hold the crucifixes they wear around their necks. Everyone mumbles prayers. Coco Liso whistles again. Everyone turns their heads, puts their rosaries away, stuffs their crucifixes back into their chamarras. His whistle is high-pitched and shrill; my ears ring. "¡Line up!" he screams. People cross themselves or hold their hands out in the air.

It's Patricia and Chino's signal to finally zip their chamarras. Chino grabs my hand. Patricia grabs Carla's. A gallon of water sloshes in Chino's backpack. Patricia decided two gallons are too heavy for her, so they traded. Some of Chino's clothes are in her backpack. She carries only one duct-tape snake in her right hand. We've already drunk a quarter of it—it's the bottle we're sharing first. Carla and I carry our medium-sized bottles—we'll drink those last.

People crowd to the front of the line, where Coco Liso points his flashlight at us, checking if anything reflects his beam.

"¡Single file! ¡Single file!" The two pale polleros line up the same distance from each other, about five meters, and tell people to stand close to them.

Carla lines up first. She's five people behind the first pale pollero. Patricia is next, then me, and Chino stands behind all of us.

A tall man rocks his body from side to side in front of Carla. We're missing our leader, Mario, and our tail, Marcelo and Chele. It feels lonely. Strangers surround us. This line must be more than fifty people long. At least a hundred feet, a hundred hands, a hundred eyes—a real centipede. *Centipede 2.0.* I'm nervous. My armpits sweat, even though it's not as hot as it was during the day.

"Walk close to the man," Patricia tells Carla, loud enough for the man to hear. Then Patricia turns her head and looks at me. "Closer," she says, pulling me toward her. My face is a tongue-lick away from her backpack. Chino rests his free hand on my shoulder. Tries to flick my ear.

"Stop," I say, looking back, and he smiles, his teeth bright like the moon should be, but it's nowhere. Behind him, the first stars poke through the dark-blue, almost black sky.

"Vamos con Dios," Patricia says, and crosses herself again. I cross myself. Chino does it behind me. The bushes look like shaggy-haired children waiting for us to walk next to them, like my friends waiting to give me high fives after a soccer game.

Coco Liso whistles. We start walking and our shoes pick up dust. I can't see it, but I taste it. Our steps are loud. Everyone's chamarras rub against themselves and make a plastic-bag-like noise. The gallons of water slosh. I recognize these sounds. Days ago, we were somewhere else, but the bushes are the same. The grass crunches the same. My heart pumps fast. I want to see the rhino's horn. The mountains to our right. The mountains to our left. The stars are more and more. I concentrate on Patricia's shoes. Her pants. Her backpack a breath away.

LAST TIME, THERE WERE trees at the very beginning that quickly disappeared. This time, we zigzag past bushes and outlines of the Lonely cactuses, and every ten or so meters, a tree juts out from the dirt. The ground is bumpy. First we dipped down, and now it feels like we're walking up a hill.

There are fewer fences, también. Chino helps Carla and me jump over them. Patricia and Chino slide under fast. No one's hair or backpack has gotten caught. Everything is moving faster. Better. I know we'll find the vans. Coco Liso knows the landscape.

We get into La USA faster than with Mero Mero. Whispers travel down the line. I'm already closer to my parents. I'll be with them tomorrow, after the ranch, after the vans. Nothing will go wrong. I saw the hawk. The moon isn't out yet, but our eyes have adjusted. We can see at night, it's our superpower.

It's colder than last time because it's windy. Sometimes a gust is hard and the bushes hit my stomach or legs with their thin arms. When we walk past a Lonely cactus, its needles zoom and whoosh. *Zoom. Zoom.* My hands get cold, so I stuff them into my sleeves. I'm not as scared as our first try, but my heart hasn't stopped bumping hard. Now I know the walk will take at least half a day. Chino is here with me. Patricia and Carla. We prayed. I follow Patricia's shoes. One step. Another.

We walk past a new type of cactus: small with thick thorns like the biggest fish bones. Someone in front of Carla stepped on one. "Pequeño pero picoso, like me," Patricia says, as she walks around it. More wind. More sounds. I don't remember the desert being this noisy. It's creepy. Makes me think of La Carreta Chillona.

Mom, Mali, and Abuelita told me if I didn't go to sleep, the oxcart would take me. They said the creaking cart has no ox, no horse, no bull, nothing pulling it. It moves on its own, possessed by an evil spirit you can't see. You can only hear the creaking. ¿What if it's here? I want to grab Patricia's hand but don't. We must walk in a single line. I concentrate on her shoes.

To our right, it's getting lighter. It's been more than two hours. We should be stopping to pee soon. None of The Four has wanted to. Chino says we shouldn't drink water until we stop. We haven't. He says this way we will save more, and not run out like with Mero Mero. I'm thirsty. I'm cold. I'm scared of La Carreta Chillona. But Coco Liso will get us there. Chino and Patricia trust him. It's our last free try. We will make it through the noises and the night. We must.

IT SOUNDS LIKE AN old motorcycle farting its way up a hill. *Toh–toh–toh–toh–toh–toh–toh*. Patricia's black chamarra freezes above the dirt. Everyone stops. Whispers of "helicopter" travel down the line. I imagine the rotor like machetes slicing a night sky full of sugarcane. We just stopped for water ten minutes ago. Water sloshes in my stomach. My heart pumps fast. I forget La Carreta Chillona, I'm scared of what's coming from the sky.

"¡Down!"

We crouch to our knees, trying to look like bushes. Carla's dark-green chamarra already makes her look like one. Chino is skinny and wears a dark-brown chamarra. I'm little.

"Bichos, get ready to run." The helicopter is close. Patricia grabs Carla's hand. Chino holds mine.

"Tree," people whisper.

We're nowhere near trees. We're out in the open. Dry grasses and more dry grasses like an overgrown soccer field. The moon is finally over the mountains to our right—it looks full, minus a bite or two. Behind it, the stars are white confetti. But right in front of us—

I can't see the helicopter, but I hear it. *Toh–toh–toh–toh–toh–toh–toh*. Closer and closer. Our heads move from side to side, trying to gauge whether it's flying toward us or away. It's like Cadejo's whistle.

Slowly, we unstick our knees from the dirt, dust them, and take another step forward. It's still up there.

More whispers.

We stop.

Crouch. We might just look like bushes.

The helicopter sounds farther away. Then, the light—

From the sky, a thick beam shoots down to the dirt. A wormhole. A flashlight brighter than the moon, moving from side to side like a sword slicing through the desert floor.

"¡Down!"

We throw ourselves at the ground. A dark cloud of dust rises and my heart beats against the dirt like a drum. *Tah-tan. Tah-tan.* We look up at the beam.

Chino lifts himself a bit like he's doing a push-up or like he's about to sprint.

"If it comes, we run," he says.

I prop myself up. *Tah-tan. Tah-tan.*

We wait, hoping the beam stays far. I close my eyes. I don't want La Migra. We have to make it. *Toh-toh-toh-toh-toh-toh-toh* . . .

Chino grabs my hand. Presses his fingers into my skin. A hot comb. I feel his heartbeat. My throat closes. I dig my other hand into the cold dirt like soccer cleats. The pebbles press against my skin. Some bits shine in the moonlight. Flickering. I forgot about them.

"Hold my hand," Patricia tells Carla.

"I got you," Chino whispers, squeezing my wrist.

The beam—

The rotor—

"¡RUUUUUNNNN!"

Bushes light up. People's backpacks. A hand. A leg. Rocks. Chino runs so fast, pulling Patricia who pulls Carla. The light behind us. In front. People run next to us. Away from us. I can't feel the ground. Chino's hand chokes my arm. It feels like it's gonna snap out. People fall. Some scream.

Patricia lets go.

"¡Mamá!"

"¡Chino!"

Chino stops. Pulls Patricia off the ground. I touch the dirt. We're running again.

"¡Tree! ¡Tree!"

Chino follows the voices.

"¡Here!"

Chino throws me over a fence. Throws Carla. He helps Patricia crawl under. The helicopter circles behind us. We run toward the tree's thick shadow. The ground has holes, dips, mounds. We run until we make it under the tree's canopy, huddled around the trunk.

"It's not coming," someone says.

"¡Shhhhh!" Others shut that person up.

We're only bits of the Centipede. Eight. Ten people pretending to be roots. Rocks.

"¡Aaay! ¡Aaaaayyy!" someone cries.

"¡Shhhh!"

"¡Aaaay! ¡Aaaaay!"

Chino finally lets go of my wrist.

It's Patricia.

"¿Qué pasó?" Chino asks Patricia, scooting closer to her.

"My face." She's crying louder than when La Migra caught us. "My hands." People try shushing her.

"¡She's got needles, cerotes!" Chino yells at the shadows. Patricia keeps crying. I sit in front of Carla, who's holding her mom's arm above the elbow. Someone starts hooting like an owl.

"Shut the fuck up. Not yet." People shut the hooter up. It didn't even sound like an owl.

"My face," Patricia keeps repeating. We're all kneeled around her.

"Vieja," Chino says.

My chest moves up and down fast. I can't catch my breath.

"I'm gonna try to pull them."

"Mami," Carla says, trying to get the needles unstuck from her mom's hands.

"Está bien," Chino tells Carla, who's trying to keep her tears in. She sounds like she's hiccupping. I haven't heard Carla or Patricia cry like this. Little pinpricks jut out from Patricia's cheeks, forehead, lips, nose. Her lips have black liquid all over them. ¿Blood? She has the same pinpricks all over her chamarra. Her hands.

"Don't brush them," someone next to us says. "Pluck. Pull."

"Don't touch." Chino holds on to the clear parts of Patricia's face tight with one hand and plucks the big needles out with his other hand, one by one. He moves her face into the moonlight so he can see better as she whispers, "Puta, ay, vieja, mierda."

I take a closer look at my hands and chamarra. They're covered in the same little spikes. They *are* cactus needles. I have a few, but mostly dirt, branches, and sticks. I start plucking. Chino keeps pulling them out of Patricia's face. Her cries turn to sobs. Carla checks her own clothes and skin. She has needles in her hands and chamarra. Her pants. I look at my pants—it hurts to brush against them. ¿How is Patricia not screaming? I pull the bigger ones out. Most are too small to see, but I feel them.

"¡Ayyy!" Patricia's tears stream down.

I scoot closer to see the needles Chino is taking out. A lot are shorter than a fingernail. A few the size of a pinkie, and thick. Patricia can't even bite her lip.

"Carla, get the nail clipper or tweezers."

Carla whimpers but carefully takes her mom's backpack off of her. She's scared. I'm scared. I want to help, but I can't even talk. There are thick needles on the backpack's handles.

"Ooooo-ohh. Ooooo-ohh. Ooooo-ohh," someone next to us hoots. This time, no one shuts them up.

"Here," Carla says, grabbing a silver nail clipper from the backpack. She hands it to Chino.

"¿No tweezers?"

Carla shakes her head. Chino does his best to clip the smaller cactus needles out of Patricia's face. He holds her face in place tighter, careful to not touch where the needles are or have been. Dark sticks jut out from her cheeks, forehead, nose, her skin gray in the moonlight. Chino struggles to grab the needles without clipping them off. Another person has run into a cactus, también. Someone else helps them pull the needles out. Everyone checks themselves. More people find us. We hear hoots in the distance.

My body feels like there's an earthquake inside it. I can't stop shaking. My legs like I'm still running. Where the bigger needles dug into me, it feels like I have ice cubes there. I check myself for more, but it's my fingertips that are covered: tiny pinpricks everywhere, from when I plucked my legs.

Another hoot.

"Let's go over there," someone says.

"¿Any polleros here?" someone else asks.

No one says anything.

"Almost done," Chino tells Patricia. She's not crying anymore.

"¡Ya! ¡Stop! Let's go," she tells him.

The helicopter is faint in the distance. I can still feel the warm wind I felt when its blades were behind us. Taste the dust. But it didn't follow us. I don't see the beam, the light, the sword in the sky.

Everything is quiet again. The wind rubs the twigs in the bushes against one another. The dry grass like a broom against cold tiles. Crickets. Patricia can't carry anything. She can't even hold Carla's hand, but she asks for the backpack. Carla puts it on her.

"Puta, my water," Patricia says. She left her gallon when we ran.

¡I left *my* bottle!

Carla and Chino show us theirs. I feel bad.

"Está bien, I left one también." Chino shows us his hands and the duct-taped gallon is gone. The group under the tree forms a small line, and we try to walk to where Coco Liso's whistle is coming from.

"Oooo-oh. Oooo-oh. Oooo-oh." They hoot. We wait. We're getting closer. They ran fast. Farther than us. A shadow of a tree gets clearer and clearer in the distance.

It feels like there are ants all over my skin. I'm shaking. ¿The needles? ¿Goosebumps? The back of my neck feels heavy, like someone is grabbing it. We're walking as fast as we can toward the tree, crunching the grass. Patricia walks first. Chino pushes her backpack. I grab Chino's backpack. Carla holds my shoulder.

"It fucking hurts," Patricia says, taking deep breaths.

"No te ahuevés, Patita, almost there."

Behind me, Carla cries softly, trying to keep it in.

Tears start to form in my eyes. Every few seconds, Coco Liso whistles again. I'm scared. I don't want anything to happen to Patricia. I don't want anything to happen to us. My family. My friends.

Finally, we make it to where people are gathered, sprawled out on the ground. It's not one tree but a lot of them, with thin, leafless branches, taller than the one we were hiding under. They cover us, they cover the stars.

"Rest, drink water. We wait for everyone," a voice that sounds like Coco Liso's says.

"Lie down," he tells us. "Flat."

"Drink." Chino uncaps the water bottle in front of Patricia's mouth. He tilts it so water falls without touching her lips.

"Estoy jodida," she says.

"N'hombre, Patita."

"Cállese, Mami."

"Look up instead, look, the Milky Way." Chino points.

It's like a river cutting the sky. Patricia sounds bad. Looks bad también. Other shadows show up. Mostly groups of three or four. Some are alone and stumble into the trees, happy to find us. "I thought you were gonna leave me," they say.

We wait, blending in with the ground in case the helicopter comes back. Every few minutes, Coco Liso loudly whispers, "¡Flat!"

People clean needles from their bodies. Brush their chamarras. Check their things. Some take their shoes off. The polleros stand and count us, then report to Coco Liso. They're the only ones allowed to stand.

I feel like I'm still floating, flying. My left hand throbs where Chino grabbed it. My shoulder hurts. I don't want to get caught again. I don't know what to do except watch Chino and Carla try to get more needles out of Patricia's face.

"My hair," she says, and Carla undoes her mom's ponytail, pulling big needles out.

Someone else was caught bad by a cactus. His face is worse than Patricia's, black liquid everywhere.

"Lucky it wasn't the eye," the shadow helping him says.

"I didn't even see it," the bleeding man explains. "Big-ass cactus came out of nowhere. Simasito it poked my eyes out."

"Puta," people respond.

"Híjole."

"Oí. You're lucky," Chino tells Patricia.

"¿If this is luck, what the fuck isn't?"

Then Coco Liso stands up. "Almost everyone is here," he says in his raspy voice. "Keep checking for needles. We're not gonna rest like this again."

I want to take my shoes off—they're full of dirt—but Chino is still working on Patricia; he can't tie my shoes. Coco Liso keeps hooting for people. Whistling. The polleros keep standing up. It's like the song: *Los pollitos dicen pío pío pío. Cuando tienen hambre, cuando tienen frío.* I sing it in my head as I try moving my feet inside my shoes so the dirt doesn't bother me as much. The polleros keep counting us. We drink more water. Patricia isn't whimpering anymore. Neither is Carla. Lying down, I raise my feet up in the air to make the dirt come out. Some does. Coco Liso hoots. Sometimes we hear someone hoot back. The bushes move slightly like they're clapping their hands, saying "¡You made it!" I lie down with both my legs flat on the ground again. Stick my hands into my chamarra's pockets. I want to hold Patricia's hands, hug her, but I don't want to hurt her. I keep quiet and wait for us to start moving again.

6-3-99

IT'S ALMOST TWO A.M. The tops of the trees sway as we walk by, and some of the branch tips rattle like they're alive. Everything is awake. The moon lights the ground silver and blue. Wispy clouds dance in the sky, white ones that look like silk. With this wind and with this lighting—the blue, the grays—it feels like the bottom of the ocean. People whisper that we're walking the wrong way, that people are missing, that we're circling the same place. The grass is seaweed. The cactuses are coral. We're looking through a submarine's small circular window. We're in that Jacques Cousteau program Mali and I watched on Sunday nights. On top, the clouds are sea foam. The ground sparkles with seashells and pearls.

"Everyone heard my calls, everyone is here," Coco Liso says.

We don't walk as fast, but we don't stop. Our single-file line is sometimes two, three people wide. Carla and Patricia walk side by side. I walk a step in front of Chino, two steps behind Patricia. She's not limping, but she's slower. When we stopped resting and lined up again, we stood next to the second pollero, but we've been falling closer and closer to the end of the line.

Whenever the people behind us start breathing down our backs, Chino taps Patricia and says, "Patita, bicha," and we step to the side to let them through. It's usually a group of two, three, five people at most, staying close together like we do. It's how we hear people's complaints. Sometimes, Chino tries to speed us up by slightly pushing me closer to Patricia, only centimeters behind her. If she doesn't do anything, I tap her backpack. Eventually we let the people through. We've done this a lot, but we're still not at the very end. We haven't stopped in hours. The landscape is the same: bumpy, but not completely hilly. Mostly dry grass, bushes, and the occasional tree. Sometimes there's a Lonely cactus, but we're seeing more and more of the ones that look like flores de izote, the Spikeys. There haven't been wire fences either. Not since the helicopter.

Sometimes we're in a clearing with just grass and dirt, but Coco Liso guides us near bushes. We're closer to the mountains to our right. The mountains on our left are farther away. Sometimes mountains seem to be in front of us, but I don't see a sharp peak. No rhino like Coco Liso said. I keep looking out for the beam, the rotors, the farting motorcycle.

WE STOP FOR WATER and finish Carla's small bottle. The two gallons Chino carries are all we have left. One strapped to his chest, the other in his backpack. Every section sits together. Everyone whispering. We're the crickets now that the crickets are sleeping.

"¿What's happening?" Carla asks. Patricia and Chino don't answer.

Coco Liso sits on the ground; the other polleros circle around him. The wind has died down, but it's still colder than last time. We're slower and slower. Over the mountains to our right, the sky is lighter. It's close to four A.M.; the moon is directly over our heads.

Chino checks on Patricia. "My lips and my cheeks hurt, pero no nos ahuevamos," she says. It's hard for her to sit because she needs help getting back up, so Patricia sits on her knees, her butt resting on her ankles. Carla sits normal next to her.

"¿What's happening, Mami?"

Dawn makes me think of bad things, because it's when Marcelo stole our water and La Migra found us. I hope everything works out this time.

"I'll go check," Chino says as he crawls like a crab to the men circling Coco Liso.

We are coral. Rocks at the bottom of the ocean. ¿What's it gonna be like during the day? Coco Liso didn't promise a van at sunrise. We're walking until sunset. Looking for Rhino Mountain. Chino comes back faster, a giant fish swimming toward us.

"Puta" is the first thing out of his mouth. "He fucked up his ankle," Chino says, shaking his head, then grabbing it.

"¿Who?"

"Coco Liso."

"A la gran puta."

"¿What's gonna happen?" Carla asks.

"Jaber."

"Estamos cagados," Patricia whispers. This is what everyone was whispering about. *Twisted ankle*. It's why we're walking slower. Other people get closer to the polleros and Coco Liso. The whispers get louder. Everyone begins to form a circle around him.

"Like you've heard, my ankle is hurt," Coco Liso begins.

People mumble and shake their heads.

"Look," he says, as he puts weight on his foot. "It's twisted, not broken. I can walk. We walk until it gets hot. We sleep. Then we walk more."

Everyone whispers. We're all blue shadows.

"¡Let's go! ¡Line up!"

"See, Coco Liso is fine," Carla says.

"I don't think so . . ."

"N'hombre, Patita, the man is fine."

"He *has* to be." Patricia makes sure the strangers around us hear. "If not, we're fucked like my face is."

We line up closer to the front this time. This is our last try. I saw the hawk. We got away from the helicopter. We have to make it. Patricia wants to be close to Coco Liso to see if he's telling the truth. We've heard polleros do this: they lie and say they're hurt, but all they want to do is take our money. His ankle isn't broken; it's twisted. He *looks* fine. I've never twisted my ankle. *Torcido.* I see a rope, all the strands twisted and tied together tight.

It's almost sunrise. I don't want La Migra. *Please, if you exist, Cadejito, don't let bad things happen to us.*

WE SEE DEER. ¡DEER! I've never seen them outside of zoos or on TV. We don't have them in my town. We have snakes, turtles, crabs, all types of birds, and anteaters. But deer . . . I've only heard the song Mom liked, "El Venao."

Whenever it played on the radio, Mom told me to do the dance. When the chorus played—*Y que no me digan en la esquina*—I spread my fingers out like giving high fives, raised my hands above my forehead, and pressed my thumbs against my temples. Then I hopped around, mouthing the words, trying my best to look like a deer. In the entire video there are no deer, just horns coming out of men's foreheads.

"Deer," the Centipede whispers.

"Javier, look." Chino points at the brown animal, and we walk slowly. I can see the side of Carla's face smiling, her big eyes even bigger. She shows her mom, careful not to touch Patricia anywhere.

"We're deer," Carla whispers.

It's funny. Our skin *is* brown. The deer closest to us is smaller than I thought. She has a big black tail and big rounded ears lined in black. When the deer sees us, she freezes. Just behind her, grazing behind bushes, three others, but none have horns. All of them freeze in place, their own line, their own centipede. When someone takes a loud step, they all run away, bouncing on top of the grasses, skipping between bushes.

It's 6:35 A.M. We haven't found any green uniforms. They haven't found us. I didn't see the sunrise in the desert last time; I was asleep when the trucks surrounded us. All of the colors are amazing—some still linger at the edges of the sky, but when sunrise was at its peak, it felt like we were walking in a painting. Pinks, oranges, reds, purples, yellows, mixing together like watercolors.

I thought I liked sunsets most, but I think I like sunrises better. I can almost see mist rising from the ground that also keeps changing color. And the smells: dust, but with a hint of water—even though it hasn't rained. It's as if the dirt is breathing, sweating. I keep taking long whiffs. ¡It's what Chino smells like!

We haven't crossed fences in a long time—just one after the helicopter, and it wasn't barbwire. We did cross dirt paths that might have been roads; they didn't even have grass, but had plenty of rocks jutting out. In the moonlight, the rocks looked like toads. Sometimes we walked on the roads for a bit; other times, we walked across. We never saw a car. The dirt under our feet is no longer gray or bluish white. It's waking up to its reds, deep yellows. The mountains, también. The desert in this light is a completely different place. We can see more—not just the dirt or the trees nearby, but far into the horizon, filled with bushes, cactuses, and trees.

Up ahead on the left, there's a mountain range. It's small and dark at the tips, dark brown at the bottom.

"¡The mountain! Creo que es esa," Chino says, pointing at one peak.

"¿*That?*"

"Think so."

¡It looks nothing like a rhino! It's more like a long-faced person lying down with a rounded nose. I was expecting a curved sharp horn like an actual rhinoceros. Coco Liso lied. The mountain range is not fat, bulky, or even gray. It's skinny, short, the color of wet earth.

The wind is fainter, también. The bushes and occasional tree don't move as much. They don't shake. They don't make any sound. They're asleep. But the birds are waking up. They sing and fly in groups.

This is the longest I've ever walked. It's daylight, and no Migra. Gracias a Dios. Our pace is slowing down. Sometimes we freeze and crouch if the pollero up front thinks he sees something. We walk slower. More and more, it looks like Coco Liso is limping. He hasn't said anything, but he's not at the front of the Centipede anymore. One of the light-skinned polleros leads us. Marcelo Look-Alike is still at the very back—our tail.

Now that it's completely light out, we can see the entire Centipede snaking through bushes, grass, and more and more Spikeys. It's the first time I see us in the daylight. I don't *think* there are fewer people. I don't know. What I do see is that if we pause and stand still, we actually do look like a centipede, dark and long with many legs, because everyone wears dark colors. But we also look like some of the bushes—the ones with dark-gray trunks and dark-green leaves. And if we slide under them, we look like shadows.

Coco Liso is now the second pollero. He's a few people in front of us. Patricia looks better. When we saw the deer, she briefly turned and I saw a scratch that begins above her right ear—it's red with dried blood. Her hair isn't tied in a tight bun like she had it before the helicopter; the bun is loose and bobs up and down right above her neck. One big, thick yellow needle is still stuck in her hair.

———

PEOPLE WHISPER SOMETHING ABOUT a road. Then Coco Liso whistles—we slide under a bush, a twig gets stuck in Carla's hair.

"Ay—" she almost screams, but covers her mouth with her hands. Chino takes the twig and breaks it off. It's not a Crayon bush—the ones whose leaves smell just like wax. It has thorns.

"It's nothing, you're fine," Chino tells her.

There's dry blood all over Patricia's face, like a cat clawed her. The scratch above her right ear is the longest, the others are small. Her lip is bruised and red, worse than when her cold sore was its biggest.

Coco Liso hasn't whistled since the helicopter. I hope we're stopping. The dirt is cooler in the shade. My butt is the coldest part of my body under this bush that reminds me of the trees we call Bull's Horns, because they have thorns in the shape of a V and tiny leaves.

"There's gonna be a road soon," Coco Liso says in a louder-than-normal voice. "I'll make sure no cars come. I'll whistle, and we run across. ¿Okay?"

People nod. Others say "sí," some even say "órale." The Four, we don't say anything, but we look at each other. I look at the bush—it has flowers like little yellow pom-poms. *Cheerleader bush*.

"Same thing as last road," Chino says, "but I'll pull Carla, también."

"Va," Patricia says. Chino usually pulls my hand, and Patricia pulls Carla's. But Patricia's hands have needles in them.

I haven't been lifted over a fence in a while. I like it; it makes me feel like I'm a giant hopping over fences. Now I just wait for Chino to grab me under my armpits and I fly over the barbs, my legs close to my chest like I'm a frog. ¡Sa-sa-sapo!

WE KEEP WALKING, BUT "Rhino" Mountain doesn't get nearer. It's so hot. Sometimes we see lizards. They look at us, pretending to be rocks, thinking we don't see them, but *I* see them—like I saw Paula in Oaxaca. So many lizards on our path. They're the color of dirt with dark-brown dots on their backs; their camouflage is good, but not *that* good. It's funny when they run away, their small arms and legs paddling the dirt. They look like me when I slide under fences. Other times, black grasshoppers shoot out of the grasses. Some have red on their bodies. We crush grass and ¡boom!—they fly off, bursting in flames.

"Don't drag your feet," the other light-skinned pollero tells a section of the Centipede. "No dust—we're near the road."

We keep hearing about *the road,* but I don't see any road. I make up another game: I step on rocks, avoiding the grass, so I leave the lizards and grasshoppers alone. At night, I didn't notice how much grass stays on my pants. It didn't bother me. But now that I see it, it's annoying. When we stop, I wipe off the broken pieces from my pants. Coco Liso said we would stop when it was really hot. It's *really* hot, and we're not stopping. Everyone has their chamarras wrapped around their waists. We sweat, but it dries up fast on our arms and necks. Sweat forms in my armpits and on my back. The ground is less bumpy, but there are occasional holes and more cactuses. It's strange to see the plants we couldn't see at night. During the day, it feels like we're in a completely new place.

We've seen a lot of Lonelies: fat and with so many hooked needles at the top, sometimes with orange and red flowers—beautiful and paperlike. I didn't see them at night. A lot of Spikeys también, and sometimes cactuses that look like nopales but that aren't as tall—they stay close to the ground and have rounded sections that remind me of bunny ears.

My new favorite is a cactus that looks like a small tree, fuzzy all over. At the trunk they're black or dark yellow, at the tips they're bright yellow. From far away, they look like yellow paint rollers. But when we walk close, the needles are longer than my fingers and very pointy. The Fuzzies, I call them.

"Careful," Patricia told us when someone in front of us brushed against one and a small section of the cactus got stuck to their chamarra. They tried to get it off, then it got stuck to their hand. I think Patricia got hit by a Fuzzy when we ran from the helicopter. These are Paint-Roller Fuzzies, but others aren't as big, and look more like mascara brushes. Their branches are almost purple or green. Paint-Roller Fuzzies and Mascara-Brush Fuzzies.

Close to the ground, small cactuses with pink needles. We watched someone else's shoe get harpooned. I never take my eyes from Patricia's feet. Because of her, I haven't gotten hurt. No twisted ankle, no needles, just the grasses that bother me, and dust and rocks in my shoes. I'm not as tired as our first try. We keep stopping.

The Four are almost done with our second-to-last water bottle. We keep taking small sips whenever we stop, but it only makes me thirstier. I want a lot of water. We hear people whisper, "¿Where's the road?" "He's lost." My legs are beginning to hurt below the knee. I hope we find the road soon.

Then we stop. "¡Down!" Coco Liso almost yells. We crouch. Pick a bush. I hold my breath. It sounds like an ocean wave is approaching the shore. A loud crash. Then it keeps crashing, but softer and softer until we can't hear it anymore. *Shhhhhh*. It quiets down like sand absorbing water, fizzling.

"Car," people whisper.

¿A car? ¿*That* was a car? ¡It sounded like the ocean! I look at Carla, who looks at me. Her eyes are big. I smile. She smiles back. I look at Chino, and he nods, doing his lip thing, meaning he thinks it's cool también.

We wait until there aren't any noises. We move again. People look back and whisper, "Stay low." I don't have to. Most bushes are taller than me. At most, I tilt my head. Carla has to bend a little, but she's also not that tall. The road is real. We hear it. We crouch from Crayon bush to Cheerleader bush. Past Fuzzies and Lonelies. We stop when we hear a wave forming, nearing, crash—then it fizzles away. I love it. ¡This *is* the ocean! The asphalt road is the ocean water, the cars the waves.

We approach ¡a fence! Except this time, there aren't as many bushes, and steel poles rise from it, holding white and blue signs with English writing. Coco Liso gives us signals with his hand. He puts his hand up for stop. Grabs at the air toward himself when he wants us nearer.

Coco Liso is flat on the ground, his eyes at the same height as the lowest fence wire, his backpack next to him. Chino and Patricia take their backpacks off también, drag them along the dirt under their armpits. We're as close to the fence as possible, our bellies on the ground like sea slugs. Then we hear another car.

"Down, down," people whisper. I kiss the dirt. Some of it gets in my nose. I want to cough but hold it in. The car is so close. The tires are right there. When it's in front of us, the wave is loudest. It's a big truck with a front door and then a box in the back like a trailer, but smaller. The truck is painted white, except the box has the word *SEARS* written in blue letters. *Flash*. It drives off.

"Se-ars," Carla whispers.

"Sepa pepa," Chino says.

"Shhh," Patricia tells them.

All of us watch Coco Liso, waiting for him to tell us "go."

"Don't forget your chamarras," Chino tells Carla and me, whispering. We untie our chamarras from our waists and hold them in our hands. I feel like I'm standing at the edge of a pool about to jump in. We're gonna run across a road, the black ocean. Hiding from cars, from the bad guys, from La Migra, like we're playing a game. My heart beats fast. I'm ready, my hands ready to press against the dirt. We wait—

"¡Goooo!" Coco Liso yells. Chino picks me up, drops me on the other side of the fence, then Carla.

So many hands slide under fences, a swarm of lobsters and crabs. Then legs. So many legs run past us.

The asphalt feels sticky. I run past yellow lines painted in the middle of the road, Carla behind me.

"Bichos," Patricia says as she's sliding under the first fence.

"¡Keep running!" Chino shouts, sliding under fast.

Carla and I make it to the other fence. We look back. Chino makes it across the black, into the dirt, picks me up. Throws me over. I land on my feet. Then he throws Carla.

I look behind and people are still running.

"¡Wait!" Coco Liso yells. "¡Car!" he screams.

A few are still trying to crawl under the first fence. They stop and slide backward.

A car *is* coming. Chino slides under this second fence. Patricia is under already. I hope no one saw Chino. We hide in a Cheerleader bush. The black of the asphalt like a machete splitting the Centipede.

"¡Wait!" Coco Liso yells when he sees someone across the road trying to slide under the fence. We don't see it yet, but we can hear it, rubber against asphalt. We hold our breath until the car drives off. Coco Liso waits a few seconds. Minutes. Looks both ways. Listens. Then yells at the people to run to this side.

We watch them slide under and run. I see faces I've never seen before. Everyone has scratches all over. They're strangers, but their clothes are dusty, and they're holding backpacks, chamarras, and water bottles like us. Behind them, Marcelo Look-Alike makes sure everyone runs across.

My heart pumps, like after the helicopter. Like I just got away with lying to Abuelita. To the nuns.

"¡Let's go!" Coco Liso yells, crouching toward another bush.

"No dust," another pollero says.

"Crouch," another pollero repeats.

We crouch from Cheerleader bush to Crayon bush, but this time faster. When we get to a flat space, Coco Liso tells us to stop. My body isn't as tense.

"Line up."

And we're back to a single-file line. Coco Liso isn't up front. He says he's ok, but he walks slower. Leading the Centipede is the same guy, the pale pollero.

We keep walking until we don't hear cars, not even the faintest ocean wave. The only sounds are the crunch under our feet and the occasional grasshopper buzzing out of our way. The slight breeze. Bushes recoiling when we brush past them. Rocks in our shoes. The backpacks and the empty water gallons moaning like frogs.

"WE HAVE TO MAKE up time," Coco Liso says. But we're not walking fast. It's a furnace. He's limping. The insides of my shoes feel like the hottest sand at the beach at the peak of summer.

"Look look look, not even birds can take this shit," Chino says as we rest under a leafless tree for a few minutes and watch small, light-brown birds panting with their beaks opened. We can see their tiny pink tongues. Below their beaks, some birds have a black beard, and around their eyes, they wear white eyeliner.

The tree is so skinny it provides no shade. Some branches have tiny pebble-sized leaves we can hardly see. *Skinny green smooth tree,* I whisper. SGS tree for short. I like naming these weird-looking bushes and trees. I'm an explorer. Javier Cousteau. I like looking up at the sky while lying down in the dirt. The tree branches look like a squid's tentacles reaching for the sky.

A few meters away, a section of the Centipede rests under another SGS tree. I like to stop because we notice other things moving in the sky or on the ground. I've seen pinkie-sized black beetles that walk with their butts up. Black bumblebees. Ants. Flies. I even saw a dragonfly—or maybe it was a hornet—buzz past us.

We're thirsty, but Chino keeps reminding us we have to conserve water: "Drink only un poquitito."

There's no wind. "Rhino" Mountain isn't closer. The ground is bumpier in places, and it feels like we're walking up a hill. This is the hottest I've ever been. My lips are dry. My hands are dry. My entire body feels hot to the touch, and my skin feels like it's cracking. I don't hold Chino's hand.

The single-file line is broken again. People keep whispering things like "¿Why don't we stop?," "We're lost," "He's lost," "He left them . . ."

"They don't know shit," Chino tells us.

I hope Coco Liso isn't really lost. I hope he's ok. The Centipede *does* look smaller. We're really slowing down. We haven't crossed a fence since the road. Everywhere, Fuzzies, Spikeys, grass, and bushes. I want real shade. We drink small sips, wait to get up, and repeat.

"LET'S SLEEP HERE," Coco Liso says, loud so everyone hears. "We're stopping until it gets cooler."

¿Sleep? I hadn't thought about sleep. We've been walking almost an entire day.

"Eat. Sleep. We'll keep watch," another pollero says.

Finally. My forehead is a frying pan. My chamarra is a hot belt tied around my waist. My black hair is a skillet. My legs hurt. The dirt in my socks really bothers me. I can finally ask Chino to tie my shoes.

"Drink and sleep," Patricia says under a Crayon bush next to the one Chino and I are sprawled under. She's in her special squat: her thighs and butt resting on top of her ankles and feet. She sits on her butt and lies face up.

Chino takes out the water and two shirts from his backpack. There's less than half a gallon left for the four of us.

"Here, put this on." He hands me one of the shirts. "Like this." He puts the shirt around his neck, but instead of wearing it, he flips it on top of his head, turning it into a hood.

"Wow. You think now," Patricia says sarcastically, but asks Carla to open their backpack and take two shirts out. ¡The shirts give us shade! We look like wizards or nuns. We laugh. People look over and we shush.

"¿Te pica la tripa?" Chino asks me.

It's what Grandpa would say, but I don't know if I'm hungry.

Sleep and food. I hadn't thought about either. All my thoughts were around water. I want to get to the vans.

"¿You two?" he asks Patricia and Carla.

"Not really," Patricia says, and Carla shakes her head.

"N'hombre, bichas, ¡we haven't eaten in a day! Coman," Chino says, searching his bag.

The wind is back. I feel it on my arms. It's warm, but it feels good. The shirt around my face makes me feel hotter. I start taking it off and Chino stops me.

"Wait."

He unzips his backpack again and takes out a clear plastic bag with about a dozen tortillas and something wrapped in white butcher paper. Water droplets cling to the inside of the bag. Chino opens it, and the smell is pungent in the best way possible. My stomach growls. I *am* hungry. *Mmmm.* Those tortillas smell so good.

Chino hands each of us one tortilla. They're not the giant, flat flour tortillas we ate at the albergue and at Doña's. These are small, palm-sized, and almost as thick as Salvadoran ones. Patricia notices.

"Vieja, vos, ¿where you get these?"

"Around. Me las rebusqué," he says, grinning.

We haven't seen this type of tortilla since Guatemala. If we take two, they're as thick as Salvadoran ones. ¡And they're warm!

"¿How are they still warm?"

"The sun," Chino answers.

"Obvio." Carla laughs at me.

Chino opens the plastic bag again. Opens the white butcher paper and displays it like a treasure.

"Queso fresco, papá," he says, proudly, his small teeth showing. The queso fresco is so white and the right consistency. It shakes like Jell-O when he moves the bag, its sides melted.

"See, it's the heat." Chino shows me the melted edges, then digs into the cheese with his dirty hands. None of us care. All of our hands are dusty, our nails have dirt in them, and we have needles stuck in our fingers.

Chino places big fat pieces of cheese on top of the tortillas we hold in both our hands like a plate. Some of the queso fresco's pale juice drips onto my tortilla. I look at the white butcher paper and, pooled at the bottom, light beige juice. My piece has bits of dirt around the edges, left over from Chino's fingers. I try to blow the dust off, but some stays; I don't care.

All of us smile. The cheese is salty, but it's not overpowering. It's soft in the middle, but not too soft like requesón. The slightly melted parts are hard and rubbery like queso chiclado, but the taste is so good. This is better than canned tuna or sardines.

We nod as we eat. I look around at the other bushes. Most of the people are eating. Some clean their shoes. Others sleep. The wind is soft on my face, but it picks up dust that lands on my cheese. I blow every time before taking a bite.

I remember eating at the beach for Semana Santa. Mali or Abuelita packed a dozen pollo sandwiches wrapped in pink napkins for us to eat under the sun after swimming in the waves. My hands, lips, and tongue were still drenched in salt water, each bite saltier because of it. Sometimes I'd eat a grain of sand. But it didn't matter. It's the same here. Sometimes I bite and there's dirt. My stomach isn't growling as much. We're still hungry, so Chino hands us each another tortilla, except Patricia, who hasn't eaten hers, but she asks for more queso fresco. All of us get one more piece.

"We're only missing avocado," Carla says.

"And beans," Patricia adds.

"But this hits the spot," Chino corrects them.

This is just right.

I'VE LEARNED THAT SHRILL whistle by heart. It's Coco Liso.

"Bicho." Chino shakes me. Patricia does the same to Carla. My head rests on my chamarra, cooler now that it's been in the shade. We fell asleep after eating. We each have one tortilla left for whenever we get to the ranch, but no queso fresco. It was too good. We're almost out of water. One or two sips for each of us left. We're saving them.

"¡Line up!" Coco Liso shouts. The Centipede wakes and rises from the ground.

Chino leaves the white butcher paper in the dirt, "for the ants."

We're bushes turning into people like Transformers, but this time, we're wearing our T-shirt hoods. Others copied us. It's a bit after five, and it's still hot. Chino tied my shoes after I cleaned them. I feel much better. People huddle up around Coco Liso. The adults smell bad. They have sweat patches everywhere. The Four get closer to the people talking. I sniff Chino and Patricia; I don't *think* we smell. I sniff myself. We smell like dust and sweat, but not bad like the men in front of us.

"You said we were gonna get there at sunset."

"We're running out of water."

"We see no ranches."

"You're lost."

"We're out of water."

"We paid you to get there fast."

"Quiet. Quiet," the polleros say with their hands up.

The Four sit back down near a bush while all the people still shout at Coco Liso as loud as they possibly can without being too loud.

"Quiet. ¡Quiet!"

Coco Liso is silent until most everyone shuts up. He stands in the middle of everyone and says, "Señores, señoras, we *are* close. We just haven't walked fast enough."

"*¿We?* You're leading us," someone says, pointing at Coco Liso, who's wearing his cap. We can't see his eyes because of the bill's shadow.

"¡Your fucking ankle is gonna kill us!" Someone else points at Coco Liso's feet, his black boots full of dust and needles like all of our shoes.

"We don't have water," someone else says.

"We're out también," Patricia lies, joining in. "We have kids."

"I know," Coco Liso says. "You have to trust me, chingado. We're almost there," he continues, stern, harsh. "If you don't fucking trust me, ask *them*." Coco Liso points at the polleros.

All three of them nod.

"I wouldn't put anyone at risk. I'll get you there."

"We'll see." Patricia turns to Chino.

"Callâte vos."

ANOTHER SUNSET. THE WIND is stronger. I hear a bird's call a few meters away. It's black, but not a crow—I know those. This one has hairs sticking up from its head and it's much smaller. *¡Hu! ¡It!* it repeats in twos. *¡Hu! ¡It!* Almost a squeak, but soft. When we approach, the bird flies off, squeaking, white patches flashing from its black wings.

I'm tired. My legs feel weaker. Wobbly. I don't know how to tell Chino. Carla looks tired. Patricia también. All of us except Chino, who *is* strong—maybe stronger than Marcelo. We keep dropping places in the Centipede. One or two sections have passed us. Everyone looks exhausted. There's a lot of space between people, making the Centipede look longer.

Our shirts around our heads make a difference, but I still feel sunburned. My lips feel like crumpled-up paper. I think I have a fever, but Chino checks me and his palm is the same temperature.

"Estás bien," he says.

We keep walking. Slow, but forward. "Rhino" Mountain to our left is darker, the sun already over it. The mountains that look like a boat to our right are bright orange like they're on fire. The grass is gold. The few leaves on the bushes light up bright green. The dark-blue sky over us begins to change at each end. I like this time.

There's a new tree or bush. I don't know what it is. Looks like tentacles coming out of the ground, a squiggly crown. Thorny and dark brown, but the thorns are silver. Sometimes there are small green or yellow leaves on each stick. Yellow and green scratches near the base. A crown of sticks. ¿Thorny upside-down octopus?

Thorny Tentacles.

"Careful." Patricia points at the first Thorny Tentacles we walk near—she doesn't miss a cactus.

The land dips a bit. I think we're headed ¿downhill? I wish it was a real hill with no cactus so we could roll down.

Then, a buzz. *Bzzzzzz*. It's faint.

"¡Stop!" the polleros yell.

We freeze and look around. There are no trees to run to.

I look at the sky. Nothing. Not even clouds.

"It's not a helicopter," Carla says.

I make a full turn. Nothing. Just the ground, dark orange, almost red.

¡Bzzzzzzzz! It's louder. A familiar sound.

"¡Down!"

"¡Facedown!"

I turn so my left ear presses against Chino's shirt—the hood around my face pressed down against the dirt, rocks, and sticks. The ground hums. I cover my face with the black shirt but leave a slip so I can peek through.

"¡Bees!"

¿Bees?

"¡Don't move!"

One. Ten. Twenty. Hundreds of bees right on top of us. *Huuuuuummmmmmm*.

Oh my God. I hold my breath. The cloud isn't yellow but dark brown. Four, five, ten seconds—gone.

"¡They're gone!" the polleros shout.

"¡Up!" Coco Liso yells.

I stand and look at the horizon in the direction the bees were moving. I can't see them. From the ground it looked like a blanket. A single sheet of wings and brown bodies.

People start dusting themselves.

"¡Coma mierda!" Chino says with a gasp, full grin on his face.

"A migrating beehive," someone from another section explains, palming their thighs to get dust off.

"¿An entire beehive?"

"Yup."

"¡Vieja! ¡Once in a life!" Patricia shouts, smiling.

"¡An entire colony!" Chino taps me in my back.

I can't believe that just happened.

"They're like us," Patricia says, looking back at Chino and me. She's already in line. But ¿where is the beehive's honey? ¿Why are they moving?

We dust ourselves and walk. The sky is changing. The temperature is dropping enough to wear my chamarra. I'm thirsty, but we can't drink. Maybe next time we stop we will be near the ranch. Maybe we'll make it before midnight. The bees must be good luck.

"HE'S LOST."

"¿Where the fuck are we going?"

"El maitro doesn't tell us shit."

Chino and Patricia whisper to each other. We're walking side by side. Chino holds my left hand; Carla holds her mom's chamarra. Carla and I look at each other across the adults and shake our heads when Chino says, "Ya la cagamos."

The Centipede is spread out thin. We've been walking and stopping. Adults keep arguing. Some people pass us. We move to the side. We pass people. They move to the side. Some hold their legs as we walk past them. It's dark out. Just stars. The Milky Way. The cactuses have disappeared in the dark, but I know they're there. I know what to look for now. Outlines. Their shadows. Thorny Tentacles, Lonelies, Fuzzies, an occasional People cactus, sometimes with one arm, or an arm on each side, facing up like a boxer. One had so many arms it looked like a city skyline.

Other people stop to pee, and they either nod or point to where the Centipede is moving. My calves are bags of water about to burst, making my knees ache. My thighs. The back of my neck. The top of my back. Everything hurts. My throat is filled with dust. My nostrils clogged by dry boogers. I don't feel like peeing. My stomach growls, it stings like I ate a lot of lemon juice. I can't walk anymore.

"Come on, Javiercito," Chino says, pulling my hand.

He repeats that when I start dragging my feet. There's less grass.

Less things in my shoes, but they're heavy. Suddenly, people ahead of us stop. More gather. People behind us catch up. All of the sections join and form a circle around Coco Liso, who's sprawled on the dirt, holding his hat in his left hand, surrounded by the polleros. In the darkness, his bald spot is almost white, an opened coconut.

"Things are really fucked," Coco Liso says in his voice, raspier than usual. "Está cabrón." It's hard for him to breathe. His head leans on his backpack, which is propped up by what looks like a rock or small bush. "Old age is not for cowards," he says. "I'm out of water. Can't find the tank that was around here."

"Puta."

"La cagamos."

"Faak."

"Mierda."

Everyone whispers.

Then people start yelling.

"¡You piece of shit, you took our money!"

"¡Stop faking!"

"¡Son of a bitch!"

"¡Get up!"

"It's my fault." Coco Liso holds his hat against his chest.

People keep yelling, asking what the plan is.

Patricia's head can't stop shaking. Chino pats her back. I hold Chino's torso. Coco Liso was doing fine. We were walking fast before the helicopter.

"The fucking ankle," Chino whispers.

"I won't slow you down anymore." Coco Liso takes a big breath. "I'm gonna stay right here."

"¿What the fuck?"

"Cállate," Chino tells Patricia.

"These guys are the best." Coco Liso points at the polleros. "They will walk faster. They know the way."

"¡We paid *you!*"

"¡*You,* cabrón!"

"¡Hijueputa!"

"Get up. ¡Walk!"

People scream. I'm scared.

"¿What do you want me to do? ¡I can't walk for shit!" Coco Liso screams back, as the polleros push people away from him.

Chino holds me tight in his right arm. "Está bien, Javiercito. Todo está bien." I look up at Chino's face, gray in the night.

"They will take you to a ranch. There's a red house. Red. Two large pointy trees in front of it, and nothing else. That's where the vans are. Two vans," Coco Liso says.

Red. Two trees. Two vans. I repeat in my head.

I look at Patricia, who slowly shakes her head from side to side. Carla hugs her.

"Puta," Chino whispers.

"¡Go! ¡Leave! I'll be fine," Coco Liso shouts. "¡Leave!"

"Órale," the polleros mumble.

"¡Line up!" the pale pollero, the same one who was already leading the Centipede, screams. His voice isn't raspy like Coco Liso's; it's deep, like the pollero is speaking from the bottom of his throat. It booms throughout the Centipede. People break the circle and start lining up. Marcelo Look-Alike walks backward and is at the end again. The front starts moving, shadows walking into the night. When people walk past Coco Liso, still on the ground, they tell him, "Be careful."

"We're going to the same hole," he says.

"Careful," someone else says.

"Careful is for kids. Cautious is for adults."

"Take care."

"I got both feet planted firmly in midair." Coco Liso smiles.

He's got an answer for everything.

We're a few people behind the second pollero. Before he walks past Coco Liso, the pollero leans down, whispers something, and leaves a gallon of water. I can't see if it's full or not. Carla walks past Coco Liso. He raises his hand when Patricia walks past him, his skin gray and pale like the dirt around us. He looks directly at me, his eyes the same height as mine.

"You're lucky, morrillo." He smiles.

I wave back and nod. His teeth white. His eyes white. His hat on his chest.

"You'll make it."

I don't know what to say. I walk past and get goosebumps.

"Gracias," Chino tells Coco Liso. I don't want to look back. *Don't look back. Stare at Patricia's shoes. Her backpack.*

I don't think Coco Liso heard Chino.

¿Is he gonna be ok?

¿Are *we* gonna be ok?

The pace picks up. Our feet make more noise, there's more dirt than grass. More rocks than twigs. We walk toward the light coming from the horizon in front of us. The light between the mountains. I hope it's the ranch. I hope there's water. I hope we get there soon. Before the moon shows up. Before the sun. Before the heat and the doves wake up.

6-4-99

THE MOON RISES OVER the hills to our right. It's a bit more lopsided than it was yesterday, less full. The hills shine purple, and they look smaller. We haven't stopped walking since we left Coco Liso. A lot of people pull off to the side. Every time, we hear the pollero in front of us telling them, "Someone will wait for you until you're ready."

"Pajas," Chino said after we saw the second section pull over to the side and collapse on the ground, rubbing their feet. Chino picked me up and threw me on top of his backpack. I wrapped my arms around his neck. Half an hour went by—or more, I don't know— I slept. Then he put me down. I walked for half an hour and then went back up.

We've been doing this the past few hours. It's 3:30 A.M. Patricia can't carry Carla, but Chino pulls Carla's hand. I like riding on his back. I'm Aladdin in the desert. Chino is my carpet. ¿Where's the genie? I don't know, but I'd ask for a lake. A Pollo Campero. And a plane. Not the Fuzzies and Lonelies we see more and more of. The moonlight paints everything gray: the dirt, the bushes, the needles. Fewer and fewer trees in our way. People tell the polleros to slow down. That we need to rest.

"We won't leave you, we will wait," the closest pollero says, pointing to the end. He means Marcelo Look-Alike. But we can't tell if he's actually waiting.

"¡Stop!" people shout, up and down the Centipede, but the polleros don't listen.

"*Water.*"

"¿Do you have water?" people ask us when we walk past.

It's mostly older men and older women who step to the side. Patricia and Chino are young. Carla and me, the youngest.

"You're strong," strangers keep telling us. "Spare water."

Chino and Patricia don't say anything. We walk in silence, crunching the ground. Carla drags her feet. I hold on to Chino's neck.

"Puras mierdas, el pollero," Chino says, angry and clenching his teeth. I can feel his voice in my arms, in my hands, and in my stomach through his backpack. We walk fast enough to not be near Marcelo Look-Alike, but we can't see the front anymore.

Chino puts me down and tells Carla, "Your turn." She's been dragging her feet. My legs wobble. She climbs on his back. He pulls my hand. Another section passes us.

"You'll alternate," Chino tells us. Carla and I nod. We follow Patricia, who walks in front of us.

People whisper, "Stop."

We catch up to the front. People are on the ground, lying down. Some have already taken their boots off and are rubbing their feet.

"Rest," the pollero says. His deep voice carries in the wind. Twigs from the bushes brush against each other. Leaves shake. My heels and big toes sting. I want to sleep. We choose a patch of dirt under a Crayon bush. Chino drops Carla from his back and holds me closer.

"Breathe, relax," he tells us.

Chino helps Patricia take her bags off, then he takes the four torti-llas out from his backpack. Through the plastic bag the tortillas look like the moon, pale with black marks—their craters.

"Má." He hands me one. "Comé."

The tortilla is a cold plate in my hands. There's no steam. I bite and the dough is hard. My mouth is too dry; swallowing is difficult. No one says anything. We chew loud. Slow. Everyone in the Centi-pede looks exhausted. I untie my shoes so my feet can breathe. I take the dirt and dry grasses out of my shoes, flip them upside down.

"Not the socks," Patricia says.

But I want to see my blisters. Instead, I pull sticks and needles stuck to the socks.

Up near the front, where the deep-voiced pollero is still standing, we hear people questioning him.

"¡¿Why haven't you stopped?!" people shout.

He stays quiet, or mumbles something we can't hear.

"We can't walk anymore."

"I'm trying—"

"We—water" is all I can make out.

"It's almost day."

"I know—I'm—get—possible."

Chino and Patricia can't hear. We lean closer.

"Stay with the bichos," Chino tells Patricia, getting up from the ground, swallowing the last of his tortilla. He walks toward Deep Voice.

The tortilla helped the hunger, but it made me thirsty.

"Your pillows," Patricia says, handing Carla her backpack and handing me Chino's. "Sleep."

I want to know what's happening. I don't want Chino to argue like he did with Don Dago. Marcelo flashes in my mind. He would be fighting the polleros. ¿Where are we? It's past four A.M.

"¿What you think?" Carla whispers, so her mom can't hear.

"¿About?"

"¿Are there fewer people or not?"

I don't know what to tell her. I look at the shadows. I don't know if there *are* fewer. I don't remember how many we started with. ¿Forty? ¿Fifty? It feels way smaller than that.

"I don't know," I say. But I know we have at least one less: Coco Liso. Like Marcelo, except *we* left *him*. Chele ran away. Mario ran away. Mero Mero, también. I don't want to get caught. I hope Coco Liso and Marcelo are ok.

"¿You scared?" she asks. Patricia is still looking ahead. I *am*. I don't want Chino to fight. I want to see my parents. I want water. A bed. I want to stop walking. My body hurts. I don't know what to tell her.

"Sí," I finally say, digging my hands deeper into the sleeves of my chamarra.

"Yo también," she whispers, her face on top of her mom's backpack.

"Todo va' estar bien," I say without thinking, repeating what adults tell us. It feels good to say out loud.

"Ajá," she says, but not sarcastically. Then she stops looking at me and looks up at the stars. The moon climbs higher and higher. I'm scared. She's scared. I'm glad she said it. I'm glad I said it. I hope I'm right. People keep shouting. I take my hands out from the sleeves and dig my fingers into the dirt. The cold feels good around my fingers, in my palm. Chino isn't back. The breeze is faint and brushes against my face.

They're arguing. Shouting. More people start getting up to check what's happening. I lift my head higher to look around.

"Sleep, burros." Patricia finally looks at us. "He's coming back, sleep."

I rest my head on Chino's backpack. I can't sleep, like when Grandpa used to come home drunk. Mom would tell me to sleep, but I couldn't. I was afraid he would hit Abuelita, Mom, Mali. Grandpa shouted too loud. People here are screaming at each other. Deep Voice also shouts. Then, scuffling. The bushes around us shake. It's Chino.

"Puta" is all he says.

"¿What? ¡¿What?!"

"People are desperate."

"Puesí."

"Javier, sleep, necio." Chino's face is fine. He wasn't fighting. I don't say anything, but look over at Carla, whose eyes are open. Her lips move, mouthing at me to "pretend."

We half close our eyes and listen to Chino and Patricia whisper to each other. The shouts are getting quieter.

"¡We leave in fifteen!" Deep Voice finally shouts.

"¡¿Fifteen?!" people complain.

"Calm down," Marcelo Look-Alike tells people.

"Shut the fuck up," the other pale pollero barks.

"We know the way," the other two say.

"¿What the fuck do you want *me* to do? We walk or we're fucked," Deep Voice says, firmly, shutting everyone up.

Patricia and Chino look at each other. They whisper something. Then they look at us. We don't close our eyes fast enough, and they see us watching.

"Sleep, burros," Patricia says, annoyed.

I try my best to breathe. To stay warm. I pray to myself. Whisper the usual things. I look up at the stars. The sky is beginning to fade from black to blue. Primero Dios we'll get to the vans before sunset.

IT'S 5:45 A.M. SUNLIGHT paints "Rhino" Mountain's horn bright yellow and orange. It's almost directly to our left. The smell of rain without rain returns. Doves rise from the bushes. Smaller birds fly across the painted sky. The ground is orange. I'm still half-asleep, but I'm walking. Every few steps, Carla and I look at each other to see who's gonna need to ride on Chino's back first. It's our game without ever saying it's our game.

Deep Voice walks fast, but not as fast as last night. The Centipede looks smaller. ¿Did people stay with Coco Liso? ¿Did they leave while we napped like Marcelo did? No one says anything. No whispers, no shouts—just walking. It's less windy than yesterday, but when there's a breeze, it's so quiet we can hear the twigs of Cheerleader and Crayon bushes. Last time, I listened for Cadejo's whistle; now I know for sure he doesn't exist. Bad things keep happening. He's just a myth. Just like Marcelo, Cadejo is full of lies. If Cadejo was real, we wouldn't have gotten caught. Patricia wouldn't have gotten hurt. Coco Liso would still be here with us. Our prayers haven't helped either.

It's mostly bushes again, and the ground is flatter—not much grass. The dirt is yellow and orange. The dawn sky isn't as pretty as yesterday's. Not one cloud. We walk and I wish for water, for clouds to rain on us. My throat is dry. We haven't walked past ranches yet, but there are dirt roads. Barbwire fences. Cactuses. I hope we're getting there soon. My throat feels like someone is choking me, my lips like they're being lashed by the breeze.

THERE'S A HOUSE FAR in the distance surrounded by its own barbwire fence. There are three armless People cactuses and one one-armed People cactus rising from the front of the property near the gate, but no trees. We hide in the bushes as Deep Voice thinks.

"It's not it," he says. "Walk."

All of us rise from the dirt that's more and more become our mattress. We're wearing our shirt-hoods again, our chamarras tied around our waists. The air heats up. The moon is about to crash into the mountains. It's nine A.M., and my watch's plastic band begins to burn. I'll keep it on. I have to know the time when I see my parents.

Whenever I ride on Chino's back, I sleep. His backpack is warm and dusty, but it's comfy. When Chino puts me down, he picks Carla up. She also sleeps when she's on him. Chino doesn't carry the empty gallon of water anymore; he can grab our hands so we don't fall off. I'm thirsty. The thirstiest—

The Centipede looks like the heat took a machete and hacked it into pieces; the space between each section is longer. People keep stepping off to the side. No one has water. No one says that they will wait. When I'm walking, there isn't much grass so I try to step into Patricia's steps, two points. One point if I step into the footprint of whoever left it before her.

"Walk."

"Get up."

"Get up," the people in line say to those who rest and lie in the dirt. Chino and Patricia don't say anything, but Chino grabs my hand when we walk past someone taking a break. I don't know if we're moving faster, but it doesn't feel like it. In front of us, the valley between the mountains is wider. *A house with three trees in front*. I think that's right. *A red house and three trees and two vans*.

"¿WHAT WOULD YOU WANT right now?" Chino asks, turning his head back to see my face next to his neck, waking me up by tapping my hands. He stops grasping my arms and I cling to the straps of his backpack.

"¿Huh?"

"Like if you could have anything, ¿what would you want?" The dark shirt he wears like a hood is sweaty. I can smell him, which means I stink, también.

"Oh . . . jamaica from Los Mochis," I tell him with a smile. But I'd drink anything—even Mexican horchata.

"¡No jodás! Hoy sí estás en algo," Chino says, putting his hand out for a high five. I look over his shoulder and tap his warm palm.

"But with a lot of ice." Ice is what makes them refreshing. Ice for my forehead, for my cheeks, for my lips, for the back of my neck, for everywhere.

"Puesí. Con un vergo de hielo." He emphasizes the *vergo* by shaking an invisible object between his hands. "¿Y vos?"

"¿What?" Carla asks, walking next to us. She's wearing her shirt around her face. She wasn't paying attention. Patricia walks in front of us, wearing a shirt around her head, también.

"¿What would you want right now?"

"A plane," she says.

All of us laugh. "Bicha bayunca," Patricia says.

"¿And to eat or drink on that plane?" Chino asks between laughs, his eyes smaller when he laughs.

"A really cold Coca-Cola, almost frozen, like in the commercials." All of us nod. *Mmm.* That sounds good. I love those polar bear commercials.

"Y vos, ¿qué?" Patricia asks Chino.

"N'hombre, Patita, I asked first."

"Easy. Un fresco de chan from La Niña Nofre's stand," she answers quickly.

Carla and Chino nod. They know exactly what she means. I nod también. I don't know who they're talking about, but I remember Abuelita's chan she made on the hottest days with so much ice. She made it so tangy, with so many chia seeds floating in the cold water, which she tinted very red, sometimes magenta.

"¿Y vos pues?" Patricia asks Chino.

"Was gonna say the same." He pauses. As he thinks by looking up at the sky, he almost trips us on a rock.

"¡Pasmado!" Patricia shouts at him for almost dropping me on the ground. "Be careful."

"Una minuta de limón y sal," Chino answers. *Mmm.* I think of the minutero who stopped in front of the clinic. Inside his wooden cart, covered by blue plastic, he'd scrape a huge chunk of ice with his metal tool, shaving the ice. Lime and salt is *my* favorite. I can taste it . . . I look around and realize there's a lot fewer people. The polleros are gone. The Centipede is only ten pairs of feet.

"¿Where is everyone?" I ask Chino.

"We're up front, we're walking fast. We're close. Todo está bien." I check my watch. It's minutes to one P.M. The sun is torching our heads. My legs are almost numb, like there are pins and tacks all over them. The ground looks like it's steaming. I remember the people at the albergue saying that the desert gets so hot you can fry an egg on the rocks. I believe them.

"Your turn," Chino tells Carla, stopping for a bit, bending his knees so I get off. She wraps her arms around his neck.

Today is hotter than yesterday, hot as the clay ovens outside The Baker's house where I'd pick up pan francés on Christmas mornings for the panes rellenos. Near the ovens, the air felt like coals were touching my face. The air now feels like that, like coals. A blanket of ash. We're walking so slow. I pretend my saliva is water, but that only makes me thirstier.

"We're almost there, Javier," Chino says.

"Walk," Patricia struggles to say. Both of them sound tired. Carla doesn't look good. My hands are scratched up. I move my watch, and the skin under it is so much lighter than the rest of my arm. My lips have cuts all over them. My eyelids are heavy.

"Water," I finally say.

"Water." Carla backs me up.

The adults don't say anything.

"Water," we repeat.

Finally, Patricia speaks first. "Chino, stop. Ya no. Let's find shade."

He doesn't say anything. No one says anything.

We keep walking. ¿What are we looking for? There are no houses. No farms. No trees. Chino holds my hand tighter. Carla is asleep on his back. Patricia walks sideways, like she's drunk. ¿Why aren't there any clouds? My stomach hurts like someone's stabbing it. I drag my feet. I eat the air pretending it's fog or clouds. I bite as I walk like I have a fish's mouth.

"LET'S OPEN A CACTUS."

"N'hombre, vos," Chino tells Patricia. "That's only in movies."

People open cactuses for water in cartoons, también. The shape of a sweetsop flashes through my eyes. A green dinosaur egg. Pink inside—sometimes white. The soft dark brown seeds wrapped in its meat.

"Let's try."

"We don't have a knife."

My forehead and the sides of my head hurt. Without Chino or Patricia noticing, I look back, forward, there's only one more section with us. Two people. The sky is almost white, it's so bright. The pale polleros and Marcelo Look-Alike are gone. Everyone in the Centipede, except us four and those two men behind us—gone. Everyone walked faster. They left us.

We drag our shadows through the dirt, and catch up to a group we didn't know was in front of us. They're next to a small People cactus without arms—just a trunk jutting from the ground. Broken. They've tried to open it with rocks.

"¿Water?"

"Nothing," they say, looking up at us from the dirt. There's something on their arms. Their faces.

"Don't look," Chino says, pushing my face the other way.

He pulls Carla's hand and turns her head.

My belly feels like an ice pick is stuck in it. The shirt around my head isn't working, it's wet with sweat.

"¿And to eat? ¿What would you want to eat?"

I don't know. I want to look back to see what the people are doing. He catches me, taps my arms, tells me, "Don't look," and repeats the same question.

"I don't know."

"Think."

I just want water. I don't want to eat. My stomach hurts.

"To eat . . ." Chino taps me again.

I can't think of anything but my house. The fruit trees. The giant avocado tree where iguanas lived. We could eat a lizard. But we haven't seen those either.

"Javier," Chino says, slightly jumping up so I shake. "To eat," he repeats.

"Bean soup," I whisper, and I can see Grandpa's shirtless torso in front of his clay pot warming on top of a fire.

Chino laughs.

"¿*Soup?* ¿Right now?" Patricia raises her voice and shakes her head.

"Sí," I say. It was the only thing that flashed through my mind.

"Sí, Pati, to sweat everything out." Chino backs me up.

I can see old newspapers thrown in between the wood Grandpa cut from our backyard to keep the fire going. A ripe avocado diced on top of the soup. Queso duro crumbled on top. Lime to squeeze. Tortillas to dip into the thick, brownish-purple broth.

"I'm hungry," Chino says, and puts me down. "Okei, climb up." He taps Carla's arm and she almost runs into a bush.

"¡Gentle!" Patricia shakes her head at Chino.

Carla rests on Chino's back, wraps her arms around his neck, he grabs my hand, and we walk.

"Rhino" Mountain is behind us. Our shadows look like asphalt. Bushes look like people. We haven't seen a road, heard the ocean, or seen a car since yesterday. Not even helicopters. Only dirt.

"Trees. Look, over there," Patricia says, pointing in front. The air is still steaming. From a distance, it looks like birds are on the ground. ¿Crows? ¿Vultures?

When we reach them, we see they're Lonely cactuses. The grasses look like dry spaghetti—yellow sticks rising from the ground. I look back, and the two people who were with us are nowhere.

"That way," Chino points. My stomach feels like I'm gonna throw up. The boats—that was better. Water, more water, and flying fish. It was hot, but not like this. We weren't walking, and it was only one day in the waves.

To the right of us, there's a slight rise, like a hill.

"¡Trees!" he almost shouts, waking Carla up. Chino walks faster than Patricia and me. He's meters away when he starts jumping.

"¡Trees!" he yells this time. "¡Trees, vos!" he yells again, pointing at something. Carla points in that direction también.

We catch up to them.

"N'hombre."

"No estamos tan salados," he tells Patricia through his shirt-hood. I can see his little-toothed smile.

We walk a bit more, and ¡yes! Not one, or two, but ¡multiple trees! Giant, woolly, grayish-green trees.

"Almost there, walk walk walk," Chino says. My feet hurt.

"Push," Patricia says. It works. It's like I just ate a star in *Mario Bros.,* and we're moving faster and faster. Closer and closer to the trees swaying in the wind, moving like they're alive. They remind me of Taz the Tasmanian Devil, because they're skinny at the bottom and bigger on top.

The huge trees rise from the grasses and the almost-white dirt. They're as tall as the avocado tree in my backyard. Two, three stories high. We slide near the trunk where the shade is darkest, and it feels like stepping into a cold curtain. We collapse, tired but laughing.

"A real five-star hotel," Chino says, pointing at the dirt, cool like night is trapped below the rocks and twigs.

"I think this one is twenty stars," Patricia jokes back.

I immediately pick a spot and lie down, use my chamarra as a pillow. Carla laughs.

"You're a cat," she says, and then she does the same. Patricia, también. We're all cats resting in the shade, except for Chino, who keeps looking at the trees.

"Someone planted these," Chino says, inspecting the trees.

Maybe. We've never seen this type of tree in the desert.

"Look, look, houses," he tells Patricia.

¡¿Houses?!

"¿Are they red with three trees up front?" Patricia asks while lying flat on the ground.

"No," Chino responds.

"Doesn't matter then," she says.

Chino keeps looking toward the houses. He snaps a few leaves from the tree and brings them to us. They feel like plastic and look like twigs. Each section of the leaf is like a tube. The color and smell remind me of the trees in front of Abuelita's yard.

"Looks like a cypress," I tell Chino.

"Usssh. ¡No, niño! ¡Not cypress!" Patricia shouts quickly, shaking her hands like she's swatting a fly.

I don't understand.

I look at Chino, who doesn't say anything.

"Cypress is the smell of death, niño. Usssh," she says, and crosses herself.

"Ohh, ¿like the wreaths?" Chino asks.

"Cabal," Patricia says.

"¡Uyyy! ¡Sorry!" I say, crossing myself. I'm scared. I remember the cypress wreaths for Día de los Difuntos. Ever since Great-Great-Grandma Fina died in 1996, we've visited her every November 2. We'd take her a cypress crown and retouch her name on her cross with black paint. I like how cypress smells.

Chino finally sits down, Carla and me between my pretend parents. Our family. We're The Four again. Everyone else is gone.

"I want a really cold coconut," Chino says out loud. We laugh, the sky so blue behind grayish-green leaves. I wish for clouds, but they don't come.

"A Pizza Hut pizza," Patricia says.

"McDonald's hamburger," Carla's response.

In my mouth, all I can taste are onions and cilantro—the tacos we had in Mazatlán.

"Tacos," I say. Then it's easier to imagine food dangling from the branches. *Green papaya with salt. Green mangos with salt, alguashte, and lime. Pepetos. Paternas . . .*

CHINO SHAKES ME.

"You passed out," he says, but it feels like I didn't sleep at all.

"We should keep walking," he tells Carla and me. Patricia is behind the trunk, peeing.

"Ush," she comes back saying, "yellow yellow, almost orange."

I wonder what color my pee is. I haven't had water since yesterday.

"Let's walk," he says again.

"¿Where?" Carla asks.

"To look for the ranch," Chino says. "No hay de otra."

"It must be one of those." Patricia points to little dots in the distance. The ground dips down from here; we're on a small hill.

"Telephone poles are a good sign," Chino adds.

They look like giant crosses, taller than anything else around—besides these trees. People cactuses also rise from the dirt like giant, dark-green Cheetos.

"A caminar se ha dicho." Chino dusts his pants.

"Water," I say again. There's another ice pick in my belly, but this one is in the bottom right, close to my waist. "I can't walk anymore."

No one says anything. My legs haven't felt like this. I can't stand. Chino paces while rubbing his head. I notice empty water bottles everywhere, and trash: plastic bags, empty sardine cans and bean cans, torn shirts, pieces of shoes. ¿Were there people here before us? He picks up the bottles, tips them over, hoping something drops in his mouth. Patricia does the same. Carla and I watch them from the ground.

"Ni mierda," he says. "Jump on my back, Javier. ¿Carla, can you walk?"

She nods.

"Up."

My legs wobble when he pulls me up, my shins like there are needles all over them. I climb on his back. He hands me his shirt. I make a hood again. He puts his on, and we start walking.

"IT'S NOT IT." PATRICIA clicks her tongue.

This is the third time we've crouched under a bush to decide if the house in front of us is *the* house. Chino thinks it's four trees. Patricia says it's two—but those aren't trees, they're cactuses. I want water. The AC from Pizza Hut in San Salvador. Mom and Dad. Mali. My mouth is heavy. My tongue dry dry dry. The sun is a grapefruit squeezing its juices, turning everything red. Orange. Pink. Lavender.

"¿That one?" Chino points to another house up ahead. It's only bushes and Lonelies now. Rocks. Birds smaller than doves. Then—

"¡Down!" Chino yells.

Rocks hit metal. Nails and screws rattle. It's a dark-blue truck with a dust cloud following it. We're as flat as possible. We're far from the dirt road. It doesn't see us.

We stand, and I ride Chino's back again. He's my camel. I'm his hump on top of his backpack. The sky keeps changing. Our shadows, longer.

"I'm sweating a lot," I whisper to Chino, and show him my drenched palm, my wet forehead.

He doesn't say anything.

"Let's stop," I whisper.

I haven't cried. I don't want to cry. My heart pumps fast. The fastest. Faster than when we saw the helicopter. My stomach hurts. My legs. Everything. My skin is sunburned. My lips are ripped. And then—I can't stop. I try keeping the sobs in by crunching my belly. My chest pops up. I can't breathe.

"¿Estás bien?"

I can't—

"¿What's up?"

I want Mom. Mali. Abuelita.

"Todo está bien. We're gonna stop, hermanito. Look, the sky, it's so pretty," Chino says, pointing at the purples. The People cactuses are yellow and olive, Fuzzies golden, Crayon bush bright green, all the colors bright and mixing together.

"Let's try this one," he tells Patricia. I don't want them to see me crying. I wipe my eyes and hide in the shirt-hood. I bite my lip. *I'm strong. Todo está bien. I'm strong.*

Chino puts me down. The ground is bright orange. Bats flap over us. The birds fly to wherever they go at night. I can't see straight. The house is close, then far away.

"It's fucking red," Patricia says. "*And* trees . . ."

Three of them. Two trucks are parked in front. A steel gate. And a van.

"It's three trees, ¿right?"

"Jaber. But look." Chino points to a bright-green, almost neon hose, glistening.

"¡Water!" Patricia shouts. Her dimples deepen, her scratched-up face brightens.

Carla smiles.

"Gracias a Dios." Patricia looks up at the sunset and crosses herself.

My tongue waters. My stomach growls. My headache stops for a second.

"We can pull it," Chino says. "Squeeze the hose tip through the fence."

"Careful."

We crouch behind Chino, from bush to bush. The hose is wrapped around some plastic thing at the very corner of the property. We crouch closer until we have to cross a dirt road. We're under the telephone poles—they're huge, and the sun makes them look like they're covered in honey. There's no one in the house, no one on the road. We run across.

There are no bushes, nothing next to the hose. Just dirt and dry grass. We're flat on our bellies, lizards waiting to drink. And then—

Dogs.

We can't see them, but they're barking.

"Puta," Chino says as he pulls the hose through the barbwire.

"¡Turn it on! ¡Hurry! ¡Turn it!"

He turns the knob. A waterfall rushes out. Chino sprays all of us. Our bellies flat to the ground. Our mouths open. The water is hot at first. Warm. Clear. A puddle forms around our heads. It feels so good. White bubbles at the edges of the puddle. The red dirt turns even more red, then a brown like the color of our sunburned skin. Mud.

"Drink," Chino hands me the hose's metal tip.

I crawl up to the hose and rise up a bit, trying not to stand. The hose is warm and feels like how I think snakes must feel to the touch. Water doesn't stop rushing out. I put my lips on the metal. A gulp. Two. It tastes like rubber—warm rubber and metal but it's good. I pour some on my face. My neck. Drench my shirt-hood with water.

"Hurry up." Patricia taps my shoulders. I take more gulps and give it to Carla, who pushes only her upper body up from the ground. And then—

Two giant German shepherds sprint directly at us—the barbwire right in front of us stops them. They won't stop barking. We scoot back with our elbows. Patricia pulls the hose a bit farther, and starts drinking frantically.

"Callate, chucho de mierda," Chino whispers, trying to calm the most aggressive of the two dogs. Their teeth, big and bright white. Drool spews out their mouths. Behind them, a thin gringo walks toward us. Tall like a pencil.

"A la gran puta, run, ¡run!" Chino says, beginning to stand.

"Alto! Parar!" the gringo screams, firing a gunshot into the air. It's loud. I feel it in my chest. My stomach. None of us move.

"Don't be dumb, don't move," Patricia tells Chino, choking the hose, her hands shaking. We're flat on the wet dirt.

The gringo keeps stepping closer. He wears a long-sleeved shirt tucked into his blue jeans. A hat on top of his skinny face full of wrinkles, and his pale hands hold a giant black gun—a shotgun he points at us.

"No corer disparar," he repeats in the thickest gringo accent, mispronouncing the *r*'s. He wears brown boots. He dresses like the polleros, like he's in a Mexican ranchera. "Okei. Okei," Chino says, now kneeling with his hands up.

"No malos." Patricia kneels, drops the hose, and points at her chest and then us.

He points the gun at her.

"¡Mamá!" Carla screams.

The man points the gun at Carla, then me.

"¡No me le haga nada a mis hijos!" Patricia screams.

Water keeps rushing out of the hose.

"No corer," he repeats, taking more steps toward us. "Migra venir."

"No, señor, por favor. Ya nos vamos," Chino says.

"Por favor," Patricia begs, her hands together. "Niños." She points at us.

"Migra. Venir," he repeats.

I don't want the cage.

"No, por favor, Migra no, niños, mire, aquí, mis niños." Patricia keeps pointing at us.

"Llamar Migra. No corer."

Then Patricia walks on her knees closer to the fence, closer to the dogs that don't stop barking, her hands like she's praying. "Por favor."

He says something in English. He sounds mad. He's still pointing his gun at Chino, who's also on his knees.

Chino tries to scoot closer to the fence.

"Parar!" the man shouts.

Chino stops. The gringo tells his dogs something, and they sit, frothing at the mouth, showing their teeth. Carla and I get on our knees. I can't stop shaking.

"Puta, este gringo cerote isn't gonna let us leave."

"Está pelado," Patricia whispers.

"Agua," Chino tells the man, nods at the hose. "Agua."

The gringo nods. "Tomar," he says, pointing at the neon hose with the tip of his gun.

Chino grabs the hose from the dirt, now turned mud. All of us are wet, our shins, knees, pants, belts.

"At least the water tastes good." Chino smiles, his mouth full of water, the sunset behind him—more and more purple.

"¿Want more?" he asks us.

We shake our heads.

I can't stop looking at the man's house—its red tin roof, the truck. Its walls are made of the same cement blocks that Abuelita's house is made from.

We hear tires. A white truck parks next to us. The green stripe.

My eyes water, and tears rush out. The doors beep open. A green uniform steps out. He says something in English to the gringo, who continues to point the shotgun at Chino's chest. My cheeks are drenched. My pants are muddy. The gringos continue to speak. Carla is also crying. Chino's veins pop from the side of his face. His hands are up in the air, and his right hand chokes the hose; not a single water drop touches the ground. Chino doesn't look at us. The back of my neck is heavy like I have rocks pressing down. My head hurts.

"Hola, buenas noches," the uniform says. His Spanish has an accent, but it's not as thick. We understand him fully. He gets closer. I don't look at his face. His olive-green clothes darker now.

"Buenas noches," he repeats. I stare at his dusty black boots. "Familia?"

"Sí," Patricia and Chino answer. Carla and I nod.

"Qué país?"

"México," they say in their best Mexican accent.

He walks closer. I look at his face: clean-shaven with short black hair. He's young—can't be older than Patricia, his face is without wrinkles like Chino's. His skin darker than all of ours.

"Cuantos años tú?"

"Nueve."

"Tú?"

"Doce," Carla answers.

"Sus padres?"

"Sí," we say.

"Quieren agua?"

"Ya tomamos," Patricia says.

The uniform turns to the gringo, who is still pointing his shotgun at Chino, and tells him something.

"Quitar esto," the uniform says, touching Chino's backpack. Chino grinds his teeth, his veins thick near his temples. "Manos detras de espalda."

The handcuffs click.

"Usted, también," he tells Patricia, whose cheeks are puffy. Her backpack falls on the wet dirt.

"No, señor, ¡no!" she cries.

"Está bien, procedimiento, no más."

Then he turns to the gringo, tells him something in English, and the shotgun finally points at the ground.

"Arriba," the uniform tells Carla and me. "Voy a poner a padres en carro, okay?"

We nod.

He takes Chino into the truck first. Patricia next. Then throws their backpacks into the back of the truck. The gringo watches us. We're standing but can't move. My legs wobble. My headache covers my head like a heated-up baseball hat. The uniform talks to the gringo, who finally turns the hose off and begins to walk toward his house, its windows shining a dim yellow light. It's officially night.

"Amigo." The uniform points at his chest. "Ven," he says, as he motions us to follow him. He opens the door. Chino and Patricia sit behind the driver's seat. Same metal divider like last time. Carla steps in first. I sit near the window. It's warm in here. The door shuts. The lights make the truck look like a spaceship.

"Okay, vamos," the uniform says, turning the engine on. "Yo, Mister Gonzalez. Ustedes? Nombres?"

Patricia gives him our Mexican names. The wheels start to hit rocks and dirt below.

"Primera vez cruzar?"

Chino looks at Patricia, who makes her eyes wide like a cat's. I look at the gringo's house. It looks so lonely. There isn't another house around.

"No," Chino answers.

"Puta," Patricia whispers, and shakes her head like Chino said the wrong thing. "You fucked up." She looks Chino in the eyes.

Chino seems confused.

"Jail," she mumbles.

"No problema." The uniform wags his index finger. "Cuántas veces?"

Patricia is still staring at Chino, and she answers for him. "Dos."

"Verdad?" he turns his head to look at Chino.

"Sí."

"Verdad, niños?"

We both nod. It's dark outside the window. After a few minutes, another house on another dirt road. I look for a red one with three trees in front. Two vans. It's hard to see. The adults keep talking.

¿What's gonna happen? We had to make it this time. I might never see my parents. I don't want to sleep in that cage. I don't want to sleep without Carla and Patricia. I want my parents. I want a real bed. I want McDonald's and snow and a swimming pool. I don't want to walk the desert ever again.

WHEN THE UNIFORM STOPS asking questions, it's finally quiet. The truck turns onto more dirt roads. Rocks in the dirt flash dark silver when the headlights hit them. Everything else is dark. Night to the sides, night above the headlights, night behind us. After five, ten minutes, the truck slows down. The tires rattle. We pull over.

"Tienen hambre?"

Chino and Patricia narrow their eyes. Look at each other. I look at them.

"Hambre?" the uniform repeats.

"Sí," they say. Carla and I nod. We haven't eaten since the cold tortilla.

"Quieren chocolate?"

¿Chocolate? ¡I haven't had a chocolate bar since El Salvador!

"Caliente." He makes the motion of a cup with his brown hands. I'm disappointed.

"Sí." Patricia nods.

"Ustedes?" He looks at us.

Carla elbows me. She nods. She elbows me again. "Sí," I whisper.

"Okay, esperar." The truck is on, but the engine is off, its headlights pointing directly at a group of leafless Cheerleader bushes. I look for trash, water bottles, signs anyone has been there, but there's nothing. The truck's back door opens. The uniform's boots are loud against the gravel. Cool air rushes in. Patricia and Chino still have their chamarras wrapped around their waists. We do también. It's cozy in here, warmer than outside. I hear liquid rushing out of something and hitting the bottom of a paper cup.

The uniform opens my door; he's wearing a dark-green chamarra, unzipped. I look at his chest and read a patch that begins: *Gonz—*. He's not lying.

Mr. Gonzalez says something in English and hands me and Carla the hot chocolate. The paper cup is hot, but not too hot; it doesn't hurt my hands. Steam rises from the light-brown liquid. He closes my door and walks to the back. More hot chocolate hits another cup.

My door opens again. "Aquí, para padres." He hands us each another cup. It's not my favorite. Abuelita used to make it when I didn't want to drink milk, but I still knew there was milk in it.

"Por favor, nada estúpido, okay?" He stares at my pretend parents.

"Okei," Chino says, eyebrows crunched together.

Mr. Gonzalez looks at Patricia. "Sí," she says, staring past the metal divider.

"Quito." He points at their handcuffs. "No correr, por favor. Yo amigo." He points at his chest.

"Okei," Chino repeats in his best English.

Mr. Gonzalez motions for Carla and me to hold the cups tighter by clenching his fists.

"Aquí," he tells Patricia, as he reaches for her wrists. His arms brush against Carla's face and my face. Patricia scoots over and turns so he can get to the handcuffs easier. I smell his cologne—it's faint, but it smells like firewood mixed with cypress.

He takes the handcuffs and presses himself up from the seat, then closes the door. We look at each other, confused.

"Buena gente," Patricia whispers, reaching for her hot chocolate.

Chino looks at us. His veins aren't popped anymore. "Cabal," he whispers, nodding, almost smiling. Patricia holds the cup funny.

Mr. Gonzalez taps my window again. "Nada estúpido."

We nod. Mister hands us pan dulce, conchas: two pink, one white, and one yellow.

"Aquí." He hands them to Carla and me. They're cold but still fluffy.

Then he walks around the truck and taps Chino's window and points at Chino's handcuffs.

"Okei. Sí." Chino turns toward us, showing Mr. Gonzalez his hands. The door opens, and the handcuffs click. "Amigo," Mister repeats. Chino smiles, rubs his hands. I hold my breath, afraid he's gonna run out the truck—

"Gracias," Chino tells Mr. Gonzalez, who shuts the door and sits in the driver's seat.

"Está bueno?" he asks, looking at me through the rearview mirror. I don't know what he means. "Chocolate, bueno?" he asks again.

I nod even though the hot chocolate tastes like water, which I liked back when I didn't like warm milk. But now I miss the milk because it makes hot chocolate thicker.

Patricia doesn't eat or drink anything. Chino already finished his hot chocolate and pan dulce. Carla también, so now she holds her mom's cup and bread. I'm almost done with mine.

"Puedo ayudar con labios." Mr. Gonzalez points at his lips. "Labios, verdad?" Keeps pointing. "Cactus? Nopal?"

"Sí, me duelen mucho."

"Okay," he says, followed by English we don't understand. "Alguien más tiene espinas?"

I look at my hands. I'm fine. No thorns or needles. Carla looks at her hands and arms. They're more scratched up than mine, but she shakes her head. Chino shakes his también.

"Okay, esa puerta." Mister points at my door. I drink the last sip with wet crumbs at the bottom of the cup.

He opens the back again and grabs something, then walks back to our door.

"Ven." He signals to Patricia, who pushes her eyebrows together. "Afuera," Mister says. "Está bien. Ven."

Carla and I stand inside the truck and lean closer to the cold metal divider so Patricia can scoot over little by little until she lands on the gravel and Mr. Gonzalez shuts the door.

"Señá," Chino whispers, grabbing our empty cups and stacking them inside one another. Carla sits facing forward, holding her mom's hot chocolate, and takes a sip so it doesn't spill. Chino doesn't try to open the door. Doesn't scream. We don't either. We know we're locked in.

I get on my knees to look at Patricia sitting on the truck's ledge, Mister standing in front of her, gently turning her face into the back light. So many scratches with dry blood and dirt inside them. He wears white plastic gloves like a doctor and holds something metallic.

"Tweezers," Carla whispers.

We watch him pull tiny broken needle pieces from Patricia's face. She grimaces as the tweezers dig in, but doesn't cry like she did last night when Chino was doing this exact same thing with a nail clipper.

"Por cuál ciudad el primer cruce?" Mister asks as he pulls out another broken needle tip, stuck deep in her cheek.

"No sé, señor."

I don't either. Polleros didn't tell us which town we crossed through.

"Cuantas personas?"

A tear falls down her face. He asks again.

"¿Cuál de las veces?" Patricia asks him.

"Esta."

"Treinta o cuarenta."

"Cincuenta o sesenta," Chino corrects her. I think Chino is right.

Mr. Gonzalez stops asking questions, and we watch Patricia's scratched-up face. Her pain. Her sunburned patches. The light turns her hair light brown again. After pulling needles, Mister pinches her skin to squeeze the dirt out, which bursts tears from her light-brown eyes, making me want to cry. I can't stop watching.

"Mamá." Carla's voice turns shrill like it does when she's concerned.

"Está bien, mija," Patricia squeaks out in her best Mexican, batting the air in front of her.

I don't know how Patricia is doing this. ¡She's not even crying-crying! Reminds me of Mali taking pimples out of her face. Or taking splinters out of my hands when I had any. I have some now, but they don't hurt. My legs still do. The space between my hip and thigh. My knees. My lower back. My shins. Ankles. Everything is heavy, like I'm made of cement. But my head is light like it's filled with air.

"Okay," Mister says, wiping the sweat from his forehead after also pulling needles out of Patricia's palms.

"Gracias. Gracias, señor."

He taps her shoulder and smiles. "No problema." He seems proud. He pulled everything out. They walk up to my door. She comes in, cold air like a shadow behind her. "Quieren más pan y chocolate?" Mister asks.

"Sí," all of us say. I'm still hungry.

"Okay, dame." He grabs at an invisible cup in the air. We understand. Chino passes the cups to me, and I give them to Mister, who walks to the back and brings two more hot chocolates. Then another with a concha. Then two more conchas. Patricia is still working through her first one. She bites slow. Swallows a little bit at a time.

Mr. Gonzalez shuts the back door, walks to the driver's seat, and starts the engine. We start moving. It's dark in here except for the numbers and lights on the dashboard. All of us in a Migra truck again, except this time Patricia's and Chino's hands are free. The truck stops shaking on top of dirt and rocks. We finally make it to an asphalt road.

We merge left, and I think I see the outline of "Rhino" Mountain. The road is a smooth blanket underneath us. The yellow lines in the middle are two thin snakes with little yellow plastic dots reflecting the headlights. No cars drive past. There's no one in front of us. Mister stays quiet, and we keep eating, drinking. I feel less light-headed. My temples still hurt. My body.

After twenty minutes, Mister says, "Hoy es día de suerte."

We look at each other and shrug. Doesn't *feel* like we're lucky. Chino does his lip thing and tilts his head. Patricia tilts hers and mouths, "¿What's he saying?"

"Próxima, descansen cuatro días, okay?"

All of us are still confused.

"Okay?" he repeats louder, turning his head, both hands on the steering wheel.

"Sí," Patricia responds.

"Rest four days." Mister holds up four fingers. They're fat and smooth. "Desierto, es malo."

"Think he's gonna let us go," Chino whispers to all of us.

Patricia's face lights up. "Sí," she answers Mister, louder.

I look at my hands. *¿He's gonna let us go?*

"Niños." He points at us. "Descansar importante por ellos."

"¿Nos va a dejar ir, señor?" Chino finally asks, slowly, pronouncing each syllable.

"Sí," Mister answers without hesitation. "Es día de suerte."

Patricia looks at us, rubs her shoulder against mine. Keeps pushing, so I get closer to Carla, who looks at her mom and smiles. I smile. We're all smiling. "¡Gracias a Dios!" Patricia exclaims loudly, like we're in church. She whispers something to herself, looks up at the roof of the truck, and crosses herself.

"¿De verdad?" Chino asks.

"Sí. But prometer you'll eat más and drink más agua."

"¡Sí! Absolutamente. Sí, señor."

¡I'm not gonna sleep in jail! ¡I'm not gonna pee in front of men! No more bad gringos. Mister Gonzalez *is* amigo. No cage. No zoo.

"No todos who say they're a coyote is telling la verdad. Cuidado." Mister looks at Patricia through the mirror. His eyes dark brown like mine. "Okay?" he says loud, turning around again.

"¡Sí!" all of us shout, and Mister almost laughs.

We keep driving. The road is straight. No curves. No cars.

"Ya la hicimos," Chino whispers. Mouths something to himself.

"Ojalá," Patricia whispers back.

Gracias a Dios, I think. I'm not gonna sleep away from Patricia and Carla tonight. No handcuffs. No strangers and no toilet next to where I sleep.

We drive until the road twists. There's a house to the right. Another to the left. Lights. The road dips. We go up a small hill. The road gets straight again. The headlights shine on a small cement house that looks like an outhouse. We park on a patch of white dirt.

"Okay, amigos." Mister turns the keys and the engine shuts off, but the headlights remain on. He opens my door, and says "Fuera." "Ven," he tells Carla, once my feet hit the dirt.

"No correr, okay?"

"Okei," Carla and I answer.

His hand waves at himself.

"Tú," he tells Patricia. "Okay, tu turno." Chino slides across the seat and we're all out.

He shuts the door. "Esperar." Mister walks to the back, gets our backpacks, and hands them to Chino and Patricia. The breeze is back. The headlights shine on a big tree next to the cement outhouse— La USA flag flaps next to the house.

"Allá es México." Mister points out of reach of the headlights, but we can make out another flagpole. "Caminar," he says. "No correr."

"Walk fast," Chino says, grabbing my hand. Carla holds Patricia's waist. We walk on the asphalt. It's dusty.

"Chamarras," Patricia tells everyone. I untie mine from my waist, dust falls off. I stick one arm inside, the other. Carla does the same.

There's no one in the outhouse, we can see through a window. Chino turns around and waves at Mr. Gonzalez.

"Vieja, he's a really nice maitro, ¿huh?"

"Requetebuena gente," Patricia says.

"Gringo bueno."

"Un ángel."

¿An angel? Maybe. I don't understand.

"¿Why was he so nice?" I ask them.

"Because he's one of us," Patricia says louder, and she's right. He looked like us. The only difference was he spoke Spanish funny, but it's the best Spanish we've heard a gringo speak. ¿Maybe that's why?

The truck's headlights don't reach once we walk past the flagpole with a Mexican flag. This side is dark. Everything around is dark. There's no moon. The road slopes in front of us. We're walking down a hill. We're in México.

CHAPTER NINE

———

Todo va' estar bien

JUNE 7, 1999

———

WE'VE BEEN HERE THREE DAYS. TODAY, OUR NEW POLLEROS
told us we leave tomorrow. We've been resting, just like Mister said. Mostly sleeping. The polleros keep us locked inside because
"it's safer," because "someone might see us and call La Migra." There's
no furniture in this house, so we sleep on the floor next to other
strangers who say they're coming with us.

"We won't be that many," the main pollero says. He's a gringo; occasionally he says one or two words in English, like "trip." "El trip por
el desierto," he says when he means our cruce. Every day, he wears the
same cowboy hat, a button-up shirt with two chest pockets, the same
blue jeans, the same brown boots, and a brown leather belt with a
buckle that has the outline of a bull stitched in white thread. Ramón,
he told us to call him, but we know it's not his real name.

After Mister dropped us off, we slept on a cement slab under
someone's roof next to the asphalt road. I don't remember that night,
just that Carla and I cuddled between Patricia and Chino, all of us
sleeping like that, sandwiched because of the cold. In the morning, an
old woman asked if we needed a coyote, a pollero, "un cruce." She
took us to her house, fed us beans and tortillas while we waited for a
man who said his nephew did "cruces." Chino and Patricia explained

we had no money, but we had people in La USA. By lunchtime, we were inside an old truck with a different stranger. I slept on top of Patricia's legs. When I woke up, dogs barked as we drove into this town—bigger than where we'd woken up, but much smaller than Nogales, and smaller than my town back home.

Ramón says he knows the way. Says his cousins will be waiting for us inside two vans "bien perronas." I like how he talks. Saying words I haven't heard. *Perronas*. I imagine a giant dog with giant teeth. Every pollero we meet promises vans we never make it to, but these polleros are different. They don't know Don Dago, Coyote, Mero Mero, Coco Liso, Mario, or Paco.

"It's gonna be easy. Quick," Ramón reminds us every lunch when he comes and gives us updates. "There won't be many, twenty-five at most."

He's not lying; we're fewer than twenty-five. The polleros feed us rice, beans, and a tortilla—the big flat ones I like—three times a day. There are two big pots in the kitchen, a big bag of rice, and another of beans. Spices next to the sink. Ramón made the first beans that didn't taste so good. Now the adults take turns deciding who will cook. At lunch, Ramón brings freshly baked tortillas—they're the best part.

We can't go outside, so we sleep a lot. It's like Guadalajara, except roosters wake us up at dawn and street dogs bark at all hours. If one starts, it sets off all the others. Instead of beds, there's a big pile of blankets we share with everyone. The blankets have different designs: roses, la Virgen, all sorts of animals. Ours has a tiger on it. We choose an open space and sleep on the cold tile floor. Ever since we slept on the cement under someone's roof, the four of us cuddle together like bananas. I love it. Patricia is the big banana, then Carla is wrapped around me, my face to Chino's back. It keeps us warm at night, and during the day, the tile keeps us cool.

We drink a lot of water, not from bottles but from faucets. The water tastes funny, metallic, "pero es agua," Patricia reminds us. Her face looks better. The cold sore is gone, but we can still see the scratches. The first day, Patricia washed all of our clothes. We showered. No Zote here, just the small and pink Rosa soaps, lots of them in a bag in the bathroom. Every day we smell like roses.

Ramón comes in at lunch. Roberto, the other pollero, comes for dinner and checks on our supplies. Roberto says he's not a gringo but knows the way. He's older than Ramón and has a thick mustache, his hair a really dark brown.

"You're in good hands, morrito," he tells me.

Roberto doesn't dress like Ramón. He wears blue jeans, T-shirts, and black boots.

"Okei," I tell him. It's all The Four say since Mr. Gonzalez.

"Írenlo, you're a gringo, a *gabachito*." That word reminds me of Mario. I hope these polleros get us to La USA. I want to be a gringo. I want to speak English and be in the movies.

Yesterday, a mom and her son arrived. They're from Guatemala and the son is eleven. His name is Tarsicio. I'd never heard that name, so I kept getting it wrong. He got mad. Tarsi is what his mom calls him. They mostly stay in their room, and only come out to eat. Everyone does that. It's boring, but better than the heat, better than walking kilometers, better than a cage.

My legs almost feel normal, except my shins feel like someone is squeezing them hard, like I'm in the middle of a river and water is rushing around me. My headaches are almost completely gone. Just one more day. One more walk. We leave tomorrow at dusk, Ramón said. Always at dusk in the desert. Sunrises, sunsets, I'm starting to hate them both.

6-8-99

RAMÓN AND ROBERTO COME early in the morning. They never show up together. They gather everyone in the living room, where we're still on top of our tiger blanket.

"We can't leave today, primos," Ramón says. "We're waiting for another group."

"Púchica, ya van con babosadas estos cerotes también."

"Tranquila, Patita," Chino tells Patricia quietly, so the polleros don't hear them.

"It's been hell out there—thirty-five degrees Celsius the past few days. Better we leave tomorrow," Ramón continues.

"Puta, it's even hotter here." Patricia elbows Chino.

"Out there, it feels like more. Drink lots of water." Roberto's boots click as he moves across the tile floor. Roberto is his name, but the polleros have nicknames for each other. I know Beto is short for Roberto. But I'd never heard of "Monchi." Reminds me of Los Mochis, the aguas frescas.

Monchi and Beto, they're our polleros. They say we're not crossing mountains. That the trip will be short, "one night and one day in the desert at most." At dusk, the vans will pick us up from the side of the road. Sounds familiar. Chino and Patricia stay quiet. Carla and I look at them. Patricia has been threatening to go back to El Salvador if we don't make it this time.

"Too difficult," Carla and I watch Patricia mouth to Chino. She's been saying this since the day after we got caught a second time. "This is the last try," she says every morning. Every night. She's scaring us. If she leaves, ¿what's Chino gonna do? Carla doesn't want to go back, but if Patricia leaves, Carla goes with her. I don't want to go back, but I can't stay here by myself. I don't trust anyone else. If Chino leaves, I *have* to go with them. I want to keep trying. I'm tired, but I'm a van ride away from my parents. We can do it. We've been so close. Every time Patricia acts like this, Chino calms her down. Right now, he's whispering to her, "We try and try until we make it, doesn't matter how many times." She always agrees, tells him he's right. I hope she's not lying.

When he's done talking, Monchi comes up to us and asks Patricia for her husband's number in La USA. "You don't have feria, that's okay, but we must talk to your contact so they pay us in Tucson." When we first got to this house, Monchi only asked for Chino's number—he believed we were a real family.

After Patricia writes ten digits on a piece of paper, she has to remind Monchi I'm not with her either.

"A cabrón," Monchi says, and asks for my parents' number. He waits for me to reach for a piece of paper, but I don't have to look. I tell him from memory. He writes it down in a booklet.

"¿Can I talk to them?" I ask.

"The phone is at another house, morrito. We'll talk to them," Monchi explains, and walks away.

"That's what they do. They didn't let me talk either," Chino says to make me feel better.

"Coco Liso never asked for their number," I tell Chino.

"Monchi and Beto are different polleros; they need different money," Chino says. He explains that our second attempt was included with the price of our first attempt. My parents had already paid for it.

All of the hidden dollars in my clothing are gone. Patricia and Chino still had some that they used to get us here.

"Don't worry," Chino and Patricia say.

"Primero Dios, you'll see your parents tomorrow." Patricia sounds better. Hopeful.

I miss Mom's and Dad's voices. This is the longest I've ever gone without hearing them. Every other week they called The Baker's house. I miss walking up the four blocks to talk to them.

"Rest," Monchi and Beto say before they leave. "Tomorrow you'll be gringos."

6-9-99

PATRICIA AND I WEAR the same clothes we've worn every time we get on the back of a truck to drive to a patch of empty dirt next to a road in the desert. All of us wear the same chamarras: black, brown, gray, and dark green. The polleros bought each of us one gallon of water, one sardine can, and a loaf of Bimbo bread per group. They passed out rolls of duct tape for us to cover the white plastic, and people who never walked the desert, like the Guatemalan mom and Tarsi, asked why we taped the water bottles. Carla and I smile; we're experts.

As much as we can, we don't move our bodies. We've napped, drunk water, eaten more than usual. I'm ready. *Tenemos que cruzar. Vamos a cruzar,* we keep repeating.

"La tercera es la vencida," Chino says, as we finally walk out the door.

The trucks waiting for us outside are black. We don't know the drivers, but it doesn't matter—only Monchi and Beto are staying. Monchi is dressed differently, his button-up shirt, belt, and dark jeans are the same, but he's now wearing a baseball hat and tennis shoes.

This time we're thirty-five, including the five who arrived last night. Two from Ecuador, two from Cuba, and one man from Brazil. *The Thirty-Five.* We split up and board the two black trucks. Carla and I are allowed up front. Chino and Patricia sit directly behind us, looking through the glass from the truck bed. The mom—who never told us her name—and Tarsi are in the front of the other truck. We sit between Beto and the driver, an older man with white hairs in his scruffy beard.

They don't say much. We start driving and Beto turns the radio on; norteñas I've never heard spew out of the speakers. Dogs bark as the truck moves past this town's cement roads. The horizon in all directions is pink.

"That way," Beto tells the driver. "That way," he says again, until we're on a two-lane highway, dry grass on each side, gold in the light.

I finally recognize a band: Grupo Límite, Alicia Villarreal's voice through the speakers: *Soy la sombra de tu vida. Tú me elevas y me tiras . . .* We drive away from the sunset, away from the volcano mountain, now a shadow in front of the sun in the side mirror. I love the chorus: *Y te aprovechas, porque sabes que te quiero . . .* We drive until the dark anthill mountains are in front of us, painted orange by the light.

Not many cars drive past us. The other truck is behind and no one else. Just the sound of the tires on the asphalt. I remember thinking this sound was the ocean, but it sounds different inside the cabin: sticky, or like opening Velcro straps. The sky keeps changing. The norteñas también, but they keep the same beat: *Pom. Pom. Pom. Pom-pom-pom. Pom. Pom. Pom. Pom-pom-pom.*

After thirty minutes, Beto tells the driver, "Primo, primo, take a left here."

"¿Here?"

"Sí, pariente, right here." Beto points to a dirt path. The ground is red and filled with rocks. The truck dips into the dirt, and a bunny sprints across the road. *Huit-huit, huit-huit,* birds sing in the bushes.

A red dust cloud forms behind us, covering the truck following close by—Chino and Patricia cover their mouths with their chamarras. In front, the slate sky keeps getting darker and darker. Already, I see the first stars and more mountains. We rattle our way deep into the road, until the path ends in a thick group of bushes.

"Here is good," Beto tells the driver, pointing to a clearing with a lot of trash bags, clothes, cans, water bottles. I wrap the chamarra sleeves around my fingers, ready for the cold.

Beto opens the door. *Pom. Pom. Pom. Pom-pom-pom. Pom. Pom. Pom. Pom-pom-pom.* "¡We're here!" he screams loud, slapping the door.

The dirt in this lack of light almost looks like blood, the grasses a dark yellow before turning gray. Everything will change soon. I see a rock in the ground and pick it up. It's shiny, like there's silver in it.

"¿What is it?"

"Silver," I lie to Carla.

"N'hombre, fantasía," she says.

I take a last look and throw the rock at the nearest bush. I was hoping for birds, but nothing. Farther away, they chirp: *Huit-huit. Huit-huit.*

"Here," Monchi says loudly, pointing to a flat patch with trash everywhere. "Sit."

Everyone sits, and we listen to the polleros give us instructions.

———

"THERE WON'T BE A moon, so stay close," Beto cautions.

"We're gonna see lights to our left. Lights to our right," Monchi says. "Those are Migra spotlights, watchtowers. We'll stay far away from them."

"No matter what, we try until we make it," Chino reminds Patricia, who nods.

"We're looking for a railroad," Monchi continues.

"We'll follow it away from the mountains," Beto says.

The polleros finish their instructions and check people's clothes. Our clothes don't reflect anything. I count the bats above.

"Line up!" Monchi yells, walking to the front. Beto is all the way in the back. Before we line up, Patricia says a prayer. We cross ourselves. Then we start walking.

IT'S THE COLDEST TEMPERATURE we've started in. I already have goosebumps. For a few minutes, when some light was still visible, mist formed on the huge mountains in front of us, a thin line of white, like the mountain was wearing a skirt. This time, The Four are closer to the front, near Monchi, The Thirty-Five's head.

After an hour of heading directly at the mountains, we find railroad tracks.

"Like our first try," Carla whispers. I'd forgotten the tracks—wood, gravel, wood, gravel—in the middle of a raised mound. An endless snake.

"If a train comes, we run!" Monchi shouts.

"¿Why is he shouting?" I ask and squeeze Chino's hand.

"Because it's still México," he clarifies. It's dark dark dark, but our eyes adjust. I can never tell whether I'm in La USA or México—the same bushes, the same Lonelies and occasional Fuzzy. Instead of trees, more rocks and a new bush that looks like a tequila plant, except it's smaller and its leaves aren't as fat or long. It has a huge stick that rises from the middle of it, like a swab.

The mom and Tarsi are near the back. They looked scared listening to the instructions. We probably looked like that our first try, which now feels like a long time ago. I wish they were closer so Tarsi could help me name plants.

"In an hour, there's an airport to our right—stay away," Monchi says.

¿An airport? I went to the airport once. Grandpa took me to look at the planes take off. I've always wanted to be inside one.

"Mirá." Chino points to a flickering dot in the distance. Red and green lights turning on and off.

"Plane," Patricia whispers.

Carla's head and my head turn directly to the sky. It's not *that* far up. We can hear it. A small plane, not the big TACA ones I watched lift off with Grandpa.

"Hope it's not Migra," Chino says, and I flinch. I want to drop to the ground and hide, but Chino grabs my hand.

"Don't worry."

"La tercera es la vencida," Patricia and Chino say.

¡¿La Migra has planes?! Planes, helicopters, infrared binoculars, dogs, trucks, ¡they have everything! The other polleros didn't scare us like this. We walk a few more minutes on the railroad tracks until, in front of us, smaller mountains. I don't see another light, just the lights behind us.

"Break left!" Monchi yells.

We start walking away from the tracks. There's a path with different dirt, more like sand and without grasses.

"Dry river," Chino says.

After a while, we sit around bushes.

"Over there"—Monchi points down the riverbed—"is Gringolandia."

"From here on out, no more screaming or shouting," Beto says.

"If I whistle, you drop to the ground," Monchi continues. "Stay

close. If we run, I won't whistle. You see people running, you follow."

"But watch where we're running, run with us, not away from us,"
Beto adds.

"Okay?" Monchi asks.

"Sí," people mumble.

"Okei," Carla and I say in English, because we're almost in La USA.

"Pee, drink, we won't stop until we make it past the road."

¿Road? ¿Already? And we haven't seen barbwire yet. All of us pee.
I'm nervous and cold, but my legs don't ache. There's no grass stuck
inside my shoes. Everything is fine. We're gonna make it.

"Vení." Patricia calls me closer. We're huddling to pray again.
We've prayed like this before, but nothing's worked. I haven't tried
crossing my fingers . . .

"A rezar." Patricia puts her hands around us. Chino hugs us. I
cross my fingers and my toes. "Diosito, guárdanos de todo mal para
que lleguemos a nuestra destinación. Amén."

Amén.

6-10-99

WE'RE AVOIDING ALL LIGHTS: lights to our left and lights to our right.
Planes land and lift off in front of us. We pick the darkest path between everything. I know we're in La USA because there are more
and more barbwire fences. Chino lifts Carla and me over them, without a hurry. Everyone helps each other.

Maybe it's true that Monchi has "the best route no one else knows
about." Whatever he says ends up happening. The moment we left
the train tracks and started following the riverbed past the small hills,
we saw the lights. "Migra station" was the whisper that traveled down
The Thirty-Five.

Monchi and Beto don't shout anymore. They said there would be
dirt roads, and we've crossed them. The next thing is *the road*.

We haven't stopped. We dropped flat on the dirt once because

Beto thought he saw truck lights. He whistled and we became dirt. It was nothing.

The asphalt road we're looking for has "two lanes," Monchi said at the dry riverbed. He gave us instructions to run across the asphalt, but only after we hear his whistle. We haven't gotten there yet.

MONCHI GETS TO THE fence before the asphalt. I think of Coco Liso. "Get closer," Monchi whispers.

We're on our bellies, right in front of the barbwire.

"Same thing," Chino tells Carla and me.

Monchi whistles, and we spring up from the dirt and run across the road. There are no cars. Everyone makes it to the other side. My heart beats, but not because I ran fast. I'm scared. I keep imagining Beto and Monchi twisting their ankles, The Four running into cactuses, everyone running out of water—

We take a short break. My heart slows, and Chino gives me water. We line up again. I follow Patricia's backpack in front of my face. We're so close together. No one is tired. We have more than enough water. We're only halfway through our first gallon. The other three are in Chino's and Patricia's backpacks. We got this. Then, the whistle. A motor in the sky. We freeze, down on the dirt.

Helicopter flashes through my head. The beam slashing the ground—but it's only a small plane.

"Crouch."

"Airport," people whisper.

I thought it was farther away.

"Vieja, I think it's another one," Chino says.

¿Two airports so close to each other? There's only one in El Salvador, but it's for big planes. This plane is smaller than the last, a flying microbus. Green and red lights flash over us. That sound reminds me of el estero and the lanchas. I remember our boat from Guatemala to Oaxaca. I'd almost forgotten about that. The Screaming Man. *No. Nothing bad. Nothing bad,* I tell myself. *La tercera es la vencida.*

———

I LOVE LOOKING FOR the big white moon. Seeing it change. It's better than looking at my watch. The moon has been up there watching me since the dawn I said goodbye to Abuelita, Mali, Lupe, Julia, the dog, the cat, and my parakeet. It was there with Grandpa, when Marcelo left us, when Chele and Mario ran. It reminds me of all of them. Polleros said there wouldn't be a moon, but they're wrong. Like a slice of watermelon bitten to the rind, it showed up over the mountains to our right. I like its gray light before the sun paints the dawn, our clothing changing from black to gray to blue like we're chameleons.

After the airport and the road, it's been dirt roads and barbwire fence after barbwire fence. We haven't seen anyone. No trucks. No Migra. No helicopters. Gracias a Dios.

"Farm" travels down The Thirty-Five.

"Walk fast. Run." It's the least windy night in the desert; the whispers are loud.

We're all in a line about to jump a fence. In front of us, huge metal structures—wheels. A thin metal pipe connects the giant wheels four meters away from each other. They look like monster spiders. Chino throws me over the fence, and underneath my shoes I feel grass—but it's different from the crunch-crunch we've been walking on. Chino grabs our hands and we start walking fast. Running. Following the people in front of us. We run under the metal structures and feel wetness on the ground.

"Cow shit," someone says.

I laugh. But then step on something dry.

"For mosquitoes," Chino says, kicking a dry cow pie to the side. This *is* a farm, but I don't know what for. No corn. No beans. No squash or watermelons. Just poop and grass that reminds me of soccer fields. We run across and make it to the next fence.

Then we hear Monchi's whistle.

We pick a bush and slide. I miss the different cactuses. The trees.

My chest rises up and down. I'm sweating. I check my shoes to see if I stepped on wet cow poop. I don't see anything, but I smell it. Chino hands me his gallon of water. I tip it up and finish it.

"Open yours," he tells Patricia, who's been carrying the fourth gallon. When Carla and Patricia are done drinking, Chino grabs the gallon and carries it.

"Throw it," he tells me and I throw the empty bottle into the next bush where no one is resting. I look over to the mountains, where the moon shines a faint yellow. The sky is beginning to lighten up. The Migra watchtowers are fainter behind us. I finally look at my watch: it's 4:30 A.M.

"That shit is not Migra," Chino realizes, pointing at the lights in the distance.

"¿What?"

"Look, they're cities."

"N'hombre, vos," Patricia says.

"Cómo no, the polleros are bullshitting."

¿Cities? They *are* bright, and there *are* a lot of little lights.

"Last rest, before another road," Beto whispers. We can hear him clearly. It's quiet.

"We'll sleep then," Monchi follows. "Almost there."

¿Almost there? ¿What "there" does he mean? ¿The vans? He said dusk, not dawn. I look at Chino.

"Gracias a Dios."

Patricia crosses herself. Our skin is beginning to change in the light. Everything is turning gray. I whisper a prayer. *No Migra*.

"Go piss," Patricia tells Chino and me, when she sees others peeing on the nearby bushes.

We know the routine. We crouch our way to a big bush. Chino picks one, I pick another and face away from him—release. My pee is dark in the moonlight.

"Yellow," I whisper to Chino.

"Same," he answers.

We laugh. My pee smells. It's loud as it falls on the dirt. *No Migra*.

———

OVER THE MOUNTAINS, ONLY a few skinny clouds remain. Wispy clouds that, like tissues, soaked up the sunrise's brightest colors. We haven't stopped walking, and we haven't found the "other asphalt road." We hear planes to our right. The landscape in front of us is flat. We're in a valley. Telephone-pole crosses rise in the distance to our left; there must be a road.

"Crouch."

All of us crouch from bush to bush. It's morning, but it's not hot-hot yet. My chamarra is still on. In the distance we hear my favorite noise: an ocean wave. We crawl as close to the road as possible. There's no fence this time, but there is trash. Another group must have been here. Monchi and Beto lie flat next to each other, looking in both directions. The road is long, a black tongue with a yellow middle. No cars.

"¡Go!"

We sprint to the other side, sliding into the bushes five meters from the road. We wait, making sure everyone is across, and then crouch deeper into the bushes. The dirt is chalky, almost white again. Rocks jut out from it. Giant ants crawl in front of us. We walk until we find a thick group of adult-sized bushes.

"Let's rest a bit. Pick your shade," Beto and Monchi say, almost at the same time.

"Take a little nap," Beto whispers loud. "Thirty minutes and then we walk."

"We won't stop again until it's really hot. We're close," Mochi adds.

"La Migra has infrared binoculars. When I whistle, drop. Pick a rock to hide if you can."

There are no rocks anywhere.

"Va, let's sleep." Chino smiles like he didn't hear about the binoculars.

Patricia and Carla are already lying down with shirts over their faces. Chino takes two shirts out. "Our hoods," he says.

¿Why doesn't anyone care? I'm scared.

Flies buzz over us. Birds are already awake. I hear a crow in the distance. *Caw. Caw.* I don't like their calls. They sound like they have something stuck in their throats.

"Time to dream." Chino taps my arms.

Smaller birds chirp in the distance. The desert is awake. I take my chamarra off to use as a pillow. The dirt is cool. I shake to get deeper into the dirt like we've seen birds do, and I close my eyes.

KILOMETERS AWAY BUT VISIBLE to our right is something that looks like a town: more and more houses crunched together and tall trees around them. ¡Trees! The air feels like we're in front of lava.

"Todo va' estar bien," Patricia and Chino whisper to Carla and me.

We have water. Two gallons left, and it's not even noon. I look at that town, the houses, the skinny trees rising from the ground like dark green beans, and I imagine shade, water, AC, a swimming pool, fresh food, a bed . . .

I'm starting to get tired, but not like last time. Chino doesn't have to pick me up. I can still walk. Our steps the only sound around.

We walked by what remained of a dead coyote again. Some fur was still on it. It was dirty. Gray. The rib cage and the spine were already turning white. Flies all over. Vultures circling above. "¿Quién dijo miedo?" someone in front of Carla said as we walked past it. Patricia crossed herself, which made me cross myself. I hope it's not a bad omen like last time.

We keep walking and there are fewer birds, less noise, fewer cactuses. I want a cold drink. The water is warm inside its plastic. The heat is unbearable, the hottest we've felt. No shade. No trees, just bushes. We keep walking. The polleros said we'd stop when it was the hottest . . .

The moon has traveled across the cloudless sky, watching us all dawn, all morning, and now into the afternoon. I want to stop. My legs are beginning to throb. My toes feel huge, they're beginning to tingle.

The Thirty-Five freeze. Patricia's backpack on my face. Chino bumps into me.

"Last stop before the vans," Monchi whispers loudly.

"Rest," Beto clarifies.

Everyone tries to pick the biggest bush. Chino starts drinking the second-to-last water bottle, and then passes it to us.

"Drink a lot," Patricia tells Carla. We gulp as much water as possible and get comfortable in the dirt. My belly is full; I can't lie down flat just yet.

"Má." Chino gives me his backpack just like Patricia does to Carla. I use it to prop myself up. Water sloshes in my belly.

"Sleep, bichos, you need to be strong for the vans," Patricia tells us.

"Almost with your parents, Javiercito."

I smile and keep nodding, imagining my parents' hands. Their house. Their lawn. Their garden. Their swimming pool and cars. I want The Four to meet my parents. I look over at Patricia and Carla. At Chino. I'm gonna say goodbye to them soon. The sun is a bit over the center of the sky, shining in every direction. Our shadows are so small, but they touch. We're one big shadow. Our own family. I hope we rest a long time.

IT'S AFTER THREE P.M., and the sun is following the moon we can no longer see over the horizon. The air doesn't feel cooler.

"Final stretch, parientes," Monchi says when we line up again.

"We're looking for a road, tall grasses, and trash," Beto tells The Four, checking to see if Carla and I are all right.

I'm tired, but I can make it. Sleeping helped. My skin is warm, I'm thirsty, but we have water to last us the night.

"If you need to, hop on," Chino tells me every few minutes. But I don't need to yet. In the distance to our left, close to the mountains, there's a dust tornado.

"Usshh, the devil is over there," Patricia says, and crosses herself. Whenever she does that, I do también. We keep walking. In front of us, telephone pole after telephone pole. The black wires between them droop like jump ropes. The Thirty-Five stop. We crouch, and Beto walks forward, telling us to follow him. The bushes here are even closer together. They're hard to walk through. In front of the telephone poles, we can see grasses taller than some adults.

The road must be there.

Everyone crouches around Monchi, who is smiling. "What did I tell you? I'm the best, cabrones," he boasts, taking a sip from his water bottle.

"That's the road. We're early," Beto says, pointing in the direction of the poles.

"Gracias a Dios," everyone says, almost in unison. I say it in my head. Through everyone's shirt-hoods, flashes of white teeth, smiling.

Patricia hugs Carla. Chino looks at me and hugs me. His smell is thick with sweat and dust. Carla smiles at me. Her dimples show, her brown eyes bigger than they've ever been. Then we switch: Carla hugs Chino, and Patricia hugs me, grabs my cheeks, looks me in the eyes, kisses my forehead, and says, "Gracias a Dios." Her face is still scratched up. It's the first time she's kissed me, her scratches bumpy on my skin. She looks like she's about to cry. "Gracias a Dios," she repeats, and I mouth the words with her.

"We stay here, far from the road, flat on the ground." Beto looks at everyone, nodding his head.

"When the vans come, they'll honk three times. We'll get closer to the road, they'll honk again, and we'll run inside, okay?" Monchi pours a little of his water over his face.

"¿When?" someone asks.

"Anytime before sunset," Beto responds.

"Rest, but don't sleep. We're here." Monchi slaps the ground, continues to wash his face. "Lie down. Hide."

"Va, pongámonos trucha," Chino tells us.

"Trucha," Patricia repeats.

¿We're here? ¿This is *it*? It doesn't feel right.

"Ya la hicimos." Patricia looks at me.

I don't know.

"¿What's up?" Chino asks.

I shrug.

"Don't worry." He taps my shoulders.

"¿Y La Migra?" I ask.

"¡Don't think like that!" Patricia scolds me. "No nos echés sal."

Carla shakes her head.

I lie on my tummy and get sticks to play with. We're under a Cheerleader bush. I take the needles that look like horns and pretend they're cows. I don't want to go to sleep. I need to be ready. I want to run into the van and make it to my parents. ¿Is this really happening? I don't know what to feel. It feels weird, like I'm playing soccer without a goalkeeper. Something doesn't feel right.

"Está bien, bicho." Chino taps my back. "La Migra won't find us. Monchi is too good."

"The best," Patricia adds.

I concentrate on the cows. I have them crash together with their horns. Maybe they're bulls. Maybe they're dinosaurs. They'll protect me. Protect us from La Migra. *No Migra, por favor. No Migra, ¿okei?*

THE WAVE CRESTS NEAR US. Then, like a trumpet, the three honks thunder over the crashing wave. The water washes on the sand, and the honks are gone.

"That's them!" Monchi whispers loudly, careful to not shout at the road. All of the bushes rattle. We shake and rise from the ground. For two hours, we've been shadows underneath Cheerleader bushes. Cars have driven by, and our bodies tensed up—*¿Nothing? ¿No honks?*—then softened.

But now, ¡real honks! My heart beats fast. My forehead feels like someone dropped cold water on top of it. The sweat on my lower back like ice cubes. ¡I'm going to see my parents!

"Let's go!" Monchi says loud.

"¡Crouch!" Beto yells at the people in front.

We're moving faster than normal. Twice the speed. Bush to bush. Cheerleader, Crayon. We want air-conditioning. Cold water. A shower. Clean clothes. Out of this desert. Out of the sun.

"Down!" Monchi says, and we're all flat, leaves and twigs on the ground.

A different car. The waves crash and fizzle down. Everyone carries their backpacks next to them.

"Flat as possible!"

We move closer and closer to the telephone poles. It's 5:20 P.M.; the ground is the color of chalk. We crawl until we get to the grasses, thick and taller than most adults. The leaves look like skinny sugar-cane leaves, and most of them are dry and yellow.

"Sharp," people whisper.

"Those cut—careful," Patricia warns.

Everyone stays close to Monchi and Beto, who hide under a Crayon bush.

"Okay, when the vans come, we sprint inside." Monchi turns back to look at us and points at Carla, Patricia, and me. "You three with me," he says, and taps the dirt behind him. Chino looks at us and nods his head toward Monchi.

Beto points at the other mom and Tarsi.

"Everyone else split evenly. In a line," they say.

"My group runs toward the first van." Beto looks back at the men forming a line behind him. They look like toads waiting to hop across the road.

"Big and tall men first. Run and lie flat on the floor. Then another row on top."

"Women and kids, wait and jump on top at the end."

Everyone looks at each other. Patricia, Carla, and I wait off to the side next to Monchi. The men and women are lined up on either side of the polleros. Everyone is flat on the chalky dirt. The ground in front of us is cracked. Everyone else tries to see if they're smaller than the next person, but everyone is lying down. Chino isn't the biggest and positions himself near the end of Monchi's line. Seventeen people plus Monchi. Everyone carries their backpacks in their arms.

A dark-blue car approaches. We get flatter, dust blows up. Three honks. Gravel shoots up.

"¡Go go go go!" Beto tells his line of people and they hop to their feet and sprint into the grasses.

"Stay!" Monchi barks at us. My heart beats fast. Patricia grabs Carla. Chino gets closer to us. He chokes my hand.

"¡Open the door!" Beto shouts.

Dark-blue metal slides open. The engine is still running.

"¡Get in!"

People throw themselves at the floor, one on top of the other, until they're all inside.

The doors close.

"¡Go go go go!" Beto says from the passenger side, tapping the car.

Wheels spin against the gravel. The back of the van has a ladder on its right back door, and a wheel attached to the left. They speed off.

My hands are sweating. My heart is gonna crack my chest open. I hold my breath.

We hear another car approaching.

"Get ready!" Monchi shouts. Then, "Gogogogogo!"

The men run. Monchi stands up next to us, grabs my hand, and my feet move faster than I want. Patricia and Carla are steps behind. We cut through the sharp grass. The sun feels stronger next to the road. The door flings open. Monchi lets me go and puts his hand out in front of Patricia.

"Wait," he says. "Gogogo!" he tells everyone else.

The van is white with a blue stripe and tinted windows. The engine stays on. Men jump into the van's dark insides. More throw their backpacks and slide in behind them. Six. Eight. People jump on top of each other like a dog pile.

"Jump!" Monchi tells Chino, who's at the end of the line. "You three!" Monchi yells.

Patricia jumps on top of the bodies. Then Carla. Then Monchi's hand pushes me. A man is right there. His teeth. It's dark. I jump on top of the man's belly. My hands touch someone else's neck. Face. I kick someone's hand. The door shuts behind me. The front door opens. The van starts moving. We're driving.

"That's what I'm talking about!" Monchi's voice is loud behind the thick black curtain that separates the back of the van from the front. "Eso, cabrones!" he shouts again, clapping. The AC is on. People groan underneath me. There's nothing in here. No seats. Just a dark blue carpet. Dark red curtains. The air smells like dust, like sweat, like cow poop.

"Move a little."

"¡You're on my face!"

"¡Get off!"

Carla and Patricia are nearest the side door at the opposite corner. Chino is near the back, like me. I can almost touch his bony shins.

"Come here," he says, and I crawl on top of body parts to get closer to him.

"Ya la hicimos." Chino is half on top of someone, and someone else is on top of most of his legs. It's smaller in here than it looked. The side curtains don't let much sunlight in. I want to look outside.

"Quiet! Don't move too much!" Monchi yells from the passenger seat.

A thin slit in the front black curtains lets the smallest amount of sunlight in. I try to spot Monchi's face through it, but just see a light blue something. ¿The sky? ¿Windshield?

"¿Water?" Chino asks, reaching for his backpack somewhere in the pile of bodies. People groan as he moves his arms. He finds it, unzips, and brings out our last gallon. "Drink as much as you want."

I grab the gallon. It's heavy. Full. I struggle to put it in my mouth. A stranger's hand beneath me helps me balance it.

"Gracias," I tell his shadow.

"¿Want some?" Chino asks the arms, legs, necks, faces, around us.

They whisper, "Sí."

The gallon makes it to the lips in the back of the van. Another gallon travels across the opposite end. Hands and legs. Backpacks. We made it. We have AC. Water.

"Quiet!" Monchi yells.

Everyone shuts up. My head is directly over the back wheel on the driver's side. I hear it stick and unstick to the asphalt underneath us.

We're inside a car, not hiding from one. I hope everyone made it. Marcelo. Chele. Mario. Coco Liso. The other people I didn't know. *Shhhhhhhhh.* I like that sound. This sound. I close my eyes and pretend I'm at the beach with Mom, Abuelita, Mali, Lupe.

THE PERSON I'M ON top of elbows me, and I wake up. "Thirty minutes!" Monchi shouts from the front. "Thirty!"

We're moving faster. The tires are loud, like we're shaving ice for minutas. The sunlight breaking through the curtains is orange now. I try to prop myself up to look out the window.

"Don't touch." Chino bats the air in front of my hand.

"I know," I tell him, and push my way closer to peek through the space between the curtain and the tinted window. Buildings. Cars. ¡People cactuses! The multicolored sky. This is a big road. Two lanes, dirt in between, two more lanes the opposite way. Someone snores loud. Those who are awake quietly laugh when the man almost chokes but somehow stays asleep. It reminds me of Mali.

Patricia and Carla look like they're sleeping. I can't see the whites of their eyes. We look like a matchbox. Sticks on top of each other. A human cake. I'm the cherry on top, the smallest one riding on the carpet. I'm Aladdin. I finally made it through the desert.

I'M INSIDE A ROOM without any furniture. It has a dark-brown carpet, and people everywhere. The blinds are closed. Next to the white wooden door, beige tiles and a sink with a silver faucet. A white refrigerator. White walls. A carpeted hallway where Chino tells me the bathroom is. When I woke up in his arms, I thought him carrying me into this house was a dream.

"¿Where are we?"

"Tucson, La fucking USA, vos," Chino whispers, smiling and nodding.

Some people sit on the carpet and lean against the nearest wall, still holding their backpacks. Others sleep in the middle of the room.

"¿Monchi y Beto?"

"Gone."

Patricia and Carla sleep next to us. Carla's face rests on her mom's belly. I touch the wall and it's smooth—not cement. The front door is meters away. It has brown smudges everywhere, and its golden doorknob shines in the darkness. Our gallon of water is full again. People get up and refill their bottles in the sink. No one talks. Only the hallway light is allowed on.

"More over there."

"¿More?"

"People." Chino points at another white door down the carpeted hallway. "Other polleros brought them."

I count, and there are at least forty people in this room.

"Está bien. We're here. Rest, sleep. Relax, hermanito."

My head hurts again. My body aches. I'm exhausted. My eyelids are hard to keep open. Chino touches my forehead. "Estás bien," he says.

"¿WHAT'S YOUR PARENTS' NUMBER?" a man asks right in front of my face. He has a brown mustache, deep wrinkles, and bad breath.

I look at Chino, who nods.

I wipe my eyes and give the man the number. He presses the buttons in a pad on the receiver. I've never seen a phone like this. The cord leads to a thing that looks like a beige shoe resting on the carpet in the hallway. The house is fuller now; people cram in the living room, cram in the hallway. Another noncurly cord stretches in front of people's shoes into the room.

"Hello. You the parents of—¿what's your name, morrito?" Brown Mustache asks.

"Javier," I tell him as he covers the phone.

"Javier," he says into the beige receiver bigger than my face.

"¿How old are you? ¿Where are you from?" he asks, pressing his hands tight, so whoever is on the other end doesn't hear.

"Javier, nine years old, from El Salvador," he tells them. "Órale. Yes, we got him. It's fifteen hundred dollars. ¿Can you get to Phoenix tomorrow morning? Órale. Bring cash. When you get to Phoenix, call this number." He presses a button and stops speaking. He smiles. "Your parents are coming tomorrow at nine A.M."

¿Tomorrow? I don't know what to say.

"¡Tomorrow, Javier!" Chino smiles and shakes me. I'm still half-asleep. I don't know what time it is. I'm happy, but now I have to pee. Everything is darker. More strangers I've never seen. Backpacks. Shoes. Water bottles. It smells like sardines. Someone is eating. Or maybe it's Chino. ¿Me? I don't think I spilled that smelly red juice on me.

"Tomorrow. Gracias a Dios," Patricia says, crossing herself. Carla is barely awake, but she smiles.

I stare at the ceiling. I hadn't noticed how white and bumpy it is; it looks like another wall. It smells weird in here. My hands smell like a dead animal. I haven't used the bathroom. Brown Mustache wakes more people and asks for telephone numbers. People who don't have a number answer with names of cities: Wachingtón. Atlanta. Los Ángeles.

"Chino, bathroom," I whisper in his ear.

"Let's goooo, pues," he says playfully, and leads me through feet, heads, and backpacks in the living room, and through the shoes and knees in the hallway.

"Get in," he tells me, and closes the bathroom door behind me. "I'll wait."

It's so stinky. The light doesn't work. There's a white toilet seat with pee splattered on it. The water inside looks dark yellow. The trash can next to it is overflowing with used toilet paper with poop on it. I hold my nose and unzip. There's no soap.

We walk back to where Carla and Patricia are sitting, leaning against the wall, their faces light gray in the dark.

"¿What city you going to?" Carla asks me when I sit directly in front of them.

"San Rafael."

"¿*Where?*"

"California."

"That's on the other side of the country, ¿ve'á, Mami?"

"¿I think?" Patricia answers.

"¿Y vos, Carla?" I like how her name comes out of my mouth. I haven't really said it out loud.

"Virginia."

I don't know where that is.

"It's far, but we'll keep in touch," Patricia interrupts.

I didn't realize we were going to opposite sides of the country. I thought they were gonna be near. Close. We're The Four. I want them to meet my parents. To tell Mom how good I've been. I want to see if Patricia is shorter than Mom. I look down at my shoes. I don't want to be separated from my second family.

"Give us your number, and we'll call," Patricia says, getting a pen and paper out of her backpack.

"¡Sí, vos! We'll stay in touch," Chino promises.

"¿Where are you going?" I ask him.

"Allí merito, Virginia." ¿Chino is going with them? ¿They're leaving me?

"Bicho, está bien. I've always wanted to see California." Chino elbows me.

I look at his eyes to see if he's lying.

"Sí, bicho, we'll visit," Patricia reassures me.

I wanted them to be my neighbors, to go to school with Carla. I can't imagine them not being there.

"¿You want to clean your feet?"

Chino pulls my shoelaces loose. It distracts me. I swipe his hand and take my shoes off and dump dirt on the carpet, wipe the twigs and grass from my socks. There's dirt in between my toes. They smell, but no one says anything.

"Wash them." He opens the water bottle.

"¿Here?"

"Sí, vos, everyone already did it." He nods at the people sleeping around us. "It's why it stinks." He pinches his nostrils together.

Patricia and Carla laugh.

It smells terrible in here, like Mali's worst pata chuca. It reminds me of the cage. How we smelled of dust, and the toilet made everything stink.

He pours the water on my toes, and I wipe them clean with my hands. The water seeps into the carpet. Chino stretches his pants so I can wipe my feet dry on them. I don't want to talk to Chino on the phone. It won't be the same. Patricia, Carla, and Chino won't be near me like this anymore. I want to explore La USA with them, learn and speak English together.

"Put your socks on." Chino grabs my dirty socks from the carpet and hands them to me.

"¡Uffa!" Carla jokes.

I sniff in her and Patricia's direction. "Uffa, ustedes," I say.

They smile.

I put my socks on and wait for Chino to tie my laces.

"¡Eso!" he shouts when he finishes and taps my dusty shoes. "Now you can walk bien pimp-it-is-nice in La USA." His small teeth like flashlights in the dark. I love his smile.

"Okei," Patricia says in English. "We have to rest for tomorrow."

"Yo no," Carla protests. "¿Aren't we leaving soon?"

I don't know what she's talking about. "¿You're leaving?" I ask quickly.

"Not yet, but that big mustached man said that a van is gonna take us to Virginia at dawn."

¿Another van? ¿To Virginia? It's too fast. Finally, we don't have to hide from La Migra, from helicopters. We're inside a house in La USA. We're not hungry. Not thirsty. I want to talk more. No one else will understand the bees in the desert, the flying fish, Doña's cooking, Paula, that fried fish in Acapulco, getting dragged out of the bus, learning what *faak* means.

I want them to help me tell my parents what we saw, who we met. My parents won't believe me. No one else will believe me. They weren't there. Now Chino, Patricia, and Carla won't be here to meet the new people I meet. To try the new foods. Help me feel better in a new place, another country—the third new country we've experienced together.

I want them to tell my parents Marcelo left us. That he's a bad person and owes Grandpa money. That I rarely cried, I followed orders, and that I'm strong. I want to take my new family with me to California, learn how to tie my shoes and show Chino I can do it like him. Chino, my older brother I never had . . .

"¿Is Virginia close?" I finally ask after thinking for a long time.

"N'hombre, the pollero said two or three days in a car."

Carla's eyes get bigger when Chino says that. "¡Three days!" she shouts.

¡¿Carla won't see her dad and sister for three more days?!

"Why we must sleep, monitos," Patricia says, pulling Carla closer to her and whispering something in her ear.

"Vení también," she tells me, swatting at the air with both her hands, Carla's back between them.

The three of us haven't hugged in so long. I miss the motels. Lying in bed and watching Patricia play with Carla's hair. I kneel my way to them. I can feel my heart in my stomach. My eyebrows get heavy. I close my eyes and take a long sniff. Their sweat, the smell of loroco and masa, is faint, but it's them. The smell of dust, pata chuca, and sardine blankets all of us. Rosa soap is there también. Patricia pulls me closer. The back of my head begins to hurt.

"Vos. No seás bayunco," she says, calling Chino over. I miss cuddling on the cement slab. On top of the tiger blanket the last few mornings.

Chino puts all his weight on us, crushing Patricia's hair against the wall. Carla's face pressed against her mom's chest, my face pressed against Carla's back. Chino's chest on my cheeks. I love them. I really love them. A pond, a lake in my eyes. I don't want to let go. None of us wants to let go. A river.

"Ya. Ya," Patricia says. My head hurts all over. I hear Patricia sniffling. My tears fall on Carla's back. Chino's tears fall on my face.

"Bayuncos," Chino says. "No chillen."

"Vos estás chillando," Patricia says, wiping her snot on her daughter's hair.

Carla doesn't care.

"We'll miss you, Javiercito," Patricia says.

"Sí, hermanito, you're strong," Chino adds.

"Very strong," Patricia repeats.

Carla nods, her big eyes filled with tears, and she smiles at me.

"I'll miss all of you," I say, crying, looking down at the carpet.

"Está bien," everyone says. "We'll stay in touch."

"Rest now," Patricia keeps saying, tapping my back, playing with my hair. "But look, after we leave, this lady will take care of you." She points at the Guatemalan mom with Tarsi.

"Ana and Tarsi are not leaving until tomorrow afternoon," Chino adds.

¿They know her name?

I wipe my tears and look at Ana hugging Tarsi, who's asleep next to her. She waves at me.

I wave back.

"So sleep without a worry, ¿okei, our little gringuito?" Patricia and Chino say, scooting closer to me.

"But we're staying here until you fall asleep." Patricia rubs my head. Carla next to her. Chino next to me, on the other side. Patricia kisses my forehead again. They both rub my hair until I pass out.

6-11-99

DAYLIGHT ENTERS THE ROOM through slits in the closed blinds. Most people have already left—only a dozen are still sleeping in the living room. The hallway is empty. I look toward Ana, who's sitting with her back to the wall; Tarsi is stretched out next to her.

"Good morning," she says softly.

I touch the carpet—they're gone. I think I watched them leave. The room was dark, a lot of people standing up with their backpacks, waiting in line. Patricia kissed my forehead. Chino combed my hair.

"The van is here," they both said.

"Salú." Carla waved at me.

Then they each hugged me one by one. Even Carla. The door closed, and I closed my eyes and slept. I thought it was a dream.

It's getting warm in here. The pata chuca smell is thicker and thicker. A woman in the kitchen fills her water bottle. My body hurts all over. I'm alone. I don't really know anyone here.

"Sleep," Ana says.

I smile at her, look at my watch—it's only seven A.M. Two hours until my parents get here.

"Sleep," she repeats.

I nod and pray nothing happens to Patricia, Carla, and Chino. That their vans get to Virginia faster than three days. That they don't ever forget me.

I SIT UP AGAINST the wall, watching the front door. It's 8:55 A.M. In the living room, fewer than ten people remain. Sometimes, Brown Mustache goes out "for a walk," and another pollero who is short and muscular comes to guard the door. They have a secret knock: three distinct taps, but with something that sounds like a metal ring. I keep listening, my hands on the carpet, ready to bounce up and run toward the door.

Whenever Brown Mustache returns, there's someone with him. The stranger steps into the living room, just a few steps, so the door can lock. They sniff around—it smells terrible in here. Brown Mustache yells out a name. If no one in the living room responds, he sends the short pollero to shout the same name to the people in the other room.

There have been three knocks since seven A.M. Once, the name was a woman sleeping next to me. From the hugs and kisses, I think it was her husband who picked her up. Twice, men walked out of that room with their backpacks, smiling but dazed. Both times, I'm sure it was a brother or uncle picking them up. We watched them awkwardly hug each other. After the cries, kisses, or hugs, Brown Mustache tells the reunited to go outside and leave. No one complains. The reunited quickly walk out into the sun.

I haven't really slept. My heart beats so fast, faster than in the desert. My hands sweat. I keep thinking about my father, Papá Javi, Dad. ¿What will I call him? I don't really know what he looks like. ¿Is he gonna hug me? I know I will run into Mamá Pati's arms. I remember her. I miss her. I miss them both. I'm excited to see if she's changed. If she still smells the same. ¿How is she gonna wear her hair? ¿Her makeup? ¿What perfume?

My hands are drenched. I check my watch constantly. I stare at the short pollero's thin gold chains around his neck. His shirt and pants aren't as tight as the other pollero's, who walked outside minutes ago. Then the ring against the door, *tap, tap, tap.*

I stand up before the door opens.

The door unlocks. Tarsi is awake, and he watches me. His mom smiles and stands up with me.

The door opens, a bright flash.

My name booms throughout the room.

Two shadows appear. At last.

Once I knew, then I forgot. It was as if I had fallen asleep in a field only to discover at waking that a grove of trees had grown up around me.

—Charles Simic
The World Doesn't End

April 5, 2021

For seven weeks (from April 20, 1999, to June 10, 1999), no one knew where I was. Grandpa handed me over to Don Dago in Tecún Umán, and Don Dago never called my family in El Salvador again. None of the coyotes or polleros called my parents in California. The first time my family heard anything about me was when Marcelo called my parents on June 1, 1999. I don't know how Marcelo made it to Los Angeles, but he told them that I was "in good hands," "that I was 'so positive and sure' that I was gonna see them again." Before hanging up, he said, "Don't worry, he's a special one."

My parents became insomniacs. At night, their phone slept next to their bed as they waited for it to ring. They couldn't drive to look for me near the border because they feared Border Patrol would stop and deport them. All they could do was wait and hope that I would make it across safely. They went to work, called El Salvador twice a day, borrowed money in case a pollero called, and attended their ESL classes at College of Marin. Their teacher at the time was Carol Adair. Carol's partner was the future poet laureate of the United States, Kay Ryan. My parents told their classmates, Carol, and Kay about my state of limbo. Everyone feared I could be dead, and each time the class met, they prayed for me and lit a candle. Three countries away, Abuelita Neli lit a candle every single night, and prayed I made it to my parents.

On June 10, 1999, at around eight P.M., Brown Mustache called my parents. They took a taxi to SFO, bought plane tickets, flew with their Salvadoran passports to Phoenix International, and then took another taxi to Tucson. Their instructions were to take the very first exit and head to a Texaco right next to the freeway, where Brown Mustache waited at nine A.M. sharp near a telephone booth. They handed Brown Mustache the money, and he walked them to the two-story apartment complex. The walk wasn't long. I remember the three knocks, my heart beating so fast as the door opened, and running into Mom's arms.

My parents and I have only spoken a few times about what happened to me those seven weeks. The first occurred immediately after Brown Mustache closed the apartment door, on our walk to the gas station, where the same taxi was waiting to take us to Phoenix International. From there, we flew to San Rafael, the town I would call home until I left for college in 2008. The second happened years and years later, when I began writing poetry and started to process all of my emotions about—and the repercussions of—my migration. When I confronted them, they both cried as they remembered what I smelled like when they first saw me—"piss, shit, sweat, a nasty stench" they've never forgotten. The other times we talked about those seven weeks were random questions via text or a quick phone call during the writing of this book.

My parents are the ones who reminded me that Chino called a few times, that they thanked him for everything he'd done. I spoke to him, but don't remember the conversations. Mom says he sounded like a very nice young man. "You could tell by his voice," she says. She still remembers Chino telling her that I reminded him of his younger brother who had died. Patricia called once or twice. My parents thanked her, and plans were made to stay in contact with both of them, but after a few weeks, they changed their phone numbers and we lost touch. Mom likes to call them my "angels," but I worry that takes away their humanity and their nonreligious capacity for love and compassion they showed a stranger.

Similar to my parents, I didn't dwell on what happened to me those seven weeks from El Salvador to California. I never forgot

Chino, Patricia, Carla, Chele, Marcelo, and every other person I encountered, but remembering them was painful. It wasn't until I started writing poetry and, later, this book (an impossibility without massive help from my therapist) that I felt courageous and healed enough to revisit the places, the people, and the events that shaped me. My hope for this book is that somehow it will reunite me with Chino, Patricia, and Carla, that I will find out what happened to them after we separated and learn what their lives have been like in this country. I don't believe I ever thanked them. I want to thank them now, as an adult, for risking their lives for a nine-year-old they did not know.

For years, I couldn't travel to El Salvador because of my legal status. It wasn't until 2018 that I finally returned, as a twenty-eight-year-old, to see Abuelita Neli again. By then, Mali had migrated to California, gotten married, and had a son. Tía Lupe also migrated and now has another daughter. They both came to California when I was in high school, and still live in the same neighborhood. Tía Lupe's older daughter, Julia, lives in the same house in La Herradura with Abuelita, Grandpa, and her two dogs, Max and Nina. Grandpa was able to visit us in California three times between 2002 and 2012 because he got a tourist visa—the only member of my family to ever be granted such status. He's still burning trash every afternoon.

I never found out what happened to Chele, or to any of the countless others who were with me. I fear they died in the Sonoran Desert. This book is for them and for every immigrant who has crossed, who has tried to, who is crossing right now, and who will keep trying.

ACKNOWLEDGMENTS

——

Un millón de gracias a:

El pueblo centroaméricano, immigrants from all over the world, and the ancestors who watch over us.

Grandpa Chepe y Abuelita Neli, los quiero mucho.

Mamá Pati y Papá Javi, I can't imagine what reading this book must be like for you, what those weeks must've felt like. I hope you carry no guilt because I've long forgiven you. I love you, every single day.

Tía Mali y Tía Lupe, gracias por su apoyo, allá y en este país, siempre las llevo en mis pesamientos.

Julia, Adriana, Toñito, I'm always thinking of you, I'm proud of you, I believe in you.

Josephine Blair Cipriano, my first and best reader, my most giving and cutthroat editor, gracias for shaping this book into what it is now. For holding me when the trauma got to be too much. For helping me become the person I never believed I could be. Gracias for your Reiki sessions, your joy, your care, and never-ending love. This book would not exist without you. Te amo a vos y a nuestra gatita, Loka.

Wendy Carolina Franco, PhD, our weekly therapy sessions helped me tap into the well where I kept this story hidden. Gracias for helping me bring it into the light and for being the most perfect guide/bruja for my healing.

Dora Rodriguez, gracias for showing me that we can help those going through the same traumas we have, in the same place where ours occurred. You're a warrior who inspires me every single day. Gracias for founding Salvavision. First, in your heart; and now, a brick-and-mortar resource center in Sasabe, Sonora. I'm here to spread the word and help with anything this beautiful Salvadoran-woman-led organization needs.

Paco Cantú, thank you for shedding one uniform and for stepping into the uniform of our friendship, mi Arizonan hermano. Gerardo del Valle, mi hermano Guatemalteco, gracias for your films and your friendship. Thank you both for helping me retrace my steps in the places where this book takes place.

La Herradura, San Rafael (The Canal), Berkeley, Brooklyn, Hamilton, Cambridge, Harlem, Tucson, and all the friends I made in these places I've called home. You've helped me more than you know.

The Lannan Foundation, for the support that helped me finish this book.

The Radcliffe Institute, for the time and space that allowed me to gather all the notes I'd kept since I came to this country and begin to call it prose. To my cohort there, and especially to Lauren Groff, for seeing something in my work that made you think, "Hey, my agent should see this."

Bill Clegg, I can't imagine what my life would be like without you. Thank you for believing in me from the day we met. You were a stranger along my journey who has become family. You deserve all the donuts in the world!

To David Ebershoff, my superstar editor, for your care, honesty, and that call that changed my life. Thank you for everything.

To everyone at the Clegg Agency and at Hogarth (Penguin Random House) who has helped *Solito* come to light, I appreciate you, I see you, my most sincere gratitude.

And to Chino, Patricia, and Carla, wherever you are, I owe you my life, I carry you with me, siempre.

SOLITO

———

A MEMOIR

Javier Zamora

Random House Book Club

Because Stories Are Better Shared ™

A BOOK CLUB GUIDE

1. "*Trip*. My parents started using that word about a year ago—'one day, you'll take a trip to be with us. Like an adventure.'" (3) The result is a harrowing migration story, a narrative that is immediate and intimate, in which the reader is essentially there, in the boy's shoes and inside his head. What did you learn through Javier Zamora's experience? What surprised or shocked you?

2. This memoir is told from the perspective of the author as a nine-year-old boy. How do you think that adds to the narrative? Would the book have a different effect if it was the story of an adult's journey?

3. From Don Dago to others who remain unnamed, Javier relies on a network of coyotes to get him to the United States. What was your initial opinion on these coyotes? Did it change over the course of the memoir?

4. There are many legs to this journey: boat, bus, on foot. Describe the ways each leg was uniquely challenging and dangerous.

5. The journey wasn't just physically taxing, but mentally, too. Discuss all the information that young Javier had to memorize—from Mexican cities to political facts—and why might he have to pretend he is Mexican?

6. Aside from Javier, which characters stayed with you, and why?

7. The author is a poet. How do you think this serves the story he tells, and how does it affect the interplay between intense circumstances and beautiful images and writing?

8. The natural world is a character itself in *Solito*—the animals, the plants, the landscape, the full moon, the sunrise—particularly in the scenes in the desert. Which natural elements stood out for you, and why?

9. How do you think Javiercito survived during the seven-week journey? How did you think he sustained himself mentally and emotionally?

10. *Solito* is set in 1999—twenty-three years ago—and yet we still need immigration reform. Name three ways you think the United States immigration system can be more efficient and humane. Is it possible to change the existing system?

11. Javier Zamora's story is also the story of millions who have had no choice but to leave home. Have you or someone you've known faced similar circumstances? If so, how has this shaped your life or theirs?

12. How much did you know about United States' immigration system before reading *Solito*? Did your view of the issue change? Why or why not?

13. Toward the beginning of the memoir, Javier lists all the ways he and his mother tried to immigrate "legally." Discuss how these attempts are thwarted.

14. What could you or your neighbors do to welcome immigrant families into your community?

15. How did you feel at the end of *Solito*?

JAVIER ZAMORA was born in La Herradura, El Salvador, in 1990. His father fled El Salvador when he was a year old, and his mother when he was about to turn five. Both parents' migrations were caused by the United States–funded Salvadoran Civil War (1980–1992). In 1999, Javier migrated through Guatemala, Mexico, and the Sonoran Desert. His debut poetry collection, *Unaccompanied,* explores how immigration and the civil war have impacted his family. Zamora was a 2018–2019 Radcliffe Fellow at Harvard University and has held fellowships from MacDowell, the National Endowment for the Arts, the Poetry Foundation (Ruth Lilly and Dorothy Sargent Rosenberg), Stanford University (Wallace Stegner), and Yaddo. He is the recipient of a 2017 Lannan Literary Fellowship, the 2017 Narrative Prize, and the 2016 Barnes & Noble Writers for Writers Award for his work in the Undocupoets Campaign. Javier currently lives in Tucson, Arizona, where he volunteers with Salvavision and The Florence Project.

For more information on Salvavision and The Florence Project, visit their websites at salvavision.org and firrp.org.

To inquire about booking Javier Zamora for a speaking engagement, please contact the Penguin Random House Speakers Bureau at speakers@penguinrandomhouse.com.

This book was set in Bembo, a typeface based on an old-style Roman face that was used for Cardinal Pietro Bembo's tract *De Aetna* in 1495. Bembo was cut by Francesco Griffo (1450–1518) in the early sixteenth century for Italian Renaissance printer and publisher Aldus Manutius (1449–1515). The Lanston Monotype Company of Philadelphia brought the well-proportioned letterforms of Bembo to the United States in the 1930s.

RANDOM HOUSE BOOK CLUB

Because Stories Are Better Shared

Discover

Exciting new books that spark conversation every week.

Connect

With authors on tour—or in your living room. (Request an Author Chat for your book club!)

Discuss

Stories that move you with fellow book lovers on Facebook, on Goodreads, or at in-person meet-ups.

Enhance

Your reading experience with discussion prompts, digital book club kits, and more, available on our website.

Join our online book club community!

f **g** randomhousebookclub.com

 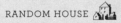